AUGUSTO BOAL

Hamlet and the Baker's Son

My Life in Theatre and Politics

Translated by Adrian Jackson and Candida Blaker

ROUTLEDGE
Taylor & Francis Group

LONDON and NEW YORK

First published 2001 by Routledge
11 New Fetter Lane, London EC4P 4EE

Simultaneously published in the USA and Canada by Routledge
29 West 35th Street, New York, NY10001

Routledge is an imprint of the Taylor & Francis Group

© 2001 Augusto Boal

The right of Augusto Boal to be identified as the Author of this
Work has been asserted by him in accordance with the Copyright,
Designs and Patents Act 1988

Designed and typeset by Sutchinda Rangsi Thompson
Printed and bound in Great Britain by T J International Ltd, Padstow, Cornwall

British Library Cataloguing in Publication Data
A catalogue record for this book is available from the British Library

Library of Congress Cataloging in Publication Data
Boal, Augusto.
　　[Hamlet e o filho do padeiro. English]
　　Hamlet and the baker's son : my life in the theatre and politics / Augusto Boal
　　　　p. cm
　　Includes index.
　　1. Boal, Augusto. 2. Theatrical producers and directors–Brazil–Biography. 3.
Dramatists, Brazilian–20th century–Biography. I. Title

　　PN2474.B63 A3 2001
　　792'.0233'092–dc21
　　[B]

00-062746

ISBN 0–415–22989–8 (pbk)　　ISBN 0–415–22988–X (hbk)

University of
Chester

He is c

Theatre

the worl

and worke

as a produc

and social re

But this

politics — onc

passionately cre

From his chi

ment to his mc

democratic politic

one. He has devise

disempowered, and

Rio to the rehearsal st

A distinctive warn

Boal's commitment to h

contents

introduction

the translators

Adrian Jackson is Artistic Director of Cardboard Citizens, a leading proponent of Forum Theatre in the UK. He has translated four books by Augusto Boal, collaborated on a number of occasions and taught Theatre of the Oppressed widely in the other countries, including Namibia, South Africa, Hong Kong, Mauritius and Finland. He has made theatre in and with a broad range of communities, as well as with trained actors.

Candida Blaker has lived and worked in Brazil. She is an international social development consultant and is increasingly involved in the arts and cultural sector.

preface:
a woman in the mirror

She was in the dressing room, crying.

Why? The show was over.

Success. And Mary was crying.

She was a housemaid. The cast, that evening, was entirely made up of housemaids, all Marys. Their group was participating in a Festival of Theatre of the Oppressed, November 1999. All the groups had told me: 'We do theatre in our communities, in streets, in open spaces: now we want to do theatre inside a real theatre.' I said: 'Why not?'

We hired the Teatro Glória for a weekend. All our groups came to play, one after another, to enjoy the rituals of the theatre: the spectators buying their tickets, the curtain going up, the applause, the curtain call . . . Oh, how they loved it! How different it was from the public parks and the street, where dogs bark, and drunkards exercise their right to speak, everyone is on the move, in transit . . . Here everyone was so educated, so well behaved!

Mary was crying. 'Why, Mary, why are you crying?'

'I am a housemaid. Housemaids must be invisible: that's essential to our profession. The food must be cooked, meals must appear on the table, the dishes must be washed, the house cleaned, the children prepared for school in the morning . . . who does it? No one: the invisible housemaid. If, while serving at the table, I hear a conversation about something I have an opinion on, I must shut up: besides being invisible, I must be mute. And deaf: I never hear my employers talking.

'This afternoon, when we were rehearsing, a man came to me and showed me where I should stand or move, for the lights to illuminate me better, so that I would be seen by all the spectators; another man hung a small microphone on my dress to make my voice be heard throughout the theatre. For the first time in my life, people were busy making me visible, making me audible. In the evening, wonder of wonders: the family I work for were all there, seeing my body, listening to my voice, understanding my thoughts, my feelings. They were there in the audience, they were silent . . . in the dark.'

'You should be happy: why are you crying?'

'I cried when I came to the dessing room and looked at myself in the mirror: I saw a woman. For the first time in my life, I saw a woman in the mirror . . .'

'What did you see before?'

'Before, looking at the mirror, I used to see . . . a housemaid. Tonight, I saw a woman. I am a woman!'

This is the theatre I believe in: the place where we can stand and see ourselves. Not see what others tell us we are, or should be – but see our deepest selves!

Theatre is the place where we can look at ourselves and say: 'I am a man, I am a woman: I am me!'

A draft of life!

Chekhov's 'Three Sisters'

Hamlet
And the Baker's Son!

introduction

I
Did
What
I Could!

That's my nature! Closing statements!

Choice and Chance!

Augusto Boal's autobiography

I think growing old is wonderful. One becomes more intelligent, more experienced, wiser. The only disagreeable thing about ageing is that it is irreversible.

★  ★

Every text one writes is autobiographical: anything else would be plagiarism.

The beginning of the conversation

In a psychiatric hospital in Rio de Janeiro, where the patients were working, playing, painting, sculpting, and were – in their own way – happy, a reporter interviewed an inmate, one of the so-called 'raving mad'. In an exhibition which had recently opened, the man had dazzled critics and public alike with his fantastic sculptures. The reporter asked if it was difficult to sculpt.

'It's easy; anyone can do it. It's just a matter of keeping calm – that is the key to it: keeping very calm! When you are calm you can do everything better.'

'Calm, I can understand. What do you mean by *doing things better?*'

'It's like this; you get a nice large piece of stone. Then, think of a person, think hard, you need to see that person in your imagination, whole, with your eyes closed, not in the way the whole world sees, but in the way that only you can see, because you are the sculptor, not anyone else. Sculpture is not about doing a portrait – portraiture is what cameras are for. You are an artist. So, thinking about someone, seeing them, you pick up the hammer and chisel, and then you remove from the stone everything that is not that person. Which is to say: you chuck out the rest, and leave in the stone only the person!'

It is easy to be a sculptor or an artist: it is just a matter of being mad! Stark raving.

It is easy to be mad: it is just a matter of being an artist.

★  ★

'Why don't you write your autobiography?' – asked Talia Rodgers. I was nonplussed, thinking about *that person*: me. Would it be worth the trouble to sculpt my biography? To draw out coherences from the impure and excessive stone of my life, to mould the profile of the man, even presuming the trajectory made some sense? To chuck out 'the rest', and describe what I feel today, what I think I think, what I think I am, or have been?

Biographies smack of the end, of final utterances. Mission accomplished. I, by contrast, am always at the start of some new path or other. I want more. More, more. I am given to excess. It would be awkward to talk about myself: in what I do, the important thing is the deed, not the doer.

Talia, who had already published three books of mine in this imprint, reminded me that in them deed and doer are mixed up together. She insisted: for my theatre to be better understood, it would be good if I unravelled the threads of my life in my own way, not in minute meticulous detail, dotting the I's and crossing the T's, but by means of stories, facts and deeds.

When all is said and done, who am I? What use am I? Instructions for use. The Theatre of the Oppressed – where did it come from, where is it going? It exists in the four corners of the earth, but in which of those corners was it born? Where did it pass its childhood?

I seemed unnecessary to me; after all, this method can be used in Calcutta and Ouagadougou, Paris, New York and London; what difference does it make to know that the lengthy birth began in Brazil, that the child grew into its body in the three Americas, before it spread through Europe and into Africa and Asia?

To me it even seemed immoral: a man relating his life, Narcissus admiring himself in the mirror, thinking himself handsome, seeking to be admired. Such presumption should be cleansed with holy water. Vanity. I would not write it. I refused.

Nevertheless, as someone who didn't want to – not by a long chalk! – I began talking with my sisters, Augusta and Aida, and we reminisced. At each meeting I would say: 'Start, talk!' And we would talk.

I began to see the Church in Penha, at the rocky height of the cliff, a working-class district of Rio, where I was baptised at the age of 11, tolerating the holy water on my head, shying away from the salt on my tongue. My father, who worked constantly, missed the opportunity to baptise me when I was a baby, and the time came only when he became godfather to a nephew: 'Baptise them both at the same time, it's cheaper with the same priest; that way, we discharge all outstanding duties.' 'God will understand the delay', asserted my mother with authority and affection; she knew what she was talking about.

Remembering, I felt a huge tenderness in my heart for these people, these characters who were coming back to speak to me. I started to sense the smells of childhood, voices, sounds, the taste of warm bread, fresh out of the oven, melted butter. Not Proust's *madeleines*, but *marias-bentas*, *barrigas de frade*, *quindins of Iáiá*.[1]

I even felt tenderness towards myself, just imagine! I did not know if I deserved it. . . . I took the solemn decision, saying to myself: 'I will not write a biography, no way! Autobiography has to be posthumous: when all is done . . . I will not! But . . . if I did, if I were to write it . . . what would it be like? How do you write an autobiography?'

In my imagination, I started to write memories. These brought up others, which in turn obliged yet others to arise.

Memory is invasory – when one remembers even the smallest thing, a thousand other images are aroused and jealously demand to be remembered; they show their faces. Memory is contagious: if I remember, others close to me remember more. Memories are envious, vain; they have to appear, like stars. The fleeting memory-ette, the detail, thinks it deserves headlines. Memories are like us.

When I took stock, the reams of material seemed to amount to a book. With multitudes of tardy memories beating at the door, wanting to come in: 'Me too, I want to tell!'

I took flight, terrified: I wanted to look forward, and they were pushing me backward. I wanted to make plans: but how do you plan the ending, the time when you are dead? Memories came limping in, seeking me out, deformed and stumbling, lacking arms, *sans* eyes, *sans* nose; they woke me in the middle of the night, jolted me at the end of the day, grimaces at dawn, at play and at work, at home and in the street, cutting into important conversations or halfway through a drink. Unbidden, whispering things into my ear: 'Tell that story, tell it; they'll like it, no doubt about it!' We made an agreement, a truce: I would write down the awakened past, alive. Afterwards, with the memory buried, defunct, we would see if it was worth the trouble of resuscitating it.

I was typing, calmly, happily. Trying to understand, on the trembling screen of the computer, that which had happened in my trembling life, had happened to me: family, *compaheiros*,[2] and also enemies, of which I have had many, more than I deserved!

I went in search of *temps perdu*. I sought to tell only that which had to

do with my theatre and its genesis: no intimacies. Very important characters remained out of the story or were dealt with in passing: I denounced
no one. Ever. That's not my way.

I changed the names of people, transformed them into characters.
Though the narrated facts were genuine, they did not happen the way
I told them: there is such a thing as style! I joined a few people into
one person, I divided a few into many; I related, earlier, things which
happened later, and later, things which didn't happen but might have.
When the events are incontestably true, then sure, I even included the
names and surnames, fax and telephone numbers, postcodes, e-mails,
fingerprints, physical descriptions, the lot.

I know what I am writing and I swear to tell the truth. I don't
measure out my candour. But I do not swear the whole truth, nor the
cold truth: it is impossible. Memory and imagination are inseparable,
conjoined twins, but they are not born of the same egg, identical: they
always seem alike, though one is white and another dark-skinned! Who
am I to divorce them, when it was God who joined them?

I hope you like it. And do not ask: 'Is it true ?'

Today it is. . . . It has been.

the landscape, the family

Uncle Miguel and the best solution

From conversations with my family came images. Uncle Miguel, my father's eldest brother: white beard, black hat. He remained the same with the passing of time, in the only picture I had one day seen of him. In my memory he was mixed with other, hatless whitebeards: my grandfather and Dom Pedro II, the last Emperor of Brazil, exiled by the Republicans in 1889.

Miguel was a strange man: in life he never smiled. He smiled for the first time at the moment of his death. Not before, still less after. He didn't have time to smile, as if smiling used up life. He came to Brazil at the beginning of the century, with a wife and three children. He left his widowed father and three sisters in Portugal; the brothers had either emigrated before or came over to join him. Emigrating was the best solution to the problem of raising children and securing an easier way of life than that of a peasant in the north of Portugal. With funds advanced from his future inheritance from my grandfather, Miguel bought a bakery, *A Chinezinha* (The Little Chinawoman), in Benfica, in Rio de Janeiro.

The work was unremitting: to gain some respite, the best solution was to offer partnership to my uncle Antonio, already in Brazil, and to my father, who arrived in 1914, aged 22. My father was exiled for having refused to take part in the war in which Portugal had involved itself without consulting him, for who knows what reason.

For reasons of economy and amity, Miguel and family shared a house with a childless Portuguese couple, Catalina and Celestino, who were also traders: they kept a grocery selling dry and wet goods. They all lived in harmony, the women washing clothes in the tank, sweeping the yard and cooking; the men setting off to work early and coming home late, each couple in their own room, and the children in another, with the living room, bathroom and kitchen shared between them all.

A flower, with corpses adorned

It was at this time that the *Espanhola*, the famous plague which killed millions across the five continents, reached Brazil, causing devastation. In the fierce battle between supply and demand, the price of cloves, of lilies, and *copos de leite*[1] rocketed. Ashamed of their own cost, roses withered unbought and scentless – so that the cadavers stank still worse, because of the price of flowers. In the streets, each solitary flower was adorned with several cadavers, sharing their single floral tribute.

Among those who died were Miguel's wife and Catalina's husband. Their bodies were buried and the widower and the widow went on living together – it was the best solution – bringing up the children as if they were husband and wife, helping each other. It was understandable, and no one was alarmed by this mutual aid, since all were fully occupied, in heart and mind, with the mortal enemy they faced: the plague.

The *Espanhola* came to an end. And when its occupation ended the rumours started: Miguel, a widower, and Catalina, a widow, were living under the same roof, openly. As well as looking after the bakery, Miguel was taking care of the store; Catalina washed their dirty clothes: as everyone knows, dirty laundry is the most intimate thing a family has, it hides shameful secrets. This intimacy gave rise to suspicions, fantasies. Underpants cannot be washed openly with impunity.

Plausible explanations calmed the gossips: to go on living like this was the best solution – Uncle Miguel ran his friend's store as a father would, and Catalina looked after her friend's children with as much care as a true mother . . . the tell-tales were silenced. There was nothing going on between them, nor would there ever be, apart from mutual respect, sincere friendship and sweet memories. That was how they explained the light which shone late into the night in one of the rooms: they were remembering. To remember is to live. And they did a lot of living, with gusto.

Some believed in the purity of the widow's and widower's intentions, others placed more credence in the conspicuous reality. Until Catalina's belly began to swell; all doubts died when a beautiful girl was born, whom they named, with much love and little imagination, Catalina. No father registered the child. Too little time; too much work. From then on, Miguel and Catalina were seen as man and wife.

Saudades *for Trás-os-Montes*

The bakery prospered and the partners decided to start over on their own, separately. Antonio bought out his brothers, my father returned to Portugal, the war having ended, to marry my mother, as he had promised. And Uncle Miguel was homesick for his fatherland and decided to visit the family.

Apart from his *saudades*,[2] he had to sort out some land matters, which were at least as strong a motivation for his return; as the eldest brother, he wished to exercise his historic rights over the estate of my grandfather, who was still of sound health for all the eighty-three years expressed in his bowed figure. The family needed to decide who would have what after his death, and to put his affairs into a proper legal framework. In those days in Portugal, as is still the case in Brazil today, land and documents did not always tally: there were constant wrangles. Although no one was willing the patriarch's death, it would be better to clarify the hectares and the monies beforehand, so that this discussion would not have to take place after death, over a still-warm body, in the midst of flowers and condolences. A matter of good taste.

When it came to sorting out passports, my uncle realised that *vis-à-vis* the accursed bureaucracy, he had forgotten to legalise his marriage to his new wife. Before the law, which did not recognise the priest's blessing – hurriedly given to safeguard morality and to baptise the offspring, on a Tuesday afternoon, in a moment snatched between one baking and the next – the couple were worthless concubines, which, in that epoch – Victorian even without Victoria – was the worst of all badges.

Two problems: how to travel on a family passport, on the cheap, without being a family, in those censorious times when even a tender gaze, lest it ruin the honour of those in love, had to be officially sanctioned on headed paper, and signed and sealed. And how to document – in capital letters and in legal form, before setting off on their journey – their fructiferous union, which had escaped the attentions of the registrar. Impossible: no time. Second problem: how to present the new wife to my old grand-father? For in these matters my grandfather was the guardian of insatiable and inflexible moral principles and ends.

My uncle resolved the most pressing problem first: given that they could not travel as a family, he convinced his wife that the best solution, to deceive the maritime police, was that he should board the ship with his three older children and she with the latecomer, as though they were single mother and bewildered child. Both widowed, they would not need conjugal authorisation to travel with their children: death certificates would suffice. They would be two families. They agreed not to speak to each other during the crossing: it was the best solution, to avoid suspicion.

On arrival in Lisbon, Uncle Miguel solved the second problem: the two Catalinas would go to Obidos, and he, with the three offspring from his first liaison would go to the grandfather's house.

Catalina did not like this, but wanted to trust her husband. According to him, it was simply a strategy to avoid a possibly fatal surprise for the patriarch. It would be too emotional a business for him to see his first-born Miguel, remarried and, what's more, rewarded with a fourth daughter. My grandfather might be shocked – which would not be good timing, as he had the flu. Later, with the passing of time, when he was up and about again, there would be time to regularise the situation and, when the right moment came along, to convince grandfather to accept the new state of affairs, time for him to accept his new grand-daughter and his new daughter-in-law, and time for new marriages and new legalities. It was simply a matter of time. And time went on passing. . . .

A niece full of nerves

Tempus, tempest. Although the elderly relatives were not informed about the new family (with a slap on the mouth and a pinch on the bottom, the children were forbidden to speak of their youngest sister) Miguel heard stories, and not always good ones, about the relatives.

The main news concerned his niece Maria Eduarda. Imagine: a backward region in Portugal called Trás-os-Montes, where Vila Real was situated, and not even in Vila, a town, but in a distant village called Justes, which even today lives sequestered in the past. Imagine how in that far-off time, they lived in the past of that present. Imagine Maria Eduarda, brown, pretty, aged 18, shut away in the house after supper, washing and breaking plates (careless indeed: soap is slippery, of course), sweeping and dirtying, pressing her nose and mouth to the window-panes, her sidelong glance looking for the hotheaded *joaquinzinho*.[3] He was young like her, a vagabond law unto himself, *joaquinzinho* who refused to tend goats and sheep, and, if his family obliged him to tend the animals, left them unleashed and lost them, off in search of his own little shepherdess Maria Eduarda.

She sighed onto the fuggy windowpanes, while *joaquinzinho* blew her kisses and pulled faces; more than that they did not venture, given their distance apart and the window between them. Only the occasional amorous swoon, from one or other, on each side of the dim glass. A bump on the head, a scratch: the pains of love.

Scandal. They said that *joaquinzinho* was mad, beyond the pale: apart from convulsive weeping, he howled, as if he were a wolf. He roared, he bellowed, as if he were a beast. He croaked, he mooed, as if he were an animal. And, after these stertorous exploits, he tore his hair out, he groaned. As if he were a lover.

In all the village, no one talked of anything else (to be absolutely honest, there was no other subject for conversation, apart from the constant dreary routine: driving cattle, picking grapes, making wine; planting wheat, making bread, washing the house and the little church).

The war had ended without any certainty as to which country had won, the consequences of the conflict and, still less, its causes. No one knew anything, not even the venerated pharmacist: 'Either the Germans won, or the English . . . no doubt about it. . . . We did not win nor did we lose, we stayed the same . . .' he said one day, sagely. And all agreed: an illustrious man, the pharmacist knew much, like the pharmacists of old.

Maria Eduarda — hidden behind the smoky panes of the window, her chest and whole body heaving and panting, from her toe-nails to the tips of her hair — would kiss the window's glass and frame, she would make herself faint, smashing plates on the wall, with cut hands, bleeding, clinging to the window, and then be carried hurriedly to bed. She was given sugared water to drink, cooled with Spanish fans, her forehead rubbed with garlic, given limes to suck and threats of poultices. To have called the doctor or even the pharmacist would have brought shame. Shame on the whole family, since they were not dealing with a regular illness; this was witchcraft stuff.

Maria Eduarda's sighs scandalised aunts and neighbours — everyone except my grandfather who decided to ignore everything, out of filial loyalty. Eduarda scandalised Justes and beyond. The family's greatest fear was that they would come to hear of it in Vila Real, to which the women travelled by donkey every six months to buy lace and embroidery, rugs and table cloths, and whole trousseaus when someone was getting married, including the lace-trimmed nightgowns which brides used to sleep in. The family's honour in such a seignorial town could not be destroyed! Ah Vila Real!

It was imperative to hide the fact that the young woman was sighing deep sighs behind the window, clinging to the curtains, which had more than once been pulled down, amid groans and protests. The lass wanted to go out on to the street, it was an 'attack of nerves', but she could not be seen in this state: for shame! She must stay imprisoned until the attack of nerves passed.

Uncle Miguel heard about the tumult and, intrigued, asked his sister Esmeralda, Maria Eduarda's mother, why they did not let her marry that *joaquinzinho* in peace. Aside from his vagabondage, he seemed like a good lad, when he calmed down, since all he ever did was to position himself in front of the window of the one he yearned after, moaning and groaning. His sister replied that it was not possible. This vagabondage could be seen to, a way could be found to deal with it: a good lash with a whip to the back would temper the most obstinate rebelry. Blessed remedy.

But the young man had another illness which was incurable: poverty. *joaquinzinho* did not even merit a capital letter in his own name, so poor were his washerwoman mother and his worm-eaten father, rotting from an unknown illness – a useless illness, since it did not keep faith with the obligation and destiny of every illness which is, as everyone knows and laments, death. *joaquinzaozinho*[4] – père, equally unmeritorious of the upper case – that is what everyone called him, with the augmentative[5] rendered into miniscule diminutive! – when his name was pronounced, everyone spoke in a low voice, eyes downcast, so that his name would fall to the floor, if possible into the gutter, in the grate. *joaquinzaozinho* had been paralysed since the end of the last decade. Where eating was concerned, expensive though it was, he ate – but when it came to dying, as was his obligation, ah, no, that he would not do.

Esmeralda explained that this marriage would be ruinous, since they no longer lived in the times when only one son inherited the entire estate. In times past, Miguel would have been the sole inheritor of all my grandfather's lands. In those days of yore, the second son was destined for a career in the army, and the third for the monastery. Every family wanted all powers: over land, war and the salvation of souls! Daughters still unmarried at age 30 went to the convent without a word. They could not remain single all their lives – they married Jesus! They had to marry someone.

Now, the world had changed, things had moved on, everyone had a right to part of the inheritance. If Eduarda married this good-for-nothing, my father's other brothers, and maybe my father, the youngest son, would not accept that she and the good-for-nothing should inherit even a pin, whatever the circumstances. She murmured:

'Land is not to be divided! Land is family, and you don't cut a family in half. . . .'

Miguel wanted a just resolution to the problem of the inheritance. He wanted the lot. Without a doubt, the most convenient way out of this mess would be to find someone suitable in the village to marry Maria Eduarda. As quickly as possible, for the sake of her nerves, and to add money and land, for the sake of convenience. Maybe a man from the town, a rich man. Or a 'Brazilian', as the returned Portuguese were called.

Miguel considered the future, imagining the best solution: 'If the girl's destiny is to marry, and it can't be to the son of a poor man, because he is poor; and if what is wanted is to increase the inheritance rather than divide it, let's give destiny a hand and marry her off quickly, on account of her nerves. Since the joaquins are out of the running, let's find her . . . a miguel!'

'A miguel?!. Don't come to me with miguels or manuels. As if joaquins weren't enough, I have to endure a miguel? And what miguel, since I can't see him? There aren't any miguels around here.'

'Marry her to her uncle . . .'

'You? Give my youngest daughter away to my oldest brother?'

'Well, it is obvious that, with all this moaning and groaning at the window, the girl has to marry someone, and quickly. No convent would take her with all that caterwauling. Better that she marry in the family, then the family inheritance stays within! We don't have to divide up the lands, or the cattle, or the wine. . . . This is the best solution: she should marry me.'

'In the latter aspect, you're right. But there are many aspects to this question: the lass is a child in most things and you . . . you already have three children. . . .'

'I managed to raise them. I can raise another. And others, when they come along.'

So thought Uncle Miguel boldly: he too had his nerves, albeit hidden, and was in a hurry.

Esmeralda was almost convinced. Almost. She just needed a final push. Miguel remembered that marriages between uncles and nieces were not so rare in European courts between princes and princesses. Queen Maria I, known as the mad queen, had married an uncle seventeen years her senior.

'That's why she went mad,' Esmeralda said, in a fit of lucidity. She seemed to reject the idea, but in fact she was happy to be likened to the mother of a queen. At least in the matter of the age of her son-in-law. A good start.

So they drank some old Port with biscuits hot from the oven, and steeled themselves to announce the news to their closest relatives. Not to the grandfather, on account of his advanced age. Nor to the main interested party, Eduarda, before the day and the hour, for fear of resistance.

Marriage was the best solution

They made plans for a wedding at home, including inviting many nuns to accompany the priest: if the bride did not agree to the nuptials, the nuns were under absolute and irrevocable orders from her mother to bundle her away to the convent – to marry Christ! So as not to waste the journey the nuns were authorised to sing some short psalms and brief Gregorian chants, exalting the virtues of marriage and the necessity of wifely obedience to her husband. The children of the village were invited as 'pages' and 'maids of honour' – their mission was to accompany the couple on the journey from the bedroom to the altar, which was set up on the dining-room table, and thence back to the bedroom, where the nightdress was laid out and the bed set up.

They invited relatives and friends to be 'godparents', they forgot no one: symbolically binding all into the act of marriage. They came without fail, talking in whispers, as if the act were clandestine, as if the police might turn up at any moment. The lengthy party was kept at a low key, despite the pomp. Discreet exuberance. Seemly smiles on the guests' faces. On the faces of the 'happy couple', no such thing. She wore the look of a sulky little girl, doing a penance on her knees at school. He was serene, serious. A severe teacher.

The spectacular nature of the nuptials was an offering to the gossips: it gave them something more interesting to tittle-tattle about than the proximity in blood and the distance in age of the newly-weds. With such a buildup it was natural that the news should spread far and wide, over the mountains and down to the coast; all the inhabitants of Justes ended up knowing about it. Beyond Justes, to Trás-os-Montes and way beyond to Óbidos, where Catalina and Catalina dwelt, waiting.

Catalina, the infuriated mother, hired a cattle cart and set off down the road at a trot and gallop, with Catalina behind her and the oxen complaining at the speed and the equine style. 'They'll see,' she said, fury personified, smoke pouring from her nostrils, steam from her ears. When she arrived, three days later, it was too late. The marriage consummated, the niece had already been living in her uncle's bedroom for days, a girl turned woman. If she still let out groans, these groans were different, more extended, longer.

Catalina revealed the truth to the family, detailed their conjugal life in Brazil and presented her daughter, who called Uncle Miguel 'Father'. With cries, she showed photos, letters, evidence, particulars. The family, in silence and without comment, believed her . . . but preferred – it was the best solution – to pretend that they didn't.

'You're mad' said Uncle Miguel. And thus was she decreed: mad!

Crazy with anger, the 'madwoman' Catalina handed over her bewildered daughter to the hunchback Isabel, one of Miguel's sisters, to raise her as her own. Isabel had never married because a fall from horseback had deformed her spinal column, which made both marriage and the convent difficult. For an inheritance, Catalina left only a medical prescription, which she had not had time to collect. This prescription was the only memento the daughter kept of that woman who disappeared for ever from Trás-os-Montes, from Óbidos, from Portugal, from the world. No one ever knew where she ended up.

My grandfather died, and Uncle Miguel certified the inheritance and dealt with all the formalities. He decided to leave his children in Portugal in the care of that same Aunt Isabel, who had had no children of her own, because she was hunchbacked, and now had four of someone else's . . . It was the best solution! He returned to Brazil and went to live with his new wife, his ex-niece, in the same house in which he had lived with other people, in other times. This time, he occupied the whole house. Progress.

Maria Eduarda had four sons, all of whom she gave the same name – Frederico. All died before they were a week old, two in more of a hurry before they were born. Maria Eduarda photographed them all, already dead, dressed up in lace and embroidery, looking beautiful. She kept the photos on top of the bedroom wardrobe, next to the mirror. When she looked at herself, she saw her sons.

Her mother, Esmeralda and her uncle turned husband, Miguel, both met tragic ends. Esmeralda committed suicide, throwing herself into a deep well at her homestead. She had fallen in love, aged 40, and wanted to marry. The same relatives and friends who had stopped Maria Eduarda's marriage to the simpleton, now opposed this one too on the grounds of her advanced age. Esmeralda threw herself into the well. She was in love, like her daughter had once been.

Uncle Miguel, prosaically, was run over by the only registered automobile in the entire neighbourhood of Sao Cristovão. He must have been very distracted, because it was the only car which was going along the Bela road that midday. Instant death: his smile, which had been alive but imprisoned behind his face, finally showed itself then. After his death, Miguel let loose the only smile of his life, the longest smile in eternity.

The night before his death, my mother had a dream or vision of relatives at a wake in Miguel's house. My mother had visions, premonitions, and I also inherited this gift.

All the other characters in this story have already died, in a more conventional manner, in bed even – except Catalina, who is still alive today and still keeps a medical prescription. Her one and only memento. . . .

Born by a hair's breadth

My mother's father was called Antonio Rodrigues Alexandre, and her mother, Maria Vilela Pinto. As a young woman Mum lived with her parents on a farm called 'Martim', where they produced grapes and wine, olives, olive oil and firewood – and, during the war, minerals, which were sold to all the combatants, irrespective of race, creed, colour or ideology. Opinions differ as to how the family ended up there, in a land which was hot in the summer, mild in the winter, and good for wine all the year round – but far from Lisbon, ever so far. In my grandmother's house, people used to talk only of the Court, in a suitably courtly Lisbon accent, and gossip about royal affairs, just as they did at Court. Those were the days of the boudoir – the ideal place for gossip and double-dealing.

My grandmother's grandfather, a certain Count Saldanha, was very well known among the intimate friends of Dona Maria, *A Louca* – 'the mad queen'. He was madder than her, and mad about her. Possessed of an unparalleled talent for fencing, he was also – of necessity – an Olympic-standard jumper from windows, like a cat. Some called him 'Saldana, the

Angoran', because he was more feline than any kitten. He also had a weakness for flamboyant outfits.

There were rumours, eagerly circulated, that Saldanha was involved with the Queen – to whom he had access even late at night, any night. He seemed to be even more involved with her principal lady-in-waiting, a young marquise, who was part Jewish, part Arab, an even more explosive mixture than Irish Catholic and Protestant. These rumours only ran to suggestions of intense and reciprocal affections, but . . . who knows! The Marquis, the affronted husband of the presumed adulteress, secured from the Queen Saldanha's banishment to avoid the scandal of an inevitable duel, and the copious spillage of blood which would result. I don't know if the dates tally, but the rumours do. There were ample vestiges of the Court in my grandmother Maria Pinto's family. Splendid on horseback, she rode side-saddle as befits a princess – and as everyone knows, a princess does not spread her legs. At least not in Portugal, in those days. By no stretch of the imagination.

True or not, the family coat of arms still emblazons the heraldic room of Sintra Castle today. It is beautiful, an item of great splendour. I have seen it. Apparently I am associated with it.

Saldanha received endless estates as a royal gift. He was an exile who gained land instead of losing it. The family was left with its morals intact and its finances restored, banished far from Lisbon and close to Justes, a tiny village. Time passes – till finally we get to my grandmother, Maria Pinto.

My mother's father, Antonio Rodrigues Alexandre, by contrast, came from a peasant family. One of his duties was to fetch firewood and wine from Martim. There Maria Pinto could be espied from afar, on horseback, both legs slung to one side. An enchanting vision: the side-saddle montage is a thing of beauty, especially when you happen to be pretty, and noble with it. After collecting so much firewood, my grandfather ended up getting scorched himself: he fell in love with Maria.

She too was captivated, seeing a man so different from her delicate brothers and uncles, men who dressed in lace and were totally unsuited to a hoe in the hand or sweat on the brow. Sweat has its attractions, it emits a strong scent. This man sowed the earth with a variety of seeds, and made it give birth to ripe fruits and colourful flowers. He was irresistible.

They got married. The woman followed the man and they went to live in Antonio's homestead, without a trace of luxury to remind the exiles of Lisbon and of Martim. Maria had been educated as if she were at Court. She had never in her life done anything productive with her hands, which proved she was indeed genuine nobility. In the Middle Ages noble women went around with their elbows glued to their sides, strapped into corsets, and never showing their armpits, to make it absolutely clear that they did not, under any circumstances, work. Heaven forbid: over their dead bodies! If they needed anything, others would see to it: that was their duty. Justes may not have been the Portuguese Court; but medieval it certainly was!

Children were born. The eldest, Tefé, displayed a virulent authoritarianism as he grew up, inherited not from his father, who was meek and mild, but from several centuries of Lisbon nobility. He was a tyrant. Everyone obeyed him, without so much as a whisper of dissent. Neither understanding nor questioning; Tefé's will was law. Woe betide anyone who opposed him: punishment was a horsewhip.

His brothers, Aníbal and João, enjoyed a degree of freedom: they could wander around the village with friends after supper. Their sisters — five buxom lasses, rosy cheeked as in all the best romances, good-hearted and healthy, with my future mother, Albertina, among their number — remained locked up in the house, looking after my grandparents and talking of things befitting their gender in those days. There were plenty of the usual giggles. Every now and then, one friend or another would drop in to pour out her troubles or to share a farewell to her unmarried state. For ever. Many tears would be shed. Marriage was the only viable way out for a young woman, who would pass from one prison to another — this second with more duties and keys.

Tefé was the first to marry: a young girl called Gracinha, who was promptly promoted to womanhood. Aníbal was the second. Before long, so as the sisters would not end up on the shelf, Tefé chose a husband for the eldest who, in this as in all things, obeyed him, and went to live on another property. The tyrant thought the other four girls still too young, and decided they should wait. That was it, the end of the story, till further notice.

Aunt Lúcia did not appreciate such a long wait. There was someone who thought her shapely and radiant: the young lad Lúcio. To their shame, Tefé and Lúcio had exchanged blows years ago over some idiotic matter, and they were not on speaking terms. When they met on the street, they would spit on the ground. On various occasions they even ended up wrestling with each other; but oddly enough, they only became so embroiled if there was someone else in the vicinity, on hand, ready to break up the fight. When they were alone, a spit on the ground would do – the gravity of this moral offence was sufficient.

Generally, they hurled insults at each other. They snarled. They spoke ill of each other, and of each other's families. But one fine day Lúcio did not respond to Tefé's provocations. The more Tefé provoked him, the more Lúcio smiled back at him. He even committed the supreme offence of offering Tefé his hand and sending him messages of praise and admiration. Messages, sent via third parties, which sought to take back any unintended offence, to ask pardon for the spitting. He promised, always through these third parties, that never again would he spit on the ground. He wouldn't dream of it!

Tefé could not sleep for thinking of his friendly enemy, his courteous adversary. It would have suited his temperament better if they had continued to fight, because he felt more at ease with hate and anger than with warm friendship. Quarrels are difficult when they are only one-sided. The two enemies did not sign the peace, but nor did they prolong the war.

Then Tefé had a stupefying revelation: 'That scoundrel wants to go out with one of my four sisters. That's the only explanation for this! When he forces a grin as I pass by, and smiles at me and sends me messages, it is because he wants to try and steal one of my four sisters.' Tefé started to keep an eye on the most developed and buxom of them. (My mother, as a young girl, escaped such control.) 'Just my luck: God gives me two brothers to till the land, and five sisters to stand guard over!' The blame lay with God, as always.

He questioned his sisters one by one. What had they done that afternoon, what had they talked about, who had they watched from the window? They replied that they hadn't looked out of the window or spoken to anyone, that they had worked all afternoon, at home, silently praying. They were tired from so much praying, they were going to bed. But as soon as they turned off the lights, Tefé heard conversation and laughter. It was draining. To stand guard over four sisters was a huge amount of work – a task for medieval convents. And Tefé did not manage to pin anything, any sign of love, on any of them. There was nothing for it – he would just have to put up with his enemy's kindnesses and his sisters' mysteries.

In those days, it was the destiny of dynamic men to exile themselves to Brazil, to earn a better living overseas and thus secure their family's future. Tefé received a 'call-up letter' from a Brazilian General, the owner of the Santa Eustaquia slaughterhouse, inviting him to be assistant to the under-manager of his butchery. Tefé had aspirations to get rich in Rio more quickly than he knew would be possible in Portugal, so he asked his relatives to make arrangements.

Before setting off, he called the family together. He was the head, since my sick grandfather was more concerned with Maria Pinto's health than with his own well-being or that of his estate. Tefé nominated Aníbal as his representative and Second-in-Command – with express orders that he was to prohibit premature courtship. Tefé would announce the correct moment and the right fiancé from afar. Aníbal was to send fortnightly reports on the economic and emotional activities of the family. After nominating Aníbal as guardian of the women, who could not be left on their own, ungoverned, he set off with his wife and his first two children.

As repressions go, the atmosphere improved. A slow easing, gradual yet secure; the dictatorship continued, but the terror gave way. My grandfather returned to the fray with a new lease of life, and sacked a hulking fellow whom Tefé had taken on, a braggart who used bad language even in front of the young girls, whose function it was to collect firewood. In his place, my grandfather employed a young, healthy, handsome man with a moustache. This was José Augusto, who was later to become my father.

When she saw the new arrival on the farm, Albertina, the youngest (later to become my mother), asked: 'Won't this one be as bad as the other?' My father heard and replied: 'No, don't worry, I'm not a bad person. . . .'

And as he looked at the young girl, he forgot that she was 12 and he 20: 'The girl is very pretty. . . . Thanks be to God.'

'She is indeed,' replied my grandfather. 'Now get to work, which is what you're paid for.'

So my father went off with his wheelbarrow to collect firewood, thinking of my mother. Family folklore suggests that José Augusto even had time to murmur to Albertina: 'I'll go to Brazil, earn some money, and come back to fetch you. Wait for me. I'm going to marry you.'

'Yes, sir!' my mother is said to have answered, intimidated, but fascinated.

I don't know whether this encounter actually happened as they described it, or if it is just a story, a legend. But with that intense look in the eyes of both of them, I was certain to be born sooner or later. With all that love in their eyes, it was inevitable: I had to be born. Luckily for me, later on, I was.

The second sign of the new democratic times was when Lúcio took a stroll close to the house, from which three young girls studied him from behind the curtains. He passed by less than a stone's throw away. It soon became clear that Lúcia was his favourite. And the girls now had the right to go out for short walks after supper. My mother, the fourth girl, washed the dishes at home and helped with the family business, a kind of grocery store, on the ground floor of the two-storey house. Dreaming all the while.

Love and tyranny

In those days even serious and committed courtship, with a marriage date and hour arranged, was not a matter for only two people: it always involved at least three. Lúcio and Lúcia's courtship began in a foursome because two sisters (Dora and Teresa) accompanied them. As a girl, my mother stayed behind at home, looking after Maria Pinto, who was always sick, with *saudades* for the Court, which she did not know, and for Lisbon, which she had never visited.

Aníbal was torn between fraternal loyalties. Out of fear or solicitude, he decided to write the letter informing on them: 'My dear brother. You should be aware that our dear sister Lúcia . . .'

He only told the truth, the whole truth, modest and small as it was: Lúcio and Lúcia went out for a walk after supper and spoke lovingly to each other. Utterances which were sensible, and yet verged on the sensual. Words heard by two of the sisters – almost hypnotised in their busybody curiosity – and relayed by night to Albertina, who was looking after her mother and nearly asleep.

Tefé's boss, the General, the owner of the slaughterhouse, was delighted with Tefé, who thought only of work, work, work. Tefé inspected the cattle and oversaw their slaughter and the sale of the quartered animals. A man in a hurry, he had attained the highest level of his new profession: General Manager. All subordinates obeyed his orders, their eyes cast down in fear.

Tefé asked the General's advice. The General, serious connoisseur of the art of discipline that he was, sided with Tefé on this matter. The order of a superior could not be disobeyed by a subordinate, in this case Aníbal. Just or unjust – it was hierarchy, not justice, that was being called into question here. Hierarchy was the only indispensable foundation of society; the basis of the army's effective operation. Regardless of any hurt that might be caused to anyone, it was imperative to bring the erring sister to Brazil, and also of course to give a good dressing down to the brother, lacking as he had been in the necessary competence.

Tefé commanded that Lucia must come and live with him. But . . . how could she travel alone? Wanting to protect her from a wolf, Tefé could not place her among a pack of dogs, in a boat full of immigrants. So all the sisters would have to come. Are you mad? Four young girls travelling alone? So, if four are too many, the youngest, Albertina, should stay behind to look after her parents. She runs less risk of getting involved with Lúcio. Let just three come. But not alone. Then Aníbal should come too. But Aníbal was married, so if he came his family would have to come as well: the cost of cabins was rocketing.

'I too am married,' Tefé replied in enormous letters. 'You should come, it's all your fault!'

'João should go: he is single and could fix himself up with a rich Brazilian,' Aníbal replied firmly. The family's discussions seem to have been limited to who should come, rather than whether anyone should come at all.

In the end João came over to Brazil with the three sisters. Tefé put them all up in the widowed General's house, who had two sons and many empty rooms, in Santa Teresa overlooking the Guanabara Bay. João went out alone. He adored Rio de Janeiro, especially Praça de Mauá and the Cais de Pharoux, where the European ships docked. João stayed for two months, didn't fix himself up with a rich Brazilian woman, and went back to working the land in Trás-os-Montes.

The young girls were allowed to go out after lunch and return home to the kitchen before 4 p.m. Dora and Teresa smiled at the General's sons, who, though also in pursuit of military careers, did not yet display the same discipline as their father: they pinched and played with the two young girls to their hearts' content. Lúcia remained apart. Other young friends always came by, to meet the little Portuguese girls. They settled in the living room distributing affectionate pinches. That was how one courted in those days: being courted meant red skin. And Lúcia would be at the window, sighing.

One night, as she sat sighing, Lúcia heard her name, uttered in a voice more sweet than her ears had ever heard, in a country burr typical of Justes: 'Lúcia. Little Lúcia . . . oh my love . . . oooh . . .'

It was enough to make anyone faint. Lúcia craned her neck and then drew herself up, both body and desire at full stretch, and jumped down into the garden, which was separated from the street by two sets of railings three metres apart from each other. No-man's land, with an owner – the gardener. He was the only one who went there, to take care of the flowers.

Lúcia remained inside the inside railings, and – just imagine – who was the other side of the outside railings? Her beloved Lúcio. The young man had sold all that he had ever owned or borrowed, bought a one-way ticket, and there he was all of a tremor, three metres from the woman he loved.

Courting behind bars. They made all the impossible promises, they promised love for all eternity, but the railings were high and made of iron. Growing more confident, they spoke more loudly, they made vows of love, while the gardener overheard their conversations. For three evenings he stayed hidden, writing down what he heard. On the fourth day the young lovers were caught gazing at each other, their arms extended in an impossible embrace, their lips pouting for the promised kiss, hearts beating with forbidden desire, when the boorish gardener appeared, stepping on the flowers. 'Hey! What are you two up to there?' he asked severely.

Without waiting for an explanation, he made a threat: 'I have here ten sheets of paper. Everything you have been saying and doing is written here. Each page will cost you a thousand *réis*. If you buy them all from me, you can tear them up and I will also tear them from my memory, because I'm not a spiteful man. If you don't want to buy them, I'll give them to the General, who, being a widower and an upstanding soldier, will hand them over to your brother. And your brother, who is an honourable man – well I don't even want to think what he would do with you two. . . . Best hide the knives and daggers!'

The lovers promised to ransom the ten sheets of paper, one by one. Every afternoon they went back to the railings, but now they only spoke with the eloquence of their eyes, the sad smiles of their bodies. In the silence, the gardener's new pages stayed blank. Of those he had already written, they bought the first four with some money Lúcio had saved. Then, doing odd jobs to raise the money, they bought the fifth and sixth. When they got to the seventh, the treasury ran out.

'Well,' said the gardener. 'You haven't bought them all from me, as we had agreed, so I will have to do my duty, since I still have the three. . . .'

He handed over the remaining sheets to the General who, as anticipated, handed them on to Tefé who, as anticipated, collapsed with shock.

Tefé's first thought was slaughter – a habit acquired in the Santa Eustaquia abattoir – but he did not know who to slaughter first. He called Lucia, took off his belt, and threatened to whip her. The General, who, ironically, did not like bloodshed, pacified Tefé. He advised him to avoid violence and to have a holiday in Portugal, taking his three sisters with him. The General himself was far from keen on the little games his own sons were playing with the two remaining sisters: he had very different matrimonial plans for his sons among the emerging society of Rio. Thus, with one single journey, three marriages, or at least dangerous liaisons, were aborted.

Tefé, surrounded by devil-possessed women, resolved to return to the more conservative Justes. He was helped by his meek and mild wife Gracinha, a sweet thing who spoke only when spoken to. Lúcio, abandoned again, stayed behind in Rio crying, thickening the tropical sea.

In Portugal, Tefé made arrangements. There were too many young women to look after all at the same time, on top of which he had to see to the business of the estate. He cursed the system of primogeniture, attributing to it brotherly duties which were certainly not due.

To lighten his load, he agreed to Teresa's marriage, and she went to live with a neighbouring farmer. Dora married a Portuguese-Brazilian who, on seeing her leaving, had realised how much he loved her. And he brought her back to Brazil.

Lúcia, poor Lúcia, remained in penance: prohibited to marry, or court or even go out after supper! Lúcia did not mind: she wanted to stay on her own, and thought of no one but her beloved Lúcio. She grew fond of railings, and wherever she saw them pressed them to her chest, and kissed the iron bars waiting to hear the voice of her love. But the cold railings stayed silent, they were not the sweet Brazilian railings . . .

Tefé decided to bring his holidays to an end and return to Rio. He nominated Gracinha to stay in Portugal and be Lúcia's guardian, since Uncle Aníbal had shown himself to be unreliable. Until further orders, which would arrive by letter, Tefé was in charge from afar.

By coincidence the two ships crossed in the open sea: the one bearing Tefé, who was returning alone to the slaughterhouse, assured of his sister's virginity, and the one carrying Lúcio, who had sold everything he had again to buy his ticket — except his soul, since no one would give anything for such a lovesick soul. The young man travelled with the clothes on his back and mortadella sandwiches in his pocket, love in his heart and hope in his eyes. His destination — Justes, in Portugal.

Destiny played its hand — as it always does:

'She has given herself to him!' a relative said ingenuously. 'What do you mean "given herself to him"?' 'Just like the rest of us, but . . . but . . . willingly. . . .' She stressed the difference.

As they assumed Lúcio had stayed in Brazil (whereas in fact he had gone to live in a nearby village, disguised with a beard and moustache) no one bothered to monitor the poor virgin Lúcia, who was melancholic and reclusive. Lúcio soon found a way of revealing himself to his loved one and the two of them began to meet in the stables of the farm in which he worked. After love-making there were loving rides on the back of a donkey, back to Justes. . . . Everything would have been pure joy if it wasn't for the sacred laws of biology. Everyone began to notice that God had blessed the couple earlier than might have been hoped.

God, who is understanding and just; God, who forgives humans their weaknesses and also their strengths; God, who allowed their happiness but did not take responsibility for the consequences. And the proud belly, untamed, did not hide. It showed itself in all its splendour.

The postal service worked apace. Uncle Tefé soon heard of the happy disgrace, the disgraceful happiness.

The first victim of vengeance was his own wife: 'You are hereby unmarried, disinherited, disaffiliated! Disloyal! Divorced! How could you let my sister sink so low? I don't ever want to see you again, or hear you, or read your letters. I will tear them up even before you have written them! Accursed woman! As for my brother, don't let that damned filcher of honest maidens' honour enter our house. He must never see the baby! Lúcia is prohibited from going out of the house. Put one lock on her bedroom door and a load more on the windows. And the child must be registered in only the mother's name. It will never have a father. To be a father is to be a man, and this traitor is no man! Lúcia must stay under lock and key for a while, and then come back here – while I find her a husband who is to my liking.'

That was the way he thought, that was the way he wanted it to be, and that was the way it was. Lúcia gave birth to a beautiful girl, the daughter of a lone mother. She was so pretty that they could find her no name other than Linda, which means pretty in Portuguese. She was surrounded by the love and attention of close relatives, and by distant hate. Grandfather and grandmother – still alive – brothers and sisters, uncles and aunts: everyone loved her.

Lúcia was forced to travel to Brazil, and leave her baby behind in the care of my mother, who was growing ever more womanly. She obeyed the tyrant's command and went back to the railings, waiting for Tefé to find her an adequate and suitable husband.

The husband appeared in the person of the amiable Mr Azevedo, who lived in his own world. Whatever the circumstances, he used to repeat the same phrase: 'It's a serious matter. . .', and then break into an extended smile, for no reason. He took no notice of anything, not even moving cars. He ended up getting run over. Another one.

(In those days, with so few cars about, accidents were frequent, on account of the difficulty people had getting used to the existence of vehicles bigger and faster than themselves. Passers-by had not yet become aware of their condition of mere passer-by-dom — vulnerable, fragile mortals that they were. Some people were so obstinate that they would not move out of the tram's way, expecting it, the tram, to let them pass. There were many machos who would kick the trams, trying to divert them from their rectilinear trajectory.)

My mother's responsibility was to look after her own mother – Maria Pia, she of the disoriented arms, who had never done anything useful or necessary in her life. The poor woman paid the price for keeping her legs tight together: one sunny and beautiful morning, while she was out happily riding her horse in open countryside, the animal took fright for no apparent reason. The horse shot off, in fear of the horsewoman. My grandmother, with her legs crossed to one side, slipped and broke both arms and a leg – and ever after was confined to her bed. My grandfather, at her side, watched over her devotedly, twenty-four hours a day, effectively as paralysed as her. Only my mother worked. My grandfather was in love until the very last second.

Until Maria Pinto, the noblewoman, the princess who rode side-saddle on horseback, died. She died, tired of doing nothing, with her arms crossed on her chest, as useless in death as they had been in life. That was in March. In April my grandfather died, gazing at the empty bed. He had never recovered from his wife's death. He died for lack of anyone to look at.

My mother looked after her niece Linda. Uncle João, who had deserted the army and gone off to Spain to sell minerals, returned to Portugal and was a true father to his niece. And many years later Linda, then in Brazil, was our dearest friend, and second mother to me and my siblings.

But in the meantime, Albertina remained alone, with a babe in arms. The store in the basement of the house sold everything: ham, savoury snacks, cheeses, olive oil, olives, dried cod, corn-cakes, eleven-litre barrels of wine . . . fabric, tape, buttons and all forms of merchandises proper to a small haberdashery. Every once in a while a relative would come by to see how business was doing, and would always lend a hand. But the person who saw to it that the store ran smoothly was my mother, and she alone. Later she had the assistance of her niece Linda and a maid, Angelina, five years my mother's junior.

★   ★   ★

Marriage was on the cards

At 24, Albertina, the youngest daughter, had many suitors. She was pretty. (I am not saying that because I am her son – there are witnesses: she was beautiful!) Requests for the young woman's hand came even from Vila Real, but her sense of her responsibilities was greater than her desire to marry. Some said she was already getting too old, and what a shame: she wasn't a hunchback, and she wasn't ugly or devout; on the contrary, she was capable, healthy, sturdy, knew how to read and write, never got the accounts wrong, and was a hard worker. That she, of all people, should run the risk of being left on the shelf.

My mother talked to relatives and friends, thought about it, saw that there was no alternative, and decided to marry. She had awaited the Enchanted Prince for many years, but the Prince had not arrived.

She was not enthusiastic about any of the suitors, so she chose the most passionate, a certain João Marcelino, educated and hard-working, accepted even by Tefé, and a man who had the virtue of being silent. They would meet, always with aunt between them – one did not court *à deux*: the witness was indispensable.

They fixed the marriage date: 10 September. They went to the Priest and confirmed it: 10 September. They agreed the cost of the ceremony and the flowers, of the music and the prayers, and all was ready for the marriage. In Justes people talked of nothing but my mother's marriage. Relatives and friends began to sort out wedding presents.

On 1 September 1925, Justes awoke all of a fluster. A 'Brazilian' had arrived (this term was used to mean those who returned from Brazil, having made something of themselves). And the 'Brazilian', with a hat of coconut straw and a cane, well dressed and be-whiskered, was called José Augusto. It was 1 September, nine days before the tenth.

Everyone wanted to see the 'Brazilian' who talked animatedly, re-counting all the news from Brazil, and all the while keeping one eye fixed on the door of the store. Inside, young Albertina, now betrothed, also spied on him. And everyone stared at the 'Brazilian', with his walking stick and his smile, which proudly displayed the first gold tooth ever seen in Justes! A genuine Brazilian gold tooth. When the local peasants saw that tooth, its glint and sparkle, they dreamt of Eldorado, the Incas, Shangri-la!

It was getting late, and before my mother closed up shop for the night, my father felt a sudden urge to drink a glass of wine. Where? At the store, of course. He went in, asked for a local red, which was excellent, and took a few sips to pluck up his courage and polish his words:

'Albertina, do you remember when you asked me if I too would be bad like the other one?'

'What other one?'

'The other one who brought firewood. He was a hulking great fellow, and swore. Your father sacked him and asked me to start bringing the firewood, in his place. You asked: "And won't this one be as bad as the other?" Do you remember?'

'I didn't ask you, I was talking to my father.'

'I'm not so bad.' Silence. 'Now . . . I've come back.'

'Why?'

'To marry you!'

Albertina thought about the tenth. She paused. It was a long pause – eventually broken by Albertina herself, who said sincerely: 'It's a bit difficult. . . .'

'No, it's easy to get married: you go to the priest and pay him whatever is necessary; in Vila Real, you go to the Registry Office, pay for the stamps and seals, and that's it: you are married! Then you go to the shipping company, you buy the tickets, pay and that's it, we're on our way to Brazil. . . .'

'Yes, it's easy but it's also difficult. . . . Because . . . because. . . .'

'Why?'

'I'm engaged.'

'Ah! That I hadn't counted on!' said my father-to-be, sadly. 'So. . . you didn't wait for me?'

'FOURTEEN years . . . I waited as long as I could.'

'And I came back . . . to get you . . . I made a promise and I kept it. . . .'

'The wedding is arranged for the tenth.'

'Well, we've got nine days. . . .' Hope was reborn.

Another pause, a lot shorter than the first. My father adduced and seduced: 'When I was in Brazil I had a dream, and I dreamt that I was returning to Portugal to marry you and take you with me. . . . I even dreamt where we would live, in a house in Bela Street. . . I dreamt the same dream many times. And each time the house was bigger and prettier, more brightly painted and colourful. . . . With each dream, the garden got bigger, along with the boys' room and the girls' room. . . . I have already rented the house. . . . But if you're engaged, yes, it's difficult. . . .'

'But it isn't impossible . . .' said Albertina the realist who, in that moment, decided my life and future. 'You must give me a bit of time. . . .'

'How much time?'

'Come and see me here tomorrow at this hour, and I'll tell you what I've done. . . .'

Before they bid farewell to each other, my mother asked:

'Is it true that you have a gold tooth?'

'I do, yes.'

'Would you let me see it?'

My father smiled: the Brazilian gold tooth shone in the Lusitanian sun. The pact was sealed.

They said goodbye to each other. He wanted to give her a little kiss, but she would not let him: she was still betrothed, and a faithful woman.

The following day when she awoke, my mother went to see João Marcelino, having dreamt of Jose Augusto all through the night. Before she got round to saying 'hello?', she explained that she had changed her mind and could no longer marry him. She made it clear that she was unsaying what she had said, taking back her word. She said that she knew he would find a way to understand her and to forgive her, and that there was no shortage of pretty and hard-working fiancées, and that soon he would meet a more adequate one. And a very good afternoon. Goodbye. Never again. And 'put me out of your mind!' My mother did not want to leave her fiancé with even the vaguest memory of her, with even the slightest *saudades*.

The stunned João Marcelino did not even have time to open his mouth or focus his eyes. Though unpersuaded by her speech, he could not dissuade her. And just as well: by a hair's breadth, I escaped not being born.

Unbetrothed, Albertina went to the church, not knowing whether she had been forgiven: she did not have time to wait for her ex-fiancé's reply. Though the priest was still half asleep, Albertina was in a hurry and would brook no delay (she had to open up the grocery on time). So she called Eufrosina, the priest's woman – sorry – the woman who looked after the priest, a respectable woman, of course, as all priests' women tend to be –

Albertina Pinto Boal and José Augusto Boal, 1924

sorry, I mean as all women who look after priests tend to be. Albertina gave her some money to get the priest up before his usual breakfast in bed, Eufrosina went to fetch him, and the priest came down rubbing his eyes, still clad in his long johns, with a crucifix under his nightshirt. Albertina informed him she had two urgent changes to make to the matrimonial plans. First the date, which was too soon. It had to be about a month later, on 10 October.

'I quite understand . . . preparations for a solid Christian marriage take time. The betrothed need to get to know each other better, it's a big decision, a decision to which both the children to come and the Holy Mother Church are party. I understand, I understand. So, what was the second change you wished to make?'

'The second change is the name of the fiancé: he is now called José Augusto Boal. . . .'

'But I don't understand!' spluttered the priest, open-mouthed, thinking he must still be asleep and dreaming. 'Wasn't he called . . . what was the fiancé's name? João something. . . . Or Manuel, or Joaquim?'

'No matter what he was called, the important thing is what he is called now! And, now, my fiancé is called José Augusto Boal.'

When my mother had to make decisions, she didn't waste any time. At the end of the afternoon, towards the close of day, a worried José Augusto turned up, glancing timidly at her, a living embodiment of the expression 'to cast a sidelong glance' at someone. His glance at my mother was as 'sidelong' a glance as it is possible to imagine. She did not keep him in suspense. Without hesitation, she said:

'It is all arranged. Our marriage will be on 10 October. The tickets for Brazil, when are you going to buy them?'

'Tomorrow morning, I'll go to Vila Real. They sell them there.'

'Buy three: Linda is coming with us, I can't leave her here alone. We don't know where her father is, but her mother is in Brazil. . . .'

José Augusto saw that Albertina was determined and did not argue. He bought a double cabin, and another smaller one next door. In the days remaining before the marriage, my mother first of all got rid of the goods and the furniture in the store, which was to be rented out, and then of her maid Angelina, especially when the girl started throwing flirtatious glances in my father's direction. My mother wasted no time: she sacked the girl. Once again, I escaped by a hair's breadth!

It was a family wedding, with a few very close friends, on 10 October 1925. Neither of the couple had ever heard of Stanislavksi, but the emotion was enormous. After the wedding the ship set sail from the port of Lisbon, on the river Tejo. Looking into his wife's eyes and seeing the beginnings of a tear, José Augusto promised: 'In a few years' time, we'll be back to see the folks, back to the old country.'

My father died in 1963 on 7 June, the very day he turned 71, without ever having returned to Portugal. After his death, my mother went to Portugal only once. She met few of the characters in this story. She had gone to visit me in Lisbon, where I was in exile. We were in Bairro Alto, where I was a teacher in the National Conservatory, and we were standing looking at Sao Jorge Castle, in front of us. She said to me: 'It was here that I came with your father, before travelling to Brazil. He wanted to come back after a few years, he wanted to come back to the old country. . . . But he never did, I was the only one to make it back. Never mind, he's here with me now. If I am here, then so's he.'

Albertina Pinto Boal and José Augusto Boal, 1950

a long time ago,
I was a boy

Three children crying

Sitting on the bridge at the entrance to my house one Sunday night, I cried and cried. I was 9 years old, a sensitive and emotional age.

That Sunday lunch had left an indelible mark on my life. It was a savage episode. I can remember the characters of that gory story quite clearly. Each time I cast my mind back I recall other forgotten details, and my eyes threaten tears.

On that Sunday, my sadness was provoked by a painful ethical question to do with individual responsibility. For a child of 9, ethical questions are spectacularly important. Was I, or was I not, the person responsible for the savagery? Nine years old, and already so responsible!

We had many animals in the backyard of our house. When the chicken-coop was full, it was as overcrowded as a Brazilian prison. We frequently

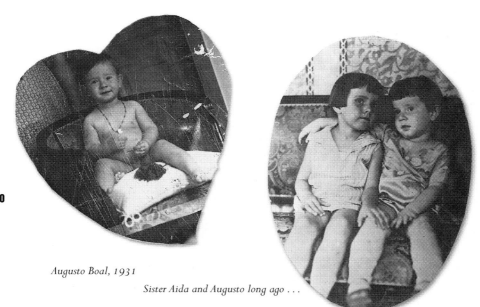

Augusto Boal, 1931

Sister Aida and Augusto long ago . . .

ate chicken stew, often roast chicken, and occasionally *coq au vin*. More rarely, we ate domestic duck and sometimes wild mallard.

The feathered ones spent their lives imprisoned in an overcrowded chicken-coop, at the end of the yard, with the right to roam about scratching for worms and exercising their muscles. The chickens' playtime began in the morning and ended when the sun set, when they would politely and voluntarily return to their roost! Our dog, Leão (Lion) helped to drive the hens and their partners back to jail.

The yard was large, with room for bulkier beasts as well. When the goats at the market looked well-proportioned and friendly, my parents would buy a billy and two or three nannies. Soon there would be kids, inevitably. Occasionally we kept pigs.

This modest zoological garden had, to my child's eyes, a sense of tragic pastime, because it was also a gastronomical garden. I became attached to these creatures, I liked to play with them, to baptise them – I even engaged the cocks, hens and kids in long and intelligent conversations. I spoke in Portuguese, and each of them spoke in their own natural language which I translated, trying (like any translator!) to improve the style and to clarify any misunderstandings provoked by the exuberance of their personalities.

We appeared to be friends: we weren't. The truth tormented me: I lived in the big house, destined for a brilliant university future, I would be a 'Doctor'. They, on the other hand, lived on Death Row, destined for the cooking pot, the oven, the stove and the spit. Even the corn and the other rations we gave them, in our generosity – and for which they, in their naïvety, were grateful – had this culinary intent. Our backyard was a huge concentration camp: all the guests had the date of their death fixed. Only I would live for ever, for all my life! True friendship cannot exist between two individuals when one is eternal and the other perishable.

Playing with the creatures at the end of the day, I felt like the priests charged with administering the last rites to the condemned, in the prisons of Alcatraz, or Devil's Island. I frequently suffered from a restless insomnia, wondering which would be condemned the following morning; I would run through each animal's features in my mind. I felt a tremendous relief when, on my return from school in the afternoon, I found that my favourite chickens and ducks and drakes and goats were still alive.

It was only the pigs I didn't care for. Nor they for me: there was a certain reciprocal antipathy, verging on hostility, between me and the pigs, even the youngest ones. But although I had no particular fondness for any

*Augusto, Albertino (brother), Albertina (mother), José Augusto (father),
Augusta (sister), Aida (sister)*

of the pigs, it was they who moved me to pity the most. Because they refused to die! They fought bravely, they cried out, horrifying the neighbourhood with their vociferous struggles – and managing to secure only the futile solidarity of the other animals, impotent companions in the same misfortune. None would escape its tragic destiny, come its allotted hour.

The death of a pig was a hideous spectacle: blood spitting like a fine London rain, squeals, uproar in the chicken-coop, and a difficult struggle with the knife. Cousins and friends would come to help: it was not a job for one man. From the moment of the 'catch', it was a dramatic and unequal combat. The executioners approached the pig, which emitted a groan, hoarse and nasal. Then the rest of the porcine family came out in solidarity in terror and panic. The brutes seized the pig and tied its trotters in pairs, while the principal executioner sharpened the knife. At the sight of the knife, the pig became aware of its tragic destiny. By intuition or instinct, it knew the true intentions of the blade and vociferated in anticipation.

The knife would puncture the swinish throat, and the first gush of blood would spurt out, whipping around like an untended hose, soaking everything around it. Meanwhile the cacophonic cries and clamour of the other animals redoubled. The struggle – armed on one side only – would last half an hour, a whole hour, an hour and a half, or more. That is when things went well, from the executioner's point of view. But it could be worse: the intrepid pig might free itself from its bonds, break loose from its captors, and run screaming around the yard, shedding blood everywhere. On such occasions, the women would close the windows and observe the proceedings from behind the glass, while we children would spectate from a distance, as the men closed in on the animal with ropes and chains and, in cases of extreme necessity, a sharp axe destined for its head.

One day a 300-kilo pig, whose death had been planned as meticulously as a military campaign, hurled itself against the chicken coop in its death throes, ripping open the fence and freeing the prisoners. The demented fowl then used their wings for the first time in their lives and flew like songbirds out of the yard and into neighbouring gardens. I didn't even know that chickens could fly! We can all fly! It just depends how urgent it is. Some neighbours kindly returned the gallinaceous escapees. Others only gave up the creatures when my father threatened to call the police.

Once the pig was dead, the corpse was gutted and quartered in sombre silence. Everyone felt guilty as they cut the porcine fat into small pieces for crackling, with the ears, knees, tail and snout kept for *feijoadas*, and every part of the body destined for a different earthenware pot and its own seasoning. After the assassination, the pig's executioners had to bathe from head to foot in soapy water, and apply rice powder to their armpits, talc to their ankles and eau-de-cologne to their clothes, before they were able to return to civilisation.

Chickens were strangled with less spectacle – it was a routine event. The maid was charged with the sacrifice. After a couple of deceptive little caresses, she clasped hold of the victim's neck with a single flourish and wrung it. Then a small knife would appear as if from nowhere, and be used to cut the victim's head off. Blood poured out and was placed in a large jar: this gave colour to the *cabidela*.

(My mother only tried to kill a chicken once. It was a disaster. In the middle of the bloody business she took pity on the bird, which then, with its neck half-severed, ran into and around the drawing-room, spattering the furniture with blood. Never again!)

Rabbits were murdered with ease: a sharp blow at the back of the head and that was it: dead. But then the ugly part would begin. The white neck would be cut and the skin stripped down to the knees, and the body hung up naked, skin and fur still attached to its lower legs, like Finnish boots in midwinter. The skin was treated with chemical products and made into rugs. The skinned body was thrown into an iron pot and braised in butter, plenty of garlic, onion, chilli and sweet pepper, tomato, salt and flour.

And what of the goats? I have never seen a goat die. In my house, when the death of a goat was decreed, the execution would take place on a Saturday morning, when I was still at school, and the body would be laid in state in the fridge for the rest of the day and one night, in a garlic marinade. We ate goat only on certain special Sundays, for lunch. Before I went off to school early in the morning, I would see the frisky goats, gambolling playfully; by the time I saw them in the afternoon, they were already marinaded in garlic and stuffed with bread, tripe and olives. I was spared their martyrdom.

It was a goat that was responsible for my first moral dilemma. That goat was called Chibuco. I do not know whether it begins with an 'x' or 'ch':[1] this is the first time I have written his adored and *saudoso* name.

He was born at home, the son of a nanny-goat for whom I nurtured a certain affection, and a billy who looked cross, like all billies, but who I admired for being genteel, elegant, affable, respectful, of good heart — which is not the norm in your common-or-garden goat. I ended up adopting Chibuco, who became my favourite animal.

Our friendship grew with time, and my family was amazed. Chibuco played with me and obeyed my orders, understanding words which not even a stunned Leão (my dog) would comprehend, though dogs are more intelligent than goats — they have a much higher IQ.

Chibuco was the greatest! He ran, he did somersaults — extremely rare in a goat — and even (uniquely, I believe) leapt over ropes: without great dexterity, it is true, but leap he did. Yes ladies and gentlemen, he leapt over ropes. I tied a rope to the basement railings in the yard, and Chibuco leapt over it, obeying my orders. A rope-leaping goat, every child's dream.

When I think about it, Chibuco was my first actor. I became a theatre director because of a goat. I was very authoritarian, it is true, as immature directors are. But I began my career in theatre with Chibuco: I directed goat shows, without ever consulting or swapping ideas with my cast. Only later did I learn the joys of team work.

Boys, my friends — and girls, sort of friends — came to see the prodigy: Chibuco leaping over a rope, Chibuco skipping on the pavement, Chibuco affectionately butting the trees and people's legs. And me directing, proudly. When I could think of no other instruction, I would tell Chibuco to imitate a dog. And Chibuco, an excellent actor, would roll over on his back in imitation of Leão.

Everyone liked it: *dona* Angelina, a widow living alone in the house next door, would abandon her household duties and come to catch the act. Even Aunt Lúcia, already a wizened little old lady when I knew her, also liked to watch through her round glasses.

'He is like a child . . . so innocent. . .' Lucia would say.

'That is not a normal goat. . . . Goats don't do that sort of thing. . . . This is more in the way of witchcraft . . .' Angelina diagnosed.

Chibuco, happy Chibuco, even smiled when I called him — or almost. And when I sent him away, he was sad, almost wept, like a little lamb — almost. There was a solid friendship between boy and goat. This friendship grew with time, along with Chibuco's horns, which lengthened with age. Chibuco emancipated himself from his mother goat. He transformed himself into an elegant adolescent goat, entering confidently into adult life, as proud of himself as a preening peacock.

Until, one day, tragedy struck. With no ill will, perverse or treacherous intent, but rather out of an undisciplined audacity, Chibuco went too far. He overstepped the agreed mark and showed me a lack of respect by ramming his horns right into my chest. Blood flowed.

Chibuco, more astonished than I, looked at me as if to ask forgiveness, without finding the right words. He approached, to kiss my wound better – I imagine – but I was so disgusted at being butted and with the blood that I rejected him with a cold and haughty glare. And decided, as a punitive measure: 'I'm going to tell my Mum about this.'

That was my tragic mistake, the first of the tragic mistakes I have made in my life. First, my mother saw to the wound. Then she went to the yard to give Chibuco a few slaps around the head. He was hiding, ashamed. Over supper, my mother told my father what had happened.

He finished his soup, calm as ever, and said something I did not fully understand, something like – 'He is already fully grown enough . . .'. I left the table and went to the veranda to gaze from afar on my ex-friend Chibuco, who was still shocked and sad. When I returned I heard my father say something like 'He could be next. . . .' I went to the bathroom to look at the wound which I cleaned up myself. I then came back to the dining-room, and heard my father say something like 'Maybe this Saturday coming. . . .'

The three sentences danced around my head, but they did not find a logical order. He is fully grown enough . . . who? He could be next . . . for what? On Saturday . . . why Saturday?

I then heard another paternal remark, and this one I did understand: 'We must baptise the child!' The child was me, a pagan until I was 11 – the promise of baptism used to be reiterated each time I fell ill. In truth, my father wanted to baptise me in Portugal – a journey always postponed.

I went to bed with pain in my heart. My mother came to kiss me and tell me it was nothing. That was Wednesday. I stopped playing with Chibuco and suspended the theatrical shows, which used to occur daily. I spent each afternoon, before going off to play football with my friends, in the yard watching Chibuco with haughty indifference, and he retaliated with the sad, repentant look of one who has inadvertently wronged a friend.

On Saturday afternoon I had a presentiment that something irreparable had taken place. I went indoors on my return from school, and after lunch I did not look in the yard or hunt out Chibuco, I went to bed, sick. I had respiratory problems and a fever. My mother thought it was better for me to spend the day in bed; I would be better by Sunday. I had premonitory nightmares, my dreams were full of blood!

Come Sunday morning, I continued to be ill. Still in bed, I heard my mother inviting relatives to lunch.

'Today we have goat . . .' she said. All the bells of all the cathedrals in the world on Christmas night, with the rippling peals of the Vatican on top, could not have reverberated more than my mother's voice did then.

I got up, in my pyjamas, and went running to the yard. I looked for my friend everywhere: in the cellar, in the street; I looked around where his billy and nanny parents were, I went to where the pigs rolled about in the mud, I went into the chicken-coop, stepping in the shit and treading on an unwary and surprised chick.

Chibuco had disappeared. I went running back indoors and bawled out: 'Where is Chibuco?'

'On the table,' my brother answered insolently.

And he was . . . stuffed with bread, tripe and olives.

That is why I found myself sitting on the bridge at the gate to my house crying, after the evening feast, too late. I cried out loud to think of Chibuco dead on the table, thinking of the happy games we used to play, and the unhappy injustices of life. Why are we carnivorous? Why did God, who can do everything, not make us vegetarians? If He can do everything, he could feed us on tasty stones, sweets of white sand for dessert, he could make us drink rain-water, or even foaming sea-water. Why meat; why does life eat life? I had lost a friend and an excellent actor.

I was weeping buckets when I saw my friend César in the doorway of his house. He saw me, and came in my direction. I quickly dried my eyes, ashamed lest he see my wet face, red and hot. Oddly enough, he too was crying. 'Big boys don't cry!' That is what they told us. But suddenly there we were, two 9-year-old men, crying.

'Why are you crying?' I asked.

'Well, why are you crying?' he returned.

'*Marraio*! I asked first!'

César decided to speak:

'My father . . . I never imagined he could do this to me . . . to my sister. . . . My father. . . . shit! To do that to us.'

'Do what? Go on, get on with it! Do what?'

César did not know how to say it.

'I am not going to say anything in front of Zeca Carvoeiro. . . . See him there, he's coming over. Look. . . .'

Zeca, the son of the coal-man Antenor, was indeed coming towards us. People sometimes called him '*Carvoeiro*' (little coal-man), since he helped his father transport sacks of coal.

'That's odd. . . . The coal-man hasn't given Zeca a beating today. . . . Have you heard him shouting? I haven't.'

'I haven't either. That's funny: Zeca hasn't been beaten at all today . . . I wonder. . . .'

Antenor was cruel to his son. Every day, Zeca would end up with |filthy clothes and a black face from working with the coal. But at play-time he only had to get a smear of red earth on him, in a game of football with us, for Antenor to turn up with a rope or a fine chain or even a stick, and bear down on the lad's back and legs with these bruising weapons as the boy shouted: 'Dad, daddy, please God, don't beat me! For the love of my mother!'

Every day, the same ritual. No one got involved. They respected the head of the family's rights to repress. Afterwards, the bleeding Zeca would go back to carrying coal sacks. Antenor justified himself to the neighbours, who looked on sullenly but did nothing, saying: 'He has no mother, so I have to beat him for two: I have to educate him.'

Zeca's mother had died in childbirth and the stout lad was born by caesarian section, which at that time was very rare. These days, as the federal government's health system pays a higher price for a caesarian than a natural birth, Brazil is champion of the world league for this type of operation.

Antenor felt humiliated at having to look after a small child, and change nappies, and do bottle feeding – this was women's work. In fact the maid, *dona* Joaninha, took care of the boy from an early age, as well as looking after the house, polishing, gardening, preparing their food and washing their clothes. Unfortunately she had the defect of being a woman of strong convictions: a more religious person you could not find, she was religious to the core. Religiosity exuded from her mouth and ears like a vapour. She obstinately remained a virgin at 50, refusing to have sex with Antenor (which would have been more practical and advantageous for both of them), and demanded time off each weekend to attend various masses from 6 a.m. onwards. She adored processions, *kermesses*, midnight mass on Christmas eve and funeral masses. She adored burials. She adored climbing the 365 steps of the Penha Church. Once, to fulfil a vow, she went up there on her knees. On other occasions she did the same even without a vow to fulfil, but for pure pleasure! Wounds on the knees were proof of quasi-sainthood. The more steps she climbed, the closer to God she would be in Heaven, the more snugly ensconced in Christ's armpit. She adored adoring.

At weekends, in obeisance to the dictates of his flesh, Antenor had to go to the prostitutes at *O Mangue* (The Mangrove), when it was full and you had to queue. Antenor would leave Zeca to be looked after by the dog or by a neighbour. On return from *O Mangue*, it was nappies, a bottle and re-heated food: woman's work.

At age 9, Zeca was now paying for the humiliation of those early years. Deep down, Antenor blamed the innocent Zeca for his woman's premature death in childbirth. Zeca would always say: 'It's my fault . . . it is – my father is right. . . . Why did I have to be born?' And how he suffered the lashes on his back. 'I should have died, not her!' But it was so good to be alive, and Zeca would implore his father: 'Daddy, for the love of my dead mother, don't beat me any more, let me live.'

César felt sorry for him, commenting: 'I am luckier than Zeca. My father only beats me on Fridays.'

Why not on Saturdays or Sundays, or public holidays? 'Friday is the day he goes out on a drinking binge! Then he really beats me – he's drunk, what can you do?' – and thus was the father excused.

I felt superior. My father never used to beat me. He only ever beat me once. With a belt.

César and I were sitting there, our tears dried, and along came Zeca, crying. 'You too? Why are *you* crying?'

No one wanted to be the first to tell. In the end, Zeca agreed that having been the last to arrive, it should be him.

We all made an oath of secrecy and Zeca told us why he was crying. The widowed *Galega* [women from Galicia] of Sintra Street, a fat red-haired, freckle-covered woman from northern Portugal, ran a small store. When her husband died, it was hard carrying on the business, but the *Galega* managed for a while longer. Her main area of inability was in dealing with the tax inspectors; the *Galega* of Sintra Street did not follow the common custom in Rio de Janeiro which was to bribe inspectors. She reasoned that if the accounts were balanced, and the bills true, there would be nothing to fear. Big mistake! And big fines! The tax inspectors surrounded the store, after their money. Piranhas.

After a few years, the *Galega* took the historic decision to begin a new life. She asked for an audience with Antenor, who that Sunday morning took a long, slow bath, paying particular attention to his toes and armpits, in order to receive her in a fit manner. He opened a bottle of sweetened 'Setúbal' wine and bought biscuits from my father's bakery. The widow arrived at the end of the afternoon, bedecked with jewellery, lace, a Spanish fan, and fulminant good intentions.

Zeca had heard the conversation from behind the door that very day. He heard words and sighs, and a marriage proposal. The *Galega* pointed out that as they were both widowed it would be sensible for them to marry each other, with all the stamps, fees and headed papers this entailed. This matrimonial contract would resolve everyone's situation; on her side, she could sell the store and enter into the new partnership with the money from the sale as if it were a dowry – it was the bride's duty to offer a dowry, this was not open to discussion. She would move out of her rented house and come and live with him, taking charge of the domestic chores, and doing the heavy work which *dona* Joaninha could no longer undertake on account of her age and her swollen knees. Everything would be put in order. Zeca, clearly, was part of the 'everything' in question.

Last but not least, the *Galega* would on no account refuse, except in case of extreme illness, to sleep in the same bed as Antenor, for 'come what come may, whatever God wills, let His will be done'!

'I will be the lady of the house, mistress of the bed and the table, and responsible for such bodily tasks as are the lady's responsibility. I want you to know that I use only Lifebuoy soap.'

'Of course, of course . . . me too . . .' Antenor hurriedly agreed.

They drank the whole bottle of 'Setúbal' wine and began to remove the jewellery from the heaving breast, the necklaces and then the bracelets. When the *Galega da Rua Sintra* closed the Spanish fan to signal 'Why not?', Zeca got out of there, guessing the denouement. 'My father is going to marry the *Galega* . . .' and tears flowed. 'In the *Galega*'s arms, he cried out louder than I do when I'm beaten.'

I tried to console him: 'It's great: you spend your whole life moaning about not having a mother! You have always envied those of us who have mothers. . . . Now you'll have one too. . . . We'll all have mothers. . . . We'll be able to be rude about yours as well, and we won't feel sorry for you.'

Unconvinced, Zeca carried on sobbing: 'Not a mother: a stepmother!' – and he cried buckets.

'Stepmother' was a swear-word in my childhood. It sounded like 'torturer', 'hangman', 'sadist', 'Creature from the Black Lagoon', 'witch'. There were some people who preferred having no mother or father to having . . . a 'stepmother'. A spooky, threatening title!

Realising that he was the only one who had told his story, Zeca complained. César agreed to tell us his drama. 'There was a marriage at my home today too. . . . You know Zé Luiz, the wrestler? That guy with arms thicker than my legs?'

We knew him. Zé Luiz, together with some of his friends, had put on wrestling demonstrations in the yard of Santa Teresa School, where we studied. He wore green shorts and a white shirt, which showed off arm muscles thicker than any of our legs, or even all our legs put together. Zé Luiz's arms were bigger than his own legs. It was frightening. And he laughed uproariously to see the fear on the children's faces. He made noises like a cornered cat in his quest to frighten the fearful. He barked like a dog, howled like a wolf, and snarled like himself. These were the wrestler's games. . . .

Well, this terrifyingly muscular athlete had gone to César's house to ask for his sister's hand in marriage, and – height of cruelty – the father had consented. He had merely asked him a few questions about his salary, exactly how much he earned, his possessions, how many houses he would receive in his inheritance when his parents died, how much time they had to live, etc. Practical questions about the future, where they would live, would it be nearby or far away, things like that. And then he said yes. The fiancée arrived and the two kissed in front of everyone. Shameless! And they too drank Portuguese 'Setúbal' wine – it was all the rage.

'César, what is wrong with that? It doesn't harm anyone.' Zeca and I were in agreement on this point.

'Can you imagine what this guy is capable of doing to my sister? His arm. . . . Look . . . it's this thick . . . I don't even want to think about it. . . . The treatment he is going to dole out to her . . . I'm sure this guy is going to force my sister to give in to him, I'm sure she is going to end up giving in to him, she's going to give in. . . . I'm sure.'

'Well, she's bound to give it up to him. . . . Sure, she's gotta give *it* to him, she's bound to.' Once again we were in agreement, first Zeca and I, and then all three of us. 'From day one!'

'Can you imagine that guy taking her clothes off . . . doing . . . doing . . . nasty things. My poor sister. . . . A guy like that, as strong as that, is capable of anything. . . . He's going to tear her to pieces . . . I don't even want to think about it. . . .'

César, contrary to what he said, did want to think about it, wanted to imagine what a sexual act could be, in reality. Our information on this area was scant, we had no teacher, and he was imagining all kinds of violence, wrestling holds in the nuptial bed, rounds of 'catch-as-catch-can' – and, worse still, a naked man would see his sister, naked! 'It is all my fault . . .' he mumbled, crying again.

We were confused. If it was his father who had said yes and his sister who had said amen, how could it be his fault?

'I should have been bigger, older, I should have already been grown up and had a job – and if I earned money, a lot of money, I would build a big house, with another smaller one next to it, which I would give to my sister, and I would give her maids, I would even give her a car and a driver, and then she would never need to marry, and she wouldn't let Zé Luiz, she wouldn't let Zé Luiz or anyone else see her naked, and do what he is going to do to her . . . do . . . do . . . well, whatever it is he is going to do to her. . . . He'll tear her to pieces, he'll tear her to pieces. . . .'

'No he won't. He'll only do good things. . . . What are you afraid of?' We continued to reassure him, Zeca and I, in the hope that César had discovered something new and dangerous about sex and would tell us. (Although in our heart of hearts we harboured some doubts, we also thought that there was some degree of risk for the bride in marriage. In all good things, some danger lurked. The greater the pleasure, the greater the risk.)

'My father and mother got married, and no one tore anybody apart . . . No one ended up in pieces. Who do you know who ever has?' I offered encouragingly.

'Fathers and mothers is a different matter! You keep fathers and mothers out of this!' The anger he felt towards the two of us made his tears dry up and he stopped crying.

'Well, we can keep fathers and mothers out of this business, but fathers and mothers . . . is the same business.'

All three of us felt guilty of something. Zeca, for the death of his mother in childbirth, César, for the marriage of his sister to the wrestler. And me, what was I guilty of?

'What about you? It's your turn to tell now. . . .' The two of them looked at me, waiting to hear one of the greatest tragedies in history. 'What are you to blame for?'

'The death of Chibuco. . . .'

While my friends dried their eyes, mine welled over. In tears, I told them the details of the death of my friend and actor, Chibuco, the one and only!

'It wasn't your fault. You didn't kill him. You don't even know who did. . . .'

'Yes it was my fault, it was all my fault . . . all of it. . . .'

'Why? You didn't kill him. . . . They killed him. . . .'

'That's right . . . I didn't kill him . . . but at supper that evening . . . I was very hungry. . . . And he smelt so good . . . I couldn't hold back . . . and I ate a piece of Chibuco. . . .'

The three of us, in chorus, burst into a convulsion of tears.

The marriage request

To assist his relatives, my father was kind enough to send *cartas da chamada* (literally 'letters of calling') back to Portugal, to anyone who wanted to emigrate. These letters were required for visas, and the sender agreed to take responsibility for the immigrant's upkeep in the country.

In my father's case, the relative would get 'board, lodging and laundry' for six months, and in exchange would work in the bakery, earning a salary which was deposited in a bank. After six months the contract ended and each person decided their own future: whether to continue as an employee, to set up on their own, to change professions or to go back to Portugal.

My cousin Roberto was one such immigrant, who came to Rio, liked it, and stayed. A quiet man, he made friends with others as quiet as he was. Two or three years went by. He contracted tuberculosis and my parents paid for his treatment, which lasted months, in a sanatorium in the mountains of Petrópolis, surrounded by trees, in a forest with a stream running through it, which has since dried up. There was no lack of birds: they were a positive orchestra. And he was cured, a rare thing in those days. Roberto came back rosy-cheeked and podgy. Five or six years went by: Roberto became Brazilianised. He turned 33, a grown man, but still lived alone. And even as a fully grown adult, my father continued to be his point of paternal reference. My father had the face of a Father. He had the knack of it.

One night Roberto turned up at our place unexpectedly, just as we were sitting down to eat. My mother invited him to dine with us. We talked about the bakery, the customers, the suppliers, the bread, and the 'mixture'. (This was during the Second World War, when there was wheat rationing and the bakeries had to mix the wheat with corn or rye. White bread was prohibited. I actually preferred rye bread, but the bakery staff would not let me eat it, saying that it was 'poor people's bread', like the so-called 'slept bread', which had spent the night on the shelves, and was sold for half the price.)

Taking advantage of the first lull in conversation, Roberto said that he had a serious matter to discuss.

'How serious?' my father asked.

'Very serious. . . .'

'In that case we will eat first.' Supper was also a serious matter, a sacred time, and two such serious things could not be mixed.

In fact, for my father all times of day were a serious matter. He rose at four-thirty in the morning, went to the bakery at five, raised the iron shutters at five-thirty, by which time the first batch of bread was ready and a few customers were already waiting outside, ravenous. He came home at half-past twelve, lunched at one, and was asleep in bed by two for a siesta which lasted until four; at half-past four he went back to the bakery and worked until nine, when he closed the iron shutters to be back home by half-past nine and take his soup shortly after ten. Soup, in my childhood, came after the main dish and before the dessert.

The only alteration to this routine came on hot summer days when we would go to the beach at dawn, in darkness, before the sun rose. Our dog, Leão, a huge black mongrel, as punctual as a Swiss watchmaker, would go and knock on the door of the parental bedroom at four in the morning when it was hot, and go on knocking with his paws until my father gave him one or other message: 'We're not going to the beach today, Leão.' Or 'We're going to get ready now, Leão!' And then the fat beast would either sit down sadly or wag his tail in joy: he loved swimming! The beach was named after the sailor Marcilio Dias (who drowned there, no one knew exactly where), but everyone knew it as 'the beach of the brown women', and everyone knew where they lived, these beautiful *mulatas*.

When we went to the beach we had to negotiate our way round two enormous obstacles. The first was a road with two mountains of rubbish, one each side, which attracted vultures even though the rubbish was burned every day. There was no treatment station, just the fire. In those days, few roads in our neighbourhood had basic sanitation, and rubbish was dumped right next to the sea. The second obstacle was a marsh, full of *siris*[2] and other crabs – which presented a threat to careless feet. Despite the obstacles, at the end of the bay the sand was white and the sea calm. The only major danger were the jellyfish which stung one's feet, as dangerously alive as their name, *aguas vivas*, suggested.[3]

Roberto had a serious matter to discuss, but he understood that, despite the urgency, serious issues were not to be addressed during supper; at mealtimes one supped and exchanged pleasantries, which aided digestion. A serious matter merited the opening up of the parlour, a visitors' room, which was almost always shut up. It was only used for my sisters' piano lessons and for serious conversations. Or when visitors came, which was rarely.

And my father ate slowly – a habit I have inherited. For pudding, he liked pineapple with red wine and sugar. (I inherited the taste for wine . . .)

After about an hour at table, my father rose and my mother opened the door to the visitors' room, so that the two men could go in. She and my sisters went to wash the dishes, which they did when there was no maid. My youngest sister had to get up on a box to reach the sink. My brother went off to play dominoes on his own, and I went to sit on the bridge which connected my house to the street, to watch the people going by. As it was drizzling our fine London rain, I opened up the black umbrella and sat there hugging my knees, with the umbrella hiding my head.

This was a habit of mine: I used to sit on the bridge and watch people go by, imagining who they were and what they did and what their families were like. Imagining whole stories. Every half-hour the trains came into the station, and five minutes later a procession of people arriving home would start, eyes cast to the ground, hurried and hungry.

It was night, it was raining, the street was deserted, but I was watching out anyway, listening to the croaks of the toads and frogs in the rain-water ditch under the bridge and in the wastelands around. I gazed at the silhouettes of people framed at the windows at the front of my house. Imagining intrigues.

'So, what is the matter?' my father asked, sitting down on one of the two spindle-legged chairs, next to the spindle-legged sofa, around the small marble table . . . with the spindle legs. Roberto stayed standing in front of him and spoke nervously.

'Uncle, I want to get married . . . I really need to now. . . . It is a matter of necessity . . . I am already 33 . . . I want to have my own family. . . . My father got married at 33, and my grandfather too, and so it must be for me . . . I would like to have children one day. Uncle, I want to marry . . . I really want to. . . .'

'And do you already have someone in mind?' – a simple and timely question.

'Her name is Anamaria, and she is a very responsible woman. She is 26, already a little on the old side, but younger than me. And a hard worker. . . . She is a customer of the bakery, she buys on credit, but she has always paid on time. . . .'

My father called my mother in.

'Roberto wants to marry. . . .'

'He's a grown man, he can marry when he likes,' said my mother, who had a good fund of common sense.

'But I want to ask for my aunt and uncle's permission before I do so. . . .'

Though unnecessary, permission was granted.

My father wanted details. 'Is she thin, fat, tall, short . . . ?'

'The best thing would be to bring her here,' suggested my mother, sensible as ever.

Roberto agreed that he would bring her round, as soon as he had permission to do so. My father, to show that the serious matter was closed for now and the permission granted, asked for a glass of Port for each of them. Visits and serious matters always came to a close with a glass of Port. When the matter was very, very serious, it began with one glass of Port and ended with a second. In the case of a pre-arranged meeting there would also be biscuits. My father liked to soak the biscuits in the wine, a habit I did not inherit.

They drank up and my father stood: it was bed-time. 'Don't my aunt and uncle want to see the young woman?' Roberto asked. 'Well, when would you like to have her over?' my mother asked in turn.

Around an hour and forty minutes had elapsed since Roberto's arrival, what with the conversation and the supper and the glass of wine. 'She is outside. . . .', he said.

My mother and father were united in astonishment: 'She is outside . . . the young woman . . . your bride-to-be. . .? You do know that it is raining?'

'I couldn't let her come in just like that, without permission,' affirmed Roberto, for whom my father was a true father.

My mother went to open the door and asked the shy Anamaria to come in. She extended her hand to greet her. 'My hand is wet,' said Anamaria apologetically, trying to dry it on her wet dress.

But not just her hand: she was drenched from head to foot! An hour and a half standing outside in the drizzle. And there was I sitting on the bridge, with my umbrella hiding my face, and I had not even noticed the young woman flattening herself against the wall, trying to escape from the rain.

My mother served another round of Port and, while the others drank, she went to get a towel. A quarter of an hour later the ceremony was over, Anamaria was dry, and Roberto escorted his fiancée back to the door of her house.

They took my umbrella. . . .

The umbrella of discord

My umbrella was not just any old umbrella: it had history. It was black, as all umbrellas were in those days. (It was a transcendental revelation to discover later on that an umbrella could be colourful – pink or yellow! – without thereby losing its main functions: to keep its user dry, and to protect young women from troublesome drunks.) And it was coming unstitched at the ends, which progressively reduced the area it protected as the material retreated. But as I say, it had a history. In 1942, when they commemorated the tenth anniversary of the suicide of Santos Dumont, the inventor of flight in a machine heavier than air, the radio and the newspapers were eulogising aeroplanes. On several occasions the Zeppelin dirigible floated gracefully over our heads in low-level demonstration flights.

'Oh Auntie, come and see the Zeppelin,' my cousin Linda would shout.

That was when I first heard of parachutes and their use in the war. I exalted the courage of fighters who would throw themselves into the vertiginous void, far from *terra firma*. 'When I grow up, I'm going to be a hero!' I swore to myself, and then immediately received my own oath with all seriousness and indeed astonishment: ('Will I?')

I used to engage in dialogue with myself frequently; one part of me did not believe in the rest of me. The rebellious part of me challenged the confident part:

'I want proof!'

'You'll have it!' I replied to myself impetuously.

I was not satisfied with the reply, and argued heatedly with the arrogant me which faced me.

'You don't have the courage to be a hero. To be a hero you have to be brave, and you're not brave. A hero has to be truly heroic, and you're not heroic. Heroes have to face dangers and take risks, and you don't take risks or face dangers. You're even afraid of wrestling with Zé Luíz . . .'

'Zé Luíz is twice our age. . . . Just you wait till I grow up. . . . I'll smash his face in, and yours, I will so. . . .'

'You killed Chibuco. Anyone who kills his own Chibuco can't be a hero. . . .'

'I didn't kill him: I ate him! Which is totally different! I ate Chibuco because he was already dead, but I didn't kill him! I'd never do that!' (I defended myself against me.)

'You *ate* him: even worse! When did you ever hear of a hero eating his best goat, his best friend?'

I was furious that I was being tremendously unfair to myself. I knew I had never killed a friend, let alone Chibuco, the best friend anyone could have, goat or human. Relations between me and myself were nearly broken off completely. Part of me, the more mature part, would not allow this tragedy to devour me any more – if it had been up to the other, insolent part I would never have talked to my self again! Sworn enemies, for life![4]

We fought so much, I and myself, that sometimes we would both storm off at the same time . . . and leave me alone. This really panicked me; the two 'me's' abandoned me: I would be no one! Unless I was that Other who kept looking at me suffering alone, abandoned, or even the Other who observed that Other, bothered by the presence of so many other Others. . . .

It was disturbing to be me without 'Me', alone with myself. It was then I discovered that perhaps 'Perhaps' does not exist, but that 'Yes' and 'No' do. To clarify: the 'Perhaps' which is almost 'Yes' exists, as well as the 'Perhaps' which is no longer quite 'No'. The 'No' and the 'Yes' dressed up as 'Perhaps'. That is why we are deceived. Or perhaps only 'Perhaps' exists: the 'Perhaps' that is no longer 'No', and the 'Perhaps' on the way to being 'Yes'. But . . . perhaps one of the two 'me's' which had left me alone at the same time with slams of the door, perhaps they knew. . . . But perhaps not even they did. . . . To be or not to be? Both! I never just drink a glass of water, I have to drink the sea![5]

I decided to put an end to my anguish and demonstrate my valour, show who I was, and what I was capable of. I told myself: 'I will prove it, before supper. Heroism should be practised before eating. Above all, dessert should be prohibited before any heroic act. Dessert and heroism do not mix, even if the dessert has sugar in it, which gives you energy. Rice pudding is fatal. We'll see, you and me. I'll prove that I can be a World War hero. When I grow up, I'll help the Allies win the war. And when I get involved in the war, watch out.'

And I replied to myself: 'The war will end before you grow up, that's why you are saying that. And what's more, Mum wouldn't let you sign up to the war. She'd grab you by the scruff of the neck, and lock you in the maid's room! If the General wanted to get you, she wouldn't let him, she'd slap the General in the face, medal and all. *She* would be brave, for sure; and you wouldn't!' I told myself, contradicting myself.

I have always fought with myself – sometimes I live in a state of internal strife. Even as an adult, mature, even at this moment writing this very story, I battle with myself, I argue, dispute, agitate, provoke, contradict. I should tell that story! – no I shouldn't – who knows?

I always watch myself doing things, hear myself speaking – and I do not always agree with what I do or say. I hold back, take stock, assess, before going ahead. When I disagree, I do so wholeheartedly, disagreeing with the disagreement. It both complicates and enriches things! I am envious of straightforward people, those who never doubt themselves, always in agreement with themselves, thinking that what they think is just, justifying what they do.

I took an oath of patriotism. 'Before this war is over, the Allies are going to win, with me in the front line!'

'Hmm, I'll believe it when I see it!'

'See this umbrella?'

'What about the umbrella?'

'I'll show you.'

I no longer knew whether I was dealing with a 'me' or a 'you'. 'Come with me!' I said to myself, and I followed me, wary of me. I never know what I am plotting, nor whether I am telling the truth or lying – so it is better to be cautious, given that, with good reason, I do not trust myself.

a long time ago, I was a boy

As far as I am concerned, I used not to be trustworthy – now I am; but in the past, God forbid! I went along behind me cautiously, casting sidelong glances at myself.

Umbrella in hand, I went into the pantry, climbed on to a chair, reached the window and climbed out on to the roof. It was no easy task because, of course, I did not help myself: I came up behind making fun of myself, censuring myself, making accusations:

'What are you going to do? Spy on the naked Olympia, the maid? In her bath? Again? Just wait until Daddy hears about this. . . .'

'Keep your voice down, otherwise everyone will hear about it, not just Daddy!'

I persecuted myself, mercilessly: 'The poor young girl takes her clothes off thinking that she is alone in the bathroom, and there's you with your big bulging ogling eyes, watching what she does . . . staring at her little breasts. . . .'

Divided I suffered, and in turn each part of me also split, and every 'I' left over from this division gladly subdivided itself. The shameless I, the kaleidoscopic I, had been capable of spying on Olympia's nudity, but the moralist I condemned the abuse. With infantile curiosity, I wanted more: 'What is Olympia like naked? If you don't tell me, I'm going to tell Daddy of you. . . .'

Sometimes I found living with myself unbearable.

The shame! I did not want to touch on this subject, even to myself, because I thought that if I gave voice and ear to what I was thinking, in no time at all the whole world would know about it. The frightened I asked myself to shut up, but the severe I continued to accuse: I broke the roof tile on purpose. . . .

'That's a lie: it was the wind!'

'The wind does not concern itself with naked women, it's busy with the leaves of trees: you broke the roof tile and, when Olympia comes to take a bath, you spy on her through the gap, and after her bath you put the fragment of tile back in its place. *Shameful.* Oh, if daddy gets to hear about this. . . .'

Since I was curious to see what it was I had planned to do as proof of heroism – I shut my mouth and spied on myself as I placed one foot carefully in front of the other, advancing along the top cornice, terrified that I might fall. I watched myself as I went along, and the part of me that was so cruel to myself almost pushed me off to make me break a leg, or in the best of worst hypotheses, two or three ribs or my collarbone.

I have never before confessed this, but here goes: I was very jealous of my brother because he had broken his collarbone and I had not. Breaking a collarbone gave one high status when I was young. Only people whose courage was beyond doubt had the right to break their collarbone and bandage up their whole chest. It was prestigious. I, poor devil, never managed to break even a toe. . . .[6]

To avoid committing an act of heroism about which I could boast, I was prepared to break a leg. Not my own leg, but that of the other me, because I now wanted to show that I could be a hero. 'He' wanted to be a hero, when the person talking was the 'me' over there – and 'I' wanted to prevent myself from committing an act of heroism, when the 'I' speaking was the other: I could not bear to witness my own heroism – I was jealous of myself!

'I can do it!' I said defiantly. As I unfurled the umbrella, only its wire frame opened, minus the material, which was torn. . . . But not realising this, and pumped full of courage, I leapt off the roof, complete with Tarzan ululations (except without his handy jungle creeper-rope!) uuuuuaaaaauu- uuuu . . . Let there be heroism.

I remember an alarming descent, the ground coming to meet me too fast. My jump, though not quite mortal in its effect, caused more than enough pain; unable to gauge the consequences of the impact, I sprained my ankle. What hurt most was the fear, but also my own sarcasm. What hurt least was the pain, maddening as it was. One pain was bad, the other was mad.

I spent several minutes making fun of myself, laughing at myself, crying with pain, laughing from crying, and crying from laughter, lying on the grassy earth, wiping my eyes, while the other me was above the window, sticking out my tongue and baring my teeth.

'Of course no one can be a hero at my age! I am still too much of a boy!' I don't know which one of me uttered that sentence, but know that it served both as defence and accusation. It was the only time we spoke in unison, me and myself.

When I was having a lie-down, after my mother had scolded me and I had eaten a plate of food in bed, I switched me's: 'Do you see? You wanted to make me into a young man, just look at what kind of young man I am now: a silly boy, with his mother dressing his wounds. One tiny injury on the foot, and he's drinking chicken broth. . . .'

I replied, indignant: 'Oh, shut up! Most heroes die, don't they? But dying is not heroism: it is an accident. To save a life, now *that's* heroism! Well I am more of a hero than a true hero: I jumped and I didn't die! I saved a life – mine! Go away and leave me in peace. . . .'

I never followed my advice, I never left myself in peace.

That duality, that dichotomy, between me and myself, has pursued me ever since I have been conscious of myself. Amidst happiness I am sad, in sadness I find happiness. In the face of courage I am afraid, and fear gives me courage. When I love, I doubt it: I love the doubt. I doubt the love. I know what I say, and I disagree. I pronounce the word I do not want to hear. I hear what was not said.

One day, decades later, I discovered the Portuguese poet Sá de Miranda from 1500. I experienced upset, tremor, stupefaction and shock, when I read:

> *'Comigo me desavim,*
> *sou posto em todo perigo;*
> *não posso viver comigo,*
> *nem posso fugir de mim'*

> [I am at odds with myself,
> I am in all kinds of danger;
> I cannot live with myself,
> Nor can I flee from me]

The poet, without knowing me, revealed my hidden secrets.

> *'Qual deverá ser o fim*
> *da triste sina que sigo,*
> *pois que trago a mim, comigo,*
> *grande inimigo de mim?'*

[What should the end be
of that sad fate I follow,
since I bring to myself, with me,
my own great enemy?]

Watching the world go by

The world went by out there. . . . And I sat here, the spectator on the bridge over the ditch which connected our garden to the street, toads croaking beneath me and the smell of sludge wafting up my nose.

During Carnival, people danced in the '*blocos sujos*':[7] dressed as down-and-outs, in costumes made out of cleaned up recycled rubbish. Men dressed up as women or imitated legendarily dubious characters such as the pharmacist and Pedro. The uglier they were, the funnier. But the women were a different kettle of fish: the more beautiful, the better!

The revellers went from door to door, soliciting small change, food, *cachaça*.[8] Some gave them nothing but dirty looks – especially the angry cat-owners whose pets had been stolen and metamorphosed into *cuícas*, *pandeiros*[9] or tambourines.

Before Carnival, the cat fraternity would be perplexed to find itself locked and bolted indoors. The cat that jumped out of a window was effectively signing its own death warrant – it was impossible to escape the frenzied pre-Carnival revellers. The lives of these hapless felines were even at some risk during the rest of the year because they could find themselves being devoured at any moment – although in those days hunger was not as popular as it is today.

We used to buy 'perfume squirters' (bottles of scented ether one could get in those days: the ether merely gave one an icy cold tingle in the head, a funny dizziness, which was an innocent enough diversion!). We would fire the perfumed jets at the legs of young girls in their cheap fancy dress, got up as gypsies, geishas or babushkas. The young girls would protest – and the more fuss they kicked up, the more we – and they – enjoyed ourselves, in these displays of infantile sensuality. Cold jets of icy perfume on warm, sweaty legs: the more exposed the knees, the greater the ecstasy. I used to adore spraying perfume on those precious legs.

Some lads sprayed perfume on the women's breasts and on their own handkerchiefs: to sniff them. Today no one would even think of it. Cocaine, yes, it's sold all over . . . but perfume sprays? Absolutely prohibited.

Father Ricardo and Dalvinha

We even let off perfume spray in front of the young Father Ricardo, recently graduated from the Seminary, the only resident of the neighbourhood who had blue eyes and curly blond hair, as if he were German or Danish.

There were two conspicuous priests in Penha. There was a very old one, Monsenhor Rocha, the rock of virtue his name implied. He used to travel up the church steps in an electric car, and then get off halfway up and climb two or three steps gripping his stick for dear life, in an act of pious sacrifice. Then he would get back into the car and travel up to the top, his legs forsaken, shaking.

Legends abounded about Father Rocha. On certain lunar dates he liked to shut himself up in the church all alone and fast, prowling around it by night. He would not even drink holy water, however cruel his thirst. The faithful faithfully observed through the keyhole the cleric clericking alone, inside the church. Frightened ears, glued to the locked doors, would hear strange voices. Who knows whose? Rocha was certainly not a ventriloquist: *ipso facto*, there was someone else in his aged company! Oh my God! (What have I said? Could it be God?)

One night three thieves broke into the church intending to steal the gold-plated image of the Saint – whose face was painted emerald green with diamonds for its eyes. Legend has it that they saw Monsenhor Rocha conversing calmly with the Blinding Light as if it were the most normal thing in the world, as if Blinding Lights were a frequently encountered feature of churches in poor neighbourhoods. They exchanged ideas, the priest and the Light, tossing thoughts back and forth, with the priest virtually patting the Blinding Light's broad and sturdy shoulders.

That was what they testified. They swore on oath that they saw this, and signed and sealed it in the registry office![10] According to them, Monsenhor Rocha and the Blinding Light were very good friends of long standing, great comrades, despite their difference in age. The Light was much older than the old man, positively ancient, but well preserved and robust, a Light ballerina.

The three thieves stumbled down the Penha steps and on up the road, filled with fear and repentance (and without the holy image, which escaped unmolested). Still panting, they turned themselves in, with their 'hands up', to the incredulous and grumpy policeman and confessed ther crime.

According to the various sweat-and-tear-sodden accounts, delivered to a resonant accompaniment of piercing sobs, the Blinding Light gave paternal advice, the sort of thing a great-grandfather might say, in a leisurely and measured pace. The priest listened, an obedient son, respectful but with enough pluck that, Father of the Priest's Father as he was, the Light had to listen to filial disagreements. The priest's voice was hoarse with a cold; the Light's was strong and solid as a rock, meek and mild, but quite severe. (God may be capable of smiling, but he is not given to raucous laughter.)

It is said the thieves then applied to join the police force, and went on to win prizes with commendations, and that they stood to attention and swore never to steal gold-leafed saints again, however emerald green and attractive they might be. It is not known whether they kept their promise, but they did progress in life, that is certain: they became rich. One day, the Saint was found without its gilded cover and damaged with penknife scratches. No one ever knew who did it. I never asked, keeping my suspicions to myself.

Before the Monsenhor, everything was holy, sacred, respectful; the most trivial 'God bless you' was dressed up in liturgical solemnity. But in front of the young Ricardo, lads let off perfume spray without the slightest respect: the priest smiled, blessing them, not knowing why he smiled, still less whom he blessed. What innocence. . . .

Ricardo smiled constantly, promenading through the church gardens, greeting the ladies at their windows, administering a gentle pat to the bottoms of unruly children, who did not like that provocative caress at all. His devoted lips murmured fluttering blue Hail Marys. (As everyone knows, Hail Mary is blue, Our Father green, Save the Queen[11] pink, and the Creed, of course, is deep violet. Everyone knows that, it needs no explanation.)

Ricardo, in a class of his own in the smile athletics, used to exercise his body as well as his soul. He did routines from *capoeira* and boxing, on his own, without launching into actual combat – or rather as if fighting a fat, out-of-condition little devil. On his own, he executed elegant basketball and volleyball movements, without team mates to pass to, or even a ball to pass! Smiling, victorious. Ricardo was only serious during mass, and was more serious still during the sermon, when he spoke of the multiple tribulations endured by the saints and apostles, during ancient eras of persecuted Christianity. To have smiled then, when dealing with such a delicate subject, would have been too much. Ricardo described these past tortures as if he was talking about the repression of our own time.

Many people were perfume spray-crazed during my childhood. Innocent crazy people: they did not know that they were sinning. . . . Oh, the good old days, a time of unconscious sins, no blame. . . . Pardoned sins. Generous Ricardo. 'Bless me, Father!' – 'God blesses you, my children!'; 'God watch over you, girls!'

One day some children wanted to teach Ricardo how to let off a perfume squirter – the good prelate did resist, I swear! They ended up grabbing hold of the young man, just for fun, and making the priest press the nozzle with his finger – it was against his will, I swear, the crazy people forced him to do it! The jet hit Dalvinha's legs – by chance, I swear!

Of the young women who made most fuss about the perfume squirters – and was secretly most enraptured by them! – Dalvinha was the foremost, a provocative girl-woman of 15, daughter of a family of discreet 'believers' – followers of sects inclining to the Protestant, with a pinch of religiosity inclining to the autochthonous, and dances inclining to the African. A blend of many inclinations. But true believers all the same, and more sincere in their religion than many a professed religious devotee.

Under the pretext of still being a child, Dalvinha wore short skirts; under the pretext of already being a woman, she showed her thighs. Dalvinha was the preferred target of nine out of ten ether jets and, naturally enough, the victim of the priest's perfume spraying induction. But afterwards the girl-woman had an attack which appeared to be apoplexy, complete with flailing legs and falling over. There was shock across the whole neighbourhood – 'call my father, my mother!', 'call the doctor!', 'ambulance!', 'police!', 'call a lawyer', 'call the pharmacist', 'call Pedro, he knows about death rattles!'

After half an hour thrashing her legs about in her tight skirt, with the inevitable consequences, Dalvinha calmed down, and smiled blissfully at the terrorised messenger of God, who was on his knees praying. The girl-woman told her friends, a few days later, that at that moment, feeling the cold jet emanate from the priest's hand, she had a vision of Paradise, complete with Father, Son, Holy Spirit, Virgin Mary and a huge multitude of rejoicing angels and short-skirted angel-dancers thrown in. A strident host of angels, applauding. Looking at the priest, she saw two of him, as if she were drunk!

We children reckoned he didn't do it on purpose. But the girls' mothers saw deliberate evil intent: for one solitary tragic second, the Devil, in flesh and blood, with boots and trident, had entered the body of the young man who was now praying with the fervour of a seminarist, though he was already a fully-fledged priest.

The mothers wanted to punish him. How? It was impossible to tell on the outrageous young man to the old priest, since they couldn't be absolutely and irreversibly sure, sure without a flicker of doubt. Even if they had been, it would have taken some temerity to tell Rocha, occupied as he was in conversation with the Blinding Light: at his advanced age, a heart attack was a definite possibility. They decided to keep silent: they would not tell anyone, not even their husbands (that is, those who were not yet widowed), or their friends (that is, those who already were). Sacred silence. And yet. . . . In the confessional, the dear priest had to listen to moral thrashings. From that day on, and for as long as the fiery maternal indignation lasted, Father Ricardo listened to them. In fear and panic, the novice priest went to confession and suffered so much that he almost denounced himself to Father Rocha. But he decided not to because his heart was guiltless, although blame for the freezing spray might be laid on his clumsy finger.

When Ricardo took confessional it was the priest's sins that were catalogued, and then punished, with medieval severity. 'Father, do you have no shame?'– 'Did you not renounce those things, did you not take a vow of chastity, did you not promise not even to think of such things?'– 'What would pious old Father Rocha say? Worse, what would the Holy Pope in his Mercy say?'– 'Father, what do you think of when you look at me? Look at my eyes, look into me, go deep, very deep!'– 'Father, take care! Don't think

a long time ago, I was a boy

those carnal thoughts, no! A priest's body does not speak, does not cry out! Priests don't flail their legs about! They aren't like us! Oh, Father . . . Father, Father. . . .'

Among the mothers who castigated Ricardo the most was Dona Rosa Cascadura. She was buxom, with slim hips and skinny legs below, and she was always saying 'This is Calvary!'— whatever the circumstances. If she climbed the 365 steps of the church, every twenty or thirty or so she would sigh: 'My Divine Our Lady of Penha . . . there are far too many steps: this is Calvary.'

If she got on the tram at the hour of push and shove, when it was over-crowded inside and covered with hangers-on outside, and she found herself trapped between two seats, she would murmur: 'My divine Sao José, here you have me at your feet: this is a Calvary.'

If she set off home and it started bucketing down, she would not hesitate to invoke again: 'Blessed Saint Barbara, whose name is inscribed in the heavens and on paper with holy water for ink, free us from this torment . . . this is a Calvary!'

Well, this Dona Rosa de Cascadura decided to seek satisfaction from Father Ricardo, even though Dalvinha was someone else's daughter, not hers. Even better: she could remain cool-headed about it.

'Father, tell me what you are thinking. Confess here in this silence, to me alone. I know you want to . . . You are a man, and you have needs, just as we women do. But, my lad, you should not seek relief for your desire in poor defenceless creatures. . . . Even if you had aimed your perfume at Dalvinha's mother's legs, she has her needs, or at the legs of any of the mothers who were there, full of desire, or at me, for example, Father, at me, at my legs. . . . If your perfumed jets had landed on my thighs, I would have understood. . . . If you had aimed at me, well, we could let it pass. . . . We could forget about it. But that young girl is a virgin through and through. . . . Think about it, father, think about it. . . . Virginity is danger . . . seduction, luxury, crime and sin . . . purgatory, hell . . . flames, fire!'

'For the love of God, spit it out!' cried out the desperate priest, shouting *sotto voce*, wringing his hands and feet, wriggling in agony. 'Tell me now what my penance is: I want to pay, even for sins I have not committed! Like Christ, who paid for what he did not do: who paid for us! I want to pay for you!'

'For the time being, go and say a hundred Hail Marys . . .' she pronounced in sentence, severely. Then she thought perhaps this was too little, that he wanted a heavier punishment: 'and one thousand Our Fathers! God will forgive you. . . . Pray with faith and afterwards come and see me.'

But the priest rebelled:

'I will do the penance only because I take pleasure in praying – praying is my spiritual workout! But one thousand Our Fathers is . . . too much devotion. I do not deserve this retribution. This is a Calvary, yes madam, Dona Rosa de Cascadura! It is a Calvary, and a long one too, with many steps, and many falls!' And he left the nave quivering and spitting out the first verses of the first blushing Hail Mary, mauling the surprised Mother of God with his wronged lips.

In confession, Ricardo's ears turned redder than the firewood embers in the bakery oven. In time, embers cool and fade to grey, the fury sleeps and the comments are silenced. Never again did Ricardo look at Dalvinha, at least not in front of us. Dalvinha looked, though, she looked daggers at the religious athlete. Zeca, César and I cried on the bridge of the big house, not knowing why, watching Dalvinha, as she watched the scurrying wind – Dalvinha looked at no one else: she heard the wind and gazed. Dalvinha, too grown up for a girl, too fresh and green for a woman. . . .

One day, Zeca, César or I, or maybe all three of us, lamented: 'I wanted Dalvinha just for me. . . .'

The other two nodded urgent agreement: 'Me too . . .' We were of one mind. 'Just for us, three Dalvinhas, or the same one for all of us . . .'

One day, Dalvinha appeared wearing a long skirt: it was now decreed that she was a woman. She converted, in her heart, to Catholicism. She started going to church regularly, and would not miss Father Ricardo's Mass. She not only took Holy Communion, she did not miss a single Communion. Not a wafer was allowed to escape nor a penitence or absolution be passed up. She became the most communicated communicant of all the faithful of the neighbourhood. When she forgot a sin – obsessed by confession as she was – she would tear back, up all the steps she had just come down, panting her head off, find the priest in the courtyard, and she would add a PS to her regimental confession on the spot. Devotion of a level you would not even encounter among the fans of Flamengo and Corinthians.[12]

Dalvinha . . . We have long lost our hopes of bedding you. . . . God be with you.

Football, dogs and little carts

As well as Carnival, in terms of sporting and social activity I played football. I was always on the attack, and loved to score goals – with feet, knees, bottom, stomach, back-heels, toe-kicks, whatever; the header was the only shot I would not countenance. Perhaps that's why I did not make a career as goal-scorer emeritus. Sometimes all the ball needed was a little nudge of the head, for God's sake, but my neck contracted and I would not head it. Never! I missed incredible goals, ready-made goals, below the crossbar, on the penalty spot. I endured shaming, put up with all sorts of insults and jostling and rudeness. But serene, poised and haughty, my head avoided high balls. Football is played with the feet! Foot-ball! There is no such thing as 'head-ball'– and if there was, I would not play it. The head, however poor, was made for other, less jolting usages.

It was while playing ball that I first perceived the relationship between economic power and the respect it inspires. I noticed that the owner of the ball scored many more goals than did other boys. It was as if, as a mark of respect, space was created around the ball's owner, and the goalies became sluggish when responding to a ball kicked by its owner's foot. I started buying balls . . . and began to shine in the backyards of Penha's Suburbs.

On the way to the Santa Teresa School, I broadcast fantastic games in my mind, in which I took on the right-half of Fluminense FC, a team which always won with epic goals. Our irresistible and devastating front line was made up of Pedro Amorim, Augusto Pinto Boal (student, son of José Augusto Boal, trader, and Dona Albertina Pinto Boal, housewife), Rongo, Tim and Carreiro.[13] I was proud of my Christian names and surname . . . the more names the better! In my internal sports-casts, we always won. Naturally, I was master of the ball, or rather of the microphone and the narrative, and I used to score the greatest quantity of beautiful Olympic goals – always with my feet! – and I made wonderful passes which my crack team mates merely had to tickle into the net, past the unmanned goal posts – I having dribbled the ball past everyone up to the goalkeeper.

Today, I ask belated forgiveness of the great right-half Romeu for having substituted him, in my radiophonic locutions. It was him or me! You understand, Romeu, I had to come on in someone's place, we couldn't put on twelve players, have twelve stars on the pitch at the same time: that would be cowardice.

Even more than football, more than anything, the thing I used to love to do, when I was not yet 11 and we still lived in the big house, was to sit on the bridge at the end of the afternoon, and watch . . . people passing by, horses grazing, municipal donkeys carting off the rubbish. I imagined and invented whole lives. On Thursdays, the little cart which went round catching dogs with a metal noose would come by, taking the mongrels to sacrifice. They would be heaped up on the barred cart – healthy dogs beside leprous and mangy ones, massive dogs next to well-groomed miniature ones. When running free the dogs would fight. In the cart they became friends, in solidarity: they could foresee their collective destiny – death.

Death was all too present in my childhood. It was a constant round of flowers, wreaths, funeral vehicles decorated as for a gala, sober hearses. I saw daggers thrust in people, I saw blood, heard gunshots. I saw people cut with knives: fat Dona Mariana slashed by her lover, on her breast and her arm . . .

The child owners of the dogs, who'd been distracted at the moment of their charges' capture, would go running out when they became aware of the kidnapping and their loss, wailing and yelping behind the little cart, begging for the return of their canine friends, swearing to take good care of them from now on. The dog catchers did not even turn round: they were paid per animal caught. Hearts of stone! The children went home crying, and there would be more crying after the beatings . . .

When parents were sufficiently moved to go to the depot in search of the caged canines, they would have to pay good money to retrieve the animals if they were still alive by the evening, after they had been vaccinated. And the parents did not always have that kind of money, and so would sometimes return home instead with an account of the animal's stoic, heroic death. The day the cart came was a day of children's tears. The convulsive, uncontrolled weeping bothered old and fat Mateus, who used to say, never once considering the cruelty of his words: 'They should invent a little cart for the children. . . .'

The sub-lieutenant and the air hostess

I was still a young lad when the maths teacher brought her eldest brother in to the Santa Teresa School. He came in uniform: a sub-lieutenant in the army. Dona Edite, the teacher, told of her parents' efforts to fulfil their son's military dreams, and praised his successes in the cavalry brigade – given that he had not been lucky enough to be selected to defend the Fatherland in Italy, and had to stay at home to look after the barracks and deal with the horse dung! She eulogised his respectability and cleanliness and asked her brother to say something by way of incentive, to help us plan our own futures – perhaps one of us would decide to follow his fine example and launch into a career as a horseman.

The sub-lieutenant started his speech, serious and dogmatic, mysterious and grave, looking at the ceiling: 'Every thirty years, a war is inevitable.' The inscrutability of Destiny spoke through his mouth, like Beethoven's Fifth at the opening of a gala, revealing the future, with more pomp and conviction than an organ-grinder's parakeet.[14] Worse: he spoke without ever looking us in the face. I am sure the sub-lieutenant never looked anyone in the face, at any time – he was so full of himself.

As for us, we trembled at the news that the German army was approaching Stalingrad – we understood nothing of politics at that age, nor did we even know where Stalingrad was, or Auschwitz, or Siberia, or the gulags. But we were shocked when faced with this military authority who predicted to us a future of blitzkriegs. I was sure that I did not have the slightest touch of D'Artagnan's vocation! A uniform – perish the thought!

The sub-lieutenant continued his discourse without any of us catching a full stop or comma – a discourse he had no doubt learned by heart from a lieutenant or captain who in turn would be repeating a colonel or general further up the hierarchy! He solemnly declared that Brazil, shamefully, still did not have the 'autonomy' to swallow up any large country as a whole – only the 'fringes' on the northern borders of Argentina or the South of Colombia or Venezuela, the East of Peru, Ecuador and Bolivia. Brazil could only swallow little Uruguay or Paraguay whole! Not to mention the indigestible Guyanas. . . . Good God . . . what an appetite!

In the whole of South America, only Chile, cowering shamefacedly behind the Andes, could escape being swallowed up by the imagination of the ravenous sub-lieutenant! I kept wondering about the nature of this particular streak of 'autonomy' we were so deficient in, the possession of which would enable us to 'swallow up' countries and 'fringes'. Instead of enriching our vocabulary, this preposterous 'autonomy' only served to impoverish it. For some time after we used to say 'autonomy' to designate anything, just as today one might say 'thingummy' for any 'thing', and the French say '*machin*' for any '*bidule*'.[15]

'Please Sir, will you give me *autonomy* to go to the toilet to have a pee? I am bursting.'

'Please Sir, I don't have *autonomy* to understand this multiplication.'

'Ah, if only I had *autonomy* to be Dalvinha's boyfriend. . . .'

'Look here César and Zeca, today my *autonomy* to put up with you has run out: go home, I am going to bed.'

Some boys, imagining themselves as men, dreamed of growing and awakening to find they were sub-lieutenants, full of the most varied autonomies. Not full lieutenants – never! – subs, like Dona Edite's brother, who had not been chosen to defend the Fatherland, and thus was in the Civil Defence clearing up horse manure, and doing a little nursing – girls' work really, but, ultimately, the sub-lieutenant was ready and willing whatever the task; if you did not fight in this war, you might have to wait another thirty years, 'like Jacob serving Laban, father of Rachel, beautiful woman from the hills, who did not serve her father, but herself,'[16] as Camões[17] taught us through the lips of Dona Neuma.

Not to be left out, Dona Neuma, our teacher of poetry and Portuguese, one day brought in her sister who used 'rouge' and 'lipstick', and who had been turned down for the job of Civil Aviation air hostess. No one knew for sure what this was – we only knew that it involved flying by plane, travelling afar, to Japan, China and Thailand, countries on the far side of the inflatable globe we had in our classroom!

The young woman turned out to be rosy-cheeked and pretty, with a short checked kilt, fastened by a large pin at the thigh. Though she might have been turned down for the job, this did not stop her dreaming of Paris, New York, London, oceans, seas and mountains. And there we were in Penha, suffused with the smell of the Carioca Tannery whenever the wind blew south-easterly: the smell sought out our noses, and we sneezed.

The poor reject with red lips – crimson lips we called them, for greater nobility – served as an example to the young girls in the school. One day they would all dream of being turned down for the enviable post of air hostess for Civil Aviation! For weeks, my class was made up of sub-lieutenant boys, not chosen to fight in Italy, and air hostess girls, turned down by civil aviation. Our paradigms would have been proud of us, had they ever seen us again – they never returned to Santa Teresa. In our fantasy they married each other and had lots of little unchosen sub-lieutenants and rejected air hostess babies.

The pyramids of tin

We used to talk about parents beating children.

'Hasn't your father ever beaten his children?' insisted Zeca, wanting to absolve his own. 'Everyone hits their children, that is what a father is for . . . to straighten out the crooked. He has to use a stick! My father is right. When I too am a father . . . see if you can hold me back! My son is going to suffer at my hands!'

César confessed to beatings, but only on special occasions when his pranks deserved corporal punishment: breaking a glass, for example, leaving food on his plate, stepping on the plants or on the dog, failing at school – serious things. But not for having dirtied his clothes playing football like Zeca – no way!

And me?

I was proud of never having been beaten by my father – apart from the one time. My mother, every now and then, gave me a cuff round the head – but you never know if a mother's blows are a reprimand or a caress. Fathers are another matter, they mean business. Only once, on account of throwing the chair at my brother's head, was I hit by my father, and even then I was entitled to a formal apology.

In my personal *sala de visitas* at the gate, we would pass comment on events. During the Second World War, Brazil had a national project: the Allied Victory. The people worked smiling and content – in those days Brazilians smiled, even when they weren't getting a fee from the television's Sunday Live programme.[18]

I remember the enormous mountains of tin which mounted up in every wasteland: the famous Iron Pyramids which the newspapers told us, without further explanation, were necessary for our war effort. They would help England defeat the Germans and protect herself from bombs.

'What does England want so many tins for?' I asked myself in amazement. I looked at the map of the British Isles and my bewilderment continued: 'Will so many pyramids really fit on such a small island? Won't it sink?'

César, Zeca and myself were the most prolific of the child contributors of tins from Portuguese sardines and Argentine peaches in syrup, of broken saucepans and bent cutlery. We were convinced that this would win the war and England would be saved. We would save England, and the Queen would say thank you very much, kissing our infant hands! I even crushed a little-used saucepan, still with black beans in it – just to be able to take it to the pyramid and fulfil my daily quota. We were soldiers, and each fought with the weapons at his disposal. My weapon, that day, was the pan!

What use could all those saucepans be? – I racked my brains. No answer was forthcoming, but the satisfaction of fighting by piling up tins knocked spots off the emotional rewards offered by the other competitions pursued by the lads in my street. They just went hunting (or was it fishing?) for toads and frogs stronger than those owned by the lads in the side-streets, with their feeble little rain-water ditches, tributaries of ours.

The visitors' room

Periodic visitors passed through my *'sala de visitas'*: the mosquito-killer came with 'creoline' disinfectant for loos and cesspits – I hated its stench. Rio de Janeiro had still not freed itself of some endemic diseases. One had to put up with creoline, in spite of its unbearable smell. Better smell creoline than catch yellow fever – people who got yellow fever turned red and green: I never understood this *danse macabre* of hospital colours.

The smell of 'Flit' was worse: on hot days, my mother, with Flit 'pump' (a tin vaporiser) in hand, sprayed insecticide about the rooms, shutting doors so that flies, cockroaches, fireflies and other similar vermin would die poisoned. Before we went to bed, we would open the window to let in a breath of fresh air . . . as well as fresh ravenous mosquitoes. . . .

'Isn't your father in to give me a few *dinheiros*?' the mosquito-killer would ask: even in those days a tip was expected, even though the employee was paid for his work. My father was not in: the mosquito-killer, in vengeance, threw creoline on the grass. I threw earth on the creoline, for fear that the animals might lick it.

Other visitors passed through. At the gate, I used to eavesdrop on adults' conversations, while they took absolutely no notice of me. One time a group at the corner was in animated discussion: friends of my father's, agitated by the new law banning spitting on the ground.

The controversy made me nauseous: Mateus said that everyone should be obliged to swallow their own spit, Filisberto thought that it was a universal and inalienable right to spit at will, the spitter's pleasure being his own business. In defence of the first argument, someone said that one's own spit did not contaminate its producer: *revertere ad locum tuum!* – it should stay inside the body which made it! In defence of the second, it was claimed that according to the Federal Constitution, no one could be obliged to swallow their own spit and the fewer microbes lodged in the body, the healthier the spirit would be. That is why roads and pavements were invented – for spitting on. Not to mention the sumptuous spittoons of Chinese porcelain, like those at the Municipal Theatre, intended for the same purpose. Nowadays, on opera nights, these spittoons are admired for their oriental beauty, and no one spits: but they have known worse days.

I felt sick!

I heard the older people saying that when Osvaldo Cruz, Minister of Health, brought in compulsory vaccination, there was a popular rebellion and the Government had to declare Martial Law. Yellow fever and smallpox came to an end, but many people had their vaccinations in prison, having been on the receiving end of a truncheon – immune to smallpox, but with broken legs and arms. The special police force did not mess about when it came to maintaining public order or vaccinating the recalcitrant. The people would be saved even if it meant giving them a kicking!

On questions of health, one consulted the pharmacist, a specialist on the subject, who would always skate around things, speaking at a tangent:

'There are cases in which spitting is unnecessary and, therefore, becomes a crime. However, in other urgent cases, there may be an imperative, depending on the logic of the distance between the mouth and the floor, the trajectory of the phlegm, it could be negligence not to . . .'

Everyone thought that the pharmacist had supported their side of the argument, and the debate continued the following day, both sides leaning on the surety provided by the doctor of minor causes.

Pedro and the pharmacist

Although people always asked the pharmacist's opinion on a variety of subjects, few believed in what he said because he was homosexual.

'A queer . . . what would he know about it? Queers only know about taking it up the ass, that's as far as it goes . . . they are specialists.'

Others added fuel to the fire: 'Have you noticed how he likes to give injections? How he grabs our arms? It should be banned. Only a certified doctor should give injections, and even then only under oath! Before witnesses! This business of a man fiddling with a person's body — that's to do with the fact that he's a poof.'

The pharmacist's wife — he did have one — was a pretty woman with dark brown skin, strong arms and an unstable temperament, who knew no middle position, no halfway house: with her it was all or nothing, salty tears or unbridled smiles.

She knew about everything, but she wasn't concerned about her husband's sexuality, despite the scandalous fuss she made whenever they told her the latest news — whom he had an encounter with, in what dubious position. How she cried! But she herself had her own lover's secrets. How she smiled! Every now and then, her own scandal was greater: she would cut her wrists and throat. No one knew whether her husband's betrayal or her lovers' abandonment were cause of her suicide attempts: sometimes they coincided.

The poor pharmacist's wife must have had much luck in gaming, because in love . . . her luck was very poor.[19] She spent her life practising death: her scars were abundant. She looked like those women in some African countries, who put a wooden or iron necklace around their necks to stretch them; they become more beautiful by their aesthetic standards. Instead of necklaces, the pharmacist's wife had scars from razors: some said seven, the more excitable said ten or twelve — the wild woman did not stay still long enough for anyone to count them. . . . On her arms — fourteen on the right and seven on the left: she was left-handed.

One day the women of the neighbourhood, moved by so many tragedies, went in a commission to the pharmacy to console her and to counsel moderation in her choice of lover. Kindly, they showed their understanding:

'With a husband like that . . . we might do the same, who knows? Far be it from us to say we would not drink from that well, if thirst became unbearable . . . but there is no need to exaggerate, no need to drink too much. . . . Even water can give you a hangover! Everyone sleeps in your bed. . . . This is taking things too far . . . an insult to your husband.'

'What is the matter with my husband?' she asked defensively.

'He is funny like that. . . . When he gives an injection, he grabs our men's arms. He doesn't need to grab them the way he does, it's not normal. Frankly, your husband is not a man . . . and a woman's husband has to be a man.'

The most forward of them, Rosalva, dotted the I's – and the Aaa's, the Eee's, the Ooo's and the Uuuu's for that matter, and any other vowel she could get her lips around, with as camp a delivery as she could manage. 'To come straight to the point – not to mince words – not to beat about the bush: everyone knows that your husband is a bender! Queer as a coot! From head to foot!'

At first, the pharmacist's wife resisted: 'My husband is a serious, competent professional – he's fine. Don't come to me with this pathetic filth. I don't even want to talk about it. . . .'

'We wouldn't dream of talking about it . . . but the truth of the matter is . . .' and Dona Rosalva waded in.

There were five neighbours, each wanting to throw in their word of consolation or criticism. They thought, nevertheless, that Rosalva had gone over the top – calling him a queen, a little woman, a pederast, a sodomite, a double-edged razor-blade, the Cantareira boat[20] and more – . . . but to be like that, openly queer? The wife's reply surprised them still more, as she shrugged her shoulders and said: 'Well, he's not as bad as Pedro. . . .'

Pedro was a homosexual who carried the stigma on his shoulders and in his biceps. In those days a homosexual was only that – a queer. He was not known by his family or his work (which in any case was hard to come by since he was 'a poof') by any other attribute: queer was queer, that said it all. At most, a small allowance was made to those who were 'active' – the consensus was that these men had not completely renounced their virility. In a way, they were regarded as even more macho than heterosexuals were, 'machos' who 'ate' 'machos'. The others, however, were much worse, they were renegades – the 'passive' encountered no pity in the severe eyes of the guardians of morality. . . .

Pedro seemed not to be bothered by this. Everyone knew about his sexual preferences and he strolled about wearing very tight trousers and a tight-fitting sleeveless shirt, with muscular arms and mouth made up with grey lipstick, extremely discreet.

On Sundays, when the games on the pitches of Penha Football Club and Maravilha Athletic Club were over, Pedro strode along the pavement, exchanging surreptitious looks with macho young men, even with the players. As night fell, Pedro would go to the football pitch, but now to play a different game. With much dissembling, one or two of the players followed along after him, on to the playing field for a second time, and queued up. . . .

Everyone commented. The children asked each other:

'Where are they going?'

'Down behind the woods.'

'Aaaaaaahhhhhhh!!!'

The older ones asked no such questions, but weighed their critiques:

'It must be bad for him, so much sperm inside the belly. . . . The organism doesn't accept it. . . . It's against nature, the intestines weren't made to take it. . . .'

'Rubbish: he gets healthier and fatter every time . . .'

'Aaaaaaaaahhhhhhh!!!'

That was the general level of their commentaries, which then moved on to events in the current round of the championship, midfield goals and suchlike.

I'll see to it after Christmas

From my vantage point seated by the gate on the bridge at the big house, I saw everything. I would often see customers from the bakery coming to ask for a loan from my father, who was not rich, though he appeared to be. My father sent '*cartas da chamada*', he had two bakeries, savings in the Caixa

Econômica Bank — these things gave him 'status'. The supplicants were after money for all manner of things: to buy a jeep, to do their house up, their daughter was going to marry some 'joão-nobody'. . . . My father was a personality in Penha. He would listen attentively and reply: 'After Carnival, I'll see to it.'

The petitioners did not leave with money, but they got to drink Port. My father only lent money — or rather gave it, since he knew it would not be repaid! — when the case concerned illness or natural tragedy: crutches for a man who had been crippled, a glass eye for a blind man, funds towards house repairs after a storm. To all others, the reply was the same: 'After Carnival. . . .'

'Mr Boal, we're still only in May. . . .'

'After Christmas. . . .' My father shortened the wait so as not to dishearten them — they were customers.

Why I am not a pianist

It was in the *sala de visitas* that I definitively gave up any ideas of being a pianist. True — I did have the shortest career as a pianist in history — a single afternoon! It began at 4 p.m. and was over by 5.30. . . .

It was like this: my sisters had a piano teacher — Dona Marieta, who came to supervise their scales twice a week. They would sit at the piano, playing and singing the same melodies: I'll never forget *Für Elise*! It was my first musical love. *The Blue Danube* — I adore waltzes. I would position myself outside in the garden, listening. One day, both my sisters were ill at the same time but, having not been informed, the teacher turned up anyway. My father did not hesitate: 'Rather than waste your journey, you can teach Augusto something. . . .' My father was progressive: 'He should study piano as well.' 'Wow, it's my turn!' I leapt in the air higher than Chibuco in my elation!

But my brother had his doubts, thinking of Pedro: 'Boys don't play the piano; start playing the piano and you don't know where it'll end. . . .' Dona Marieta poured more cold water on my enthusiasm: 'Listen. Boys play football, jump over fences, climb trees. OK? I have never seen a boy playing the piano. Just think of it, a boy playing the flute: it would be indecent. A little respect and *amour propre* never harmed anyone. Drums maybe — why not? — *cuica* or *berimbau* or *pandeiro* or *zabumba* . . . fair enough. But piano. . . . Lord preserve us — that's all we need. . . . Boys and harps do not go together, they have nothing to do with each other! As for boys and harpsichords . . . absolutely ridiculous!' — she said, without an ounce of respect for Mozart.

'But I like . . .' I mumbled timidly, inaudibly.

'Like doesn't even come into it. Do boys like playing with dolls? Do boys like sewing? Do boys like weeing sitting down? Of course not! Piano is the same thing, it is like weeing sitting down. Oh well, I don't care, I am paid for this, let's get on with it. Let's go: scales, *dó-re-mí-fá-so-la-ti-do*, solfeggio!'

Dona Marieta did her best to complicate things which were already far from simple for a 10-year-old. She threatened:

'That is nothing like it, look here, this *dó* is white and counts for two: *dó-ó*, do you see? The *fá* is black, it counts for a *fá*: *fá*. So! The *mí* is round, and counts for three: *mi-i-i*! Then the quaver and semiquaver, demi-semiquaver and hemi-demi-semiquaver, the flats and the sharps. The syncopated notes have a dot above them. . . . You don't understand anything and that's why none of this is right . . . *solfeggio!*. At once!'

'Could you repeat that?' — it took all my courage and more to make such an audacious request. Since she did not respond, her thoughts else-where, a distant look in her eye as she stared at the lampshade, shaking her head, I tried to encourage her: '*Dó-ó-ó- óóó- óóó- óóó- óóó* . . .'

I opened my mouth as wide as it would go: the piano would have needed two or three metres more keys to have reached the note I reached! Neighbours came out of their houses to witness this outrage of sound! Dona Marieta was cruel: 'It is I who have *dó* (compassion) for you . . . *Dó-ó-ó-ó-ó-ó* (Compa-a-a-a-ssion) . . . You will never be a pianist, trumpet player, harpist, saxophonist, choirboy, singer, tuner or even mover of pianos — nothing that has anything even remotely to do with music. . . . But let's get on with it, I need this lesson, this is my salary. Repeat after me: *dó-dó-dó-dó* . . .'

If I ever had any musical vocation, it was killed as dead as a *do*-do in that *sala de visitas*. Pitilessly, by the *rays* of the setting sun, she berated *me*, *far* more than I deserved, *so* that by *tea*-time Dona Marieta had knocked all musical inclination out of me. Dead as a *do*-do! Only the *la* was *la*-lacking.

. . . This has not stopped me directing musicals in the theatre, some of which have made their mark: '*Opinião*',[21] '*Tiradentes*',[22] '*Zumbi*'.[23] I cannot sing, and my fingers get tangled in strings and stumble over keys. But I can hear. And suggest. It is not ideal, but has sufficed.

(Years later, directing '*Opinião*', I demonstrated to Zé Keti[24] how I would like him to sing the theme music, so that the lyric 'You can beat me, you can arrest me!' would sound like a shout of revolt rather than a joyful carnival chant. To give him a sense of what I meant, I dared to sing. Zé Keti thought I wanted him to imitate me.

'You want me to sing like that?'

'More or less along those lines. . . .'

'I'm never going to sing like that. . . .'

'Why?'

'I've got a family to support. . . . If I sang like that, I'd never work again. . . .')

German lover, allied marriage

Before Brazil came down on the side of the Allies, Hitlerian fascism won enthusiastic converts, the sort of people who are always on the winner's side. There are people like that: always in power, on the side of those who give orders, even if this means they have to keep changing sides. Many 1970s Marxists became pragmatic in the 1990s: proponents of globalisation – they sold off Brazil for nothing! We thought they had changed, but they had not changed at all: they had always been running along behind power or prestige. They were hard-line Stalinists under Stalin, Maoists in the China of the little red books, and no one would defend *glasnost* more fervently than they, not even Gorbachev! The Dalai Lama or Chou en Lai – it doesn't matter: the important thing is to give the orders!

In Germany, it was the SS; here, *O Integralismo* (the Integralism)[25] formed paramilitary groups, known as '*Galinhas Verdes*',[26] who paraded everywhere in green and yellow, singing the national anthem angrily. Everyone had to take off their hats as they went past – in those days people wore hats, képis and peaked caps.

One day I saw a young man, enraptured, murmuring the anthem with his mouth open, sincerely moved in the face of the apparent patriotism of the *Galinhas Verdes*, forgetful of the cap on his head, drunk with patriotism. Seeing his hat, the commander of the battalion, passing next to him, gave him a tremendous punch in the face and the young man fell down into the muddy frog-ridden ditch, blood running from his mouth. He got himself out of there on his own, clambering up the bank, stumbling and dirty: no one had the courage to help him in the menacing presence of the battalion parading past. After the punch, there was the silence of a cemetery on a windless midnight.

That afternoon in the bakery, where beers were served on three tables and nine chairs, the punching was the subject of the day: 'If it is agreed that you must take off your hat, you take off your hat. . . . If you don't, you have to face the consequences. . . .' This was Mateus, drinking lager.

'Who agreed it?' said Felisberto, unresigned to this historical necessity. 'Punching someone like that isn't right.'

'I don't know, but it was agreed: when the *Galinhas Verdes* pass by, you must take your hat off. . . . That's the way it is, and it has to be.'

No one knew who the *Galinhas* were — everyone had a presentiment that they were not a good thing. They had tight faces. People talked vaguely of Nazis, assassins of Jews, communists and gypsies.

Parades were in fashion. Every occasion of any solemnity would have a parade. I myself paraded more than once before my eleventh birthday, all in white, the uniform of the college gala, with a golden buckle and a hot képi. I paraded before Getúlio Vargas, (President and then Dictator 1931–1937, 1937–1945) on 7 September, in the Central do Brasil, proud of being seen in the middle of the crowd, by the President of the Republic. Eleven years old: white uniform, heat, képi, sweat, dizziness, military march. Patriotism: it did exist.

When I, a patriot, heroically intoned our national anthem, the protests of my little friends silenced me. 'Augusto, stop singing, or we're going to get out of tune too. . . .' my little colleagues said kindly.

Still proud in spite of the affront, I murmured the words, *sotto voce*, so as not to bother anyone, but without letting my recalcitrant patriotism wither, because I was extremely patriotic, believe me. . . .

That is how I started to believe in the notion of *Pátria* (Fatherland). Qualms notwithstanding, I still believe in it. Pátria . . . until when shall I believe in it?

Paris has fallen! London is standing!

'Paris has fallen!' said my father, rushing into the house. 'Fallen where?' I wondered, amazed, running into the kitchen, where he was telling my mother the details of the fall of Paris, both of them all of a quiver.

'London still hasn't fallen, thank God! London is standing!' He went on completing his round-up of the news of the day. 'Nor will it fall! Never!', he added optimistically. My mother chimed in supportively: 'Let it be God's wish that London does not fall. . . . We will do all we can.'

Hitler frightened me. What most horrified me were the speeches in German we heard on the radio, with a translation summary superimposed. I did not know what 'Heil Hitler!' was – but I was afraid. That may be why, to this day, I have not managed to learn German. I speak several languages, four or five, but German, not even close, just a few words – '*danke schön!*' '*Verfremdungseffekt*',[27] that sort of thing. My unconscious resistances come to the fore!

Politics also frightened me, because I did not understand anything, I did not know which side to be on, or what the various sides were, or whether it was OK to change sides. The *Socorro Urgente* (Urgent Rescue) team would arrive, in the form of a family-sized Black Maria, full of police armed with stout solid rubber truncheons, who would get out of their van and, without asking any questions, launch a hail of blows! The violence was democratic: blows aplenty were distributed to all and sundry, irrespective of sex, race or creed. Anyone who happened to be within the team's field of action got a beating. People collapsed. Hours later, the ambulance arrived to tend their wounds.

When the situation was particularly serious, as well as the *Socorro Urgente* there came the *Polícia Especial* (Special Police): athletic and strong youths, *catarinas* – in the same way as the Pope has his svelte Swiss Guards in their uniforms designed by Michelangelo, so the Dictatorship of the time had its *catarinas* from Santa Catarina.[28] A strapping race, of Germanic descent, without relatives or acquaintances in Rio de Janeiro, who could rain down blows easy in the knowledge that there was no chance of their being recognised by a friend, or of their cudgels falling on a relative.

When I started my theatre

I heard the first Brazilian soap, *Em Busca da Felicidade* (In Search of Happiness) on the radio, when I was 10. The suspenseful music at the end of the episodes shocked me. The tremulous voices of the actors made me tremble.

One day, my brothers and I had the idea of creating a little piece of theatre. We read the weekly instalments of romantic novels my mother used to receive by post and dramatised them. My sisters say that I was authoritarian, but agree that it was necessary, because of the undisciplined nature of my cast.

We rehearsed on Sundays after a late lunch, and at the end of the afternoon the family would sit down in the dining-room, brilliantly discharging their role of audience. By way of curtain, we opened the doors that led to a room where my mother used to sew, which became my first stage. Siblings and cousins were the actors. As there were many characters, each person had to play a variety of roles. Perhaps it was there that I began to imagine the '*Coringa*' (Joker) System':[29] the same character was represented by various siblings, as well as each playing several other characters. There was no private ownership of the characters by the actors: each scene was told by whoever was available, all the characters interpreted by whoever liked them most. Here already I was using the form 'Arena Tells of . . .':[30] 'The Boal Brothers And Their Cousins Tell Of. . . .' We told of 'The Count of Monte Cristo', of 'Isaura the Slave', of 'The Cardinals' Supper'. . . .

We wanted the whole ritual: in order to be allowed to watch, each spectator had to buy a ticket. The price: three beer or *guaraná*[31] bottle tops, which would later serve as wheels on the cars we made from jam tins. . . .

Our little theatre lasted for several shows, with me accumulating the functions of director and prompter, making sure my brothers respected the author's text. (And that is the way I have continued all my life, a respecter of texts!) For their part, by contrast, they wanted to improvise. When one of the actors did not repeat the lines as they had been written, I would argue, cry, and threaten to bring our young artistic careers to an abrupt end. We would have to interrupt the scene, close the 'curtains' with a clatter, lock them, argue, discuss, reach an agreement, reopen the 'curtains' and then . . . go off in search of the spectators, who had better things to do than just sit there. They would disperse at the slightest pretext. We sought them out one by one, brought back our audience, returned the entrance money – the bottle tops – charged them the same tops all over again, and the show would begin again. The ritual of paying the entrance fee was important – it was the pact that we established with our audience, a sign of mutual acceptance.

Today, when I do street theatre and we go out in search of spectators, I remember those times. However, by contrast, the audience in the street is so needy they sometimes come running.

Chibuco, a good actor, did not speak, nor did he always understand my instructions, and above all, he had his own ideas. With my brothers, dialogue was possible. Much better to work with humans. Since then, I have always respected my actors: they are always my siblings.

It also happened that, as the performance was short, we would tack on a variety show at the end of the piece. Then would come the turn of my 6-year-old cousin, Marlene, to enchant the family. She had a beautiful voice, but . . . I was a trouble-maker and I mocked arias and solos. Actors represented a text, a play, a story – they were at the service of something, in interrelationship; whereas in solos, the singer showed himself to himself – vanity. Today, I know better.

I invented a prize that praised and accused simultaneously – sadist that I was in childhood. My cousin Marlene still remembers today that the prize was called '*Abacaxi*' (Pineapple).

My admiration for actors dates back to those shows. I am sure that, starting from that first experience with my brothers, I adopted the fixed idea of doing theatre from then on. As soon as my first childhood theatre season came to an end, my desire to be an artist began. I had to be one, I would be one! I am one!

I never understood why Gordon Craig[32] wasted time inventing puppet actors. If he had succeeded, they would be like the singer-dancers made by computers nowadays. They have legions of admirers and fan clubs and yet . . . they don't actually exist. They are totally fabricated, synthesised from the voices of thousands of singers, the bodies and movements of hundreds of dancers, the deadly gaze of dozens of cinematic vamps, and the perverse innocence of entire classes of high school student girls. . . . Behold the robot-star. And the task of replying to the love letters received by the thousand every day is undertaken by yet other computers, which analyse the ardour of the senders and respond accordingly.

Gordon Craig died before the advent of computers, the only means by which his dream of robot-actors could have been realised. By contrast, I, who live in the civilisation of robots and zombies, prefer to work with imperfect actors, those insecure beings, afraid before they go on stage, but with ideas in their heads and desire in their hearts.

Our little childhood theatre lasted throughout infancy. In its wake, it left an enormous desire to continue, to begin 'for real' what was merely 'a game'.

Today, when I surf the Net to the world beyond, I feel as though I were sitting at the bridge to the gate of my house, watching the world go by.

I send messages from my 'site', like one who tosses bottles into the sea . . . I write books as if wanting to reach someone, whose face has dissolved with time. . . .

I want to see the faces of those who, in my books, see my face.

The control tower, the baker and the bread

Without realising it, I started working in the Leopoldina Bakery at the age of 11, when we moved from the big house. In the beginning, I would go there bearing a message from my mother, or to fetch a can of oil. My father would tell me to serve a customer: a hundred grams of butter, a dozen buns, or biscuits made from powdered cassava. I got used to it. And there was something in it for me: I ate what I wanted. Sausages and cream crackers, from the savoury side of the shop; fairy cakes, from the sweet side. I acquired a tendency to get fat.

I began to do a certain number of hours, in exchange for an increase in my pocket-money. In the holidays (did someone say holidays?) I worked double time, day and night! In term-time, sweet relief, I only worked afternoons till nightfall.

The routine was simple, with the hard work concentrated in the morning when the first batch came out of the oven, and in the afternoon when the second was ready. On to the stage went the basket of hot fragrant, crunchy bread – and the audience of ravenous customers would explode in a wild clamour. Everyone wanted to be first; people would be trampled, there were shouts, blows, jostling – this was before the invention of that marvellous device 'the queue', a thing which would subsequently come to plague us, a necessary evil!

Today, there are queues for everything. In those days one never queued for anything, brute force was what counted, the shove ruled; social niceties were rare. It was normal to push fat people, to tread on the weak, to chat up pretty girls, and shout in the ears of the deaf.

Between batches of sweet-smelling bread, customers were scarce. I would pass the time watching people in the street. I worked at that counter from the age of 11 till I was 19, when I went to the National School of Chemistry. Now I had to take two buses – an hour and a half of being thrown about on the way there, and another hour and a half back, with no time to help my father. Once at university I worked on Saturdays; while my colleagues accompanied girls to parties in the Faculty of Medicine next door to ours, I was behind the counter. I never learned to dance. I still only dance when I am well hidden in the middle of the crowd, or when I am directing musicals. Then I let go.

While still at the *cientifico* stage, the last part of secondary school, I must have had some illness, I never found out what. I would be waiting for a bus. It was usually about 43 degrees in the shade, and I'd be clad in an English cashmere vest and an Italian silk tie, with the granite dust hanging in the air, mixed with the fetid stench of the Carioca Tannery, whose smell wafted north or south according to the direction of the wind (living in the east, we got the leftovers). Suddenly I'd feel dizzy and have to sit down on the kerb. When it came to boarding the bus, some sympathetic person would always let me sit on the front seat, where the bus swayed less. I would arrive home, feeling my old self again, and would not bother going to the doctor. On those days I did not go off to work.

At the counter, I invented an observation post, which was a substitute for my special place at the gate on the bridge. I wanted to continue watching people, imagining scenes. I found the stool, which the bookkeeper used when studying the accounts. There I sat at the counter, next to the telephone hanging on the wall. When no one came by, I would read newspapers.

I always needed a control tower of some kind or other, which would allow me to watch others – the director submerged in the darkness of the auditorium, giving instructions to the illuminated actors.

The announcer of rituals

I watched the world. I would pretend that things only happened as a product of my will, and for its delectation: as I knew the customers' habits and schedules by heart, they would always do the same things, with the same script. Everything was entirely predictable. I would joke with the staff, anticipating what each customer would do: if, in the past, I had commentated on football games like a good radio broadcaster, now I gave a commentary on the movements of these characters *before* they happened.

Mateus would appear at his veranda, and my commentary would commence:

'*Come on Mateus. Cross the road. But before you do, take a good look behind you.*' I never understood why he looked behind him before crossing the road ahead of him. Maybe he was afraid of being pushed.

'*In you come, Mateus, right foot first. . . .*' And in he would come, making sure that his right foot was leading. '*Now stop at the door, look at your house and make sure you have not left the door open, you fool!*' Mateus checked the doors and windows of his house: they were closed. '*Everything OK, you dunce? Then come on in and sit down, you old idiot!*' Mateus sat down. '*Lean your back against the marble counter and say it is very hot . . . unbearable . . . no one can put up with it. . . . Go on, you nincompoop! Say it! What are you waiting for?*'

'No one can put up with it . . . this heat . . . unbearable . . .' Mateus would say, cooling his back against the marble counter.

'*Moan, Mateus . . .*'

And moan he would.

He spoke and acted as per my 'broadcast': he would be the first to arrive, followed by fat, round Felisberto – I have never seen anyone so round, so ball-shaped, so *Mappa Mundi*! The two of them would sit at a table near the ham-slicing machine, light their cigars and puff away with a single rhythm, drinking their beers with a shared meditative fervour, and spitting on the floor with the same lack of embarrassment, the same slovenliness. Shameless. Even Mateus, the enemy of spitting, spat.

'Now, Felisberto, it is your turn . . .' I opined, in silent thought. '*It is your turn, Felisberto, you great Zeppelin-load of shit, tell a stupid joke about the marble tomb and the cold stone of the cemetery which await us all. . . .*'

Felisberto told his funereal joke.

'Come the mausoleum, no one will complain about the heat . . . I am in no hurry: I prefer the hell of the summer here on earth to the paradise of winter, six feet under.'

Everything obeyed me, like the sun obeyed the Little Prince when he ordered it to appear in the sky good and early in the morning, and go to bed at the end of the afternoon . . . and the sun obeyed him. Mateus and Felisberto, customers and passers-by, obeyed me. They were my marionettes.

When an employee was absent I would start work at dawn, rolling up the iron shutters while it was still dark. Workers from the Carioca Tannery would arrive, hurried ants – always late! I ordained that every morning they would ask for their half cup of milky coffee, with bread and butter and – none of us is made of steel – the same glass of *cachaça* or *parati*.[33] They swallowed the pure cane alcohol like a Russian downs vodka: a matutinal incendiary! Only after the fire were they properly awake. The machines awaited them, ready to start working, to start cutting hides . . . and the workers' fingers.

Every morning, coffee, milk, bread, butter and . . . *cachaça*. Lunch-box in their hands. Packet of cigarettes in their pocket. In their eyes, fatigue and unhappiness. The future . . . empty.

The blind singer

When the workers left, the morning comedy unfolded in front of my control tower: children going to study, washerwomen hanging out the clothes, the fisherman with a basket selling stary-eyed fish, the man selling live poultry, his chickens clucking nervously. The gallinaceous ones were tied by their feet to a rod which the vendor carried over his shoulders, the animals hanging head down on both sides. The bread-man passed on his tricycle. *O Ceguinho*, the blind man, who saw everything, spent the night in the street humming church music, and in the morning entered the house of a worker, every day, and no one knew why, or for what. . . .

Inside, just this woman. Neighbours imagined all sorts of things, but the skinny woman would appear all the time at the window or at the door, working outside the house, hanging out washing. The blind man sleeping . . . it was an enigma. Or it was charity, which is also an enigma.

Before the afternoon was up, before the husband returned, *O Ceguinho* would leave and walk around the place until night, when he would choose some bit of the street to lie down in, and sing sacred music and beg; as by this time there were hardly any passers-by, it was slim pickings.

Inspired by that blind man I wrote *Martim Pescador* (Martin the Fisherman), which was rehearsed years later with Grande Otelo[34] as its protagonist. We used to rehearse with Abdias Nascimento,[35] my oldest close friend, my brother, and other actors of the Black Experimental Theatre. The rehearsals took place in the shed at the bottom of the garden of the flat I lived in. Inspired by those people – blind men, women, labourers, white people and black people – I wrote several plays . . . and left them to rest; years later I would rewrite them. Like my father's bread: first you made the dough; then you let it rest; then you cut it into pieces, kneaded it, formed and shaped it; let it rest on the side again; and finally, you put it into the oven. Like this book. Writing is me making my bread, like my father.

As for my marionettes – my mechanised actors! – I felt like the director of another writer's play: I could only co-ordinate what was scripted, the rituals of those quotidian lives. The characters always behaved just like themselves, with never a deviation. The only time a day was different was when it rained, or a Sunday. Perhaps this monotony led me to invent some of the techniques of the 'Rainbow of Desire': the circuit of rituals, the ritual gestures, the masks.

★   ★   ★

The strange story of the German from Piauí[36]

The only unexpected character in my childhood was a young man who began to appear in the neighbourhood. Initially, no one gave him a second thought, despite the fact that he seemed to go out of his way not to belong, impertinent with his dark, almost black garb, such as might be worn by one who has just been to a funeral. Every now and then he turned up with a walking cane . . . in Penha, with its dusty unmade roads! A walking cane was a Northern Hemisphere thing, a thing of snow and cold. A black suit in the scorching sun? Topped off with fine gold-rimmed spectacles?

He was a weird man. No one spoke to him because his strangeness shocked them. Some swore that the man was a special kind of spectre, an ally of Satan, spying on humans. Some wanted to check whether, instead of normal feet with toes and toe-nails, men's feet, he might by any chance have goats' feet, with cloven hooves. No one dared go up to him and say: 'Take off your shoes, fellow: show your essence!' Their fear of the consequences outweighed their curiosity: what if the man *was* a goat? What if, on being discovered, he fell into a fury, and in his frenzy went about impaling people on his horns? What if his horns were poison-tipped, dipped in the Indians' *curare*? Best just leave him be.

So they left him be.

The only other people in Penha who wore black – apart from those in gloomy mourning for the first weeks after any burial, or widows who were black-clad for the rest of their lives – were the church priests and the Man with the Black Hood, a fugitive leper, who was said to capture disobedient children and lead them handcuffed to the leper house. Horrors! Why the handcuffs? No one knew. The Man with the Black Hood was a sort of children's cart (like the dog-cart), as prophesied by Mateus.

The Man with the Black Hood was not an hallucination, he existed. He did not capture anyone, except in our frequent guilty nightmares. The Black Hood was used by mothers to frighten their children: 'He will come and take you away if you don't do what I tell you, if you don't get good marks at school, if you don't do your homework, if you don't help in the kitchen, if you don't eat the food on your plate, if you don't wash up your plate. . . .'

Eventually the Man with the Black Hood lost his clout because he did not harm anyone, and no one disappeared as had been feared. One fine day, the children began to throw sticks and stones and carnival fireworks[37] at him. Wounded and bleeding, the leper fled and never came back again. He died of the wounds, not of leprosy.

Meanwhile, who was the man in mourning? Was he of the Devil, or more mundane? An enigma!

'He is from the Portuguese Secret Service. . . .'[38] iterated Walter, one of the staff at the bakery, leaning his belly up against the counter. Mateus and Felisberto, both Lusitanians, pretended they had not heard.[39]

'I wonder if you could possibly be kind enough to sell me a packet of imported Lipton tea?' asked the man in black, as if there were any shadow of a doubt about our commercial intentions.

'Everything on display is for sale, sir – I sell everything!' Walter would say – 'Except for the girl at the cash register and me. . . . The rest is for sale, you can help yourself.'

'So how much am I in your debt?' the outlandish foreigner would ask in an educated tone.

'You're not in my debt at all, but you owe the boss . . . allow me to see . . .' Walter would say, imitating his style.

One day, Mateus and Felisberto decided to discover who this pale man was, with the curious but undeniable affirmation that he 'must be somebody!'

'Sir, tell me . . . why do you go around looking so odd – so . . . unusual, so . . . indefinable, so . . . out of fashion and out of place?' asked Mateus.

'The style is the man . . .' came his *retort* – well, not for such a distinguished man the mere *reply*. 'Each of us has his own style. That of your good selves[40] is unmistakable . . .' he added in a manner designed not to offend anyone, the irony being well-disguised in his soft, fluting voice.

'Are you, by any chance, a priest? Are you connected to religion?' asked Felisberto without much subtlety, biting the end off his cheroot and spitting it out. 'Priest, Archbishop or Pastor, Rabbi, *Macumba* or *Candomblé* Shaman,[41] Saint Mother or Father[42] – any God stuff like that? Do you have anything to do with that sort of thing?'

'Not by chance nor by vocation . . .' *reflected* the strange man, not being a man merely to *retort*. 'I have always bravely pursued the path of science, and not that path which leads us to dogma. I nevertheless respect all religions, however African they may be, animism, the lot, even the commonest and most vulgar!' he continued disrespectfully, dwelling with painstaking care on each phonetic detail.

'Tell the truth . . . are you a Rosicrucian, a Thirteenth Day Adventist, an esoteric or a Freemason?' returned Mateu, bent on guessing.

'Although they do not allow themselves to be identified, I do know many of those type of men . . .' *rejoined* the outsider, not being a man merely to *reflect*. 'No, the truth is, I never joined the masonry. Perhaps . . . there was a time . . . I thought it possible.'

Felisberto, fat like a ball, gave it one last shot – his best shot!

'How come you are so peculiar if you're not a priest camouflaged as a civilian, nor a Mason dressed up as a Protestant Pastor, nor the head of the Civil Guard, nor a sergeant in the Special Police; unless you are a Black Cockerel of Exu,[43] why do you dress in black like a vulture, if you are no bloody thing known to man . . .'

'Not even Portuguese!' the elegant stranger interjected, alluding to the two friends' nationality.

'Not even Portuguese. . . . So, it is obvious that you must be German!'

A triumphant pause: they had discovered, at least, the man's nationality. A person who was none of the things they knew to exist must of course be German!

'Unfortunately I am not German . . .' the false Teuton countered. 'I am Brazilian, to my shame. . . . I was born in Cajuazeiro do Sul, in Piauí. . . .'

'Why unfortunate? There are still people being born in Piauí, so I have heard. The place is just as worthwhile as any other . . .' Felisberto defended his adoptive fatherland.

The false German protected himself:

'You are not completely mistaken: I was educated in Germany, yes, in Köln. . . .'

And he pronounced the word 'Köln' with such velveteen subtlety, with so much satin and muslin, that no Brazilian, still less any German, would have understood what godforsaken city he was talking about.

'Where? Who? Why?' The questions rained down like bullets from a machine-gun.

'The city of Köln, which you call Colônia . . . Köln . . . Köln . . . Köln
. . . That was where I was educated.'

'Cologne, like eau-de-Cologne?' asked Mateus, entertained by the
conversation with the black-clad owner of the sweaty white straw hat.

'Precisely. . . . Kölnwasser, Glockengasse, 4711. . . .' He even remembered the address. 'Next to the factory, they built a beautiful museum
which revealed the secrets of eau-de-Cologne, *Kölnwasser*! Europeans hold
their traditions in high esteem, which is why there are as many museums
there as there are bars here: you find one on every corner.'

'We esteem *cachaça* highly . . .' said Walter, full of patriotism.

'What name do you go by, by the grace of God?' Felisberto wanted to
know, and even though the German had not sought explanation, he
explained: '"The name you go by" means what the hell is your name?'

'I am Doctor *Karl Roethe* Ribamar.' And he gave fanatical emphasis to
the pronunciation of the German part of his name, fading almost to nothing
the emaciated 'ribamar' . . . the provenance of which, if truth be told, was
Maranhão[44] and not Piauí.

With this the conversation was closed, and he turned to his purchases:

'Be so good as to give me: fifty grams of margarine. If you would be so
kind: one corn biscuit. If I could trouble you for a Malzbier lager and an egg
. . . and if it won't put you out too much, a dozen eggs, separately.' (My
father's bakery was like an underdeveloped supermarket!)

On other visits to the bakery, always in response to indiscreet
questions, the Colognial told how his Brazilian father had married a
German tourist, who was separated from her Swiss first husband and who
had arrived late for the Nigerian boat on its return leg to Europe, on a
'tour' organised by a Turkish travel agency. Apparently the ship departed
before the agreed hour, taking some fugitive Lebanese smugglers, who
had paid double the price of the ticket to the Pakistani captain, who was
married to a jealous Norwegian. In sum, a maritime tale of Babel.

His mother put up at a hotel near the port while she waited for the next
ship and, having nothing else to do, she used to drink beer in a bar on the
sea front, watching the ships. And it was there she met his father, a rich and
unattached landowner, who took her for one of the other women who hung
out there, also awaiting better days, drinking beer and watching the ships,
and attending to 'customers', when there were any. . . .

They got married and stayed living in Piauí. The son was born, and when Doctor Karl was 6, as a result of insurmountable cultural differences, his mother returned to her native land taking her son. Both did all they could to wrest the Ribamar from their name, following the mother's third, more endogamous marriage, to a Tyrolean violinist who wore short trousers and a feather in his hat.

Until the war came along, and the adoptive father died in bloody battle impaled on a bayonet. The impoverished Doctor Karl Roethe and his mother decided to try life on Piauí soil, like true Piauíenses. They went to find Ribamar Senior, in search of sustenance and, who knows, reconciliation. But the old land-grabber Ribamar, now much richer, was already on his seventh set of nuptials, to a young girl of 17 who did not want — not in the slightest, not in the least of the slightest — to shake hands with the family Roethe, which as time went by shrank more and more. As Ribamar was at least a millionaire, he gave them plenty of money to buy a house and live in Rio. In a suburb, of course: in Penha. Far away from the cattle and the Colonel's[45] young spouse.

Over and over, Doctor Karl would say: 'Unfortunately, I was born in Piauí. . . . With so many beautiful cities in Europe, in Germany. . . . Guissen with its suspended pedestrian bridge . . . Cosmopolitan Berlin, Hamburg with its gigantic port. . . . Wiesbaden with its celebrated baths . . . Gauting with its bucolic main road, Mainz with its Gutenberg Bibles . . . Saarbrücken with its dancers, Wuppertal with its Neanderthal museum. . . . I have to be born in Cajuazeiro do Sul with its cashew trees. . . .'

He was disagreeable, the man in black. After all, he was talking about our fatherland. A man who uses a walking stick has no right to speak ill of other people, who don't use sticks — imagine! What do you need a stick for, if you are not lame? I was fascinated by him.

The black telephone: 30.2473

Doctor Ribamar coming up Fuas Roupinho. That was the street I had to go down each time our telephone rang, the first phone to be installed in the whole of Lobo Júnior: 30.2473! A magic number. Someone would answer: a message, please, go and fetch them. But it rarely rang. Phones in Rio were few and far between. When it did ring, it gave us a shock. The old telephone sound was shocking, other-worldly.

'Can you call Dona So-and-so for me?'

No one ever could: the telephone was always left hanging for five or ten minutes, until someone went to call the person who in turn was always busy and took another ten minutes to answer. The bakelite handset was left dangling. Inquisitive dogs would come and lick it. . . . The dogs of the neighbourhood adored licking telephones. To canine eyes, a telephone was like a black bone. The phone was always covered in dogs' spittle.

Once, a pesky meddlesome dog, the sort of dog which goes around looking for a fight, broke a tooth chewing the numbers on the black tele-phone, pulled the cord and tore down the apparatus which came off the wall. The technician from the telephone company came to reconnect it. Who should pay? The owner of the de-toothed dog, the customer who took so long to answer, or the telephone company?

My father, the owner of the line, of course.

After that, it was discovered that the handset did not have to be left hanging: it could rest on top of the counter, out of reach of canine teeth . . . it took some time, though, to make this important discovery. . . .

One of the people who frequently telephoned was Dona Hildegarde. Another German. Swearing as only she knew how! She had learned or fabricated an enviable collection of swear words adapted to all circum-stances. As it proved popular, she never missed an opportunity to deploy it! It was all the more amusing with her heavy accent, redolent of sauerkraut and sausage: Brazilian swear-words, pronounced in a steaming German accent, it was enough to make one die laughing. She swore with the inno-cence of a foreigner who does not know what she is saying. In one's mother tongue, words have a history and prehistory, but in another's language, only a history. If I say 'my mother', she is mine alone: 'ma mère', 'meine Mütter', 'madrecita' are everyone else's mothers.

When I started in the bakery, Hildegarde used to rib me: she wanted me to marry her daughter, Belinha. She would whet my appetite with post-matrimonial delights: 'You will marry her and put your little willy inside. . . .'

Inside what, where? How? She explained the details: she wanted at all costs to be my mother-in-law, or rather to be related in some way to the owner of the bakery! Without beating about the bush, I clarified the situa-tion: 'I can't, don't you see? It isn't possible for me to marry her because my mother has already decided: I am going to marry Princess Margaret! Now, as for the willy, let's see. . . . When would be a good time . . . ?'

I got excited, seduced, and I eyed Belinha from afar, in the afternoons, watering the garden – with my willy awakened. Though ready to accept the distant Princess, thus satisfying my mother, I was seduced by Belinha who lived nearby, near enough to be visible to the naked eye, with no ocean between us. (The Princess in question was English: thank goodness my mother was not ambitious and spared the Queen, satisfying herself with the latter's youngest sister.)

Another woman who spent hours on the telephone was Dalvinha, she of the perfume squirters and short skirts. She was married to the car mechanic, João Bobalhão, who was, to put it kindly, a big man and little lettered ('Bobalhão' means 'great fool'). The young girl was now a good-sized woman herself, fat even, the mother of three boys: one white, another black, and the first-born blue.

Let me explain. One day Dalvinha sought out Bobalhão and proposed to him. When the dropped jaw of the bridegroom-to-be was back in place, they agreed that the nuptials should take place the following week and Dalvinha gave birth to a premature baby boy weighing five kilos, after four months of pregnancy.

Everyone believed that the baby was premature, in spite of his being more sturdy than befitted the circumstances, and also because of his blue eyes and curly, blond hair, like that of that lay missionary or priest they no longer remembered, and very different from the presumed father, João Bobalhão, who had dark skin and frizzy black hair. The black colour of the second son was easily explained by the paternal line – there had been a black man in João's leafy family tree. Aside from this, psychological factors came into play, of course: nine months before the birth Dalvinha had converted to *Candomblé* and frequented *terreiros*[46] in Duque de Caxias and São Gonçalo – the skin colour of most of the participants was a lustrous black. Thus, by the effect of an uncontrollable religious mimetism. . . .

The belly gradually purifying itself, of course, explained the whiter than whiteness of the youngest child. That is how colour of the children was explained. God be praised! This same God whom Dalvinha now adored through her Kardecist[47] spiritism. Dalvinha loved God above all things, on any pretext and in all conditions, forms and rituals. Her new spiritualist guide in the spiritist religion, who was expelled from his church for religious insubordination, incorporated in himself some very aggressive, uneducated, athletic spirits, which loved to play with Dalvinha.

Dalvinha telephoned every day, without taking any notice of us. I think she never once realised that I existed. It was better that way: she was fat.

A writer's dreams

What I really liked doing was reading and writing. When I read a story and did not like it, I would rewrite it. I wanted peace and quiet in which to concentrate – and secrecy, so as not to be ridiculed. So I shut myself away in a junk-room, which was used for domestic chores and was my mother's sewing room. We had already given up the big house where I spent my infancy, with its backyard, chicken-coop and football pitch, and now lived in a smaller flat in the same street. My father used to say, well, at least it was our own!

'The first thing a man should do in life is buy his own house!' Boal would say 'Seu'. We agreed and accustomed ourselves to living in a cramped flat, which grew when my father bought the house next door, followed by another and then yet another.

I opened the window, which looked over the water tank in which my mother washed our clothes. In those days washing machines did not exist, everything was done by hand and, of course, washing clothes was a feminine occupation. Imagine a man washing clothes! Heresy! Infamy! Dishonour!

I wrote my first plays on the top of the sewing machine. With my mother washing smalls. Dona Ana used to wash the big things – sheets and towels – in her home.

Ana, the washerwoman, was married to Aristeu, who worked at the Light Company.[48] As he was entitled to free medical treatment, when Dona Ana fell ill, she would explain the symptoms to her husband and he in turn would describe them to the doctor at Light, pretending that he was experiencing his sickly wife's symptoms, so he could receive free treatment and medicines.

One day, the doctor exploded at him: 'According to your symptoms, you have a cyst in your uterus and complications in your ovaries! We'll have to operate!' Aristeu stuck to his guns and the doctor gave him the medicines, but with a recommendation that he abstain from sex for two months – as a punishment. Only when it came to Dona Ana's actual operation could Aristeu no longer pretend to be her. . . . Then he had to pay.

The 'Singer' sewing machine was the first 'desk' for my literary work. Today I have the latest generation of computer. In those days it was a Parker pen and Parker Indian ink. I took pleasure in drawing the letters – pretty, painted letters. I started to write with a manual typewriter, then an electric, and later an electronic machine: my calligraphy got worse. Today, not even I can understand what I write by hand. I like to see the words flowing from my fingertips and reappearing in a dance on the computer screen. Like now, right this moment. This very moment, as I am writing the word 'moment'.

Crouched over the sewing machine, I started to read Greek tragedies, and to feel that many stories in Greek myth were similar to the Nagô and Yoruba myths, brought over by African slaves. Oedipus and Orungan, for example, are similar myths. In the black version, the violence is greater: Orungan tears his own children and brothers from his mother's belly and kills them.

At that sewing machine I wrote *Laio Se Matou* (Laius Killed Himself) and other plays which mixed mythology with the lives of people I saw! Atreus in Fuas Roupinho street.

The unjust upholders of justice

The United States entered the war in 1941, shortly after the invasion of the Soviet Union by Germany. It was the beginning of the 'Good Neighbour' policy which replaced the 'Big Stick' policy (by which the United States gave itself the right to invade any country in its backyard – specifically Latin America! – which did not follow its will). They gave up their written legal rights, but they did not give up invasions. With 'Good Neighbour' we ceased to be good little natives and learned to sing: Carmen Miranda launched her career and was a hit, in Broadway and Hollywood, dressed in bunches of bananas, emerald green grapes and golden pineapples.[49]

With the world conflict, there was a serious risk of Nazism enslaving the world. The United States became flexible, meanwhile, when it came to the economy, and Brazil took advantage of this to develop industrially; the *Companhia Siderúrgica National*[50] was formed in 1941, and the *Vale do Rio Doce*[51] in 1943. They were our pride and joy: we could become industrialised, produce steel and iron, and manufacture laminated sheets, just like the grown-ups. Then came the *Fabrica Nácional de Motores*,[52] the greatest proof that we were among the most powerful countries in the world. They were our pride and joy.

In that same year, 1943, Brazil, which had entered the war the previous year, formed the Brazilian Expeditionary Force, and our soldiers went off to conquer Monte Cassino in Italy. The war was part of the agreement which permitted our industrialisation; Getulio Vargas[53] was enamoured with the Axis for a while. Permitting our economic development was part of an agreement by which the Brazilian government was resolutely to change both the side it was on and the ideology it espoused.

With Brazil fighting in Europe, soldiers' families despaired in the absence of news. There was growing hatred for the Germans, more than for the Italians; the Japanese were not even noticed in Rio, similar as they seemed to the Chinese who ran the pastry shops. Brazilian soldiers killed and died in Italy and, in Brazil, no one forgot that the *Galinhas Verdes* – taken as similar to the Germans – had for years committed violent crimes of all sorts against the apolitical population, against anarchists and communists, against Pedro and the pharmacist and the few gypsies there were. Torture *en masse* and assassination were the Aryan recipe.

Anti-Nazi groups began to be formed. In Penha, the *Justiceiros Contra O Nazismo* (Upholders of Justice against Nazism) movement was created. This was a group of angry men who intended to punish Germans in Brazil, simply for being Germans. In Penha they could number twenty to thirty men, armed mainly with knives and daggers.

The worst thing is that some of these 'Upholders of Justice' were old *Galinhas Verdes*, cunning ex-members of the paramilitary groups of Plínio Salgado, Chief *Galinha Verde*. The sort of people who are always on top, on the side of the strong. With Hitler in power, they were Nazis; if the Allies won, it was death to Nazism!

To justify their name, they had to create victims. One day (led by João Bobalhão, self-confessed husband of Dalvinha, supposed father of white, black and blue children), they went out on to the streets, having resolved to take revenge for the sinking of a Brazilian ship by German submarines. First, they wanted to get Dona Hildegarde, who had an undeniable accent: it could not have been more German. Someone objected:

'We can't beat her up, she is Brazilian, apparently she even swears in Portuguese. . . .'

'We'll see about that . . .' mused João Bobalhão.

So they went to Hildegarde's house, fondled Belinha all over and fumbled under her clothes, and then brought the old woman to the middle of the street and encircled her. Bobalhão ordered her to utter as many swear-words as she knew. The woman, a veritable encyclopedia of fearless profanity, knew all the usual swear-words as well as those no longer in use, and she invented other original ones. . . . And thus she was pardoned, for scatological reasons.

The Upholders of Justice went off to fetch Doctor Karl Roethke and his mother. Karl had already changed his name. Now he was Carlinhos Kid Ribamar, a fanatical supporter of Flamengo, a frequenter of *macumba terreiros*, who used sacred necklaces and amulets, and his mother was in bed at the time with suspected meningitis, appendicitis, stomachitis – he showed them the medical diagnosis and the prescription provided by the pharmacist, who, for all his defects, was a man who understood solidarity.

The Teuto-Piauíense was so sincere – 'Protect me, my God-daddy Cicero',[54] he said, speaking with the purest Northeastern accent, 'Ain't that so?' And the Upholders of Justice believed him, '*Ô gente*.'[55] Although they believed him, they wanted proof of the patriotism of the ex-admirer of Köln, Wiesbaden and its baths and Saarbrücken and its choristers. They ordered him to sing the Brazilian national anthem with patriotism and fervour. Both parts of it.[56] In their entirety, right to the end, up to and including the line 'Thou art the gentle mother of the children of this soil, beloved fatherland, Brazil'!

'It is very long, *Uái*, don't you know?[57] Isn't it?'

This mistake was almost fatal for him – to mix Minas Gerais[58] with Piauí was unpardonable! Nothing to do with the Northeast, and to mix 'Don't ya know' with 'God-daddy Cicero' was too much! Even so, he saved himself by saying that Brazil is diverse, and has many cultures! In the heat of the moment and with their urgency to find a real scapegoat, they decided against punishing the one-time wearer of the Black Hood, who now dressed in the most resplendent tropical rainbow colours, and sang with tuneless grace the first verses of 'Ouvirudu. . . .'[59]

With a tenor's voice, he sang what he could remember; never before had such a moving and moved interpreter of the anthem been seen. His voice trilled and trembled, and with both hands clutched to his chest, in the sections he had forgotten, with elegance and brio, he offered Mozartian variants that were better than the original: he passed the test. The upholders went on their way empty-handed, and they had to teach a lesson to one or other of these Germans. They could not just leave it like that. 'They sank the *Baependi*, on the Pernambuco coast. And are we just going to stand by and do nothing? We want blood! Revenge!'

'A German family lives over on Guatemala Street. Let's go there. . . . They are real foreigners, and never speak to anyone!' suggested one of the insatiable zealots.

'Yeah, it's a bitch hitting people we know, it even makes me feel bad! Let's only beat up people we don't know!' agreed João Bobalhão.

The party concerned in Guatemala Street was a family of communist Germans, Jewish fighters, indefatigable anti-Nazis, fugitives from Hitler, who still spoke not one word of Portuguese. They stayed in their house, sitting around the table studying the newspapers. . . .

The *justiceiros* went to the house, armed with sticks and stones, sharp knives, and daggers designed to perforate the flesh. From far off, people could hear foreign-sounding cries and broken windows. From my bedroom, I heard shouts, I heard glass shattering and the door being broken down.

At the end of the night, the *justiceiros* came back; some had blood on their shirts. João Bobalhão had blood on his mouth.

The mood was serious, few words were spoken. They emptied jugs of *parati* in the bar on the corner. Some went to their houses; others slept right there.

The following day, the newspaper *A Noite* reported that an entire German family had been the victim of a car accident: parents and children alike, they were interned in the Getúlio Vargas Hospital, recuperating. . . .

Some of the victims' bodies bore signs of perforation by penetrating objects.

★　　★　　★

Renata, the blonde –
or, the sensuality of inorganic chemistry

At the *Colégio Brasileiro* at the age of 15, my life changed. Metamorphosis. The butterfly leaving its chrysalis, exploring space and time. Fifteen years old and almost an adult.

Travelling by tram broadened my horizons by . . . ooh, at least ten kilometres. I had always made my way to the Santa Teresa school on foot, looking about me on both sides, into the few open windows; now, I had kilometres of new world around me.

Up to the age of 15, Penha was the world; going downtown was a rare adventure. The beach was a fringe of white sand, through and beyond mountains of black rubbish – we went there at night, just before daybreak. Football was Penha versus Maravilha (a neighbouring village) – no television. My idea of a popular festival was the church *kermesse*. Knowledge was the Santa Teresa School. Friendships were my friends from the street, at the gate to the bridge.

Humanity, in São Cristóvão, exploded in diversification, kaleidoscopically.

At age 11 my universe had shrunk: we had moved from a large house, with a vast backyard with animals and trees, to a cramped flat, with a narrow terrace, cut flowers, marbles on the living room carpet, a kite in the fan. Goodbye to space, goodbye to the sky; I lost the sun and the moon. When I was 15 my father was building on rooms as annexes, he was buying land, and I was changing schools – the world grew, beyond infinity – São Cristóvão! The estate of the Marquis of Santos, the Emperor's lover, near Quinta de Boa Vista.

I felt important discovering distant quarters of the town!

Cheaper than the bus, the tram also stuck to a timetable, whereas the bus would come whenever it wanted, and being a standing passenger on a bus was dangerous – school hours coincided with rush hours. People would fall over when the bus driver took a tight line round a corner – to demonstrate his virility.

The tram, on the other hand, did not invent its route, it followed tracks; the driver had his destiny mapped out. The bus driver, a free man, had to struggle with his own creativity – desire versus predetermined will – ergo, the buses swayed about.

José Maria, once in his life

There were two such bus drivers, both called José Maria. They both worked for the same company, drivers on the same line, the same route even, every day. They turned the same corners, accelerated up the same hills, stopped at the same railway crossings, respecting the heavyweight precedence of the train, at the same times.

The sum of their ages was 120 years equally distributed between them; they were 60 in the same month, separated only by a few days. The son of one was called José, and the daughter of the other, Maria. They were married. Their new-born baby was called José-Maria, in quadruple homage.

After work, they sat down at a table in the same bar near the bakery, drank *cachaça* from the same bottle, and ate *mortadella* sandwiches. They exchanged ideas which would stubbornly roll back to the same subject: retirement.

They were tired. Decades of the same journey, the braking, the passengers, the hullos, the hooting, dust, ditches, unpaved roads, pot-holes. Future years held one certainty – that they would be the same as those gone by. Getting slowly worse, actually, because the health of one of the José Marias was deteriorating every day, his lungs groaned, his hands shook, his fingers found it difficult to grip the slippery steering wheel. Retirement – let it come soon. There were five years to go. . . .

One day, in mid-journey, José Maria, the ill one, stopped his full bus in the middle of the road, a dusty track with the rain-water ditch masking the open sewer, uncovered and open to the sky. José Maria stopped the crowded bus and looked back. With the dying breaths of a fainting life, he made his final passenger announcement:

'You must excuse me, but I can't bear it any longer. Please get off and take José Maria's bus, which is right behind us. . . .'

He sat down in his seat, his place, his faithful friend all his life, gripped the worn steering wheel, gently laid his head down, and died calmly, not waiting for retirement.

José Maria, the healthy one, arrived moments later. He did not want to believe it, but he was obliged to: even in life, his friend's body had started to chill; now it was hard, as rigid as a statue.

'Oh, so this is it, is it? Well then today I'm going to do exactly what I have always wanted to do . . .' José Maria shouted.

He got back on board his own bus, put his foot down, and keeping his foot flat to the floor, he deviated from all the known routes, introduced his wheels to virgin streets, descended unsuspecting hills, broke through closed level crossings, narrowly escaping the panting steam locomotive, leaving the shocked black train behind him; he stopped at no stop, responded to no bell-ring or request, no shout of terror nor plea for mercy. In an hour and a half he drove down every forbidden street in Rio de Janeiro, invaded the *Mangue* (the prostitutes' zone), deaf to the cries of the prostitutes of the 'Zone', and crossed the Caju cemetery, leaving no time to pray for any poor dead person intimidated by the velocity of the vehicle. He only stopped when an obstinate pillar said: 'That's enough!' Many were wounded, he more badly than any. In hospital, he received the news: when you are discharged, you will be sent to prison.

'Doesn't matter! At least, for once in my life, I have done what I wanted to . . . I went where I wanted . . . I forgot the brake, I put my foot down on desire.'

Friends and teachers

Many of the passengers liked to travel on the tram's steps so that they could jump on and off between the ticket collector's rounds. But in order to save money to spend on magazines and newspapers, I preferred the even cheaper alternative: the 'paupers' tram', which carried people and luggage mixed together. I travelled standing up, conversing with the bunches of bananas, tins of butter and lard, boxes of oil or vinegar, sacks of beans and rice.

At *Colégio Brasileiro* I had a friend called Israel, who came with me from Santa Teresa. It was to Israel I proudly showed my first 'library' when I was still at primary school.[60] It was a wooden box, originally for Argentinian apples. Using wire and nails, I had put up a piece of cloth which hung over the front of the box to protect my books from the dust.

What books? Please, do not laugh. They were Vargas Villa, Eduardo Zamacois, *The Laws of Triumph* by Napoleon Hill (a kind of Dale Carnegie). Dreadful literature, momentous melodramas, mixed up with educational books, editions of the magazine *Eu Sei Tudo* (I Know Everything), Victor Hugo's *Les Misérables*, Alexandre Dumas' *The Count of Monte Cristo*, Julio Ribeiro's *A Carne* (The Flesh – an erotic novel, nothing to do with a butcher's shop!) and a Bible donated by a Protestant family next door. My reading was very eclectic!

I wouldn't go so far as to say that for me my library was a kind of altar – that sounds overly melodramatic – so I won't say it.

Israel and I became friends with Silvan, who was the son of our mathematics teacher, and a violinist. We did not even play the *cuíca*. What envy: the violin! And Israel listened to classical music. The two of them talked about Mozart, Wagner and Beethoven. Meanwhile I listened to Noel,[61] Sinhô,[62] and other popular composers and singers. (Still ashamed, I omit from this list Vicente Celestino, to whom I listened but pretended not to – I knew the verses of 'The Drunkard' by heart, from the first to the last drop of *cachaça*!)

Silvan and Israel were the best pupils in the class – I was perhaps fifth or seventh. I was not particularly bad, nor terribly good, but I only studied subjects taken by the teachers I liked. I had a teacher called Erasmo, who revealed mathematics to me and taught me to think of the world in a rational way, to seek causes and reasons for everything, and introduced me to 'formula', 'theorem', 'systems' and 'hypotheses'. He taught me to think with clarity, to discover the *whys*.

And I had Peçanha, who dictated entire lessons in a colourless drone. We copied down the sordid lives of kings and queens, the bloody Peloponnesian wars, the monstrous tortures invented by Attila, Scourge of God, the extraordinary Chinese adventures of Marco Polo. In handsome, carefully drawn aseptic letters, the Huns, the Goths and Visigoths, the Vikings inventing Russia, and Vasco de Gama encircling the world, the genocides of indigenous peoples and black enslavements – all of which barely touched my consciousness, going straight on to the white page. The only thing the pupils were concerned to know was whether they had heard a 'full stop' or a 'semicolon'.

By way of light relief, every now and then Peçanha recounted a legend. When our hands were tired, we would shout out: 'Sir, tell us just one little legend!' Suddenly enthused and transfigured, Pecanha became the excellent actor that he was, and made theatre of legends and myths, re-enacting scenes of invasions and landings, personifying heroes and villains, becoming the protagonist of wars and battles. And we would rest our right hands in the face of such theatre. The 'little legends' of teacher Peçanha were, for me, the real History – pure theatre!

Edgar was the teacher who taught me that geography was not in a map or drawing, but in the living reality of oceans and seas, continents, volcanoes, islands, peninsulas, rivers and mountains. That geography could not be understood as separate from history – the two subjects were but one. Humankind lived in one and made the other.

Vitória advised me on reading the humanities; David Perez taught me philosophy and history, an inspired old man, super-intelligent, super-cultured, super-entertaining, super-theatrical, super-everything. Super-super! One day, during an oral exam, while presiding over the examining panel, he asked a pupil seriously who had assassinated Julius Caesar, as if he were a detective conducting a murder inquiry.

'For God's sake, no, it wasn't me, sir! I am against the death penalty!' blurted out the pupil, suddenly a suspect.

'Nor was it me! *Ipso facto*, we now have a lead . . .'

Renata, the blonde

I adored Chemistry, not only because of the teacher Gildásio, but also because Renata adored chemistry. I urgently needed a girlfriend at that time, with whom, whether or not I ever got any further (and in those days there was no further), I might at least walk hand in hand and nuzzle necks with.

Israel, Silvan and I would leave school together every day, walk to the corner where Silvan lived, and stand around chatting for another half an hour before taking our leave. Sometimes the blonde Syboney would come with us, though she would not stay so long because she lived far away – in Vigário Geral – and had to take the train at Leopoldina Station.

Secretly, I believe that the three of us were all in love with the skinny

Syboney. She was as good a student as they were, better than me, and liked learning. I think she secretly fancied all three of us. But in spite of all the fancying going on, no one ever – as far as I know – admitted to any such thing. Not even to themselves. But something in the conversation changed when she was around; we would try to be wittier, more profound, to demonstrate our superior possession of general knowledge. I guess we wanted to be the most worthy of her! But Syboney was not the prettiest girl in the class: she was the third prettiest. First came blonde Renata, a natural beauty, and second . . . the other one.

Oh, the other one, oh! . . . The other one's name was Generosa. Maria Generosa, worse still – which translates as Generous Mary! Her parents were cruel: with so many well-behaved saints' names to choose from. . . .

Renata and Maria Generosa – or just Generosa, as we used to call the poor girl, out of pity – were the prettiest in the class. But they were very different. Generosa put make-up on her eyes and lips like a grown-up woman, a fully turned-out beauty; she was the only girl in the whole school who used lipstick. When she wanted something, she took your hand. But she would forgot her hand was in yours, and turn away to speak to someone else. And her hand stayed there, on your arm. Or sometimes, your shoulder. Round your neck even. While she swapped thoughts with her girlfriend. Distracted.

Being 15 in those days was enough to reduce you to a bag of nerves. Generosa generated a pulverising nervousness wherever she went. Using the mirror from her handbag, she would touch up her lipstick, look behind her to see who was looking at her, and stay looking at the person while we looked at her, with the mirror also looking, mirroring the looks of those who were looking at her looks. The amount of looking that went on in that classroom, when Generosa was on one of her exuberant days, was just not normal!

When she wanted to share a secret she would come up close to your ear, so close, right up next to you so that you were left with the tell-tale lipstick of a kiss. Then we would be left with one red ear, all of a jitter, and subjected to mockery.

If one of us was in the doorway, the brown-skinned Generosa – dressed all over in birds and flowers, the theme of her skirts always being

Amazonian flora and fauna – the dancing Generosa would somehow manage to leave the classroom, brushing against our legs, enflaming us. Apart from the lipstick, there was the perfume. It was too much, really, much too much! We, poor fools, did not do anything. We would discuss philosophy, algebra, geometry. . . . That is how it was in those days. What can one do about it now, so long after the moment has elapsed?

Times have changed. Nobody even mentions geometry any more. In those days, people remained untouched till later. Courtship is culture, it changes with time. Biology, however, is not culture: the human body desires in any era. The human body is not culture: the way we kiss can be, but not the act of kissing. The human body makes its nervy way, snuffling around anxiously, puffing, wanting, growling. . . .

 0 0

Renata was the opposite of Generosa – in the colour of her skin, the perfume of her body. What skin, what perfume! What colour, what a body! What a voice! I do not know if I am embellishing recollections and making reminiscences divine, but I think that Renata really was 'up there on her own', I do, and what's more . . . she fancied me. We would talk in whispers, huddling close together. She laughed, in that way of hers! She fancied me, for sure. At least, I thought so at the time. At least I think that is what I thought. Who knows!

Generosa's generosity was generous in many directions; Renata treated me with an affection that was just for me. That is what I thought and I returned the compliment. I think this was love-making as it was at that time – in each age it has its own character. She told me her dreams: those of the night and those of the future. No one shares their dreams if they don't like you. Renata told me her dreams and I told her mine. But I did not tell her that my greatest dream was Renata.

A doctor's career and many loves

We carried on like that for two years. In the third, we had to choose whether to go to university. My father used to say that it was a serious matter. We had to take life seriously. Teachers said we should choose well, that it was a serious question. And I? *Could* I be so serious?

Who would be what? Most of the young men would be engineers and doctors – well-paid professions, with prestige. As for the young women, some regretted having entered on the science course rather than the Classics course, others opted for Fine Arts, or abandoned higher education in search of marriage.

When I was 17, trying to help me to make a decision, my father asked Fleischmann the yeast-vendor how much he earned. Very little. How much did the chemist responsible for producing the yeast earn? A huge amount. From then on, the profession of chemist began to be valued. It was a *serious* profession! Sagely, my father commented: 'It is better to be a chemist than a yeast-vendor. . . .'

Israel chose engineering and became one of the engineers who built Brasília. Silvan, who played the violin (which is quite a diplomatic instrument), became an ambassador. And me? One day, Alzira, another stunning class-mate of mine, and I met in town. We sat down in a café, drank a milkshake and talked of our futures and our possible careers. Alzira was decided: she would be a teacher, whatever it took. She did not know what subject, but she knew she wanted to teach.

'But what are you going to learn, before you teach?'

'I know I am going to be a teacher. . . . Of what, I don't know, but I am going to be one!'

I was fascinated by this unshakeable determination. There was something wrong with me: I liked everything, but one could not do everything. I thought that perhaps I was not fit for practical things in life. I decided to decide. It had to be decided. I took a decision: 'Alzira, let's go to the cinema!' There was a cinema called Trianon: 'The show begins when you arrive!' Its programme was short features, news, cartoons. We each paid for our own ticket.

We sat down cosily close, me breathing in the smell of Alzira, who was on the edge of her seat at almost everything she saw on the screen, exhaling nervous smells in synchrony with her emotions and the scenes which provoked them: war and pole-vaulting, horse-racing, swimming, football: at every decisive moment a fragrance came forth, at every goal Alzira grabbed my arm and squeezed it tight. I smelled the goals, the leaps, the butterfly strokes, the horses trotting. . . .

Then a documentary about animal reproduction came on. A huge quantity of baby rabbits. Alzira asked: 'Augusto, why don't you get me a baby rabbit?' 'Alzira, I can't give you a baby rabbit . . .' (I did not know where to buy rabbits.)

The young animals continued to file by: 'Augusto, why don't you give me a guinea-pig?' 'Alzira, I can't give you a guinea-pig . . .' (and I smelled the guinea-pig).

'Augusto, what about a pony? Look at the sweet little foal. . . .' Me, smelling that little smell: 'Alzira, I can't give you a pony. . . .'

Then a nursery appeared on screen, with babies of every appearance and colour, European, Asiatic, African. Before Alzira could ask, I offered: 'Now we're talking, Alzira. I can give you one or two of those at the drop of a hat, you only have to ask. . . .'

Alzira frowned and did not speak to me for two weeks.

I did not know how to interpret her explosive muteness. Alzira said neither yes nor no. I knew that I fancied her, but did not know if she fancied me. I thought she did. I also fancied Renata, who *maybe* fancied me: someone had to fancy me and I was available to be fancied. At that age, we fancied fancying and being fancied. . . . We were born to fancy and be fancied, we were fanciable. Who did Alzira fancy, if not me?

Not one courtship turned into anything serious. Passion was left hanging, undefined. If one of us said: 'I am in love!', it was not necessary to say with whom. It was as if the sentence did not need a direct object. As if a vague, fluctuating object would do fine: 'I am in love with Renata, Rosinha, Ramona, Rute, Rosalva, Rosalinda, Syboney, Cydnéia, Cynthia, Cecília, Inês, Idalina, Isabel, Jaqueline, Eduarda, Eliana, Helena, Baby, Myriam with an "i" and with a "y", Madalena, Marialva, Maria Antônia, Maria Aparecida, Maria José, Maria Vitória, Mariúska, Nélida, Naruna, Alba, Albertina, Amélia, and with you, Alzira, my true love . . . and also with . . . with . . . what was that bakery customer called? Elizabete . . . No, Belinha . . . what was it? Oh, I forget. . . .' Ah, childhood love. . . .

We were what might be called 'pure people'. I was in love with all the girls in my class and with most of the young girls in the whole school, and even, if I am honest, with teachers and neighbours. Only my mother's friends escaped. Some of them, that is. An overpowering, torrential passion. I liked fancying girls, impassioned with passion!

Meanwhile, my mother had already decided: 'Augusto, one day you are going to marry Princess Margaret!' End of subject.

Marriages could wait; a profession was urgent. But which one? I wanted to be someone, someone really good, but I did not know who! The future is serious. What anguish! What fear!

I knew I wanted to do theatre. After the experience of directing the goat, four brothers and assorted cousins, having written poems and stories, a handful of dialogues and versions of old novels, I did not want to stop: I wanted theatre! Theatre, theatre. But how could I find the courage to tell my father? He would never understand, still less allow it. . . . Theatre, for him, was us playing around for the family on Sundays, charging three beer bottle tops for entry. It did not provide a professional qualification. It was either that or the musicals we went to in Praça Tiradentes.

We used to watch Beatriz Costa – a Portuguese singer who came to Brazil every year – Oscarito, Grande Otelo and artists who imitated politicians of the time, in '*cortinas*' (curtains) – which were comic sketches or songs performed out front, while the stage-hands changed the scenery behind the curtains. Cortinas were used between two scenes in which the dancers exchanged one kind of nudity for another: from scanty clothing to even scantier. The shows would end in a cascade of real water falling on to the stage, to the enthusiastic applause of the packed house, applauding the water and the near-naked dancers.

These revues traditionally included political scenes. They were therefore called revues of the year. To get round the censor, criticisms of the dictatorial regime would end with a character saying: 'That seems like an attempt to sabotage the work of our great President. . . .' So the censor would allow the show to go on.

We liked theatre, but went rarely because my father did not like the theatre district. Tiradentes Square had already become a place for transvestite prostitution; they would start work after the show but would be already promenading beforehand. My father – and my mother, though she was open to unusual ideas – would not be able to understand my theatre desire, or imagine how theatre could be studied in a serious way, at university. Good immigrant that he was, my father always said that we would have total freedom to choose a profession . . . as long as we got a doctor's degree. (A bit like the joke about the Portuguese man who says to his daughter, 'You can choose any husband . . . as long as you marry Manuel!')

We had to be doctors of something. My brothers and sisters chose medicine, architecture, neo-Latin languages. Professional careers. And me? What should I be Doctor of ? (Theatre? Perish the thought!)

'What about you, Renata, what path will you follow?'

'Chemistry. . . .'

Why not? A chemist can provide the title of 'Doctor'. Chemistry is fun, it's lively. . . . Organic chemistry explained Life! explained a sun-tanned Renata! *Viva* chemistry ! As for inorganic chemistry, don't even talk about it: *sensualissima* . . . when Renata was at my side. Microbiology, next to Renata, was pure beauty! Research into cations and anions, with Renata and I doing the researching, was more suspenseful than Agatha Christie.

Why not? I got home and announced:

'I am going to do chemistry.'

'That's good,' my father said. 'The yeast-chemist, Fleischmann, earns a fortune, much more than the salesman does . . . chemistry is serious. . . .'

From then on I began to pay more attention to the teacher Gildásio, although without losing interest in history and philosophy. I became an excellent pupil! I began to dream of the future: Renata and I, dressed in smart white coats, performing extraordinary magical experiments, with test-tubes, alembics, stunning whiter-than-white laboratories, producing dazzling yeast to make my father's bread more splendid, bigger than the *Pão de Açucar!*[63] But in truth, the only yeast which ever appeared in my university curriculum was in the microbiology lesson in the second year, when I chose to make . . . whisky. It didn't work, didn't even get me drunk, the one obligation of any self-respecting whisky. The pure malt Scots had nothing to fear.

In order to get into university it was necessary to undertake a course parallel to school, which prepared us for the rigorous entrance exam called the *Vestibular*. For the career of industrial chemist, there were 400 candidates and only forty places! We, Renata and I, were decided. It was for real. We would be chemists! We intensified our ardour studying. I was sure that, once at university, aged 18, Renata and I would definitely have the courage to say the 'I love you . . .' which was lacking, and the 'Me too!' which would be the seal of eternal happiness. Without cease, our hearts pulsated with the same message, our eyes shouted: 'I love you!' Our mouths, however, were silent. They would open in time, indeed they would!

The day of the exam arrived. There was just one small hitch: I passed, Renata didn't. By the time I realised the significance of this I was at university studying chemistry, with all the test tubes, flasks, and alembics I had dreamt of. . . . But without my beloved Renata, without my dream. . . .

Warming up *pandeiros*, *cuicas* and *tamborins*

By the time I realised what had happened, I was dressed in a white coat, sitting in a white chair, at a long white table with white tiles, colourless test-tubes and flasks, serpentine tubing, transparent retorts, bottles full of coloured liquids and powders, more iridescent than the most scintillating rainbow, sitting beside white-clad colleagues, in front of a white-haired teacher whose face was whiter than his white coat, with white-painted walls and a pure white floor, clean, white!

Even I was pale, with shock. 'My God, what on earth am I doing here?'

Chemistry had signified books, notebooks, formulae, blackboards, and, above all, the perfume of Renata. Now, instead of her fragrance, the room smelt of burnt yellow sulphur. Even the volley-ball pitch behind the school smelt of sulphur, where the young men watched the women playing games and vice versa. The bus smelt of sulphur. The stone of the mountain-side smelt of sulphur; the church, the baptismal font, the altar, the sad Christ on the Cross, pure sulphur! The garden of my house, sulphur. Flowers smelt of sulphur. My nose smelled sulphur, sulphur, nothing but sulphur. My lungs. Everything, just sulphur!

A chemist who does not like sulphur is like a doctor who fears blood; a goal-scorer who does not like taking penalty kicks. No can do. Penalty kick, blood, sulphur, whichever – you have to love it! It is difficult to love sulphur: you need a vocation for it! I prefer blood. Better still: penalty kicks!

I was overcome by the whiteness of the laboratory, where colleagues filed past like yellowing white popes in a festive Mass. I had *saudades* for Moseley, *saudades* for the exercise books, the doodles . . . and Renata's perfume. Back then, our researches into cations and anions were done on paper, in pen and ink. Now, it was a matter of mixing substances, taking care not to let them effervesce and bubble over if the calculations had been done incorrectly. I was afraid of the acids. I suffered liquid shocks studying chemistry.

At the end of the first lesson I met up with my enthusiastic family: 'Did you like it? What are your colleagues like, are they nice people? What about the teachers, are they competent?'

'My God . . . there are still four years to go!'

I had hardly started and I was already thinking about the end: my graduation! But at no point did I think about giving the course up. My father was worth sacrifices: he wanted his children to be 'doctors'! I swore that I would not be the black sheep, or the scapegoat. Whatever it cost, I would be *doutor* (doctor): neither sheep nor goat!

Copacabana, Princess of the Sea

In 1949, aged 18, I went under the New Tunnel one afternoon when two of the teachers were absent. For the first time, I saw the sea at Copacabana, and stood there open-mouthed, gazing at the immense beach, a hundred times bigger than the *Das Morenas* beach. I went back to the school with the ocean in my red eyes. I had never imagined the sea could be so big, so much water, so much sand. So many people, such women, so brown and sun-tanned. So much sun.

That night I dreamt of the sea, I dreamt of brown women. Nets and fishermen. Today, I live on top of the water, virtually. I listen, see calm waves from my window, smiling horizontal waves, or angry vertical waves, foaming: never less than seductive – changing with the day, with the restless mood of the sea. You cannot trust the sea – it calms and it shocks – it is uncontrollable. It gives confidence, it strikes fear. The sea is an irresponsible being. It is the madman in the family. It brings in sand and then engulfs the beach.

When I travel, I take the sea with me in my memory's archive of living sounds; closing my eyes I see the sea, its rolling waves. I converse with the sea, and it answers me. Not always the right answer: it says what it wants. Softly, screaming.

We have biological rhythms in our body: the rhythm of breathing – above all we have a rhythmical heart, melodious blood pumping. We have the circadian rhythms of hunger, of sleep, of sex. . . . The cosmic rhythms of day and night, winter and summer. . . . When you live beside the sea, you have the sea as an essential rhythm: you internalise it. It is necessary to harmonise all our rhythms.

When you are distant from the sea, you carry it with you in your chest. Wherever you go, it comes with you. Alone, without the sea, the heart only beats half time! Those who live with the sound of waves feel empty when they do not hear them. Something is lacking in the absence of the sea and its music.

Director of something

I studied more than my colleagues did; not being enamoured of the actual substances, I had to put in more study to understand the same amount.

I was lucky. In the very first month, there were elections for the Academic Directorate of the National school of Chemistry. All the posts were highly contested, except one: Director of the Cultural Department. I could put myself forward in the certainty of being elected: I would be the only candidate.

I almost lost: being new in the school, no one remembered my name. Most of the votes were blank . . . white, like the laboratory!

The Cultural Director was responsible for organising conferences, exhibitions, debates, whatever it was as long as it could be called 'cultural'! Even *gafiera*:[64] culture, obviously.

In the breaks between classes I used to go to the other beach, the *Vermelha* (the Red Beach). I would sit on the ground, watching the waves, thinking about cultural activities. I like seeing waves advancing, growing, dying. It is like theatre: one scene after another, each more intense than the last. I needed the sea to inspire me: for the first time, I was Director of something . . . I used to think and watch. With the rocking of the waves, the sea dissolved in the sand . . . and the ideas rolled around my head.

I saw two opportunities arising from being Director: the opportunity to meet important people I admired, and the opportunity to get into theatres free; theatre companies used to invite university students as their guests.

Mr Umberto, a short fat man, would distribute complementary tickets for seats for operas and ballets at the Municipal Theatre, to fill out the claque, in the Gods. During the shows, he would wander through the corridors of the theatre smoking the cheap, black, untreated tobacco known as '*mata-rato*' – rat poison – talking to himself and swearing and spitting into the Chinese spittoons! He would suddenly pop up out of the darkness, like an apparition, seconds before the programmed applause at the end of all the crucial arias and duets. In a low voice, hoarse and nasal, he would shout: '*Piú forte, piú forte. Mascalzones!*[65] You mob of vagabonds!' – mixing and matching his polyglot attainments.

We bellowed for all we were worth, terrorised by Umberto's face, which demanded clapping of hand-breaking extremity and stertorous shouts, in return for more tickets for the next opera, the next claque. Our party from the school of Chemistry used to applaud with such enthusiasm that some women in the audience would look our way in justifiable alarm.

Most theatres had their Umbertos. Thus I was able to see Brazilian and even foreign companies such as Madeleine Renaud and Jean Louis Barrault, Strehler's Píccolo Teatro do Milano, the Ballet of Marquis de Cuevas, Ballet Theatre, Alícia Alonso and Igor Youskevitch.

I wanted to see the plays, but also the artists, to converse with them, to talk theatre. The fall of the curtain left me bereft and I used go home to think about it on my own; I wanted to ask questions, to exchange ideas, to learn. I decided to organise a cycle of lectures. To start with, I invited the playwright I most admired: Nelson Rodrigues. He wrote Brazilian plays about Brazilian life for Brazilian spectators.

Nelson, my godfather

I went to the editorial office of the newspaper where he worked. I arrived, took one look at 'The Dramaturg' and my knees knocked together before such divinity! Nelson, a calm, gentle man, asked modestly if I believed anyone would come to listen to his talk: he did not want to address empty chairs.

Of course! In my opinion, the school of Chemistry could *guarantee* a hundred people extremely interested in his playwriting, plus dozens more students from other faculties; we were going to stick posters up on all the notice-boards. The readers of his newspaper would also grace the event, because of course the newspaper would publish an article on it. From that alone there would be a further 200 or 250 attenders. More people would come from all over . . . these things spread fast, by word of mouth . . . 300. . . . Maybe more. The best thing would be to get an auditorium downtown, because there was not a room in our Faculty big enough to hold so many passionate followers of his theatre. . . .

'Well . . . maybe . . .' Nelson said. And by the tone of his voice . . ., maybe not. I swore: '300 is realistic! Maybe a few more than that, who knows — less is unthinkable! It is like a show: no one knows the secret of success,' I burbled, spouting theatrical nostrums before the Myth himself.

I went to the National Theatre Service to ask for the big room. For free. I had been misinformed because it could only hold 200 people. The official reassured me: 'If as many people as you expect come, the latecomers can stand: which won't bother anybody. Or they can sit on the floor. . . .'

This seemed reasonable. To get to hear Nelson, my maestro — 'the' Maestro! — whether you had to stand throughout or sit on the hard floor, would be an unprecedented honour.

Nelson was the second to arrive. I was the first. After us, minutes passed, anxieties mounted, half an hour passed. The next arrival was my desperation. A timid man got out of the lift, in silence; then two thin people — Good afternoon! Three — How are you? Four — I would like you to read my latest play, would that be possible? A fifth — Is your talk about football? What about our Fluminense, eh? . . . to lose like that to Flamengo, never again, I'd sooner change sides. Six — Wow, hasn't it started yet? Seven — Now what shall we do?

'Let's start,' Nelson suggested.

I have rarely felt so much anguish as in that afternoon, when seven people came to hear Nelson Rodrigues. Playfully, Nelson began the talk by asking if it wouldn't be better to do it in the '*Vermelhinho*', a bar opposite which was frequented by artists. We could save time, mixing lecture and coffee, theory and practice.

Rumour had it that Nelson was secretly the author of a series of chronicles about 'Giselle, the Naked Spy who Took Paris by Storm'. A tabloid published chapters full of sex and intrigue, decorated with photographs of the spy naked in the arms of Nazi officials – her way of spying. The stories extended to the scatological; in one, the prostitute-heroine let herself be infected with the gonorrhoea virus in order to transmit it to the Nazis. Horrors! And all complete with forged photographs of naked patriots who, of course, sold the newspaper.

One day, I asked Nelson if what they were saying was true, if it was he who scribbled these pseudo-*reportages*. 'Are you really the creator of Giselle?'

A hurt Nelson replied: 'I know that they are saying out there that I am the author of Giselle! It is a lie, a gross and shameless lie! I am Suzana Flagg: Giselle is written by So-and-so!' and he cited a famous journalist.

Starting from my fiasco as a cultural entrepreneur, I began to cultivate the dramatist's friendship. I used to visit him in the newspaper where he worked, and timidly give him my plays, which he would read and advise me on. He really did read them: he made comments and annotations in pencil, enxugamentos underlinings, suggestions of cuts, or – 'trimmings'. 'Trimming' meant writing 'telegraphic dialogue'. All directors were obsessed with trimming. Nelson's plays came ready-trimmed.

Out of all his many pieces of advice, the one he repeated with most conviction was about deforming reality. Theatre is not reality: it is a vision of reality. Thus, there was no reason for it to be the same as reality. He vociferated against Antoine,[66] a French director from the turn of the century, who when a scene took place in a butcher's, would hang fresh meat on the set every day.

'An imbecile!' – he would explode, foaming at the mouth in anger (to use one of his favourite expressions).

Nelson was passionate about the same football team as me, Fluminense, which aroused a secret shame in us both: at the beginning of the century our club operated a ban on black players in its team, which resulted in the creation of another team, Flamengo, formed by disgusted anti-racists. In Fluminense, mulattos were accepted as long as they agreed to rub rice-flour on their faces to hide their negritude! I was anti-racist, no one was more disgusted than me, but my heart beat for the tricolor:[67] what suffering! Why I was for the tricolor I don't know – perhaps it was in the spirit of contrariness: my brother supported Vasco.

In an extraordinary proof of trust and esteem, Nelson gave me one of his own plays to read and comment on. Using two or three fingers, he used to hammer out one original and five copies, using blue carbon paper, on his dilapidated black typewriter.

The following day, I took my trophy to the school of Chemistry and showed the whole world the fifth copy, reading bits of the dialogue out loud. Even the teacher of inorganic chemistry was impressed with the calibre of my friendships.

When the lesson was over, I went to return the precious opus, in the aura of my uncontained admiration. Before returning the play to Nelson, I went all around the editorial office, exhibiting the bulky text, to make it absolutely clear to all the journalists present that I had been graced with the title of First Reader – together with another five or six people – of the works of the greatest living Brazilian dramatist, Nelson Rodrigues.

In the editorial office I always saw Vinicius de Moraes. He was already a great poet, but not yet a known songwriter, which is why he needed to work as a journalist. (When poetry is put to music, the wages go up.) I showed off the trophy . . . but the journalists were all too wrapped up in their own agendas to have time for such trifles. For them, Nelson was only one more journalist.

Other friends

Nelson introduced me to Sábato Magaldi, who was fundamental to the beginnings of my career. We watched a play and went to talk over glasses of cashew juice (me) and lager (the others). Apart from the three of us, there were five or six well-known actors and actresses, all talking enthusiastically. I stayed silent, watching. Every now and then, someone would ask my opinion. I would smile, as an answer. When I was a child, I sat at the gate to my house, watching others pass by, far away. Now I watched close up, silent in the same way. Sábato's erudition inspired my admiration; he seemed to have read every book, seen every play.

I also cultivated the National Theatre Service, site of the tragedy of the empty auditorium. At night, Luiza Barreto Leite and Sadi Cabral gave theatre lessons there. (Luiza was one of the most energetic fighters for their regulation of the profession of actor and, above all, actress. Until the beginning of the 1950s actresses had the word 'prostitute' printed by the police in their official employment documents.) I did not sign up for the course, but they let me attend their classes, sitting in the back row, observing, silent. Watching things happening.

Duque was the teacher of 'social' dances (waltz, foxtrot, swing, bolero – tango was far too audacious) and . . . etiquette: he taught how to sit at the table, how to converse with a distinguished lady, how to eat, with which cutlery, how to drink red or white wine, with which glass, how to drink champagne. It was part of the curriculum, and came up in the exams. Champagne in the acting classes and actors' exams!

The Vermelhinho bar was the artists' rendezvous. There I got to know a good number of them, well or in passing, including Abdias Nascimento, a crucial friend at the beginning of my career. Before him, my relationship with black people was one of pity: I felt sorry for those black labourers who worked so hard and earned so little. After Abdias, this turned to admiration: how was it possible for black people to excel when they were surrounded by such prejudice? In the theatre, for instance, a black character was either a slave or a servant, and even then it would often be a white actor blacked up. The idea of using a dark-skinned person for the role of Othello would have been unthinkable! Any pigment in the skin was a stigma! After Abdias, my characters became less maudlin and resigned, and more rebellious and affirmative. I began to like subversives, heroic characters, fighters. Down with melancholy!

The marvellous theatre that never existed!

I also met Glaúcio Gil and Leo Jusi, students of theatre. Dissatisfied with the existing theatre groups of the time, we decided to found a new group *O Teatro Artístico do Rio de Janeiro*, imitating the theatre of Nemirovitch-Danckenko and Konstantin Stanislavski.[68] Glaúcio would be lead actor, Leo the director and I the dramatist. We sought a theatre, which we did not have, and money, and plays.

Our search began in 1950. We carried on seeking until my journey to the United States, in September 1953. When I returned in 1955, there we were, still seeking. . . . In this long quest, for the first time, the social function and political significance of theatre lodged in my consciousness.

Before, I used to write in order to vent my feelings: I wrote for myself. Now, it would be for the 'public'. Before, I wrote as one might bellow – in truth, I did not believe that my plays would ever be put on. Now it was necessary to articulate my thoughts, because it was certain that they would be heard. What should we say to our public? Should theatre entertain or educate? 'Educate' comes from the Latin and means 'lead out'. Would we have the right – or even the power! – to lead our public? And where to?

None of us was entrenched in his own aesthetics and we were unanimous about one thing: our theatre would be of the highest quality.

But *what* quality? How is it measured? If I am an artist, I create the new, that which does not have parameters. In their absence, how can my work be measured?

In response to these questions, a heavyweight repertoire with concrete armour-plating won through, including *The Lower Depths* by Gorky, *A Month in the Country* by Turgenev, *The Cherry Orchard* by Chekhov and, on the more ambitious side, theatrical adaptations of Tolstoy's *War and Peace* and Dostoevsky's *The Brothers Karamazov* – just to start with, taking it slowly. These authors knew what to say: we would merely be their faithful interpreters. We did not know what to say: but they did! We would say what they had said.

For a group of three young artists, yet to perform, it was ambition out of all proportion. But if you want to dream, why dream in black and white on a small screen? We wanted to dream epic dreams in gigantic technicolor cinemascope.

Luckily, we soon realised that we were overly Russophile. Too much admiration for Stanislavski! We pitilessly abandoned the Russians and set off for the Classics. In this category Shakespeare was the unassailable champion. Glaúcio and I wanted *Hamlet*. Glaúcio spoke English, he had visited the United States as a tourist guide; I used to study with a private tutor – a Chinese man who lived in Lapa, right behind the current premises of the Rio Centre of the Theatre of the Oppressed! I was preparing to study in the United States and knew how to recite monologues:

> '*Oh, that this too too solid flesh*
> *would melt, thaw*
> *and resolve itself into a dew . . .*'

Hesitation: *solid* or *sullied*? What did Shakespeare mean?

Meanwhile, in the National Chemistry school I passed each year's exams – I was not one of the worst students, I was in the mediocre-to-middling section! I was always re-elected as Cultural Director – no one wanted my enviable post.

We came down to earth. Where could we raise the money for so much Shakespeare, where was there a theatre that would house such a large cast? Where was the public that would become enamoured with us? We wanted to be loved!

It would be necessary to educate the public. In order to educate it, we would first have to attract it. In Ipanema and Copacabana, we would not attract it with Gorky's miserabilists, or Chekhov's anguished souls, and even less, with Shakespeare's execrable serial killers.

Okay: first draw them in, then educate them. Considering that Rio has always been a tourist destination, we would have to begin with a repertoire which would not scare people off. Comedies – digestible, inconsequential, irresponsible. We made one proviso: we would not descend into idiocy! No superficialities, no rubbish, ever!

Ah, apologies, Shakespeare, Gorky, Chekhov! Sorry! Saintly names taken in vain.

Doctor of Something, at last

The year 1952 was my last at university. According to the curriculum, students were supposed to do an internship in industry in São Paulo.

Hotel Lux. For the first time in my life, I slept away from home – aged 21! When I found myself alone, I sat down in front of a 'vanity table' – with an enormous round mirror (which is also called a psyche, yes really, a psyche!) – I looked at my face and my body and thought – 'I'm alone'. I was unhappy. I do not like being alone, and I need to be alone – a slight complication! An endless discussion I have with myself.

I used to like being alone at the gate, knowing that the family was inside, my friends nearby. Alone . . . but accompanied. There, I was alone by myself. Alone amidst multitudes who rushed around faster than the *cariocas*,[69] 'São Paulo cannot stop' – said the local government publicity, 'São Paulo, the fastest growing city in the world', and it grew before my

very eyes, like a cartoon mushroom growing after rain. And how can this be, a city without a beach? All cities should be obliged to have a beach!

At the end of the year, I received my Diploma in the same Municipal Theatre where Mr Umberto used to bellow out his palmiferous incentives. (I still have the dinner-jacket my father had made for me for the occasion. And if I hold my breath I can still get into it, with heroic difficulty and pride.) The young women received their Diplomas clad in long white dresses. Some wore a veil and garlands: they were marrying science! Speeches and flowers, emotion, eyes brimming with tears, all that. Even I was moved. I cried secretly, and why not? I was a *Doutor*, just like my father wanted.

I received the Diploma – it was the first time I was applauded in a theatre! My hand trembled, and my conscience too: – 'Do I deserve it? Am I a chemist? Do they know I don't want to be what they are saying I am?' I had an identity crisis . . . I have had many in my life. Am I, at this very moment, who I write that I was? And will I be me? And if not, who will I be? Aaarrrggghhh!

At the end of the ceremony, the young women went back home to their families, in cars hired for the party. We men, we *machos*, in full exercise of our masculine freedom, went to a bar in the Cruzeiro Gallery, and drank cashew juice (me!) and lager (the others).

In truth that night no one received the actual, written Diplomas, as they were not ready in time; they had to be properly written out in gold gothic letters and sealed with wax. Instead, the Director of the school gave us rolls of foolscap paper, tied with blue ribbon for the boys and pink for the girls. After the third lager (when you are young, the drunkenness comes earlier!) someone suggested we should make a big fire of the 'Diplomas' and extinguish it with urine. Some were enthusiastic pyroma-

115

a long time ago, I was a boy

Boal receives his degree in chemistry at the
Municipal Theatre of Rio, 1952

The family at Boal's graduation from his
MASS Degree in Chemical Engineering, 1952

beyond his comprehension: he wanted *Doutor* sons, and the Diplomas, albeit falsely, provided that certainty.

The majority won, the fire was made and we solemnly unsheathed our penises. I confess I urinated less than my colleagues. Cashew is not as diuretic as lager.

A just man

My father was a just man. As my siblings had taken longer courses, I graduated younger. At 21, I was already an industrial chemist; 1952 was the last year in which the National school of Chemistry turned out industrial chemist graduates – from then on, it was chemical engineers. For me to have that Diploma too it would be necessary to do some supplementary subjects.

My father decided to give me the right to a year's specialisation abroad. I could study for a whole year. Chemical engineering, of course. I thought about France (I had seen French shows at the Municipal), and about the United States (I liked Eugene O'Neill, Arthur Miller, Tennessee Williams . . .). But I would have to study plastics and petroleum, mixed with theatre.

In a bookshop, I found *European Theories of Drama* by Barrett Clark, with essays by great theorists of occidental theatre. The last chapter listed North American writers. John Gassner was there – enthused, I wanted to study with him. I wrote a letter, certain that no reply would be forthcoming: he was such an important teacher, how would he find the time to reply to a young suburban lad? But a few weeks later, Gassner replied; saying that, from the following year, he would be lecturing on playwriting at Columbia university. He gave me the name and address of the Course Director, Milton Smith.

As the classes did not start till September, I studied English intensely with the Chinese man from Lapa. Studying English with the Chinese teacher, I fell in love with words rarely used. 'Flabbergasted' was my main love! No one was 'flabbergasted' all the time – except me! I was flabbergasted a lot! Me and my mirror. Instead of being 'flabbergasted' we could have just been 'surprised', 'astonished', 'amazed', 'stunned', 'astounded', 'dumbfounded'. But no, we wanted to be 'flabbergasted' and that was it:

flabbergasted *est*!

I had to learn prosaic words in a hurry; I had to learn that in the restaurant one ate 'pork' not 'pig'. It makes a difference: I understood that when I asked for pig and the waiter snorted.

New York: the impulse and the leap

Braniff, four propellers and three legs: first leg, from Rio to Lima, in Peru. Overnight. Hotel Bolivar. The waiter brought *ceviche*[70] to the room and asked me: '*Está servido, Senõr?*' I answered in the affirmative, in my first venture into Castilian: '*Como no, Señor!*'[71] I was pleased with my first experiment with the language of Cervantes. But the man did not want literature, he wanted a tip, so he slammed the door.

I went out in the street, full of indigenous people covered in ponchos of a thousand colours. In Rio you would only see as much colour as this during Carnival. In Brazil, at the time of the Portuguese invasions in 1500, there were more than five million indigenous people, living naked, as if still in the Stone Age. They were decimated because they could not adapt to what was effectively captivity, and did not know how to defend themselves. Today, there are fewer than 400,000 survivors, mostly in the forests. Others say 300,000, but no one has actually counted.

In the Bolivarian[72] and Central American countries, by contrast, there were already extremely advanced civilisations; the Incas used to perform delicate cerebral surgery through a cranial opening – trepanation. In architecture, they were masters: in Cuzco there was an Inca temple (which the Spanish transformed into a Catholic Cathedral, until along came an earthquake which swept the Spanish mortar away, and allowed the original temple to re-emerge. The Incas knew how to construct buildings leaving space between the stones, to withstand the earth's tremors).

What the Incas in South America forgot to perfect – and, in Central America, the Aztecs, Mayas, Toltecas, Chichimecas and other aboriginal peoples – were the tools of war. The Spanish and Portuguese invaders had a field day. Neither gunpowder, nor those magical tanks of wars, horses, existed in the Americas; to indigenous eyes, horse and rider seemed like strange animals – inspiring respect and fear. I knew this from reading books; but the impact of seeing those sad faces was enormous! I felt like an invader, an occupier. I felt guilt, though I was not to blame. My notion of humanity at its truest was embodied by the bronzed, hip-swinging sunburnt *carioca*. That is what a human being was: a bronzed *carioca*. Even São Paulo was already a strange humanity, with an accent. So imagine my shock: suddenly everyone has turned into Japanese Indians wrapped in colourful ponchos, with women wearing men's hats! Nightmare!

I searched for someone who might have my face; I could find none. Sure I had come across people who were different from me, I had even seen mean-looking Mongols and tiny African pygmies, Australian aborigines and tall Caucasians – but only in the cinema. Film is celluloid; it allows all freedoms and fictions. In Lima, the indigenous people were there in flesh and blood, surprising and alive. For the first time, we were face to face, eye to eye. They found me strange, because I *was* strange, I was different, white and . . . poncho-less. Imagine: a man without a poncho in Lima, in the cold – strange! I was scared. They looked at me: I was the *different* one. For the first time, I felt out of place.

I never want to forget that night when, for the first time, I realised that I was not the Other: I was not an Indian, I did not use a poncho, I had neither dark skin nor oval eyes! Before, I had so many 'I's; now, none. Void. Empty. I wanted to hang on to these images, retain these memories of difference. I bought a sculpture of a god and went back to the hotel. In my room, a mirror on the wall – hotels enclosed me, mirrors pursued me. Even with the light off, I could see myself in the blue penumbra.

Mirrors will insist on reflecting! Someone was watching me. My other I. I did not sleep: the mirror held me in its gaze. I covered my image in the mirror with the blanket, my image imprisoned in the mirror, because its blankness scared me. My body got cold, exposed to the night air. I continued to imagine my hidden image, as if I could see it. The two of us, alone. I do not remember who slept first, me or my image. I remember that I woke up frozen, with a blocked nose; coincidentally, my image got a cold too. . . .

Second leg: Lima to Miami, small plane flying low, people throwing up into little bags – which was perfectly normal then. Never since have I seen people throwing up into little bags, but in those days everyone vomited as though it were most natural thing in the world. The plane jolted about (below) Boal's first encounter with US show business: a domestic fight between an Indian and his crocodile friend, Miami, 1953

(right) Boal thinks about what he should do with his life, New York, 1954

without a second thought.

'We have crossed the imaginary line of the Equator!' The great event of the crossing, it deserved an announcement, smiles broke out. 'Tighten your seat belts . . . but not too much, or else the next time you throw up it will be in the northern hemisphere . . .' joked the Captain. In the South it was still permissible, but in those civilised Northern regions vomiting was no longer acceptable.

Miami! Another overnight stay. A roadside hotel with a mini-tour of the city thrown in. The only image I retained of Miami was of a ferocious fight between an Indian and a crocodile. I was shocked by the martial moves and pirouettes of the Indian, and by the crocodile's mouth, sharp with daggers. I feared for the human life. The rink of flattened earth, full of water and irregular stones, helped the animal more than the human. This 'stadium' was full of tourists. People more experienced than I laughed at the rehearsed blows: the meek tamed crocodile frowned menacingly, though he was as gentle as a docile white Siamese cat. In fact, Indian and crocodile were good friends, excellent folk, co-workers.

That was my first contact with US show business. . . .

Third leg: Miami to New York. Hotel America, near Times Square, at ten dollars a day. I sat on the bed, once again face to face with the vanity

(right) Boal at Times Square, 1953

(below) New York, 1954

table: it looked the same, reflecting my same tired image.

I approached the 'me' in the bathroom mirror, sought its embrace, looked deep into my mirror eyes and spoke quietly – 'We are alone. . . . Here, we are not going to argue, no. We are going to have to trust each other, to be friends.'

I accepted the truce.

In New York, I felt lost. I spent the first few days looking upwards, a country bumpkin in the big city, gawping at skyscrapers. A Brazilian friend of mine who lives in Hong Kong says that when she is indoors it is fine, she has space, and some territory, but when she goes out in the street she feels claustrophobic, even in the open air. New York made me feel claustrophobic, even in Central Park.

Every night I would change restaurants but it was always the same chicken – I knew how to pronounce 'chicken' with the most impeccable Shanghai Chinese accent! I ate chicken for every supper until I learned how to pronounce 'meatloaf and potatoes'. I broadened out to vegetables when, courageously, I said 'chow mein' and the waiter, thankfully, under-stood what I meant.

Every night, before I went to sleep, I would ask myself: 'How could you ever have had such a mad idea? What is it that interests you, in this country that is not yours, this city that is not yours, this language that you do not speak?' I was hard on myself. 'Take the first plane home and get on with founding this "Artistic Theatre of Rio de Janeiro" thing, put on your plays (and while you're at it, the complete works of Shakespeare) and have done with it! You want to be a writer, don't you? Well write then! You learn by doing! Talent cannot be taught! John Gassner — what nonsense! Go back to Rio: there you have friends.'

I had serious altercations with myself, numerous times we broke our precarious peace, cat and dog, I and I. The fault was always mine: I do not know which of my 'me's' was more to blame.

I could not look myself in the face, except in the inevitable moment of shaving. When I was mad with myself, when I came close to fisticuffs, I would throw the blanket over the mirror, and that was that: the blanket avoided a definitive rupture.

Gassner, the teacher

I was certain I wanted to return, and more certain that I wanted to study with Gassner. If I believed that talent could not be taught, I also believed, if I had talent, Gassner could only do me good. After all, he had taught Arthur Miller, Tennessee Williams and other famous playwrights. He had given them advice. The man must know a lot. He could teach me secrets. Keys that would open doors. Roads that would lead me to Rome: I knew that all roads led there, but I didn't know how to find any of them.

This struggle with myself lasted the first seven days, before I arranged the date of the first interview in the Brander Matthews Theatre, at Columbia. I went to sleep absolutely decided to return to Brazil the very next day . . . and I awoke with the determination to be a dedicated pupil studying with Gassner.

I took the first subway of my life. I looked for the word 'Uptown', knowing that I should get off at 116th Street in that direction, and I got off fine. It was just that I took the wrong train, the Lennox, and I ended up in the Bronx, bang in the middle of blackest Harlem, on the other, East side of the city — I saw only black people in dark clothes.

That was my third version of humanity: suddenly everyone had become darker! Nice-seeming people and evil-looking people, kind smiling people and angry, suspicious people. I asked where Columbia University was and people thought I was taking the mickey and did not even reply, or their replies were inaudible – in those days I did not yet understand English swear-words and always expressed my gratitude: 'Thank you, mister, thank you, madam.' I asked again, and then again, and once more, until an old black lady, in a hat with coloured feathers, maternally took pity on me, and clarified the mystery, showing me the mistake on my map: there were two 116th Streets, East and West, which were the same, except that there was one on each side of Fifth Avenue. I was 'Uptown' yes, but on this side, in Harlem, and not on that side, at Columbia University.

Taking a deep breath, I went back 'Downtown', then 'Up' again, and arrived at the appointed time, with British punctuality: I had left the hotel hours ahead of time. When I saw the statue of the *Alma Mater*, which I knew from photographs, I felt at home in New York. I caressed the stone statue . . . and dirtied my hand with pigeon shit.

Professor Smith, the Course Director, used the minimum of vocabulary. We decided I should take Shakespeare, of course, modern drama, directing, Greek theatre and, above all, 'playwriting' with Mr John Gassner! The teachers, apart from Gassner and Smith, included Maurice Valency, Norris Houghton and Theodore Apstein. I informed Smith that I would need time and space for my chemistry lessons: plastics and petroleum. Mr Smith asked me three times to repeat what I had said, thinking that I did not have the English words to express myself.

I explained: chemistry was obligatory not only because of my father, who deserved any sacrifice, but also because the Brazilian government even in those days discriminated against the Arts. It only authorised the student to purchase $200 of US currency per month at the official exchange rate if he studied sciences; the Arts were not worth anything for exchange purposes. And the difference between the official and parallel rates was more than 100 per cent. Those dollars were my monthly allowance. If chemistry was difficult enough in Portuguese, imagine it in a language I was barely master of – a language which, to be honest, was master of me. But even so, I had to take both courses simultaneously.

The university gave me a list of rooms to rent. I was lucky at first try and went to live with a couple, he a rabbi and she a housewife. The weekly rent was the same as one night in the Hotel America: ten dollars. It was close to Riverside Drive. On the way down, one was met by the icy wind from the river.

Cold differs, according to the country, the geography, the culture. The cold of Rio is cross-looking, it knows it is out of place, an insolent invader, a foreign cold. It attacks, wounds, leaves victims in its wake and goes away, back to its maternal home in Argentina and other glacial retreats. The cold of Rio Grande do Sul barges in without asking: it wrestles its way inside ears and nostrils. The cold of London, grey, wet, overflowing, clothes-drenching, soaking. The cold of Stockholm, dark, night falling at three in the afternoon, and yet it knows respect, it is sincere – sure, it is cold, that is its nature, but it means no harm.

All colds are sincere, only the treacherous cold of New York lies: it is a blue cold. New York's winter sky is as blue as Rio's summer sky. In an instant, the New York cold settles in the spinal column, straight to the marrow, where it bites with its canines and draws blood! I put up with the cold of the Hudson River, descending the hill, for two years. Two years of chapped ears and a frozen red nose.

In the first chemistry lesson, I understood absolutely nothing, not a word, not a formula, not a whisper, intention or proposition, not a look, nothing, nothing at all. I did not even understand why I was there! And in the first playwriting lesson, Gassner introduced me to the other students: 'Mr Boal lives in Buenos Aires . . .' I explained the geographical, sociological and cultural differences in South America, but I must have jumbled up the words to such a preposterous extent that my colleagues thought I was Paraguayan.

The language of words is but one of the languages we use in our dialogues. There are languages of the voice, of the body, of movement, and then there are the unconscious languages. Since words evaded me, I paid attention to the rest.

I noticed that the chemistry teachers (and their students) spoke only with their mouths, just with colourless words – as though they were speaking in silence. Those in the theatre moved their bodies and sang their sentences, lyrically. I watched the teachers' bodies, listened to their voices and thought: 'Now he must be talking about Ibsen, that rhythmic repetition can only be Norwegian, with those very precise, dry, economic gestures –

pure Ibsen! Now, this subterranean veiled manner, half words, the weight on the shoulders, the anguish, the shriek, is Chekhov. . . . Ah – Shakespeare, without a shadow of a doubt: that demonstrative and energetic way of waving his arms and then banging down the fist hard on the table, that can only be Shakespeare.'

I decided I should read newspapers in the mornings, go to the cinema in the afternoons and listen to the radio all day. And above all, speak to my self. (In that, I was already an expert.)

I would wake up at seven, buy the *New York Times*, walk three blocks to a university cafeteria, 'The Lion's Den', read the paper eating cereal and yoghurt, drinking coffee and orange juice, return home to brush my teeth and listen to the radio, and then go to the library to study. At midday, a sandwich of some sort, whatever was closest to hand, tuna or turkey. Teeth again, and then books until it was time for the classes, at six. When I did not have a class, at two in the afternoon, I went to the Thalia cinema, on 92nd Street, every day, two films for the price of one. I think I saw all the great French, Italian, German, Japanese and Russian cinematography as well as old North American films.

After a few weeks, routine took me over. I began to be more solitary than ever. Living amidst multitudes in the streets, in classes, in restaurants. No one talked to me. Ugly Duckling! The loneliness of a man surrounded by multitudes is as bad as that of the maximum security cells, surrounded by thick walls: I have known both.

No one looked at me when I went out; if I stopped, no one looked at me. I tried sitting on the pavement, made faces and grimaces: no one glanced in my direction. I let loose a shout in the middle of the street. No one heard: everyone had better things to do than listen to the cries of lonely Brazilians . . .

I was alone.

★   ★   ★

Langston Hughes and friendship

I discovered that the university had a cultural programme. Langston Hughes, the famous black poet, was going to give a lecture. I remembered a letter which Abdias wanted me to give to the poet.

I went to the packed lecture. At the end of the applause, people queued to greet the poet. I joined the queue. My legs began to tremble and I recalled the tremor I suffered when I saw Nelson Rodrigues for the first time. I imagined the emotion I would feel when shaking the hand of a world celebrity.

'Mr Hughes . . . my friend . . . Abdias, you know . . . my very good friend . . . a brother . . . this letter . . . see? It is for you. . . . He wrote it himself . . . by himself . . . for you . . . for himself . . . *não sei* . . . It is yours! Take it!' The words were, mostly, right; the style syncopated and the syntax random.

Hughes certainly remembered 'our friend and brother' Abdias, of whom he was very fond. He conversed with me for a good five minutes –

The poet Langston Hughes with Boal, 1953

MEG HAL ELLEN EU HOWIE JOAN

JEAN HAL FRED

Boal's 24th birthday, New York, 1954

I understood half of what he said, and, luckily in the intelligible half there was an invitation to a round table in Harlem.

The following week I went to listen to black poetry and literature. Hughes introduced me to several of his friends, black and white, men and women. They were all determined anti-racists – that struggle, that determination, united them. How beautiful is the friendship between people who struggle for the same just causes. It does not matter what the skin colour, sex, age, nationality is. What matters is the passion!

I was never part of his circle of friends – I was only ever a visitor – but nevertheless I would be invited to a show at the Apollo Theatre (a musical theatre in Harlem, where many stars have begun their careers), or even to conversations at a bar. I was an unobtrusive presence – silent the greater part of the time, listening attentively, only responding when asked something.

'I live in Rio de Janeiro which is the capital of Brazil, *and not* Buenos Aires, which is the capital of Argentina, which is *another country*, like Paraguay, whose capital is Assunción, and is also *another country*, and the capital of Ecuador is Quito, of Uruguay, Montevideo . . . of Chile, Santiago . . . of Colombia, Bogotá . . . and . . . well, that's it.'[73]

When vocabulary is limited, conversation tends to be on the shallow side. . . . Better to smile intelligently. To think intelligent things in Portuguese and smile in English.

I went on smiling and meeting famous people: Sugar Ray Robinson, who shook everyone's hand, smiling, and who I feared might 'sock' me (all boxers like socking people for fun, don't they?); Dizzy Gillespie, whom I almost asked to play me something . . . I met so many black celebrities that today I think I must have met everyone and I find myself wondering 'Was Martin Luther King there, was he *that* guy? Of course he was. Could that fascinating woman have been Ella Fitzgerald? Of course yes! Is it possible that it really was them? Of course not. . . .'

Little by little I lost my fear of famous people – they were just people like us. I decided I would be a reporter for the *Correio Paulistano*.[74] A friend of mine worked on that paper. I asked if they would take me on as their voluntary correspondent: they accepted. I began my career as an international journalist.

I began to seek out the people I wanted to meet. All artists like to appear in the newspaper – it is a necessity of their profession. I would write a letter to the artists requesting an interview and leave the letter at the stage door, with my telephone number. No one ever refused.

That was how I met José Ferrer, after a matinée of his famous *Cyrano de Bergerac*, and Ruth and Augustus Goetz, adaptors of Gide's *The Immoralist*. I met Louis Jourdan, Geraldine Page, who were in the Goetzs' play. James Dean played the Arab seducer; and seduce he did, but he was not yet famous.

Through Geraldine, I met José Quintero, a Puerto Rican director based in New York, the director of a theatre in the round which is still there today, the 'Circle in the Square'. I interviewed Harold Clurman, Stella Adler and Elia Kazan, following the première of *Cat on a Hot Tin Roof*, with Barbara Bel Geddes, Burl Ives, Mildred Dunnock and Ben Gazzara. I interviewed dancers from *Wish You Were Here* which had a real swimming pool on stage. And Robert Anderson, the author of *Tea and Sympathy*, with Leif Erickson, Deborah Kerr and John Kerr (not related), who was later replaced by Anthony Perkins; I discovered that Perkins was a class-mate of mine in the Shakespeare lessons, in which he was even more silent than I, and no one yet knew him as an actor.

Through one person I would meet another, and then another through them. I improved my English, chattering away. I learned to like the words, to play with the words. As if they were alive. And they were. Words are living beings: they only let themselves be known when they are loved. Like us.

Gassner managed to get me admitted to some sessions of the Actors' Studio as an auditor — though *observer* would be a more accurate description, since I understood more by seeing than by hearing. Their temporary workplace was a little theatre called the Malin, and I would be just a few metres from the actors — watching in fascination while they created characters. Since those Actors' Studio sessions, I have had a fascination for actors who truly live their characters — rather than those who pretend to. To see an actor transforming him/herself, giving life to his/her dormant potentialities, is marvellous. It is the best way to understand the human being: seeing an actor create.

The Writers' Group

Howard came along one day to invite me to join a group of new playwrights called The Writers' Group in Brooklyn. Ten future dramatists, girls and boys. Counting me, eleven. Girls . . . great. As well as being dramatists,

The Writers' Group (Brooklyn, 1954–55)

they were girls. I have always liked those two special categories, even separately. And to be a foreigner, to have an accent, conferred a certain charm on one. Excellent! I was in need of this divine assistance.

We would meet and read our plays. A *rapporteur* had to read the play beforehand and write report on it – on Saturdays we would have the reading, after which we carried on together, for hours, talking. There I felt totally loved, totally integrated. It was my first theatre group after that of my brothers. I still think of those people with tenderness.

When I felt that I was becoming confident in the language, and using colloquial English without fear, I had the courage to attack reading *Don Quixote* in Spanish. I wanted to compare Cervantes with Shakespeare, not only because they lived during the same epoch, but because I imagined that the slow passage from feudalism to bourgeois society was the essence of the work of these two authors.

Don Quixote is a hero out of his time: his values are those of the nobility of one or two hundred years before. Nothing about this hero is ridiculous. The ridiculousness of Quixote resides in his anacronymity. Hamlet, like Quixote, brings with him past values, he brings his father. Unlike Quixote, he also brings the bourgeois Machiavellian 'virtú' of Claudius. Usually in productions of *Hamlet*, Claudius is almost a secondary character. For me, the two characters are on the same level, though the size of their roles is different.

Hamlet is the synthesis of the world in transformation, two worlds co-existing (at least in the ideal): the pure nobility, incarnated in his father's Ghost, and the impetuous bourgeoisie, in his uncle. To be or not to be? In truth Hamlet's tragedy is not this. His tragedy is to be *and* not to be! Hamlet is both, he is the father and the uncle. He just does not know how to be himself. He does not recognise in himself his other I. Which of the two is 'Hamlet'? Both. I am a specialist in this dichotomy. . . .

After my first Quixotesque reading, in 1954, every January for at least ten years I would think: 'Ah, it has been such a long time since I have reread "Don Quixote"!' And I would sit down to reread it, to take notes again, to re-evaluate previous notes. 'Oh, it has been such a long time since I have read Shakespeare!' And one of his plays would return to my table. These two authors have marked and continue to mark my life, even now.

A year goes by rapidly, especially when you begin to enjoy what you do, to understand the language you speak, to make friendships, loves. When you are writing one play after another, getting feedback from such a teacher, what a luxury! The comment of his which most pleased me was that I was creating a lot of work for him, I was the student who wrote most! And studying with colleagues like mine, learning, reading all the books, watching all the films, going to all the shows, when you live like that, really living and loving, a year rushes by.

The academic year had ended. It was time to go back home. I went to say goodbye to John Gassner, the Pope of Playwriting. He recalled plays of mine he had read and commented upon, eulogised my progress, wished me much happiness as a playwright. He explained that being a playwright was a gift, like being a poet, a pianist or a painter. One can always learn more by studying, but the gift is still necessary. Rising to his feet, he uttered the explosive phrase, which moved me to the root of my hair and the tips of my toes: 'Mr Boal, you are a playwright!'

I had two choices: either I faint right there and hit my head on the cold stone, or . . . I make a heroic resolution to run greater risks. Heroism prevailed. 'Well, Mr Gassner, I think that I can improve still more, I can learn the things I don't know yet. Which is why I need to study with you for a further full year. You are a formidable teacher. I have decided here and now that I am not returning to Brazil yet, no: I will stay on here next year.'

The fulminating career of the young waiter in Atlantic City

Seu Boal, a fair man, had offered me one year of studies abroad, as compensation for my siblings' longer courses; I was now asking for two. I wrote him a letter explaining my feelings, explaining what it meant to be called a 'playwright' by John Gassner, no less, the Prince of playwriting professors! I was sure my father would understand. I wanted to stay and work, and my father decided to support me. Thank you, father, receive my loving thanks, tardy as they are. A just man. An example.

In summer there were loads of jobs going, of two kinds: picking oranges in California, or being a waiter in Atlantic City or Miami. I decided to take the bus to Atlantic City, the beaches of the south.

Arriving in Atlantic City, I went to temporary employment agencies, hotels and casinos, which is where the jobs were. By the second day, I had three offers and I visited the kitchens of the relevant three hotels. My intention was clear: I wanted to visit the cooking pots *in loco*, to smell the food, to dip my finger in and lick the sauce. I wanted to choose the best menu, and I chose the Chelsea Hotel.

I realised later my misunderstanding at the very first lunch: employees did not eat the customers' food – they got special, simplified grub!

As I did not know how to do anything, they gave me the job of lift operator, which did not require much knowledge. I have never come across such a monotonous and boring job, more senseless than sucking a nail (as we say). A lift operator does what any user of lifts knows how to, can and should do: he pushes buttons.

Worse still: I had to wear a uniform. In the United States, most hotels sport porters and lift operators, and porters are more fantastically outfitted than Carmen Miranda in her days of Hollywood glory, or a Soviet General on military parade in Red Square. I was disgusted with all the embroidery on the jacket, the green and the gold, but I had to wear it. I protested in my best Portuguese, so that no one would understand me, but obeyed in English and wore the uniform – the only uniform I have ever worn in my life.

A vacancy arose for a 'bus-boy', bus-boys being young men or women – would they be bus-girls? – who clear dirty plates from the tables and replace them with clean ones. The waiters' secretaries.

At least this job would be more entertaining, more sociable, and it offered the possibility of tips. Let me explain: the bus-boy got a tip from the waiter, who got a tip from the head of the 'station' (a group of tables), who got a tip from the customer. It was the head who collected all the coins from the tables – no one could touch the money except for the head. He totalled it up, divided it (subtracting something) and gave part to each of the waiters in his 'station'; each waiter then sorted out a portion (a minimal portion) of what he received, to be given over to us, the bus-boys. Fifty to seventy dollars a week. For me, a fortune undreamt of!

I have always been hard-working – a paternal inheritance. Even as a bus-boy, I liked to do things properly. I was promoted to waiter at the end of the first week. My colleagues called me 'Columbia Man'. To be a student of Columbia University lent one a glamour, it was one of the most prestigious universities in the world. My accent lent more charm still. And the fact of being a *simpatico* bilingual and, with some hiccups, even trilingual (including my incipient Spanish) – helped in my promotions. After three or four weeks, I was promoted to 'head of station' waiter: glory! A fulminating career, from lift operator to departmental head!

I had all that was needed to win Margaret's heart – a bus-girl who brought the drinks; Meg was not meek [*meiga* means meek], not docile, she was a rebel. Margaret did not have blue blood, as desired by my mother, but she *was* a princess. And she worked for exactly the same motives as I – money! She came from Baltimore, Maryland and studied philosophy at the university of her state. She liked music. Adored it. She listened to music all the time.

We were together everywhere, listening to hot Caribbean rhythms in the pit of a hotel I resided in (who was I to live in the Chelsea, where I worked!), in her hotel, which was a little better though also only meriting half a star, or on the boardwalk, on it or under it. Let me explain: running along the edge of the sand was a boardwalk, a wooden pathway, along which tourists promenaded. In some places, as darkness fell, the area under the boardwalk was silent and tranquil – ideal for heartfelt tenderness and passionate caresses. Ideal for anything, really.

Margaret could sing. I did not sing even in the bathroom – ah, Dona Marieta! – and I confess, with some embarrassment, that I liked Bing Crosby, yes I did, I swear, and Frank Sinatra, and Lucho Gatica, Tommy Dorsey, Xavier Cugat's orchestras . . . (well, no one is perfect). Even Liberace seemed to me to have some talent playing the piano and telling jokes and 'small talk' . . . if it were not for the Brylcreem in his hair. . . .

Meg had a musical ear and was equally up in arms about the 'American way of life' as about the romantic ambient music we had to listen to all day while we worked: 'Oh, My Papa!', 'Stranger in Paradise', 'Hernando's Hideaway', big hits of the time.

Under the boardwalk, Meg used to produce a blue plastic record-player and we used to listen to her favourite music on '78s – or maybe, by 1954, they were less than '78s, I don't know! (Who wants to count revolutions per minute when they are making love . . . ?)

What was this music? It was not yet Elvis Presley, it could not have been – 'Hound Dog' was from 1956 and I went back to Brazil in 1955. Perhaps it was a premature and premonitory Jamaican rhythm . . . but I swear that when I remember the music Meg loved, I remember Elvis the Pelvis!

Still today, when I remember the most important boardwalk of my life, it is as though I were listening to Elvis sing 'Blue Suede Shoes', which had not yet been written then. He arrived exclaiming 'That's Alright, Mama!' and hit the bulls-eye with everything he played. Everything one listened to, ecstatically, at that time, started with 'One, Two, Three O'clock, Four O'clock Rock!' But only after I left.

Imagine that kind of sound and fury invading the public spaces in hotels and casinos in which one heard soppy saccharin sounds, designed to lead to whisky, dancing 'cheek-to-cheek', and celestial peace! Elvis was the Amazonian *pororoca*[75] of music! For sure it happened, just not in my time: I was already back in Brazil. Funny how memory deceives us and, even knowing it is wrong, we swear by it! I swear that it was him . . . and I know it was not!

I think that Rock 'n' Roll, in the beginning, was revolutionary. It complied with none of the customs of the time: it came full pelt, breaking limits, moulds, chains. Elvis knew what he wanted: he was poet of discomfort, of revolt! Later, 'Rock' became the unbearable asinine noise which we are all obliged to put up with: mediocrity. But initially it was a protest, an affirmation, it was young! It demolished, it surprised. It was art. (And I admit: every now and then, it still is.) But Elvis' revolutionary content was not in the songs themselves, but in their context: their counterpoint to the slushy melodies of that era. He was revolutionary in what he negated, not in what he affirmed. Today, he is transformed into what he used to condemn.

Listening to that music, I used to think: in Rio, we had wanted to make the transition gently from what might be termed 'balnearic theatre' or theatre for tourists, to a serious, austere theatre, and we wanted to do it gently. But in music, Elvis came in kicking! Rupture is rupture. I will make it! Rock helped me to think like this. I thought: one day, when I return to Brazil, I am going to do what I want, what I think I want and what I want to think! I am not going to think about what the public wants: I will think what I think! The artist rules! Macho!

Van Gogh thought with his head, moved the paintbrush with his hands, mixed the paints by eye. He did not ask 'Are they going to like it? Is some

THE HOUSE ACROSS THE STREET
The first play written and directed by Boal, at Malin Studio, New York, 1955

marchand going to buy it from me?' That is why he knew how to paint the wind, which would not stand still to pose for anyone, not even for Van Gogh. He knew how to paint old age itself, not merely the aged. He painted colour, not just coloured things.

Rembrandt liked the ambiguity of *chiaroscuro*, not worrying about the complaints of those who wanted more light to see better. . . . Picasso always did what came to him on the canvas. An artist's canvas. Imagine if Picasso had taken notice of women who preferred to be portrayed with an eye on each side of their nose, and a mouth beneath the nostrils? He would have carried on forever painting blue portraits of his poet friend J. Sabartés, everything in its right place, irreproachable noses and ears. Picasso saw nipples and navels wherever they were in his imagination, not on his models' bodies. The public has to want whatever I want! *Asi soy!*[76] I am not going to do what they think should be done, but what I want to be done: take risks.

My second year in New York was still better. I did things I had already done before, but now I knew what I was doing.

Columbia University arranged an informal competition of one-act plays. The prize was a performance of the text by the acting students. I won with *Martim Pescador*. I thought happily how much I would learn with the director of the play, the actors and the audience. From studying, I had got the impulse: now I would make the leap! The impulse was in the typewriter: the leap, on the stage. But it so happened that the directorate of the school thought that my text, though well written and theatrical, was not suitable for staging, neither by virtue of its subject – Brazilian fisher-people – nor its form – poignant naturalism. What a letdown!

Enter the Writers' Group. They would not accept the decision that the victorious work should not be performed, especially now that we were all possessed of an invincible lust to put on our first living breathing Writers' Group play. My colleagues decided that they would produce the show themselves, together with a comedy of mine *The House Across the Street* and another, Howard's *The Old Man*. We ended up swapping *Martim* for another of mine, *The Horse and the Saint*. The cast would be made up of the group's playwrights themselves, and the authors would be their own directors. How could I refuse?

That was how, without wanting to, I began to direct. As I was not a director, I had no fear of directing. I did not fear failure, nor my incompetence. I was pardoned in advance. Even by myself. Even by my other 'I', which always disagreed with me (actually I suspect that perhaps I am that other 'I', and not the 'I' I think I am!).

And as the actors were not actors, they were not afraid to act: they were great. As we had no money, we decided we would build the scenery ourselves – as well, of course, as sweeping the floor, painting the walls, inviting friends, selling tickets, receiving the spectators and showing them to their seats, serving drinks during the intervals, thanking people for being so kind as to come, for taking the risk . . .

That really was the leap after the impulse. As I had no thought of becoming a director I directed calmly, democratically – my actors adored me. As we knew nothing of the stage, we learned together – it was great team work.

The metamorphosis enchanted me: here was the text, in written form; there, the text in the space, on the set, in light, in movement, in the body and voice of each actor or actress. Everything changed, gained meaning. I learned that dialogue, on paper, has a calm feel, it takes the time it takes to read – when read, it is time past. When it is flying between living people, on stage, it is present time!

Nilson Penna, a Brazilian stage designer, was passing through New York. We invited him to do the design. He accepted. We had no money for the production, but Nilson had a good friend, Bidu Sayão, a Brazilian lyrical singer from the Metropolitan Opera House. I went with him to Bidu's house and heard her marvellous records. She, in turn, heard about our ambitious project, and gave us some money, as well as tea and biscuits.

Imagine: my directorial debut in the theatre was produced by Bidu Sayão: how chic! With the $100 she lovingly offered, we made Nilson's sets, hired the Malin Studio – the place where the Actors' Studio temporarily met – and put on three shows with audiences packed with our friends. Not

Bidu Sayão, the Brazilian soprano at the Metropolitan Opera House in New York, who offered to produce Boal's first play in New York

a single incautious or unwitting unknown spectator arrived. All were conquered beforehand: parents, girlfriends and boyfriends, neighbours and hangers-on. It was a spectacular success!

I made my writer's and director's debut on Broadway – what luxury!

The burial

For the first time, I felt the sadness of seeing scenery being pulled apart, the stage stripped, ready to give itself to another anxious show. Prosceniums are such prostitutes!

Within fifteen minutes our sets were piled up waiting for the truck. There, on that stage where I had lived my first theatrical emotions, my very own, ours, there, on that stage, my characters had vanished. I understood why, in Brazil, some companies liked to perform a 'burial' of the play on the last night: that final time, improvisations are allowed. Each of the actors, on their own, prepares surprises: scripts out of context, costumes from another play, absurd make-up, false entries and unexpected departures. A great tragedy transforms itself into pure farce! Laughter instead of tears. Uproar instead of reflection. This is a way of mourning the show. Usually, the cast warns the audience that they are to witness 'a burial', and the spectators prepare themselves for all manner of outbursts. I understand that this burial had the same cathartic function as the burials of New Orleans, or of some African countries, full of song and dance. But without being a masochist, I prefer the suffering of the farewell, I prefer the truth.

The goodbyes

Tears flowed. For the play and for the goodbyes: my time in New York had come to an end, I already had my bags packed.

It was not only the scenery which was being dismantled – it was New York, Columbia University, Broadway and off-Broadway, the cinemas in Greenwich Village and the Thalia, Harlem and the Bowery, the libraries and the museums, streets and parks. Everything was being dismantled.

It was not only the cast of the play that was breaking up, it was not only the city that was distancing itself from me: it was Gassner and Hughes, it was my university friends and those of the Writers' Group, it was the waitress who served me, faithful to the end of my stay, it was my soup, my warm clam chowder on cold days.

When you are young, two years is a long time. Later on, the years rush by. What a shame! In July 1955, I returned to Rio de Janeiro. The aeroplane was full, and I was empty.

in the arena of arena

The Arena Theatre of São Paulo

Much of my life divides into fifteen-year periods: fifteen years with Arena, fifteen in exile, fifteen back in Brazil . . . and now what? A new track: the SambOpera ! Another fifteen years? Five will do!

Snoozing in my hammock, peacefully

On my return from New York, in the car on the way from the airport, my brother delivered the shocking news that he had got me a wonderful job as a chemist at Petrobrás: excellent salary, immediate possibilities of promotion through the firm's hierarchy. . . . My career as a chemist in Rio promised to be more fulminating than my career of waiter in Atlantic City had been! Fantastic, marvellous! Panic! If I took up chemistry, never again would I do theatre.

'You're a nationalist, aren't you? You can't get more national than Petrobrás. . . . Its our petroleum!' – insisted my brother.

Jobs were abundant. The words of my sister Augusta on starting work as a teacher became legendary – at the end of the month she arrived home with two payslips in her hand, having that day received her first wages at two colleges.

'What on earth am I going to do with so much money?' she asked, gazing in shock at the huge figures listed for her simultaneous salaries.

Teachers were demi-gods. With a diploma in hand and a degree ring on one's finger – the police stole my ring two decades later! – one could pick and choose jobs. I was Columbia-Man! Employers would be queuing up! Brazil was growing.

I told Nelson Rodrigues I did not want to be a chemist, but that I did not think my father should have to support a grown man of 24. 'Can you translate?' Nelson asked. 'I can try, but I'm not a translator. . . .' 'If you speak English, you are a translator!'

Nelson gave me the address of a friend of his, Drummond, director of *X-9*, the crime, sex and gore magazine, a forerunner of James Bond; Drummond made me go through a first trial: translating a short piece of text, generously splattered with bursts of machine-gunfire and spurts of Rhesus Negative. I drenched the text in red.

I passed. After this first translation, every week I went to pick up some ensanguined and steaming texts.

Drummond liked my versions, my visions. He would not complain when I altered the texts: paid by the page, when I was short of money I would invent sub-plots, create new characters, spin out a ten-page sketch into a thirty-page novel. If I was flush with cash, I would do the opposite and kill off important characters before their time.

As I did not read the stories before translating them – irresponsible fellow that I was! – I frequently assassinated characters who would later be necessary to shed light on the crime, and this obliged me to contrive ways to resuscitate corpses. I transformed myself into a powerful inventor of resurrections.

This was how I learned the detective novel technique, which helped me to write a novela in 1975 about the *coup* in Argentina – before it had even broken out – entitled *A deliciosa e sangreta aventura latina de Jane Spitfire, espiã e mulher sensual!* (The Delicious and Bloody Latin Adventure of Jane Spitfire, Spy and Sensual Woman!) The book was published by *Pasquim*,[1] and Guidacci did beautiful illustrations, which were absolutely pornographic and lascivious, and the book sold in tens of thousands at newspaper kiosks across Brazil . . . but not in bookshops. The book's purchasers thought that they were getting a book stuffed with pure filth – and filth there was, great spurts of the stuff – but that was not all! By means of this technique, I explained the economic and political machinations in that country.

One day, I was lolling in my hammock when the telephone rang: it was Sábato Magaldi.

'The Arena Theatre needs a director. I put forward your name.'

'I am not a director. . . .'

'If you have directed, you're a director!'

Sábato remembered that I had directed plays on Broadway. Only three shows packed out with friends, in home-made productions by Bidú Sayão . . . but Broadway! For years, this was a cause of pride for me: my debut was in Broadway, wow! As time went on, I calmed down a bit. . . .

José Renato, Arena's director, was frank and direct:

'You say that you aren't a director, but maybe you have got what it takes. We'll give it a try. If it works out, good for all of us; if not, it's back to Rio with you.'

'Do you have confidence in me?'

'I don't know you. But I need a director to split the repertoire with.'

I prefer it like that: clear and sincere. This gave me a feeling of security.

Hamlet immediately came to mind. Well, it did not actually *come* to my mind because it already had permanent residence there. I wanted to start with that much-loved text. I remembered the first time I saw *Hamlet* – I liked the show's austerity. (It was advisable for me to get used to austerity: poverty beckoned.) Austere or no, it would need space. *Hamlet* needs to breathe, it has big lungs. *Hamlet* is open air, clear sky.

When I first went to see the arena at Arena, I almost asked naively: 'Where is the theatre?' Being timid, I kept quiet, wanting to see the stage, the scenery, lights and cycloramas. Slowly, it dawned on me that this *was* Arena's arena: a minuscule five metres by five. Little larger than a regular dining-room. . . . That this tiny space was where we were to bring about aesthetic revolutions. . . . Scarcity of means is a limitation – I am not about to eulogise the lack of resources as if it were a divine blessing. But with desire and art, the lack of means *can* be a stimulus. In our enslaved countries, we are condemned to creativity! This undesired poverty ended up transforming itself into the ideal conditions for our work as actors. The stage space may be finite; within ourselves, however, we are infinite. We went looking for the infinite – within. At Arena, we dived into the ravine of our souls.[2]

Arena forced us to place the utmost value on the actors. It allowed no tricks, hid nothing: actors had to rely on one another. It was like an extension of the Actors' Studio: close-up theatre. The actors were centimetres from the audience.

I believe that the truth of all theatre is the interrelation between actors, between two human beings. It is the passion which burns between them. This is the essence of theatre – after which it can dress itself up with all manner of ornament. Not before. Lope de Vega said, 'Theatre is a platform, two actors and a passion!' I subscribe to that. I can even do without the platform.

I looked at the twenty-five square metres of floor space, thinking about *Hamlet*: would it fit? *Hamlet* close up, why not? The King is the 'emergent power', the bourgeois affirming itself; the Prince represents the values which were crumbling in the rotten kingdom of Denmark. . . . The latter, however, contains the former, and the former has residues of the latter.

Images of the play kept coming into my mind: *Hamlet*, intimidated – yes, in my reading, he is afraid of the young woman! – ordering Ophelia to a convent, in meek and sad lament; in a small voice, lovingly, asking of his mother, Queen Gertrude, that she never again make love to his uncle. It is lullaby-like, this dialogue with his mother. The conversation of the Ghost with his son done in whispers – wonderful! That is how it should be, a serious conversation between father and son, none of those purgatorial trombones from beyond the grave! Up to that point, everything *sotto voce*, fine. But . . . how to kill Polonius behind soughing curtains? How to whisper acrobatic duels-to-the-death, with blood spurting everywhere? How to murmur the triumphal entrance of Fortinbras?

I dreamed of directing *Hamlet*, but the contract had already been signed for the first play: John Steinbeck's *Of Mice and Men*.

Arena's actors were not bad but their acting was, in the terminology of the time, 'stylised'. As I had seen Molière's *School for Husbands*, with young and inexperienced actors, I said to Renato: 'I will feel more at ease working with inexperienced people like myself, rather than with people who know much more.' With his help we selected the cast, in which there were several actors who would go on to work with me for more than a decade such as Gianfancesco Guarnieri and Oduvaldo Vianna Filho.

We agreed on my wages. I cannot remember if it was six, six thousand or six million; if it was new or old *cruzeiros*, *cruzeiros cruzados* or old *milreis*. With inflation running at 30 per cent per month the government used to change the currency without even blinking. I just know that my salary had the digit six somewhere in it, in front or at the end. This impressed me: I was going to do theatre and, on top of that, I was going to be paid!

I could hardly believe it: getting money for doing the thing I loved most! Enough to live on, without luxuries. Apart from my wages, I was entitled to lunch every day, except Sundays, in José Renato's house: his mother, gentle Dona Gina, reminded me of my own mother – she was a wonderful cook! (I will never forget the Thursday macaroni. . . . Or the maternal affection she gave me.) Apart from the food, the family atmosphere made me feel protected. It was important, at the beginning of my career. To this day, in the theatre, I look for a family. I look for siblings.

Stanislavski

The best way to rehearse would be to practise Stanislavski from day one. I explained what the work would consist of, asked the actors to study the first chapters of *An Actor Prepares*, and told them we would start experimenting with it on the first day of rehearsal, at 2 p.m. on the dot. I went home – to a borrowed room – to re-read my notes on the Actors' Studio, and to review the jottings I had done in the Russian master's books.

From my professional debut in September 1956, Stanislavski has been and always will be my main point of reference as a director.

At 2 o'clock on the dot, there I was, anxious and alone, sitting on stage of the Arena. At 2.15 p.m., half the cast was there. At 2.30 p.m., the cast was complete. Then I asked everyone to open the book at the first chapter and read the violent dressing down Stanislavski gave to actors who were late.

A poet can wake up in the middle of the night and write a beautiful poem — inspiration is all it takes! A painter can paint a picture in minutes or over years, whatever feels best. But artists working in collective art-forms cannot call together their audiences at three in the morning on the pretext that only at that particular moment do they feel the visitation of their muse. Theatre is a collective art. Mutual respect and discipline are essential. The chapter ended with Stanislavski refusing to give a class that day, by way of punishment and warning. Being a mere young novice, I was more moderate: 'Let's read the play. Tomorrow, please, can no one arrive after five to two, because two is when the rehearsal starts, not when you start arriving.'

I always had this problem in Brazil. Where schedules and timing are concerned I am more British, Swiss, Danish, German, Japanese, Finnish, Norwegian, Australian, Bora-boranian, Hong Kongese, New Zealander, all of these. . . . In this respect I have nothing *carioca* about me! (You will note that I do not include in my roll of punctuality Portugal, Bolivia, Mexico, Ecuador, Colombia, Argentina, Italy.)

The next day, almost everyone was there with their script open when I arrived. That's how it always was: *almost* on time, *almost* everyone. The layout of the stage limited one's visual creativity. But it was not all bad: though the actors always had their backs to one part of the audience, they always faced another. They had to play truthfully, to be expressive in all directions. But the proximity of the audience was intimidating. During a performance of *Chapetuba FC* Vianninha was playing a footballer; in one particular scene he had to lie down right next to the front row of the audience, which that day happened to be full of young women, seated ten centimetres from his body. He was a handsome young man. One of the women, either through lack of restraint or excess of attraction, commented quietly, which in the Arena meant in earshot of everyone: 'What lovely legs he has. . . .' The scene was dramatic and we had to stop ourselves laughing.

Audience comments could often be heard and this increased concentration. When working in an arena it is interrelate or die!

★   ★   ★

The eyes

Every day we would study a chapter of Stanislavski and analyse the script. We studied the whole of the master's first book during rehearsals. It was by studying the Method – not slavishly, but trying to apply it to our reality – that we began to create a Brazilian style of playing, as against the predominant style of the Teatro Brasileiro De Comédia (the TBC), our best bourgeois theatre of the time.

A Brazilian show meant being ourselves, Brazilians. We did not go into considerations of class, the social system, etc., just Stanislavki's 'emotion memory'. It was inevitable that the excellent actors of the TBC, being directed by four Italian directors, a Belgian and a Pole, would end up with Italian, French or Polish prosody. We, in Arena, were more like our audiences.

For me, the foundation of any show has always been two actors looking at each other. The eye is the most vulnerable part of the human body! That is why at times of great emotion, out of caution we seek to hide our eyes. Or equally, why we offer them at times of great love. Actors must offer each other their gaze. It is in the gaze that the structure of the show is created. It is in the gaze that the characters are born. It is in the gaze that one discovers the truth. The open eye is not enough: I am talking about the deep gaze of which even blind people are capable.

The actor does not enter into the character; this is false. No actor can interpret a character that does not exist within him – or herself. The character comes out of the actor, who has been carrying it within. And it comes out through the eyes. The actor does enter, yes, but into the characters of the other actors, not his own. Through the eyes.

Theatre is this energy passed from one actor to another, *between the two of them*. Like love, which is not contained in one or other lover, but exists intensely between the two, so the theatrical does not belong to this or that person. Like lightning, it is the flash which jumps between two poles. Marx said that the smallest social unit is two citizens, and Brecht said that the smallest unit of theatre is two actors. (I think it was Brecht who said that, but if it was not, then I am saying it now!)

Around the interrelations of the characters, I created a simple show, in which movements were kept to a minimum. Each gesture carried a meaning. We had neither set nor costume designer, *ça va sans dire*! The set: a broken table, a dilapidated chair and two boxes. The costumes – bought at the Saturday market.

Poverty

I thought of justifying our poverty and invented an expression *selective realism*: we would select a small element or part of something, which would symbolise the whole – a few ears of corn symbolised the granary; a broken mirror, a girl's room; a horse's harness, the stable. Props and costumes fitted into a laundry bag. All the better for touring.

In the beginning, there was distance between us: Guarnieri and Vianninha knew that I had studied in the United States, and called me 'Cowboy'. They used to say that I walked as though I were on horseback. I did everything I could to swing my hips *carioca*-style, exaggerating the swing. And the more I tried to do the *carioca* hip-swing thing, the more 'Cowboy' I became.

The study of Stanislavski was a cornerstone of my career. It was he who systematised a method which helps the actor to seek, within him- or herself, ideas and emotions attributed to the characters. In this sense, one of the main functions of the director is to be *maiêutic*,[3] like Socrates in his philosophising process – the philosopher is the midwife who makes the student discover what s/he already knows, without knowing that s/he knows it, by means of questions which provoke reflection, thus opening up the path to discovery. That is how the theatre director should be: helping the actors *give birth* to characters.

The birth can be difficult. Vianninha was playing a character who was supposed to be feeling the anxiety of a person who is climbing up a gorge to save someone and is torn between solidarity and fear. When I observed that he had not felt anything and was merely coldly relating the thoughts he had had during the exercise, without emotion or feeling, Vianninha was shocked and said:

'Did you really want me, here and now, to experience the fear of death?'

'Of course. And tell us about that fear, which must be terrible. . . .'

There was incredulity. After a thoughtful pause, one of the actors commented, in a tone of outrage: 'I would never do that . . . that must be bad for one's health. . . . Taken that seriously, Stanislavski would make you ill. . . .'

I perceived the actor's fear of feeling fear. I grasped the opportunity and asked him to describe this fear, the fear of experiencing fear. . . .

I explained that Stanislavski, contrary to what certain ill-informed Brechtians would have us believe, never advocated the emotional orgy. In him, we always perceive the idea that governs the character's action: reason and emotion. The emotion always derives from a discovery, not from ignorance. Truth is therapeutic. Art is good for the health and should be recommended by all doctors. So is Theatre![4]

If the actor lets himself be swept away on a wave of uncontrolled emotion, with no direction and nothing to discover, it is madness. Or else, if it is articulated as such, it may serve purely as an *abstract emotion* exercise; two actors vigorously dispute some absurd subject, using only words which make no sense, and they must try to arrive at a state of anger, love, etc. Like abdominal exercises which serve to strengthen the stomach muscles; like pedalling an exercise bicycle, without leaving the room.

Some actors have a fear of or an aversion to everything which tends to the emotional or emotive. They invent the absurd notion of 'emotion versus technique', as if the two were antonyms, rather than parts of the same creative process. Some actors achieve their state of greatest emotion when arguing against emotion!

Emotion in Wuppertal, cradle of pre-human Neanderthal

Let me give an example from more recent times. In 1985, I was invited by the *Schauspielhaus* of Wuppertal, in Germany, to direct a play by Garcia Lorca, *El Público* (The Public). The greater part of the script had been lost for years, and having been found among the poet's papers a few months earlier, this was to be the first showing of the complete text.

I was surprised by the invitation: usually, directors are labelled according to the sort of work they do most, and are not considered capable of or interested in doing anything out of their habitual line of work. I have always been known for the shows I direct which have social or political

THE PUBLIC

The world première of the complete text of this play by Gabriel Garcia Lorca, directed by Boal
at the Schauspielhaus *in Wuppertal, Germany, 1985*

concerns – despite having directed a bit of everything, and liking everything a bit! The Lorca play was an attempt at surrealistic writing. Uneasy, I
asked why they had chosen me to direct that play. They replied: 'What
could be more surreal than inviting you to direct it!'

I loved the explanation and was fascinated by the idea of trying
Stanislavski in a surrealist play. For me, *surrealism* is one thing, *non-sense*
quite another. The latter is a succession of signifiers without signification,
or without meaning in their juxtaposition; in the former, there is a
meaning, at a subterranean or unconscious level, and it is transmitted by
the artist – through his work – to the spectator. I wanted to find this hidden
meaning, without necessarily translating it into words. I wanted to retain
all possible meanings, not to reduce them to merely one.

Some of those Wuppertalian actors, trained in another way – although
they were in the House of Pina Bausch! – wanted logical explanations for
everything. When they asked me if a particular scene was this or that, I

would reply sincerely: 'It is this *and* that!' Unsatisfied, they wanted a yes or a no, a or b, one or two, like computers. Nevertheless, I wanted *this* and *that*, and a whole host of other *thats* and *thises*: I wanted the *more*, the *also*, the *maybe*, the *apart from that*, the *who knows?*

We were rehearsing a scene in which two figures are arguing (the 'One' and the 'Other'), seeking to establish which is the 'One' and which the 'Other'. Along comes the Centurion, preceding the Kaiser, and demands that they decide. The scene ends with the arrival of the Kaiser, who chooses 'one' of them and rejects the 'other'.

The actors who were playing the figures kept asking me: 'One, what? The Other, what? What is hidden in those terrible words, "One" and "Other"?'

I insisted that, as actors, they should float on the waves, they should sail on the sea of possible meanings, musing upon exactly that: how they could make the desire to be 'One' (which both the characters wanted) and not the 'Other' (which they rejected) arouse in them the very emotion which would bring them to the right form: idea-emotion-form: the essential triad.

We always want to be 'One' and not the 'Other'. The actors had to think about 'One' and 'Other' with all their possible significations and an ample compass, and not just single out one of the possible meanings of these words, reducing them to a mere 'this alone' or 'only that'.

I explained that any connotation we might give to the 'One' and the 'Other' would reduce the wealth of possible meanings, rendering the scene into a less interesting realism. Like putting a subtitle on a painting: *The Enigmatic Smile of the Gioconda*, *The Strange Mysterious Lady Whose Identity No One Could Ever Explain and Who Is Suspected to be a Beardless Boy*, by Leonardo da Vinci; or Manet's *Two Women Lunching Naked, Just Think, Lying There in the Grass, With a Bored Look on their Faces, Watched by Men Dressed in Black*. Or, in music, *Destiny Knocks at the Door* also known as Beethoven's *Fifth Symphony*. . . . What banalisations!

'What do you mean, connotation?' they asked me.

'If I were to say that "one" is *Hamlet* and the "other" is Horatio, it becomes clear, but it obscures the range of possible meanings and reduces the conflict – which is dense and profound precisely because it is nebulous and imprecise – to a straightforward dispute between two actors for the best role.'

'It may reduce it, but if it was an argument about parts, that would calm us down, because we know about that problem. We need things to be precise.'

'Well then precision you will get! Even more than you need!' I threatened, losing patience, which rarely happens with me.

I called the stage manager and asked him to set up the following scenario: on the right, a huge banqueting table laden with anything he could find in the theatre storeroom – roast suckling pigs, chickens, turkeys, wine casks, beer barrels, whatever there was relating to gastronomy – made of *papier mâché* of course. On the left, another table with instruments of torture – leather straps, saws, chains and leg-irons. In the middle, a closed cell.

I asked the actors to get up on the stage and improvise, in the closed cell, the 'One' and the 'Other', now that they knew the destiny of each. With Germanic precision, within ten minutes, before the astonished eyes of the cast, the scene emerged, dazzling beyond all expectation.

They improvised, and we could see only their heads when they went past a little window in the cell. They were emotionally engaged, and became more so when the Centurion came in, doling out blows onto the scenery with a whip and demanding to know who was 'One' and who the 'Other'. I got up on to the stage and knocked down one of the cell walls at the very moment the Kaiser came on and asked:

'Who is One and who is the Other?'

The actors threw themselves at the Emperor's feet claiming that they were both the 'One'! The Kaiser chose one of the two and took him to the banqueting table: the actor got up on to the table and started to dance amidst the food and drink. The Centurion took the other to the torture table and, while he adjusted the instruments of torture with unnerving and horrifying noises, the actor – now unequivocally transformed into the 'Other' – undressed and lay down on the table, ready for torture. The 'One', the dancer, seeing the scene, did a grotesque striptease while he danced. Both were naked.

And there the improvisation ended. The few spectators – my assistant, my translator and some stage-hands – were moved. They applauded enthusiastically. The two actors spoke as though in chorus: 'We are professional actors and we do anything our director tells us to. Anything, except *that*: because *that* is not theatre, *that* is us! Our personal life, our privacy, which is ours and ours alone, and which here today we have exposed! We are quitting!'

It took a lot to convince them not to quit. We managed. It was more difficult to convince them that, yes, *that* was theatre, and good theatre too. The show was a hit, to general amazement. Right up to the end of the run, the two actors kept on saying: 'It is a hit, but *this* is not theatre: *this* is us. . . .' At the end of every show, moved as they were, they bowed to the audience. Who was it doing the bowing – the actor or the character? Who was 'One', who was the 'Other'?

The courses and the playwriting seminar

The rehearsals of *Of Mice and Men* in 1956 were less contentious. The play opened on 23 September. Renato invited me to stay in São Paulo and co-direct Arena with him. 'You are a director!' he said. I was proud and grateful, and remembered Gassner saying: 'You are a playwright!' I asked myself: 'Is it true?' I was never sure. Am I a playwright, a director, a teacher, a writer, a theorist? So many people are so sure of themselves, know how to define themselves – I have never known. Perhaps I am *one*, perhaps I am *other*.

Every night, after the show had opened, I would position myself beside the entrance to the theatre. I experienced, for the first time, box-office anxiety: how many spectators would turn up? The life of our theatre depended on them. An excellent opening night was not necessarily a sign that the play would have a good run – one had to hope for good 'word of mouth'.

One of the greatest successes I had was Machiavelli's *Mandrágora* (The Mandrake). At the opening, tears of joy. The next day, no one. Absolutely no one. Not one single kind-hearted spectator came to see it, not one friend or lover. We decided to do the show anyway . . . for fun, with the doors open. At the beginning, there was the doorman, the ticket collector and me. Half an hour later three drunks arrived, attracted by the music: as it was free, they stayed. Their drunkenness gradually wore off.

Rain was a bad sign, even people who had reserved might not show up. Years later, in exile in Buenos Aires, if it rained at five in the afternoon, without knowing why, I would find myself becoming anxious. Later I worked it out: if it rained at five in São Paulo, half the spectators didn't turn up. . . .

Of Mice and Men was always packed. The actors had begun to like the Stanislavski exercises, and other games I myself was inventing and which served as a basis for my book *Games for Actors and Non-Actors*. We instituted 'The Laboratory of Acting'.

Where did the name 'Laboratory' come from? I believe chemistry has helped me a lot in the theatre, not just in the nomenclature, but in the necessity I feel to systematise everything and in the rigour of all my work. Scientific thought is behind everything I do. My father was right: six years at the university were not wasted – chemistry, by a strange alchemy, has flourished in my books, in my productions and in my life.

In the Laboratory we created a feeling of fraternity with actors from other companies. We took pride in talking about the *theatre class*, as if we were talking about an important part of the working class.

The company wanted me to run a playwriting course which would be open to the public. I argued that I was not a teacher. Insisting, they said that I should stop worrying about myself and start worrying about transmitting what I had learned. 'You studied with Gassner: tell us what he told you. . . .' If you know how to speak you are a lecturer. . . . To be a writer, it is enough to put down on paper the words that come out of your mouth. To be a writer is to think: everyone thinks, so everyone is a writer.

I had never spoken in public, so it was natural that my legs should shake. Nothing excessive, just a tremendous tremble. I had intended to speak standing. I saw a hundred people awaiting my speech – amongst them well-known figures, famous people, like the writer Pagu – and I decided to ask for a chair and a table for my papers, which would thus tremble less.

When the class/talk ended, my friends asked me how I felt: 'Giving a talk is easy: it is just a matter of concentrating on what you want to say, and not on yourself. . . . If you want to convince people, think about them, not about yourself.' It is easy.

For weeks around fifty people assiduously met, and I gave classes showing that the laws of playwriting are tools to be used, not rules to be obeyed. Laws extracted from *chefs d'oeuvres*, from Sophocles, Shakespeare, Molière. Use them if you want; if you don't, run the risk. . . . I got a taste for it. I discovered that, when one is really teaching, it is the teacher who learns most. At the very least, s/he learns about the different ways different pupils have of learning. Some questions that people asked me Gassner had already answered; other answers I had to invent on the spot.

154

Fear

Fear is a curious thing: I am still shy but, in front of an audience I become so interested in convincing people that I forget my fear. NB: I do not *lose* the fear – I *forget* it. I forget that I am afraid. The fear recedes, it hides, but it can return at the end of the speech when there is no longer any reason to be afraid, or it can go on being there throughout the speech, but submerged, out of view; timidity is always there somewhere. I am not afraid just because I feel fear. I am afraid of others seeing my fear, sensing that I am afraid, because I know that fear is narcissistic, it likes to show itself at inconvenient moments – fear has no fear of exhibiting itself! When this happens, I push my timidity aside and I talk loudly to hide the fear . . . I am afraid of being afraid and I hide the fear. Where? Inside me! (How *frightening*!)

The seminar

The following year, 1957, we organised another playwriting course which was open to the public. In 1958, after the opening of *Eles Não Usam Black-Tie* (They Don't Wear Black-Tie), by Guarnieri, we decided to found the Playwriting Seminar to deepen our study.

The Seminar would be for invited participants, and the Course for all-comers. We met on Saturday mornings to analyse our plays with at least two *rapporteurs*, one of whom was always me, as they presumed that I was a connoisseur of theatrical carpentry: after all, I had studied at Columbia University! The Seminar also embraced in party politics: our debates were politicised. The Seminar got a name for being sincere, verging on the dogmatic.

The *rapporteurs* had to write detailed reports and provide information for the debates. The other participants listened to the reading and debated. The meetings ended when hunger overcame us. We used to lunch in a bar where a succulent *feijoada*[5] awaited us, in spite of the heat! The discussions continued, sweatily. Difficult to combine Hegel and Aristotle with crackling and pork ribs – in high summer! Ibsen and Shakespeare with oranges and *chorizo*. Heroic combinations: *caipirinha*[6] with Machiavelli and Euripides. Delicious!

(I observed that those who drank *caipirinha* with their *feijoada* became more generous, more able to understand the other person's point of view. I was completely abstemious: until then, the only alcohol that had passed my lips, with some difficulty, had been a modest *cuba-libre* at the Writers' Group farewell party, a glass which seriously dented my reputation as a well-behaved young man.)[7]

On Saturdays, the theatres did three showings, at 4, 8 and 10.30 p.m. On Sundays, at 6 and 9. The plays could not last longer than two hours, including the interval, which was obligatory in the interests of the smooth running of our own bar. At midnight, down to the cinema for Kurosawa, Fellini, de Sica, Visconti, Rossellini. . . .

The actors who worked at the TV studios were obliged to rehearse after midnight – from 2 p.m. for the theatre and until 4 a.m. for television. On Mondays, sacred day of rest, they rehearsed in the studio in the afternoon, dead tired, and performed live at 9 p.m. – there was no such thing as videotape then.

In 1959 I was invited to inaugurate a playwriting course in the Escola de Arte Dramatica[8] which made the resumption of the Arena courses unnecessary: anyone who wanted could go to the EAD.

We were invited to perform *Mice* on TV. Soap operas did not exist then – only on the radio. I was impressed by the TV Director, Luiz Gallon. Lennie, the protagonist, was persecuted in the forest, and Gallon created the illusion of an Amazon forest with just three cameras and two tree branches.

Come transmission time, adrenalin gushed from every pore: mistakes were not allowed, everything was live.

At the end of the year, Renato asked me to direct the next play. But what?

Thin husband, boring wife, and troublesome girlfriend

Hamlet – don't even think about it. I suggested a Copacabana boulevard comedy of mine, *Marido magro, mulher chata* (Thin Husband, Boring Wife), a play with few young characters.

After the tragic sadness of Steinbeck, a comedy of the kind we used to call, ashamedly, 'unpretentious' would be salutary. A Brazilian play was usually considered 'box-office poison', but an 'unpretentious' comedy was forgivable. The set and props: borrowed sofas, gardens made from borrowed artificial flowers, hired dinner-jackets, borrowings from family wardrobes.

I was happy. The telephone rang: it was my new girlfriend, Maria Christina, an actress recently arrived from England. She had been studying drama and was a cultured woman, intelligent, pretty and smart. She spent all her time talking about Peter Brook and I was smitten with jealousy. She spoke of the marvels of Europe, its diverse cultures, and I had just arrived from the United States, where everything was the same. But it was Peter Brook who made me most jealous. January 1957. Long ago.

Our courtship went well, we were happy. We could not have been more sincere, we always said what we were thinking – too much so. On the day of the opening, Maria Christina surpassed herself in her exuberant directness: she was so sincere . . . damn it! At openings, special attention has to be paid to the sensitivities of those about to perform. Maria Christina went beyond the limits, way beyond.

I had given her the play to read and awaited her opinion, ready to hear her sing my praises down the telephone:

'Did you like it?'

'Rubbish. I'm avoiding using the word "shit", because today is the day of the opening and you might have taken it as some kind of encouragement!' [In Brazil, like in France, we say *merda* to wish the actors luck, just as the British say 'break a leg'.]

'What did you say?! The line is terrible . . . this telephone company is really useless . . . I can't understand anything you're saying. . . .'

'Oh yes you do, you understand perfectly! This play is rubbish! How is it that you are capable of directing such a moving Steinbeck, a show which made me cry – and bear in mind that I do not cry at just anything – you do a show that made me cry, and then you go and do an appalling piece of worthless slapstick . . . it leaves me fuming!'

'Shall we talk about it after the opening?'

'I don't even know if I'll still be going out with you after the opening. . . . Just imagine, the two of us in bed, and those stupid ridiculous dialogues come into my head! It would kill any passion stone dead.'

I argued that the characters were ridiculous, and that the play was a critique of the immature youth of Copacabana. . . . At least, that is the argument that came to me, caught off guard as I was. (I had to say something, didn't I?)

'A critique of what, Augusto? What on earth is going on in your brain? It does not critique anything: it is pure complacency! Absolute horror!'

'Alright, but the script is only *part* of the show, it isn't the *whole thing*. . . . Come tonight! I'll reserve as many tickets as you like! You'll see that all the social critique is in the actors' performances. They are great. . . .'

'God save me from seeing this national disgrace . . . I've got better things to do. I'm going to stay home. In bed, with Brecht . . . rereading Brecht . . . In fact, you should start reading him. . . . He's great! He died in Germany when you were rehearsing Steinbeck. I think he even died on the opening night. And if Shakespeare were alive, he would die tonight! Of shame!'

The stuff of love. A slight surfeit of lovers' sincerity. She would not shut her mouth, and my ears were burning on the end of the black telephone, like the one in my father's bakery: I instantly regressed! She spoke again of Peter Brook. . . . (Ah, Peter, you'll pay for this!)

'OK, but Peter also does light comedy . . . I saw one, on Broadway . . . a musical comedy called *House of Flowers*. Well done, very entertaining, but light comedy all the same . . . prostitutes and policemen in pyjamas . . . I saw it myself . . . I did. . . .'

I was dying of jealousy, I didn't know if my memory was right or wrong, but I carried on remembering all the famous directors who might once have directed a little peccadillo! She would hear none of it. She argued that Peter Brook had put on *Titus Andronicus* with Lawrence Olivier and Vivien Leigh, and I hadn't. She recounted to me, not sparing the detail, the entire curricula vitae of Peter, Vivien and Lawrence, Redgrave père, Gielgud, Dame Edith, Peggy, Paul . . . I hung up on her. Macho!

On that opening night she turned up at the last minute, entering the auditorium in the dark, hidden. The audience laughed from start to finish! At the end of the show, they would not stop applauding. Maria Christina came to find me in the dressing-rooms. 'You were right: the script is not the whole show. . . .' She praised the freshness of the actors, the intelligence of the direction, she liked everything. (Women . . .!) 'No. You're the one who was right. The play is crap!' (Men . . .!)

I went home to a sandwich supper on my own. Bitter victory. Maria Christina was right: I had betrayed my Penha characters, I was a traitor to the workers' cause, to the socialist revolution, to the New Man, to Stanislavski and Chekhov, to the famous Theatre with a capital 'T', to my Ideology with a capital 'I', there was nothing left. Nothing with a capital 'N'! Traitor with the most minuscule 't' in the universe!

Maria Christina came to visit me later, after dining with friends. By that time I was serene and told her that her dressing-down had helped me to see clearly, to return to my true idea of theatre. Maria Christina was affectionate. But before things went any further I asked: 'Won't you find yourself remembering my dialogues, won't that kill your passion stone-dead?' She said not. As it was late, she preferred to stay with me until sunrise. (Couples . . .!)

Theatre for whom?

After this, I returned to selective realism and to *seriousness*, with Sean O'Casey's *Juno and the Paycock* (which opened on 5 June 1957), a master-piece about the civil war in Ireland. I invited the poet Manoel Bandeira to translate it. The translation was perfection. The cast included Sadi Cabral, from whom I had first heard the name Stanislavski.

It was a precise show – emotion with rigour. In the audience tears were shed at the irrationality of the war, the pointless deaths. Especially the scene in which Vianninha, the traitor to the guerrillas, surrounded by his excomrades and knowing all is lost, goes down on his knees and prays: Hail Mary, Mother of God. The lights faded to black, in the darkness a single shot rang out. When the lights came up again, there were tears on everyone's cheeks. Curious: the sight of suffering left us happy. The ways of theatre are inscrutable. . . . Theatre is a means of coming to an understanding with pain, dominating it. We make theatre to be masters of pain!

It was a pity that the subject did not inspire many people. The Irish civil war was so distant. . . . The audience would say: 'You know, I liked it, but . . . I did not understand it at all.' 'You know, I liked it, but . . .!' does not presage great success – still less 'I did not understand it at all' . . . *Juno and the Paycock* ran for two months. The fact that the text was a masterpiece and the show a gem was not enough – something more was needed. But what?

Who for ?

For whom is one making theatre? For oneself or for the public – and which public? I was a 'Columbia Man', and that university training made me think of literary texts, the 'great works' found in anthologies, without taking into account realities which were happening outside the theatre. It was as though I were trying to be the pride of my teachers. It was as if I was doing it for an end-of-year exam in New York, without thought for its São Paulo audience. My preoccupation grew stronger: For whom am I directing my shows?

I have always liked rigour, but how to negotiate the encounter between director and actor: the latter's subjectivity – when he is a good actor – tends to demand more time and space than the former can allow him.

The work of the Actors' Studio allowed a degree of self-indulgence on the part of the actors. 'Are you OK?' a character would ask; and the other actor would look at his glass, pick it up, roll it in his hands, lift it to his lips, take a sip, put it down on the table, push it away from him and, then reply: 'Yeeeeeaaahhhhhh. . . .'

That happened mostly in cinema. My God, were there pauses! When the actors were Marlon Brando or James Dean all would be forgiven. Unfortunately, most were not.

Stanislavski, while giving freedom to his actors, never forgot the interrelation of characters — an interdependence which is social and exists in concrete, measurable time and space, not merely in the incommensurable subjectivity of the actor. The Actors' Studio created a species of expressionist realism. . . . In such dialogues, what showed was what was going on in each person's head rather than what was going on in the relationship between the two characters. A difficult equilibrium.

When it comes to women, I know what I am talking about!

A true story illustrates this conflict.

Pedro Paulo was a well-informed theatre director; he spoke several languages, read all the theatre magazines, and was in love with the lead actress, Anabela, who also spoke several languages and was extremely well informed — on top of being pretty. Cultured people, in the sense that they possessed much accumulated knowledge — most of it useless. They were what Nelson Rodrigues used to call 'illiterate in several languages'.

They were rehearsing Strindberg's *Miss Julie*, and Hamilton Manga was playing the part of the servant; he was an excellent actor who could only speak Portuguese — they say he had a vocabulary as rich and varied as next door's parrot, which learned to speak in old age[9] . . . Manga would spend ages listening to erudite conversations between Pedro Paulo and Anabela in English, French or Italian, languages they both negotiated with an acrobatic ease.

There was Manga, cut out of the conversation, furious, but staying the course. He even felt guilty for being so ignorant of matters idiomatic, on top of his other various areas of ignorance. He heroically swallowed the quotations from Corneille, Molière, Dante, Ariosto, Homer, Racine. After such polyglot explanations, Pedro Paulo would ask, maliciously 'Did you understand, Hamilton?'

'Sort of.'

'Then say it back to me!' he would demand cruelly.

'Let's start rehearsing!' implored Manga, a man who, once on stage, was a communicator with marvellous presence, conveying everything, especially when he understood nothing.

'The cow that produces milk does not know what it is doing . . .' Nelson used to say.

These were torture sessions. Hamilton, baring his teeth, swore vengeance. The director would ask him something and Manga would reply with another stupid question; for example, what is the difference between a camel and a dromedary, a spider and a silkworm, a palm and a coconut tree? Is a table a quadruped? His was a mulish anger, which harboured desires for vengeance.

Then the day came. There was Pedro Paulo, as splendid as ever, scattering erudition in all languages; and a sullen Hamilton, a wet blanket, till he hears the life-saving phrase 'Let's rehearse!' Pedro Paulo told him to improvise a scene on the stairs after the manservant and Miss Julie have spent the night making love.

When the improvisation was over, the director gave vent to mediaeval curses, saying that Hamilton had not understood a single thing, that Strindberg was one of the greatest writers of his time and that he could not allow this total assassination of a masterpiece. . . .

'Explain in Portuguese, for God's sake! What was wrong with what I did?'

'They have spent the night screwing, do you hear? All he ever wanted in life and he gets it: the whole night long, him and the little rich girl. They went to bed at nine at night, now it is seven in the morning' – he exaggerated. 'So, the young man is ecstatic, he opens the bedroom door and comes down the stairs, vaulting them two at a time, three at a time, jumping for joy, whooping, he is a happy man, do you understand? He is not the sad character you just did, dragging himself down the stairs, staggering like a drunkard. . . .'

'They have spent the whole night screwing, from nine at night to seven in the morning?'

'That's right: he is happy as never before! Which is why he leaps the stairs two at a time. . . .'

'I quit. I resign. Today, right now.'

Shock horror: the publicity was out, it would not be possible to replace Hamilton; apart from anything else, he had a following.

'Have you gone mad? Why do you want to quit?'

'Because you may well know a thing or two about Schopenhauer and Spinoza, aesthetics and philosophy, but when it comes to screwing, I know what I am talking about: if he spent the night having sex, he is tired, he is shagged out, no way can he come down the stairs doing these prissy little leaps you're so keen on!'

He was right. The director wanted a joyful scene, with frisky tripping characters, but the actor could not pretend. Sex, if it is any good, is exhausting!

Discipline

When I directed Júlio Cortazar's *Nada Mais a Calingasta* (Nothing More To Calingasta), in the Schauspielhaus in Graz, Austria, I was working on the blocking and I asked an actor to go behind a table with a book in his hand and, book still in hand, to threaten to throw it at another character. The actor did as asked, but the very moment he raised the book with his right hand, he looked at his watch on his left wrist and said: 'It's 2 p.m.'

Cortazar's NOTHING MORE TO CALINGASTA *directed by Boal at* Schauspielhaus *in Graz, Austria, 1982*

Surprised, I asked: 'So?'

'According to union rules, the rehearsal should finish at 2 p.m.'

He stood with the book still raised in threat, looking at his watch. I asked if it would be possible to finish blocking the scene; he said he would rather obey the union's working hours. I agreed, disappointed.

The following day, on the dot of 9 a.m., the actor went behind the table, lifted the book in an attitude of threat and asked: 'What now? What shall I do with the book?'

The Germanic actor is like that: the director only has to say something once and it sticks for life. But he has to say it before 2 p.m., union rules. . . .

The Nuremberg *Schauspielhaus*, rehearsing Griselda Gambaro's *La Malasangre*. Arranging the set, I put a small table right in the centre of the stage. The next day, I thought that the table didn't work where it was and decided to change its position. I went up on to the stage and moved it to the left. I went down the steps, with my back to the stage, sat down, and had the impression that I had not moved the table enough, because it seemed to be still in the middle. I went back up and pulled the table well to the left. I went down, sat, looked, and – it was not possible! – the table was back in the middle.

Marina Vlady as the Grandmother in CANDIDA ERENDIRA *by Garcia Marquez, directed by Boal at Théâtre de l'Est Parisien, Paris, France, 1982*

To explain the mystery, I went back up on stage, changed the table's position again and backed down the stairs, never taking my eyes off the stage: quick as a shot, a stage-hand replaced the little table in its old position.

I protested: stop playing around! He replied and my translator translated:

'You may be the director, but I take orders from the stage-manager. If you want to change the table, you can do so to your heart's content, but first you must speak to your translator so that she can explain it to your assistant, so your assistant can then go and explain it to my stage-manager, and the stage-manager will give me a new order, and then yes, I will move the table wherever you want, first on my floor-plan, and then on stage!'

I had to explain to the translator, who explained to the assistant, who explained to the stage-manager, who gave the order to the stage-hand. . . . It took time, but I managed to move the table a few centimetres to the left, and counted myself lucky that no seal, stamp, bribe nor verified signature had been necessary!

One heart

The *Schauspielhaus* has a statutory obligation to provide a varied repertoire to the public of its city. Each night a different play: a German classic, a French boulevard comedy, a modern play, a musical. . . . That kind of production-line production engendered the bureaucratisation of artistic production. If even the vanguard shows are rigidly predetermined, where does that leave the vanguard? As a collective art-form, the creation of a

ZUMBI
A musical samba *play performed by Austrian and German actors at the* Schauspielhaus *in Graz, Austria, 1983*

team is vital in theatre; whether this is achieved by contractual rigour or emotional ties, there must be a team.

In my life, teams have existed on a variety of occasions and for diverse reasons. When Guarnieri and I wrote, and Edu Lobo put to music, *Arena Conta Zumbi* (Arena Tells of Zumbi), we were never apart, rehearsing parts of the script and the music as they became ready. At night, we presented Molière's *Tartuffe* and after supper, writers and actors would go back to my place till dawn. Guarnieri and I used to take turns on the typewriter, with others around us making suggestions, and Edu locked in another room, composing. Together, we created this unity, this heart, not only because we were a family but also because we were united ideologically, in struggle against the recent installation of the civic-military dictatorship, which killed so many people, and which caused so much irreparable damage.

It was the same with *Arena Conta Tiradentes* (Arena Tells of Tiradentes – Tooth-puller, the nickname of Joaquim José da Silva Xavier, a Brazilian hero who was hung, drawn and quartered for leading the movement of independence from Portugal). We opened *Tiradentes* in Ouro Preto, where the hero lived; before the opening, we did some quasi-invisible theatre: the actors played scenes in bus queues, at tables in bars, dressed as the characters, but making it look more like reality and less like theatre. The spectators were staggered to hear talk of insurrection, of non-payment of tithes to the Crown, etc. A geat way of rehearsing). It had the same writers, music by Gilberto Gil, Caetano Veloso, Theo de Barros and Sydney Miller. And so also with *Arena Conta Bolivar*, with my script and music by Theo.

In Graz, staging a play about my own exile, *Murro Em Ponta de Faça* (Blows At Knifepoint) – with actors I had never seen before, in a country I had never visited, in a language I never managed to learn – even then, we created a family; I felt an affection for all the actors, who were in solidarity with me, knowing I had written that play with suffering, a denunciation of the dictatorship. The actors felt the drama of exile – not only professional exile, the vicissitudes of the profession – but also because the themes of diaspora and exodus are tragically alive in the European memory.

Sadly, I do remember instances of the contrary. When I did *L'Incroyable et Triste Histoire d'Erendira et sa grand-mère diabolique*[10] in the Théâtre de l'Est Parisien, in the year in which Garcia Marquez won the Nobel Prize for

Literature, everything about the show was good, but it lacked a heart. The performances were good, including Marina Vlady as the protagonist; the set and costumes were admirable, the music great, the lighting masterly, my direction seemed excellent to me . . . but it lacked the essential ingredient. There were a lot of hearts, but they were not beating in unison. Every night the police came, threatening to close the theatre on account of excess spectators: it had it all, except a heart.

It was the same with *O corsário do rei* (The King's Corsair) which marked my return to Brazil; Chico Buarque's words were as beautiful as Edu's music; the actors were great, right from the heroes Marco Nanini and Denise Bandeira down to the last of the crowd; my script and direction were good; in the orchestra we had fifteen teachers chosen from among the best in Rio de Janeiro; the producers did not skimp on Hélio Eichbauer's stunning and expensive sets, including two ships on stage, cannons discharging balls of blue fire in bloody naval battles, with beautiful choreography.

It too lacked a heart: the Corsair Duguay-Trouin merely moved us intellectually. . . .

'*Que voulez-vouz?*' asked my psychoanalyst, Dr. René Major, on my return to Paris where I was living. 'You stage a play in which a French Corsair occupies and pillages Rio de Janeiro. It is natural that you should be confused with the protagonist: after fifteen years of exile, you return from France to invade the Brazilian theatre, with such an expensive show. . . . They thought you were the Corsair. . . .'

They Don't Wear Black-Tie

The second season of 1957 was not good. Our theatre was small, and one hit show did not provide enough funds to meet the following month's salary bill.

Our Playwriting Course was bearing its first fruits: many plays had been written by new authors. With the Laboratory, we were seeking Brazilian forms of representation, but the plays were all foreign. We were in a terrible economical crisis. It was make-or-break time. We either had to affirm our identity or close. We decided to put on *Eles Não Usam Black-Tie* (They Don't Wear Black-Tie) by Guarnieri.

Meanwhile, I received an invitation to direct *Society em Baby-Doll* by Henrique Pongetti produced by Dercy Gonçalves' husband. My heart was not in it, but José Renato, the owner of the theatre, had the right to direct Guarnieri's play. As money was scarce, there was not enough to pay all our salaries. I would not wish that affliction on any director: directing a play in one theatre while your thoughts and affections are in another. Fortunately, Maria Christina had gone to live in Rio and we were no longer lovers.

At the end of a rehearsal, each actor would go his own way, unlike at Arena. I used to go to *Black-Tie* to hear about the rehearsals. I realised that theatre could also be done by individuals who did not constitute themselves in a 'family', as we did. Protestations of eternal love were not necessary. At the Arena, we looked and behaved like *amateurs* in the true sense of the word – we loved theatre and loved each other! Theatre was only theatre among brothers, as it had been in *The Count of Monte Cristo*.

Both shows were hits, which was good for Brazilian theatre. That is what we most needed: to end the stigma of it being 'box-office poison'.

Black-Tie was a gigantic step – for the first time our actors played a script which truly spoke of our people. Empathy arose from this total identity, as opposed to the more distant analogy we experienced with foreign plays.

So on the one hand, our financial problem was resolved; on the other, it delayed my return to the Arena as a director of plays, although I continued to direct the Laboratory and the Seminar.

I was then invited to do *The Waltz of the Toreadors* by Jean Anouilh. For the first time I experienced the pleasure of working with a designer: Gianni Ratto. Despite being fifteen years older than me and famous – he had even directed operas in La Scala Milan, which he had helped to found! – Ratto did not impose his views and offered me alternatives for what I wanted. It is marvellous to work like that. I cannot draw, but I would talk and feel as if I were drawing with his hands; I cannot paint and I felt as if I were painting with his brushes. The sets he made were absolutely what I wanted and absolutely him. Thank you, Gianni Ratto.

A polite way of putting it would be to say that *The Waltz* was an exercise in style, but it had nothing to do with me. Anouilh left me cold. In the midst of the rehearsals I surprised myself by asking 'What am I doing here?' It was not that the play was bad: it just had nothing to do with me, nor me with it! Did anyone hear my thoughts? No: I had thought in a quiet voice . . . and I dropped the volume of my thinking further still. Infuriated, a voice from within said to me: 'I heard what you're thinking! Shame on you! Directing a show you wouldn't recommend to friends!' 'Who are you?' I asked myself: 'I am the person speaking, me myself, you: Augusto Boal. . . .' If psychological torture exists, that was it. The play was neither success nor failure, not anything, no one, no-thing.

The huge amount I learned with Dercy

Black-Tie continued to cruise along, and another invitation came my way: to direct Dercy Gonçalves in a ghastly melodrama, *Dona Violante de Miranda*, by Abílio Pereira de Almeida, which she wanted to transform into a slapstick comedy.

Abílio was not a great playwright, but had the merit of treating taboo subjects. On the *paulista* stage no young woman had ever had an abortion. With him, it was clear to all that in the days before the Pill abortions abounded.

In Dercy's case, I cannot say it was a relapse into triviality: I had a positive desire to work with her. Just as I would like to have worked with the clown Piolim, whom I knew from my youth, or with any of those circus actors or musical performers, who had their own style and their own particular mastery of the audience. I wanted to see them in the act of creation. Brecht knew about this; his *Verfremdungseffekt* brings to mind circus clowns, serious people.[11]

I knew that Dercy was un-directable, but I wanted to try: I remembered Grande Otelo (baptised Grande by Orson Welles, when he was in Brazil). He used to say that he was the only person who could play opposite her. Why?

'Because other actors try to make a fight of it, and end up losing out, because she is funnier and eats everyone else up. Not me: I let her go! She goes on and talks and talks, gets the laughs, and does what she wants, and when she pauses for breath, on I come with my act! She wins her bit, and I win mine!'

My 'direction' consisted of laughing or not laughing at things she did: if I laughed she would always repeat what she'd done . . . until she had had her fill. If I did not find it funny, she would change tack. It was very different from rehearsals in the Arena, in which we used to debate the deep significance of every gesture, the metaphysical importance of each look, doing a philosophical exegesis of each pause! With Dercy, laughter was language . . . I communicated with her through laughter.[12]

The rhythm of clown-actors, or full-blown clowns, is something you only learn by experiencing it. Dercy had so much experience of audiences that, every night, she would look through a hole in the curtain and say: 'Awful house today: it'll be three minutes before the first laugh.'

Or else: 'Today it's a cinch: they'll laugh as soon as the curtain goes up. . . .' – And it would be just as she said.

Dercy was not an actress, but an entertainer – someone endowed with specific qualities, a trade mark. In Brazil there are some excellent entertainers: whatever play they do, they do not change at all, all the characters they play are in their own image. No matter if they are playing Romeo one day, Juliet the next, makes no difference. This is not a demerit, but a condition. It is only bad when the entertainer plays a character greater than himself and reduces that character to his own petty dimensions.

In those days there used to be an 'ideology patrol': the 'politically correct' held the upper hand and Abílio was considered to be less than 'right on'. Not because of his plays, but because of his subjects: it was not 'politically correct' to waste time on the defects of the bourgeoisie. The bourgeoisie was not even worthy of a hiding!

Dona Violante was about prostitution. Everyone knew that millionaires kept chorus-girls as lovers, who were picked up at the stage door by luxury cadillacs, 'fish tails', but that was a taboo subject. Everyone had lurid stories involving suicides, romantic scandal, veins slashed with razor-blades, but . . . silence. The noble *paulista* bourgeoisie was untouchable: just silk and scent, and charity balls.

Abílio opened it up for all to see. It reminded me of a story I once heard around a rich table, when I dined with a traditional family, all distinguished and elegant ladies and gentlemen, with half the dialogue in French. In the middle of the dessert, after a lot of talk about family trees, someone asked: 'Auntie, wherever did those French and Polish prostitutes who used to brighten up our festivities end up? They have disappeared. Where could they be?'

The aunt, laconically: 'They're all married into our families.'

The worthy lady liked to shock. . . . But she touched a sore point and there was much clearing of throats before the table talk became animated again. There was truth in what she said: *paulista* millionaires used to fall in love with Parisian prostitutes who, on traversing the Atlantic, re-found their lost virginity. In São Paulo, Pigalle was sanctified.

Violante, a brothel-owner, was a serious person. In order to demystify her, it was necessary to present her, initially, as mysterious, kind of Mrs Warren.[13] The character had to appear honourable so that, later, her dishonour could be revealed.

I achieved miracles in rehearsal: Dercy playing a society lady, full of dignity. She followed my directions – 'religiously' would be the wrong word to apply when it comes to Dercy, but like an obedient student! Little by little, as the drama's revelations exploded, the true unmasked Violante appeared, i.e. the Dercy of always.

I was so amazed that I did something ethically incorrect, but forgivable given my good intentions: I invited actors from the Arena to observe a rehearsal, submerged in the dark at the back of the auditorium. They were astonished: Dercy under the artistic control of a director.

Then along came the première, along came the audience, along came uncontrollable instinct.

Like the fabled scorpion who asks the frog to carry him on his back to cross the river: faced with the reluctance of the frog, the scorpion promises on his honour that he will not sting him, convincing him of his sincerity with the argument that if he were to use his sting, both of them would die – the scorpion drowned and the frog poisoned. Halfway across, the scorpion cannot resist, he stings the frog's nape and, before they both die, asks forgiveness: 'Sorry, my dear frog – it is my nature!' Dercy, hearing the audience's laughter, could not contain herself and, from the very first scene on, unmasked and revealed herself: her nature was stronger than she was.

★   ★   ★

Chapetuba Football Club

I went back to Arena at the end of 1958 and started directing Vianninha's *Chapetuba FC*. I have never rehearsed for so long: six months. Vianna had time to write ten versions of the script during the rehearsals. Sometimes he did not accept our ideas, but rewrote it with the same angle, with greater energy and clarity.

On entering the Arena, the visitor would bump into mini-laboratories everywhere, even in the toilets. No one could say even so much as a word of their lines if they had not done a laboratory exercise. Chico de Assis tells me that when rehearsing the part of Cafuné, the illiterate footballer in *Chapetuba*, he had difficulties understanding what an illiterate would feel looking at a newspaper. Chico himself had been literate at 4 years of age. . . . Solution – the laboratory! Chico looked in all the news-stands until he found an Arabic newspaper and then spent hours trying to decipher it: a one-man laboratory . . . which produced fine results: Chico was great in the role. Knowing Chico, I am sure he ended up learning how to read and write Arabic, as well as Berber, Kabila and other geographically close languages.[14]

We went to Marília for the première. It was a town of 100,000 inhabitants, 80 per cent of whom were Japanese, or descendants thereof. The venue was an enormous basketball stadium with an acoustic quick to amplify cheers, but hardly adequate for delicate passions: the audience could hear nothing, the actors couldn't hear each other. Disaster. At the end of the show, spectators came to ask us: 'Did the ball go in or not?'

We went running back to our intimate arena and had to re-rehearse and to rein back the stertorous shouts suited to the Marília Stadium. We learned that each show is the size of the theatre it is played in: if the space changes, the size of the show also changes.

After that experience, I began to do 'spatial' rehearsals every time we went on tour. Doing *Phèdre* with Fernanda Montenegro, we encountered theatres far and wide across the country: I used to ask the actors to go up to 'the Gods' or under the stage or round the corridors and, as they walked, to practise their dialogues from a distance in order to 'appropriate' the space, rather than merely accommodating themselves to the stage.

Chapetuba opened at the beginning of 1959 and had a five-month run. It was not the spectacular success of *Black-Tie*, but it was a success. I remember some actors from other companies were shocked with our full-blooded, sweaty style. Some, from the Brazilian Theatre of Comedy, said: 'What you do is moving, but it is not theatre: you don't interpret a role: you "live" it.'

Just as in Wuppertal: What is living, what is interpreting? Can you perfrom a role without living it – can you live without performing?

Many thought the same: that our actors made the audience cry, but that they were not actors – they were normal human beings, living and not performing. As a challenge, they would ask us if we would be capable of doing the same thing in classical plays. In my head, I answered yes: but you can really only answer a question like that on stage.

Years later, during the 'nationalisation of the Classics', we gave the answer: Yes, it can be done. It is not necessary for the play to deal with the quotidian; the actor's life is not in the accessory, it is in the nerve, in the heart. Or to put it better: if a classic is universal, it is so because it is Brazilian, otherwise it would not be universal.

Artistically, we were in disagreement with those TBC actors. They were the rich cousins, supported by millionaires, they got good wages which were never late, they were unacquainted with economic crisis. If the till was empty on account of a rare failure, someone would bail them out, and the till filled up again: pure magic!

Fernanda Montenegro, on TV, said that one of the advantages she felt when she joined the TBC was that she began to eat in better restaurants, with tastier spaghetti. At Arena, we used to eat in the bars at the corner. When a show bombed, it was bread and bananas all round.

As our theatre was small and our subsidies smaller, we were con-demned to touring. If the play was a hit, we were remorseful: why do a little 160-seat theatre, when our beloved public is in the Northeast? We wanted to show it to the peasant farmers: the *people*, who, like us, wanted agrarian reform rather than the slavery of paying the country's external debt.

Before continuing to launch new Brazilian writers, we decided to make a tour to the interior.

That was my baptism of fire.

The discovery of Rio de Janeiro

In Rio in the 1950s, the Communist Party became popular among artists. Some became members or sympathisers; others observed it from afar, warily. Others joined the PSB (Partido Socialista Brasileiro), and the 'commies' teased them saying: 'A socialist is a communist who won't get beaten up by the police!'

The world seemed to be changing for the better, a habitable planet! The Cuban Revolution expelled the gorilla Fulgêncio Batista, reclaiming the dignity of what had become 'the brothel of the United States'; sputniks were demonstrating the impetuous advance of Soviet science; Lumumba was starting the African Revolution in the former Belgian Congo — down with all colonialisms! Brasilia was rising up from the dry desert.

Fifty years in five. President Kubitchek's saying seemed to be coming true. Student movements and Peasant Leagues multiplied! The world was being put to rights.

In 1961 a Soviet theatre company appeared in São Paulo. Its actors came to fraternise at the Arena. The Soviets told of marvels. They spoke of Yuri Gagarin, Titov and Laika the puppy, barking in the Cosmos. We wanted to know about theatre — they told us of their prowess in space.

Gagarin was the first man to go round the Earth in an artificial satellite, on 12 April of that year; in August Titov did it twenty-five times in one day! Glory and proof of communist superiority. Spaceships were more important than Tolstoy or Chekhov.

For ourselves, in terms of spectacular marvels, apart from the goals of Pelé and Garrincha in Sweden, the photos of João Gilberto joyfully singing 'O Pato' (The Duck), and the films of Ruy Guerra, Glauber and Nelson Pereira dos Santos, we Brazilians had only a few photographs of Brasilia, an unfinished symphony: the houses of the capital's construction workers had yet to be built. We showed the Russians photos of the Cathedral, and they asked about the shacks in the satellite towns. 'Those are the temporary dwellings of the workers who built the city: soon they are going to build social housing where the people will live in dignity and comfort.' The pioneers' homes never arrived: even today they live in slums. The people who built Brasilia were not entitled to live there.

The Soviet Union was marching resolutely towards world leadership, thrusting past the United States. The next Pope would be a communist . . . Woytilja, in fact, was born in Poland . . . but. . . .

The Soviet actors left without telling us about the theatre in their country. By way of compensation, we were given souvenir figures of a smiling bitch barking happily in the cosmic heights.

Whenever any important figures of world theatre came to work in Brazil, we invited them to a dialogue with all São Paulo's artists. George Devine, Luigi Suarzina, Jean Vilar, Gassman, Jean Louis Barrault – they all came.

1812 – cannons and symphonies

I was particularly struck by one of Barrault's visits – he came twice – when he brought shows as diverse as Gide's translation of *Hamlet*, Kafka's *The Trial*, Lope de Vega's *The Gardener's Dog*, Claudel's *The Tidings Brought to Mary*, etc.

The Arena, jam-packed with artists. Barrault was asked his opinion on the relations between politics and theatre, our daily subject. He replied that, for him, politics was as foreign to theatre as cannon fire to a symphony. Alberto D'Aversa[15] remembered that in Tchaikovsky's *1812 Overture* you can hear not just one but several salvoes of cannonfire . . . in perfect harmony with the rhythm and the melody.

A curious affirmation from someone who had shown us *Les Mains Sales*,[16] in which the purity of the French Communist Party was called into question. Another strange thing: precisely because of party political and psychological fluctuations, Sartre later banned productions of this play, and at Arena we had to abandon it when it was already in rehearsal.

The party

Leaders of the Party came to induce us to affiliate, explaining their political vision, i.e. alliance with the national bourgeoisie. This was how imperialism would be confronted. The Communist Party (PC) thought there were two capitalisms in our native conjuncture, one good, the other evil: the first was in the interests of the fatherland, the second the figurehead of the Yankees. Not all of us followed this ratiocination.

I was always averse to party life and the discipline demanded of the militant. The mere idea of joining a party gave me a cramp. I did not believe in simplistic analyses, and was unsuccessful in imagining complex ones. So I never joined the PC, but I respected most of those who did. As in any party, there were honest people and there were opportunists. Then, as now.

'The people' – who were they?

Our discussions turned more on the political than the aesthetic. The most urgent question that exercised us was: To whom should our theatre be addressed? Our audience was middle class. Workers and peasants were our characters (in itself an advance!) but not our spectators. We did theatre from the perspective which we believed to be 'of the people' – but we did not perform *for* the people! What was the point of representing working-class characters and serving them up, as a pre-dinner treat, to the middle class and the rich?

We longed for a popular audience, without ever seeing it in flesh and blood. 'The people' was a chimera. The dream was to engage in dialogue with 'the people' . . . to whom we had never been introduced. The people: we did not define what this was, where it worked, what it ate, how it loved, what it did. We knew what it was not: middle class, our audience. We wanted to be at the service of this mysterious and much loved 'people', but . . . we were not the people.

Some theatre groups had 'their' factory worker, 'their' peasant farmer – as well as more than enough of 'their' students! – these were the 'people' in each theatre group. . . . Our peasant farmer, who frequented our theatre for years, was called Manoel de Oliveira. A skinny man, with a sparse beard, he was a devoted eater. Of course we paid for his beef and onions and fried eggs: for us, he was the symbol of the peasantry, our 'people'. He lived in a *favela* and grew lettuces and tomatoes in his backyard. He was the 'people'! Is a person who plants only lettuce and tomatoes a peasant?

The participation of a peasant or factory worker, that human concre-tion of an abstraction (class), seemed to legitimise the work of the company. Our peasant liked the play, our peasant thinks that we are doing the right thing; before long, our peasant speaks on behalf of the countryside, of agrarian reform, of national liberation, of the New Man! Long live 'our' peasant!

Our peasant is right, *ipso facto* we are right too. Our factory worker said so, *ipso facto*, amen! A single being could represent the whole class, the individual was the genus, as if the whole was made from the multiplication of the one, by replication. Ideological cloning.

We knew that the 'people' did not go to the theatre. Arena, the new Diogenes, would have to venture out with a lantern in search of the 'People', just as the philosopher went in search of 'Man'. It was necessary for the Mountain and Mohammed to meet somewhere: Mohammed and the Mountain would have much to talk about, many ideas to swap. Arena and the People, face to face: what a glorious day that would be!

Cars and guinea-pigs

Arena decided to intensify its journeys in search of Utopia. We wanted to meet our true interlocutor. São Paulo – the world's second largest city, second to Tokyo but above New York, Mexico, London and other lesser entities – had become small and shrunken for us: São Paulo Lilliput. We made deals with clubs and councils which paid for shows in halls, open-air amphitheatres and the street, where part of the 'people' we were looking for were to be found, dissolved in the lumpen crowd. Was this *the* 'people' or just a lot of people? Could such a disorganised, wandering 'lot of people' be considered to be 'the people'? Or was it necessary to have a union card? Are you only of 'the people' if you attend a trade union or Peasant League? Does the Brazilian Union of Students entitle you to certificated membership of 'the people'? And what of a very progressive church? Or a Residents Association? In the end, who had the right to that coveted title: 'the people'? We played anywhere. In the open air, a frog on stage was a common occurrence, as were bats flying past the actors, curtailing their Stanislavskian interrelationships. Concentration is difficult when cohabiting with bats and dogs and cats.

I am not complaining: it was not all difficulty. The car firm DKW-Verlag magnanimously decided to lend us a fleet of four vehicles for one month.

Along with their blue bonnets came Werner, the German mechanical engineer, yellow of hair and boot, not to mention smile.[17] He barely spoke Portuguese, but he understood motors and roads. We were overjoyed at the firm's generosity: it even paid for the petrol and the engineer's wages.

Strange roads the engineer chose – the worst and most risky, full of brush and loose stones. If we had to choose between a reasonable asphalt road and one full of pot-holes, Werner preferred the mud and earth. Dancing all over the track at 150 kmph on slippery mud, risking life and limb, bathed in a cold sweat.

In the second week of the trip, a huge storm struck in the middle of the night along the muddy road. Rain and thunder. We wanted to stop at the first village, to wait for blue sky, but Werner, transfigured, possessed, wanted to press on, storm-besotted. His frenzied enthusiasm was contagious. Along we went, singing – not in the rain, like Gene Kelly, but in the tempest, torment, tornado! – dodging bolts of lightning, deafened by thunder, soaked to the marrow. It rained inside the cars – squashed up together, sweating, we would open the windows to cool down, only to be drenched by torrential splashes, as it rained rain.

We came to a wooden bridge over the river in the middle of the forest, and had to stop because there was only room for one vehicle at a time. We had to wait for buses and trucks coming in the opposite direction to cross first. Werner told us to get out of the cars, into that rain and wind: it would be better for the cars to cross the bridge at high speed, one at a time. We did not understand why, but obeyed him: a German engineer, a specialist, he knew better . . . we were wretched artists, specialists in being rained on. We laughed and sang, hysterically.

At bottom, we were afraid: there we were in the middle of God knows where, on the way to God knows what, some unknown place . . . and the night was growing darker and more terrifying, the cold was getting colder. The wind was no joke! It was cold and we were sweating! We saw the torrential river's cascading heights, galloping down, smashing against the wooden bridge, masses of water drenching the hard wood, swirling over and under. Torrents, rushing. We were afraid, and we were laughing.

Our turn came and we crossed: those on foot ran; then, each car crossed the fragile wooden bridge, at speed, bouncing on to the rolling stones to happy, nervous applause. We were afraid, and we were applauding.

As the last car passed, the rain passed too. We bade farewell to the driver of a lorry going in the opposite direction: now it was his turn. We went on. We were afraid, and we talked loudly.

We looked for a hotel on the map and there was none. Darkness. Hunger and thirst. We were afraid and we wanted to sleep.

Two kilometres ahead, the beautiful image of a roadside café rose into view – a mirage. Joy of joys, it was bricks and mortar. No one is made of steel. We made Werner stop: we were afraid of the road and the mud. We ate *mortadella* sandwiches and drank *cachaça*: some drank it neat, others took it with lemon or honey, making excuses that it was good for the throat, good for projection.

We thought the strange driving was the German engineer's mania. Germans are like that, what can you do? Till we discovered the truth: DKW-Verlag wanted to test the stamina of its cars, to study how they coped with the worst terrain: they hoped to extend their market in the interior of the country. In this marriage between industry and art, we were the guinea-pigs.

Minutes later the lorry came back and its driver told us that before he had time to cross, the river had swept the bridge away . . . torn to pieces. . . . We could have been on that bridge. . . . We had had fear, now came terror! How difficult it was to get close to the people – a calvary. Why did the people hide themselves away? Could they not dwell a little bit nearer?

By sheer luck, we were alive. We made a point of looking at each other, touching each other, making sure we were awake, counting our party on our fingers, one by one, calling out all our names, one by one: were we all alive, all of us? Did no one drown?

Alive . . . we continued our search for the enchanted 'people'.

Marriages, made and unmade

It did not always rain; there were some sunny intervals. Even in the dry, the journeys were tough. Driving in Renato's van at night, he would ask us to sing loudly, not because he enjoyed our tunes, but to avoid falling asleep at the wheel. To save money, we used to sleep in school dormitories or *pensions*; plus the odd hotel, one star or half a star, if that.

Excess of work created tensions. In our case this was exacerbated because we used to mix politics and aesthetics, ideology and love life, Brecht and Stanislavski. When the cast changed, a new set of emotional bonds would be established.

One actor couple decided to separate. The artistic director, in those circumstances and at that tender age, had various roles: emotional adviser was one of them. The ex-husband came to tell me that at 23 years of age, he did not understand women at all. I answered that it was the same with me, women were not made to be understood. Women – God bless them – are unknowable. If they weren't, they would lose their attraction.

The ex-wife came to tell me the reason: 'He used to bring me flowers . . .' she said, to my open-mouthed confusion.

'Isn't that touching? Roses are so romantic. . . . Don't you like them? Yellow roses are so pretty!'

'Boal, I wanted a steak . . . and he gave me roses.'

She wanted to eat, not look at flowers. She wanted beans and rice and he gave her sunflowers. I have seen separations of the converse nature, I have seen steak given to one hoping for daisies. People are never understandable! Real dialogue is, perhaps, impossible.

We began to think that perhaps it was not worth the trouble. For whom were we working, if it was not for money, of which there was so little? With whom were we in dialogue? Was it dialogue? We wanted to be heard. I don't remember if we wanted to hear, but I am sure that we wanted to be heard. Where were the right ears?

The audience in the interior: 400, 500 pairs of ears. In the street, a thousand. Nothing changed. In São Paulo, we played to those who could pay – the middle class. In the interior, we played to landowners and estate managers, in the clubs, and to the occasional passer-by, in the street. Where was the 'people'? The partner to whom we wanted to speak remained out of reach. We were still playing for the same public in the small cities as we did in Sao Paulo.

People Like Us

A new show: *Gente Como A Gente* (People Like Us) by Roberto Freire, from the Seminar. I liked the author's ideas but to me the play seemed melodramatic. There was a tendency among our authors (myself included) towards sentimentality. The snivelling of the Left. I confessed my limited enthusiasm, but I was the only director available. I agreed to do it. Should I have? I don't know. I thought it my duty, in fulfilment of Arena's nationalist aims (which were my own). Now, I think I should have said no. It was wrong, to stage a play I did not love.

The play required five different settings. How could we deal with such exuberant scenography in a space of 25 square metres? At Arena, each director saw to set and props by a trip to the flea market. Shows were lit according to an equation of directorial intuition and available wattage. I admitted my incapacity in both areas.

I invited Flávio Império to design the show, an architect who had never previously done any stage work but had a vast talent for making things by hand. Instead of being horrified at the task facing him, he took it as a challenge. He asked me questions and, before I knew it, I was talking and he was drawing. The miracle of Gianni Ratto was repeating itself. I cannot draw; with Flávio I drew.

Flávio used to make his students dance in the classroom, to get a sense of the space which they were to make habitable. Before drafting plans, they would dance. Some thought he was mad, others a genius. I am sure he was both. His starting point was a working unit, which would foreground the melodrama: the 'paralleliped'. Everything in the scenography was parallelipedal: of all sizes, from the room furniture to the nails on the railway line. If the dialogue was gentle, the scenery was austere and rough. The same contradiction operated in the casting: Riva, who by *physique de rôle* should have played the vamp, played the goody: the lovable Vera played the part of the evil woman. I swapped the roles, like Lana Turner and Ingrid Bergmann in *Doctor Jekyll and Mr Hyde*.

Flávio cut the arena in half with three metres of railway track and two different environments on each side of it. It looked great on the model. If everybody held their stomachs in and didn't breathe, there might even be room for the actors.

On paper, I was able to block it in such a way that each scene would not overlap into a contiguous area. But . . . in reality, how could we stop the lights bleeding into areas they weren't supposed to?

I sought help from Ziembinsky, the lighting expert. We had insufficient funds to pay such a luminary of illumination. After a chat with me, he got

1 8 0

Hamlet and the Baker's Son

to work, with us all the while not daring to ask what the cost of his labour would be.

Zimba drilled holes, hammered in nails, asked us to climb the ladder, to lower this light, change that blue cellophane, crumple it up to provide a warmer light – we did not have proper lighting gel, we were that poor! At the master's back, there we were, wanting to ask how much he would cost us, how many dinners we would be going without. Zimba ran through the lighting states, showing us his suggestion for each scene. We were dazzled by his simple and yet rich effects. Anxiously, we asked how much it would cost: 'It was a pleasure.' Often – not always – I have experienced an enormous solidarity among the Brazilian theatre class, which had the capacity on occasion to be united and strong. There were fine instances of this, some of which I relate in this book. Ziembinsky was a master of solidarity.

Gente Como A Gente had a euphoric opening, it was a huge success among friends, but not with the public. Once again, Arena was insecure. The lack of subsidies to support our project of launching national authors – a project which should have been taken on by the government – meant that we did not enjoy the slightest security.

Crisis, forever crisis

In the crisis of 1958, the Arena saved itself from disaster with *Black-Tie*. Now – at the end of 1960 – it was necessary to take another, riskier step. We decided to split the company: half in *A farsa da esposa perfeita* (The Farce of the Perfect Wife) by Edy Lima; half in *The Rio Adventure*.

Edy's play was set in Bagé, on the Uruguayan border: a young woman makes love with all her cock-fighting-mad husband's friends in order to achieve happiness for the pair of them, via the victory of her husband's cock – in the ring! She has no evil intent or unseemly lust; this is not conventional adultery, just common sense. We had a heated discussion: was this a worthy subject for us?

The play was funny, and economic verging on the beggarly (five actors, a sparse setting). It would reveal the reality of an unknown Brazil – the frontier. We could not spend the whole of our lives talking about São Paulo: Bagé was Brazil! Somewhat Spanish, it is true, with a speech peppered with *entonces*[18] and *chê*,[19] with *chimarrão* in the *cuia*,[20] but ours all the same. Brazil, *chê*! A sort of Spanish Brazil.

For me, till then realism meant speaking like a *paulista* – now I became aware of the existence of other Brazils.

We went all over in search of a 'Brazilian people' – and at every step I was seeing more 'peoples' in my people: Japanese from Marília, rustics from the interior, *paulistanos* of 400 years' occupation, *mineiros*[21] from Uberaba, *cariocas* from Copacabana, workers from Penha, Germans from Santa Catarina, Italians everywhere . . . and Swedes and Finns in the mountains. I was afraid of the Northeast: what would those 'flat-head' people be like?[22]

The people we sought were not defined by geography or history: they were a class. We were after the people in the fields and the factories, whatever their colour, whatever their clothing. 'The people' was a class.

Rio, rapture

We discovered a 'shopping centre' under construction in Copacabana, and went to speak to the proprietor, a Senator of the Republic.

The Senator had just assassinated a deputy of the National Congress[23] in the middle of a session. By accident, he explained: he was aiming at a rival Senator and – without meaning to, of course, by pure chance – killed the deputy, who simply failed to duck in time, having nothing to do with either the argument at issue or the rival Senator. He shot at the Senator and killed the deputy: impudent chance!

The Senator declared himself innocent: he had killed without malice, he had pulled the trigger at the wrong moment, pointing in the wrong direction. Poor Senator, he was suffering. . . . For this reason, he did not understand our demand to use his building, but he agreed to let us improvise a theatre where there is still an Arena today. Seating tiers made from salvaged wood.

Off we went again in search of the people. There was a contradiction, we knew: we were searching for the poor exploited worker, but we ourselves had to eat. This was the contradiction: if we went up the hillsides we would find audiences that were 'of the people', and poor; by the beach, there were the middle class and the rich.

The first show, *Black-Tie*, a hit again. Who came to see us? Those who could pay. Ideological torture. We found solace in the thought that intellectuals also came, people with whom we wanted to exchange ideas: the journey would not be in vain, even if we were not able to find the people. Why exclude the middle classes, who were trapped between hope of becoming better off and the anguish of becoming poorer – it was our duty to engage in dialogue with them, too.

The year was 1960, we were world champions at football and basketball, sports of the people; Maria Esther Bueno, Wimbledon champion, sport of the elite; Eder Jofre won with a knockout in the bantamweight boxing contest, a little-known sport. Bossa Nova was on the up, becoming a craze. Brasilia: President Juscelino was inaugurating the new capital on 21 April. The *Cinema Novo* was showing Brazil to Europe. We did not have to feel ashamed: the middle class was also the people! Since we were not encountering our 'people', we transformed everyone into 'the people'.

Then came *Revolução na América do Sul* (Revolution in South America), a play of mine I had just finished, in which the influence of Brecht was visible. José da Silva, exemplary factory worker, believes everything told him by bosses, television and newspapers: throughout the play, which was intercut with songs, José goes hungry, sustained by his belief. On election day, José is wooed by all the politicians, eventually eating a free *marmelada*[24] and dying, choked on his first forkful, having got out of the habit of eating. The politicians erect a statue in tribute to him, using his own body, complete with attendant speeches and appeals for votes. José was a sort of Don Quixote: he believed in everything politicians told him.

Renato directed *Revolução* and I was charged with the task of 'doing something' with our empty arena in São Paulo.

Arena, Godfather of Oficina

Benedito Rui Barbosa[25] had written a play about the frosts in Paraná, *Fogo Frio* (Cold Fire). Some people did not like the script. Without being absolutely in love with it, I took into account that this was a new writer showing promise. It was our 'mission' to help new playwrights take their first steps.

There were no actors left for me in São Paulo. José Celso Martinez Correia and Amir Haddad were directing an amateur group, *Oficina*

(Workshop). I proposed to them that they become professionals with Arena. They accepted. With their cast and my direction, the play opened in April 1960. It had the virtue of nurturing the professional beginnings of *Oficina*. And I had the pleasure of having José Celso as my assistant director, a man who would later become one of the best Brazilian directors.

A side effect: I got married for the first time, at 30, to the actress Albertina Costa, who was working at the Arena Theatre. I was overwhelmed by the ceremony, the ritual, the slow steps towards the altar – the bride with her father on the way up, and with me on the way back; the father's surrender of his daughter to me at the altar, in front of the guests and the priest, all in their finery, giving their consent; the raised arms blessing us. Marriage in church is a moving ceremony. (It puts the fear of God into you!)

Fogo Frio – apart from the marriage which lasted two years, and the season which lasted six months – added nothing to our work. We began to feel that our project was losing steam. Morally, it was right and useful; politically, too. Aesthetically, we were repeating ourselves, same ideas, same costumes. . . .

Other theatres had lost their fear of staging plays by national authors. Previously, theatres had been obliged by law to put on one Brazilian play for every two foreign ones! That was the only way of enabling our playwrights to be staged; now the inverse relationship operated. A Brazilian play was synonymous with success. The Arena's nationalistic line was no longer necessary.

L´Engrenage,[26] *Sartre*

Jean-Paul Sartre and Simone de Beauvoir had some trouble with the French government, on account of Algeria; having been advised to remove themselves from French territory, they came for two weeks, and stayed for months.

Oficina decided to stage a piece that Sartre had written for cinema: *L´Engrenage*, which never became a film. José Celso, Renato Borghi and I adapted it for the theatre and, once again, Celso was my assistant in staging the play, which included Ronaldo Daniel (who had dual nationality and became the famous English director, Ron Daniels).

With *L'Engrenage* I had my first serious battle with the censors, who banned a show we wanted to stage at Ipiranga, a monument to Brazilian Independence . . . as if Brazil was independent. Dozens of extras involved in our Eisensteinesque show were there when the police surrounded the square. We decided to gag ourselves and left in procession, handkerchiefs over our mouths, to the applause of bystanders and housewives at their windows. The ashamed police withdrew. We returned to the *Monumento* with redoubled fervour, and the police returned with redoubled intent to break our heads. Significant detail: they were armed with real weapons and our guns were theatrical props.

At the time I was beginning to experiment with a more open dramaturgy, outside realism. Brecht had influenced us, but more in the sense of freeing ourselves from naturalism than any sense of imitating him. The 'alienation effect', for us, already existed in the performance style of our clowns.

Revolution in South America

Revolução was my first important play. Some critics even talked of a masterpiece. Imagine my youthful delight, I was knocked out.

In formal terms, it was a revolution which provoked another revolution inside the Arena. Everyone praised it, but some bemoaned the fact that the play spoke of the poor to a middle-class audience. Always the same complaint. . . .

Vianninha and Chico de Assis thought that Arena had no future as long as it was a 'commercial' venture, living off the box-office, however much ideology we had in our heads. Ideology apart, to survive we had to fill the theatre and our bellies.

Brazil could not continue as a colony of the United States. We were not a Banana Republic, or a brothel! The theatre had to help liberate the country. How? By 'raising the consciousness' of popular audiences! Who would carry out the revolution? The people! Who would raise their consciousness? We would! Elementary, my dear Watson. . . .

At the time, 'consciousness-raising' was the new Divine Revelation. We were not raising our own consciousness: we were raising other people's. In the CPCs,[27] that was the keyword.

The Chê syndrome

Chê Guevara was our model of honesty, tenderness and bravery. He wanted to do good, to rescue the weak and oppressed – like Christ with machine-guns! He knew that Latin America was enslaved, he wanted to free its peoples: one, two, three, a thousand Vietnams, he used to say; he wanted to liberate Latin America. Chê did not want war; he loved peace and justice. To get it, there was only one way – and you had to follow it.

(Today, even Unesco proclaims in its official documents that the mere absence of war does not signify peace: while there is hunger and unemployment, sickness and illiteracy, prejudice and child labour – this is a world at war! Let us, the pacifists, make war on war. Peace, not passivity!)

Never has there been such an extreme desire for pacifism as that of Chê Guevara: with the possible exception of Gandhi, Luther King and Jesus! Before he found Fidel Castro, Chê fought in the Belgian Congo, in Mexico, and he considered fighting in Panama. At Fidel's side, he was the victorious commander of the Santa Clara battle, which divided the country in two: with eighteen guerrillas he overcame 400 well-armed government soldiers! He won, heroically. Once in power he did not adapt to the role of Minister of Finance: he was a warrior of peace. He bade farewell to the beloved people and returned to the struggle, to the jungle.

Even without the Bolivian peasantry asking for his help, Chê wanted to rescue them: he could not bear to see their miserable exploitation, their slave labour. He could not see them suffer. Chê had one desire: he could not see the wretched without wanting to free them, *even if it was against their will*! He abandoned his adoptive country and went to help them – or should I say, to oblige them?! – to bring about the same revolution that had had such a happy outcome in Cuba.

There was a difference: in Cuba the people wanted their revolution, had the capability to bring it about, and did so. Not in Bolivia. Chê was betrayed by the very peasant farmers he wanted to liberate by force.

I call this 'the Chê Syndrome', a condition to which so many of us at some point or another succumb. Wanting to free slaves by force: I have my truth, I know what's best for them, therefore let us do what I want them to do, now. I know it is right. I see what they cannot see: let them come with me, I want to open their eyes. They have to see what I see, since I see the right way! The best of intentions. The most authoritarian of practices — coming from above.

In Arena we limited ourselves to showing the life of the poor, as we were able to understand it. On stage, we dressed as workers and peasants: the costumes were authentic, but not the bodies which wore them. Unhappy sentimentality. But I do not want, today, to lament our griefs of yesteryear. We did what we could!

As our dissatisfaction grew and grew, the Chê syndrome grew with it. Theatre groups in all countries were abandoning their 'professional' audiences in search of another public, to offer them the True Word! Some of those groups were aggressive in their quest, inciting people to make rebellions. Sometimes they did the same within the traditional theatres, which made the 'message' more ridiculous still. They played out, in grotesque farce, what Che had done in tragic real life.

Many, before us, who practised so-called 'political message theatre', were in reality practising a kind of evangelical theatre: they evangelised, with undisputable dogmas, the sovereign word of an organisation or a Party. The vast majority of the CPCs, in spite of their immense and never-sufficiently-sung virtues, suffered from this disease.

What was to be done?

Dissatisfaction flourished in Arena, and thoughts started to turn to alternative forms of theatre, which would, of necessity, imply abandoning a professional structure and returning to amateurism. Guarnieri and I wanted to continue as professionals.

In Rio, the choice became clear: did we or did we not want to continue as professionals? To seek or not to seek the famous 'people's audience' of which we talked so much? How to reconcile these contradictory desires?

Foreign examples, like the *Théâtre National Populaire*, were of no use to us. We subsisted with almost no government support while they received subsidies of pharaonic proportions. We had a staff of three: a ticket-seller, a doorman, and a cross-eyed electrician-cum-stage-manager-cum-office boy; the TNP had armies of staff. *Théâtre Populaire* cannot be translated as *teatro popular* — they are poles apart! The sense of the word *peuple* had nothing to do with 'the people' we meant when we used the word *povo*. And their *théâtre* had still less to do with our *teatro*. . . .

They had a concept of 'popular' which meant 'taking culture to the people', i.e. presenting a high-quality classical or modern repertoire at reasonable prices, in a comfortable theatre, so that 'popular' spectators could sit in the same soft seats and enjoy the benefits of the same culture as the middle and upper classes. The French example was no use to us: we had to find our own way.

The idea of the Arena bifurcated. Those who stayed in Rio got in with intellectuals linked to the *União Nacional dos Estudantes*[28] where they found a welcoming home. They founded the *Centros Populares do Cultura*.

In São Paulo, I staged *Pintado de Alegre* (Made up to Look Happy) by Flávio Migliaccio, a play of tender poetic realism, endowed with a gentle beauty which the audience sadly failed to notice. So much beauty, such fine intentions. . . . Oh insensitive public! We wanted to create a national dramaturgy, we forced ourselves down a difficult road, step by step; the public wanted immediate results.

The Outlaw's Testament and the Art of the Actor

The Arena resorted to Chico de Assis[29] to save us from financial crisis: *O Testamento do Cangaceiro* (The Outlaw's Testament). Later, when the CPC wanted to have its Playwriting Seminar, it was I they approached to teach it.

I took advantage of the trip to talk to my mother, who would tell me the stories I now tell in this book, and to my sick father, who spoke little, but liked listening to me. The two of them were still living in Penha. He, a man who all his healthy life had not stopped to rest for a day, was tied to his bed, watching people out of the window. As for my mother, she did not rest.

Lima Duarte was an actor of renown on *TV Tupi*, a pioneer of Brazilian tele-theatre. He had been part of that station's first broadcast programmes, and was considered its best actor; but he had no experience of the stage. His following was rock-solid, success was guaranteed. And, being a TV actor, he was quick in rehearsals. And we were in a hurry! We invited him to play the protagonist. On the first day, Lima gave us the whole character, the finished work: he had understood it all, he knew everything there was to know about Cearim. Nothing more to do, apart from memorise the script.

I was desolate. With my laboratory training, my experience of slowly gestating characters before their laborious birth, I was now confronted with an actor who knew everything before we had started. For me it was essential for the actor to set out from the idea which, by way of the emotion, would eventually find its appropriate form. Lima had the form done and dusted. It was amusing. But . . . is that the art of the actor?

We had enough money in the till for two weeks. A war-cry: *open or starve*! In the first years, when we used to eat at the café on the corner, we used to count our money and then direct our gaze towards the prices on the menu, on the right, rather than the dishes, on the left. When money was short, we would buy three dozen potatoes and regale ourselves with this succulent supper. My father, whenever he saw me, as well as giving me money, used to hand over a five-kilo tin of Maria biscuits. And I still like them, dunked in coffee.

I suffered in those two weeks of script-memorising and blocking – I cannot call that rehearsing. Neurotic premature ejaculation. A director likes to rehearse, to sweat, to suffer, to pull his hair out, to create with his actors and designer and other artists – to work on the floor. After the opening, he goes and sits in the stalls, like the football coach for whom the pleasure goes on even if he doesn't get to shoot at the goal.

Lima told me that in television there was never time to rehearse; you got the script in the morning for recording that afternoon. He would ask the director what 'key' he should play in – there were four or five comic or dramatic 'keys'. In television that's the way it was. Every minute cost money. The 'key' or *jeito*[30] was the trick of it, the way of playing the character which the actor, obviously, did not feel. He did not feel anything, in terms of genuine emotion, but knew how to do everything. From the mouth outwards. Lima was master of four or five 'keys'. An actor of immense empathy, his contagion of the cast was such that the rest of them performed in the same style.

The only 'directing' I did in relation to him was when I realised that before every line he would make a little sound with his mouth or a little noise with his hands or, at the very least, hold for a short silence. I wanted agile dialogue, ping-pong: Lima, before he spoke, always did something or other lasting a few seconds. Then I realised that the cause of this was a vice of live television: the sound he made was to attract the attention of the cameramen who barely knew the script. In the theatre, there were no cameras; there was the permanent gaze of the audience, who did not need to be called to attention.

The opening was one of those 'indescribable' successes. I went up to my room, I felt I had nothing to do with that show. I suffered bitterly, in silence – the applause thundered on and on. Chico noticed my absence and came to find me. He was a younger brother, he consoled me.

Perplexed, I quizzed myself; if theatre is that – going on stage and being funny – it is not art, it is pure histrionics. Dercy did not need a director so much as a good traffic policeman to stop the actors bumping into each other or the scenery, or running away from her – collision avoidance. I decided not to thank the frenzied public, and pig-headedly stayed in my lair, nursing my sadness.

Lima had brought me up against an agonising doubt: if the actor manages immediately to find a form adequate for his character, is there anything wrong with that? In *Testamento* there was no other way of doing it, and to persist in my laboratorial obstinacy would have been impossible – we only had the money for two weeks!

Of course, when rehearsals go to the root of things, the show is better equipped to resist the ravages of time. In the case of *Testamento*, its structural fragility required my constant attention. It was as if the actors were improvising without knowing where they were going – each performance gave us vertigo. My much sought-after rigour crumbled.

It was another way of doing theatre. I could not complain: wasn't I the one who was so fond of those clowns? What did it mean to be a clown? At the least, this: the capacity to improvise; permanent creativity. (Many years later, this became absolutely vital in Forum Theatre.) The creativity was abundant, but I would have liked it if this freedom of creation could have existed within rigorous parameters: total creative freedom within insurmountable walls. It was possible, but . . . it wasn't possible yet.

The show's success restored our faltering finances. The play opened in

July 1961. Almost thirty-seven years later, in May 1998, I met Chico de Assis in Rio. We talked and both had a clear recollection of those events. Chico said I cried that night: it is possible. I do not remember.

Doubts racked us: were we wrong and those who had remained in Rio right? The choice was unnecessary: perhaps we were all right, each on our own provisional path. What stark madness to want to decide who is right and who is wrong when, in art, many paths, even divergent ones, can all be right. Only one is the wrong path, for sure: the path of mediocrity!

We decided to go to the Northeast in our indefatigable quest for the authentic 'people': there, surely, we would find the true Brazil. We had made contacts with the progressive church in the Northeast and with the Peasant Leagues of Francisco Julião, precursor to the *Movimento de Trabalhadores Sem Terra* (*MST*).[31]

On we went, in our search for our people.

The discovery of the Northeast and the blood on Father Batalha's hands

It was called the *Movimento de Cultura Popular* (The Movement of Popular Culture – MCP)[32] – the people had their own culture, which was independent of the official culture, the bourgeois culture. We wanted to discuss the nature of that culture and why it was the *Movimento de Cultura Popular* and not the *Movimento Popular de Cultura*. Was there not an elitism in the concept of 'popular culture' as an impoverished corruption of the true culture? Was it not another way of saying 'folklore', a dwarfish form when placed beside the 'true culture' of European inspiration?

In a suburb of Rio there is an artist who constructs musical instruments from tins, boxes, wire, plastic and zinc. Someone said this creativity was merely the result of poverty: lacking the funds to buy a German piano, our artist invented instruments. This dismissive comment ignored the fact that, before it was invented, the German piano also did not exist and needed an inventor.

Each instrument produces sounds which only that instrument can produce. Before the trombone was invented, the human ear had never heard the sound of a trombone. The *berimbau*,[33] *caxixi*, *pandeiro*, *cuíca*,[34] harp, oboe and violin all produce their own unique sounds. Naturally, some sounds and timbres are more agreeable than others, and more complex – but all are unique.

The argument was semantic because the MCP was popular and involved in culture, and it was the people who did it and participated in it. But, as Julián Boal writes in his book about CPCs,[35] there was, in their theatre, an authoritarianism in the relationship between artists and audiences: the famous 'message' came accompanied by a great simplification of political and social reality, schematised according to certain indisputable premises. Characters personifying peasants were married to the Earth, workers to the factory, in a manner reminiscent of those Soviet pictures with muscular factory workers and peasants smiling healthily at their future, chewing on fat ears of corn. . . . In fact, that movement had a strong influence on the Brazilian Communist Party.

In Pernambuco, the Left was in power. Being in power does not necessarily mean having power, but it did have some. The MCP had salaried posts: they were state functionaries. They were not at the mercy of 5 o'clock downpours. . . . They had buildings and vehicles at their disposal – they did not need the good offices of DKW-Verlag.

Having finished our season in Recife, we did a show in the *Arrail do Bom Jesus* for thousands of spectators – some on horseback made their mounts watch the play, against their equine wills. Here is a curious thing: the horses were more docile during the musical scenes. Horses love music. And, contrary to what one might reasonably presume, they prefer drama to comedy, and classics to modern work. Who knows why! They pay closer attention. But they do not applaud; after theatrical excitements, they feed! Horses are half bovine.

The extra show delayed the continuation of our tour to another faraway city, Salvador. I went to ask the Governor for an aeroplane for the cast. I went without great hopes, in an act of pig-headedness: the Governor gave me the name of a brigadier. When I made my request to him, the soldier banged his fist on the table: 'What sort of time is this to come asking for a plane? If you wanted to be in Salvador today, you should have warned me by yesterday at the very latest!'

His complaint was not about my seeking an aeroplane, which seemed natural to him, but about the lack of time. A few hours later, the plane took off and we arrived on time. *Being in power meant having permission to do good.*

The MCP offered courses in culinary art, and the arts of theatre, embroidery and philosophy. In the city of Angicos, Paulo Freire carried out his first experiments in what would later become his method of developing literacy, which today is used universally around the world.

Brazil was going through a time of transition . . . but did not know where it was heading. It was becoming radical. I was in the Palace of Princesses, at a reception the governor was hosting for our company, when the telephone rang: the sergeants in Brasilia had risen up in mutiny. Everyone was rising up. The people had discovered it had a voice and could speak out.[36]

In 1961 Brazil reached boiling point. The spectacular resignation of Jânio Quadros as President of the Republic had the miraculous effect of dynamising popular participation. The population understood that drastic changes could be made. Nothing was ordained by fate. Brazil was more politicised than ever before in its history.

The *Ligas Camponesas* (Peasant Leagues)[37] fought against the slavery which still exists today. Slavery: the peasants were not allowed to leave the lands on which they worked; they did not get wages, merely 'credits' to buy goods in the stores of the feudal *senhor* – they were always in debt. Hired guns punished and killed any recalcitrants. The Northeast lived this terror. It still does.

During our tour in the Northeast we lived in priests' houses – the church produced truly Christian prelates, as well as the most reactionary priests known to man. In the Northeast, hundreds of true sons of Christ were at work.

Father Batalha and the blood-stained cassock

All the actors had come with me to the evening mass. Father Batalha invited me to follow on foot, back to the parish house, where we were supposed to eat. The women were staying in family houses.

'The journey will whet your appetite' – the priest said, joking at the expense of a serious matter: my hunger. I had worked through lunch: in each town we had to procure the pieces of furniture we needed on stage.

We took with us only the cloths that covered them. It was now 7 p.m. and hunger gnawed!

We had done a show just for the League's local peasant farmers, which ended with the actors singing frenetic revolutionary salutations, left arm raised, fist clenched: 'The land belongs to the people! We must give our blood to reclaim it from the landowners!'[38] Things that everyone thought, which we thought needed reiteration. The art of the time.

A peasant farmer, Virgílio, moved to tears and enthused by our 'message', asked me to come with the cast and our guns and set off with his *companheiros*[39] to fight against the hired thugs of a 'colonel'[40] who had invaded their lands. Taken by surprise we replied that they had misunderstood us: the guns were make-believe, stage props which couldn't be fired, and that only we, the artists, were the genuine article. Without hesitation, Virgílio told us that if we really were genuine we needn't worry — they had guns enough for us all. We should just come and fight at their side. We were ashamed at having to decline this new invitation — an invitation to really fight rather than just talk about fighting. We told him we were genuine *artists* and not genuine *peasant farmers*. It was then that Virgílio pondered the fact that when we, the genuine artists, talked of giving our blood for a cause, in fact we were talking about *their* blood, the peasant farmers', rather than our artists' blood, because we would go back to our comfortable homes.

That episode made me comprehend the falsity of the 'messenger' form of political theatre. We have no right to incite anyone to do something we are not prepared to do ourselves. Before that encounter we were preaching revolution for abstract audiences. Now we met the 'people'. Virgílio was the 'people' we had been looking for. The peasant farmers of the Northeast were that 'people'. We had finally found the 'people'! *Viva* the *people*! How should we speak to this real people? How could we teach them what they knew better than us?

'To be in solidarity is to run the same risks', Chê used to say; we were running no risk chanting revolutionary hymns.

The political theatre of the 1960s and even before was like that. I remember a North American group in Europe, doing an anarchist play in which every night the actors tore up their passports and incited the spectators to do the same. Clearly the US Consulate did not furnish them with new passports every morning to be torn up that night: false prop passports incited the spectators to tear up their own real passports. That, we now understood, was highly immoral. We should never do that again. Yes, we have the right to do agitprop, provided we are on the front line, running the same risks!

I thought that perhaps our show had been too much of an incitement to violence, and I prepared to ask pardon of the priest, Father Batalha. Mass started and I got a shock. In his sermon, right there at the altar, the priest shouted out, loud and clear as a bell: 'They say I am a red priest. It is not true: I am as white as my cassock. But the day will come when my cassock and I will be red with the blood of the Nazi landowners!'

The priest noticed my shock and explained himself further as we walked along the sweaty street through stones and dust.

'I hate the fascists! I am a Christian. Apostolic Roman Catholic. Before all else, a follower of Christ. Things cannot go on like this. This was not what we learned with Christ, who died for us on the cross. Who is going to change Brazil, if we don't?'

'But wasn't it Christ who uttered the famous phrase: "Render unto God what belongs to God, and to Caesar what belongs to Caesar"?'

'He spoke of paying taxes, and in order to pay taxes one must have an income. These people have no salary, they have nothing. There are people working here who have never seen the colour of a ten *réis* note. They are slaves!'

Never having been of any religion (although Christian friends tell me I am like them, as do friends of other religions; perhaps some hidden spirituality resides within me!) I wanted to learn and Father Batalha wanted to teach. He talked nineteen to the dozen.

'If I had been present, I would never have let Cain kill Abel! If necessary, I would have killed Cain myself: if someone had to die, better that it be the assassin! God would understand, I am sure I would be forgiven.'

But if Cain had been dead before the assassination he would not have been an assassin. Thus, Father Batalha would be assassinating the ex-future assassin: one assassination rendering the other impossible. He would be assassinating the potential assassin, the one we carry in our hearts, unconsciously: in that profound and vast 'person', irrational, amoral, that is the source of our well-educated 'personality'; the 'person' that is Stanislavskian inspiration, where the actor goes to find the monstrous 'personages' he plays.

Batalha resumed: the intention to sin is already sin; if the sinner does not sin because he has been impeded, even then he is a sinner. The assassin is an assassin even when his victim escapes.

'If I had been there, David would have had an important ally – a brother and a *companheiro*: I would have thrown stones at that miserable coward Goliath's head. Victory would have come earlier! Strength in unity.'

This second example I was able to accept. The struggle would be in full swing and, God be praised, it would not be necessary to kill anyone: a few good stones thrown chucked at the giant's head would be enough to bring him down a peg or two. I am against the death sentence!

'If I had been there, I would have cut Herod's throat, and Salomé's, with a sharp fish-knife, before they cut off the sacred head of St John the Baptist!'

Father Batalha's pace quickened as these bloody examples came to his mind. I found it an effort to keep up with him. Fatigue and hunger preyed on me. He resumed:

'I was not there at David's struggle, and could not help him, I was not in Herod's palace and they beheaded the Saint, and I was not out in the fields and did not see Abel's bloody body. . . . But I am here today, I am present now. I am a Christian and believe in God: love thy neighbour as thyself. Who is my neighbour? Not the fascist landowners who have stolen this land. My neighbours are those peasant farmers you saw at Mass and at your play. Humiliated and demeaned, dying of hunger.'

Noting that the priest used the words 'Nazi' and 'Fascist' indiscriminately, I asked him what the difference between them was to him. He replied: 'A Fascist is someone who prohibits you from expressing your thoughts. A Nazi is someone who prohibits you from thinking!'

He continued: 'No Christian with any sense of shame can stand by and watch what is happening in the countryside, as a mere spectator; we have to be actors!'

I was a young theatre director from a big city. I talked about agrarian reform in theory, without knowing the countryside or the country people. I read about violence, I did not see it. This man was living the violence in the streets, in the confessions he heard.

We climbed the hill; we could see land as far as the eye could reach.

Tracing in the air with his hand, he indicated an immense estate: 'From here to there, those lands belong to Colonel Matusalém. The life expectancy of a peasant is thirty-five years of hard graft. Matusalém is over 80. His intestines are well lined. On that land, plant anything and it grows . . .

'But here you can't plant, it is forbidden! Did you see those peasant farmers at the 6 o'clock mass? I prayed more quickly because we were going to hand out bread and water after: they are probably still there, eating.'

I had seen them: entire families, malnourished, babies strapped to mother's hips, without the energy to cry.

'They are ill. Even so they could cultivate manioc, potatoes, soya. . . . It's just that Colonel Matusalém does not allow them to. He does not want anyone on his land, apart from his bully-boys. He is afraid that once on it, they might not ever want to leave. *Usucapion*.'[41]

'This land is abandoned . . . it is just grass . . . It isn't even good for nature. . . . Nature is Baroque or Gothic in its forests, it's only Romanesque in the desert!' I said, remembering a discussion we had about sacred art on our arrival.

'Speculation' – he replied. 'The land is kept, virgin and untouched, like money in a bank account. No one profits, only the banker and the grass farmer. Matusalém is waiting for the government to build a road on his lands. The contractor is one of his brothers, it all stays in the family. . . .'

The priest was given to explicatory diversions:

'Why on earth do those lands belong to him? Who gave them to him? Was it Dom João III, King of Portugal, when he divided up the Indians' lands amongst his court friends and gave Hereditary Captainships[42] to his toadies? Not even that. This Matusa bribed the owner of the land registry office, burnt the deeds and made new ones, he arranged for certificates to be forged. Land-grabbing, pure and simple. No one gets thousands of hectares of land round here without stealing them at machine-gun point. There are estates here larger than the whole of Portugal and half of Spain. Larger than the Netherlands. The size of the United Kingdom, including Scotland and Wales. But in God's Great Land Registry, land which does not produce is land which belongs to no one.'

He returned to his explanation of profit: 'The land stays idle, devoured by grass. Matusa goes to Brasília doling out bribes. They want the road.

Once the road is built they sell the land for a price a thousand times higher than it would be worth without the road. . . .'

'Jango Coulart [the new leftist President] is going to pass a law expropriating 80 km to either side of Federal roads. Which will be the end of speculation.'

The priest – the 'people' we were looking for! – had faith in God, but not in politics.

'The rural lobby in Congress is strong: here, even dead people vote for the Colonel. On election day, the dead don't rest, they vote in all the ballot-boxes. Even people who don't exist vote – names are invented! Even so, as the owners of the land are frightened of that hypothetical law, cruelty in the countryside is worse now than ever.'

He gave terrifying examples. He pointed out another estate on the horizon, which was productive. The producers were slaves; they worked in the heat of the sun, without rest, and continued to owe ever greater debts. Their debt to the owner grew in the same way as Brazil's debt to the international banks, our owners. This is the modern form of slavery: a country that pays almost two billion dollars a month in debt interest is a slave country – no point looking for synonyms. Governments that accept this situation without rebelling are *Capitaes do Mato*.[43] Without euphemism. Since the 1950s and 1960s no government has said *No* to the IMF, nor even *Maybe, who knows, we'll see*. . . . It's all *Yes Sir, leave it with me, Sir*!

'To prevent their slaves from fleeing, the colonels have armies of thugs, who earn much more than the peasants do, and are therefore faithful servants. When a slave runs away, the thugs go after him on horseback, tie him up and bring him back to the farm for punishment in front of everyone.'

'Punishment?'

'Last year a slave was tied to a tree right in front of the farmhouse. They cut up his body with a knife used for cutting sugar cane, and put honey on his wounds. At night, the ants came and ate the whole peasant. He was screaming, everyone heard, no one came to his aid. The slave was screaming, his body was being consumed, leaving only his bones and his scream, which the ants were unable to eat. Ants don't eat screams. He cried out the whole night long, he died early the next morning.'

Seeing my horror, my pain, Father Batalha softened the blow:

'That does not happen every day, rest assured. It was last year. Less serious are the whippings, the beatings on the palms, the imprisonment of the man naked in a sty with pigs, or in a damp windowless cell. It is true that many die, but that is not the aim, because it suits neither the colonel nor the deceased.'

I remained silent, thinking on these horrors.

Changing the subject, Batalha revealed that in his youth he had not been religious, and did not even believe in God.

'For me, God was merely a question of our fear of the Infinite. If you think about Infinity, if you try to understand Infinity, you go mad. Because if Infinity exists out there, logically it should also exist inside oneself. If there are billions of galaxies out there, trillions of Milky Ways, it must be the same inside us. In just one strand of my hair there must be quadrillions of suns, hotter than that one out there scorching our earth. When I was young that's the way I thought and I used to go crazy! It made me giddy. So giddy I had to sit down to stop myself falling over. That was until I began to believe in God. God, who is infinite, is the finity of Infinity: everything begins with him and will end when He wants it to. We need to have limits: God is the greatest limit. Other limits are this street, my house, the church, my timetable, my prayers. . . . All of these things help me not to think about the Infinite, until I see the infinite at my back. Then, I just think about those peasant farmers, who need me, and those Fascists and Nazis or the lightning which will smite them.'

I talk a lot, but I like to listen. The priest said that he had toyed with other religions before turning Catholic. His father considered religion to be an unhealthy form of relationship with the Unknown. He used to say that the Catholics were masochists in their adoration of martyrs, the Jews melancholics with their Wailing Wall, the Muslims obsessives throwing themselves to their knees five times a day to face Mecca, and the North American TV Protestant sects totally hysterical fanatics, with their live audiences and manufactured miracles made to order by the score! The conversation lost its direction. . . .

We arrived at the priest's house; my actors, who had come by jeep, were already there, waiting. The arrival of an enormous bowl of soup was greeted by applause. Despite the horrors I had heard I was the most ravenous. We ate the first course. My friends unceremoniously helped themselves to generous third and fourth servings of soup. I had only a second helping, half a bowl. I kept thinking about his words: 'We must be actors, must go on the stage and fight. To be spectators of an unjust, unequal fight is a crime!' He was right.

I have always heard it said that priests eat well: 'Gluttonous as a friar', people used to say. 'Cheeks red from so much wine. . . .' The soup was delicious: I waited for the untold delicacies that would follow: any connoisseur of religion or epicure knows that no dish should leave one with *saudades* for its predecessors.

Batalha kept insisting: 'Didn't you like the soup? Don't you want more?' 'No thanks, it was delicious. Really very good. This *macaxeira*[44] is tasty. In São Paulo they call it *mandioca*, in Rio de Janeiro it is *aipim*', I said, in an unequivocal demonstration of my linguistic and culinary knowledge.

The priest gathered up the plates. A pause. My stomach eagerly awaited the next instalment of our friarly repast. We talked about unproductive *latifundia*. I was hungry. The coffee came: panic! 'What about the rest of the meal? What about the rest, for God's sake? I am hungry!' My brain shrieked hunger, my mouth silenced it. No one heard my pensive shrieks.

'Let us retire,' the priest said. 'Early start for us tomorrow. . . .'

Before leaving he looked at me and commented: 'You ate little . . . Didn't you like the soup?' I replied, 'It was great. . . . Manioc . . . soup.'

I went to sleep with my belly churning and my stomach praying for breakfast. Smitten with faith as never before![45]

That trip to the Northeast and that day changed my life. Virgilio and Father Batalha changed my conception of art. At least, my way of seeing theatre and its usefulness.

The fat man and the thin man in the Santo André Seminar

The idea of the active spectator, the protagonist who oversteps limits instead of resigning himself to his sedentary participation, was already in my mind when I went back to São Paulo. Something beyond Brecht, who only asked the spectator to think with his head, without giving him the stage space to express that thought.

No more message-bearing theatre, I did not want to be postman for the unknown sender (the Party? Divine revelation?). I wanted the spectators, democratically, to use the same theatre language used by the actors. How could this be done? A good question, an answer to which would only come years later.

President Jango had a symbolic value: he was of the left. The military did not want him, the greater part of the Brazilian bourgeoisie detested him, the United States government abominated him, but the people had put him in place. This was irrefutable proof that the slogan was right: 'The people, united, will never be defeated!' The problem was the uniting, then as now.

I remembered Father Batalha: 'There are times when it is antichristian to be a spectator. To do nothing is to crucify Christ anew! In Brazil they are crucifying Christ every blessed day! All Christians have a duty to save Christ. It is not enough merely to swallow the wafer. Legs are for running, not for kneeling. Kneeling before God, yes; kneeling before injustice, no!'

His speech was turning radical, drawing on biblical subjects: 'We have to make the choice between Cain and Abel, Salomé and John the Baptist, David and Goliath. We cannot remain neutral, watching the massacre. Living is choosing which side to be on. The future does not exist: it has to be built! To be a Christian is to choose the just path! Abstinence is not abstention.'

I couldn't get Father Batalha out of my head. Even when he was exaggerating: 'I am not the messenger of God; I am the Message!' Who doesn't exaggerate?

Carrar's Rifles

In early 1962, Renato directed *Senhora Carrar's Rifles*, in which Brecht speaks of the impossibility of neutrality. Dostoevsky: 'We are responsible for everything, before everyone!' Let's be clear: responsible not for what others do, but for what we do in response. Or fail to do.

Carrar was written after the destruction of Guernica by the Nazis. It came to remind us that no one is neutral, that no one should hide their guns. Brecht was an aesthetic and moral reference point. In Brazil, *Carrar* was a premonition of the *coup* that was to come.

If the *Théâtre National Populaire* did not work as a model for us, the Berliner Ensemble was even less use – these were rich theatres, well fed, fat. We were condemned to invent our own path! The path of the wayfarer is made in wayfaring. . . .

The Santo André Seminar

I was invited to organise a playwriting seminar in the Metalworkers Trade Union of Santo André. Once a week I explained to a group of ten factory workers Hegel, Aristotle, Machiavelli, and the laws of dialectics – laws not to be obeyed but utilised in the carpentry of theatre.

I avoided 'difficult' words, and when I had to use one, I would explain its meaning – the workers loved discovering new words. The greater the vocabulary, the greater the possibilities of thought. We do not have to limit our vocabulary when speaking with uneducated people. Anyone who has learned to say 'daddy' and 'mummy' can also learn *catharsis*, *metaxis*[46] or *Verfremdungseffekt*. I am not joking, they can. In due course, with a purposeful approach . . . and good explanation.

At the end of the Seminar each participant had a play; Jurandir's was the most highly praised. *A Greve* (The Strike) told of a strike that had happened in the ABC,[47] where the PT[48] was founded and developed twenty years ago. I was overjoyed by his capacity to create characters that were what might be called 'authentic'. We rehearsed it over a number of weeks.

Having workers on stage and in the audience was a novelty. The curtain rose, to uproar. Spectators applauded or jeered every exchange: organised fan clubs, rooting for and against.

The Fat Man, the strike-breaking character, was jeered every time he opened his mouth and the actor who was playing him took fright. I appealed for silence and respect. I swore that the man playing the role did not in any way identify with the character politically. There was booing and hissing: it was like children's theatre when the wicked witch appears.

One spectator approached the stage shouting: 'It's a lie! I never said any of this. . . . You are liars; this is a theatre of slanders . . . you . . . you . . .' and off he went, verbally abusing the actors.

He was in reality the Thin Man, a real worker who served as the model for Jurandir's villain! Jurandir had purposefully chosen a fat actor to play the character of the Fat Man who represented the Thin Man. The longer the play went on, the more the Thin Man protested in outrage. Till it turned into a threat: 'Shut your mouth or I'll smash your face in. . . .' Never had a spectator addressed himself so abusively to a character. A world première!

Since the Fat Man continued, the Thin Man jumped up on to the stage. We were prepared for a fight; however, once on stage, the Thin Man appeared to be less bellicose, and merely desirous of the opportunity to deliver his version of events – as was his right! – simultaneously with the action of the play. His commentary contradicted the script, in a simultaneous de-translation of it, unsaying what was said and done. According to his version, he had not been against the strike but against the idea of coming out on strike at that particular time.

The Fat Man exploded, departing completely from the script: 'The strike was beaten because of scabs like you, cowards who stayed at home or went to the factory to mount counter-pickets!'

In the confusion, other workers – the real people other characters were modelled upon – got up on stage and each incarnated themselves in front of their actors, the scene fragmenting into explosive simultaneous dialogues with worker-models of characters pitted against actors and their characters.

Astonished, I joined in the heated debate (when the spirited exchanges would allow a word in edgeways), arguing that if the workers did not recognise themselves in the characters, so much the better: it was proof that the characters were not them – they were fictions! So why all the fuss? If on the other hand they had said those things, then in that case it was true, and no one could complain. But, for sure, the Fat Man (the character) was not the Thin Man (the person), in spite of the adipous[49] reference.

'Don't give me that claptrap!' disagreed the Thin Man. 'This was the way you found to speak ill of me, without actually naming me! That is why you call it theatre. . . . But I'm not falling for it.'

I asked the spectators to get off the stage, but the Thin Man was interested in restoring his tarnished image: 'Jurandir must have been hiding under his bed during the strike! Now he is telling everyone that I said what I didn't say and, as I didn't, I want the right to say what I did say and I am ready to say it all over again!'

I sought to defend the autonomy of art: 'The person speaking on stage is the Fat Man, who obviously is not you because you say that you did not say it: then the person who said it is not you, it is the character! It is not the Thin Man, it is the Fat Man!'

I don't remember which of us was more confused, in spite of this crystal-clear ratiocination.

'In theatre, Fat and Thin is all the same. When you talk about one you are referring to the other. That is what your theatre is for, to defame! Now clear off and let me show you how things really happened.'

The Fat Man did not want to clear off, and the Thin Man remained at his side:

'I will not clear off because you do not know the plot, you cannot do my character.'

'I do not know the plot but I do know the strike; I do not know your character but I do know myself. Clear off!'

Two obstinate, bull-headed men, neither would give way. As I have always liked to experiment, I suggested that they do what they were already doing, but with some kind of discipline instead of all this ballyhoo.

'Let the Fat Man say the written script and you correct him, straight afterwards. . . . In this way, working on the hypothesis that you are in part – please note, I said "in part" – like the character, you can clarify the nuances of the difference. . . .'

'He speaks and I correct him?'

'Pretty good, no? That's democracy!'

'He doesn't even need to speak, I know what he is going to say. Let me correct him before he gets it wrong.'

The argument started up again until both accepted the proposal: the Fat Man speaking his script, the Thin Man making corrections. The Fat Man spoke Jurandir's script, the Thin Man invented his own, giving us his version. The Fat Man would go on, in would come the Thin Man, an anti-guardian angel.

Who was the Actor? Who, the Character? Who, the Spectator? As he told his story, the Thin Man was not living the scene in the same way he lived it during the actual strike, but he was experiencing it, ordering the events and the speeches. He felt emotion, now controlled by reason and by the desire to convince; not that he wanted to experience yesterday's strike-related emotions all over again – today he wanted to explain them. Emotion revisited.

The Fat Man, on the other hand, wanted to accuse his interlocutor and was reliving the scene because, once again, he saw the Thin Man trying to dupe his *companheiros*. To him, the same situation as the strike was being reproduced there and then, provoking the same emotion. The Thin Man lied before, he was lying now. The Fat Man's emotion was the same: he was reliving it.

I learned a lesson there about *living*, *reliving* and *experiencing*. And what stuck in my memory was this extraordinary image of the human being fighting the character, the man against his image; an image of him that another man was showing. Struggling against himself, or part of himself, in the other. A man wanting to present an image of himself, to construct that image live, but all the while being, himself, at that very moment, another image: the image of the builder of images. He was neither the image that he was presenting, nor that which the other presented of him. He was the image of the maker of images. He was also, to some extent, all those images.

It was not yet Forum Theatre, but it was a forum inside the theatre. I was fascinated to see this multitude of people and characters. Who was fiction, who was reality? Fiction interpenetrating reality.

In Santo André I began to think about exploring this frontier: the truth of fiction and the fiction of truth.

The fat woman

A year later, there occurred the genuine intervention of a 'spect-actor', which gave rise to Forum Theatre. It was in Peru, in 1973, when I was directing a workshop about popular forms of theatre. We presented a play and, during the debate that followed, a female spectator came on stage, taking the place of the protagonist, and showed us what she would do if she were in the protagonist's place – she showed it by playing.

I have told this story twice, in *The Theatre of the Oppressed*[50] and in *Rainbow of Desire*.[51] You may rest easy, I am not going to tell it a third time. I am going to comment on it. It is strange: in each of these books I tell the same story in a different way, which gives me comfort in the certainty that the psychic processes of memory and imagination are indissociable – no one remembers without imagining, no one imagines without remembering.

Remembering today what I remembered yesterday, the thing remembered now differs from the memory before. Every day is a new day. I am no longer who I was only hours ago. My being is becoming. I never am: I am always becoming. I am that which I am not yet, and I am also what I have already ceased to be. In the act of approaching being, I become that which I shall never be, since, if I become by being it, I shall already be in transit to another being which I am not yet nor will be, as I am the first, always in transit. Inevitably.

Is it complicated? No, it is not: read it again. And once more. Who has read it three times? Are you still the same person you were three readings ago? Impossible!

Returning to our story, imagining the minimum and remembering the maximum, I remember that in Chacalayo in 1973, the fat woman came on stage when we were doing a show in which the audience was offering alternatives as to how the protagonist should behave; the actors were improvising, in accordance with their suggestions.

It was a play about a wife who discovered that her husband, who was living off her, had a lover in another town where he said he was building a house for her, the wife. The story was true and the middle-aged woman who had told us her story was seated on stage, for all to see, awaiting suggestions: the husband, the real husband, was due to arrive the following day, back from his lover. In the play, when the husband knocked at the door on his return, I interrupted the action and asked the public what the wife should do; pretend she knew nothing, react, cry, become angry, bite him on the neck, kick him up the arse?

Every idea was tried out, even that of the fat woman, who said that the wife should forgive him: 'After she has had a very clear conversation with him!' In response to the suggestion, the wife-actress tried every possible form of clarity, but the fat woman kept saying that it was not like that: till finally I invited her up on stage to show us herself what the hell she meant by 'a very clear conversation with him'.

Delighted, she came up, she took hold of a broom, and doled out a magnificent thrashing to the husband. He was an excellent actor; I shall never forget his wonderful, sincere, emotion-filled, Stanislavskian interpretation of his part when, cowering under the broom, he promised never again to betray her. I am convinced that the actor never betrayed anyone, not even the most occasional lover! Only after this beating – her 'clear conversation'! – did the fat woman forgive the treacherous husband, and not before sending him out to the kitchen to fetch her a plate of food, famished as she was after all that beating.

From then on, I adopted Forum Theatre as a way of working, always explaining that the spectators are free to do what they wish . . . apart from beat up the cast!

In Santo André, I saw actors representing characters and the people upon whom characters were based creating other characters – themselves; any given moment, they were the real person *and* the character. They leapt between one and the other. In Chacalayo, it was straightforward. Actual events, lived life, became art; on stage, that image of the real was shown. The spectators, real people, penetrated that aesthetic space: there they were dualised. They went on being who they were *and* they became characters. Their lives, dualised – themselves and their images – became more comprehensible; lives having become two, each person becoming two – the person as an actor can direct himself, tracing his own steps, inventing his own paths. The actor is he who commands the character, and the character is also himself, the actor! Within the fiction of theatre the spectator can try out actions for later use in his real life.

In Santo André, before 1964, I saw characters and actors on stage in disorderly combat. In Chacalayo, in 1973, the real democracy of the Theatre of the Oppressed began. The Northeast had opened my eyes; Santo André showed me the problem, Chacalayo presented the solution.

The metaphor and the discovery of the Classics

Renato wanted to sell the theatre. We formed a company: Guarnieri, Flávio Império, Juca de Oliveira, Paulo José and myself. We bought the Arena. We decided to invent a new path, 'The nationalisation of the Classics'. We wanted to seek our identity, no longer before the naturalist mirror which revealed crude physiognomy, but in portraits of other times and places, which would allow us to see our true face, reflected in faces of other epochs.

'Nationalising' was all the rage. Jango was threatening nationalisation of all economic and industrial activities of national strategic interest, even banks. The press was either pro-nationalisation or vehemently in favour of selling out the country to foreign investors – there was no middle way.

In politics, 'nationalising' had a strong connotation of appropriation, taking back what is ours. In theatre, it was not to be confused with the *Teatro Antropofágico*,[52] proposed by Osvald de Andrade in 1922 and taken up by our contemporary *Oficina*; in this, the appropriation was effected by means of cannibalism. Some anthropophagous peoples believed that, by eating the enemy, the cannibal would absorb his virtues. Eating the defeated hero, the gourmet became a hero like him, changing identity, becoming who he was *plus* the other . . . .

Theatrical cannibalism has always existed in Brazil. Groups like *Oficina* used marvellous anthropophagy; other, less talented groups wreak havoc on texts. Molière and Shakespeare were subjected to merciless phagocytosis, serving as a pretext for directors to say their own words – words they were not able to write!

We respected the structures of the 'nationalised' work of art, within which we sought to find ourselves. We gave prominence to what there was of us in the play, and what there was of the play in us; we wanted to rediscover our identity, not exchange it for another. Analogy can only exist between *different likes*. We retained the differences as we sought the semblances. Anthropophagic art makes the 'cannibal' resemble the 'outsider'. We merely wanted to recognise ourselves in him, to see ourselves as we were – and to continue being ourselves. Alike and different.

We chose classics: no art is universal unless it is also Brazilian. We kept our distance from the anthropophagic movements of the tropicalist mode – we never had any desire to transform ourselves into the 'Other', let alone the 'Invader'. For us Caliban is beautiful![53] Let us be Caliban and be happy! (Contrary to what some have written, Caliban is not a cannibal. If he were to make love with Miranda, he would people the island with little Calibans, not little Prosperos.)

When at Carnival, *favela*-dwellers[54] transform themselves into Louis XIV and Marie Antoinette and their courtiers, are they anthropophagically cannibalising the French Court, or expressing their own desires in metaphor? I plump for the latter hypothesis. The former would only make sense if the *favelados* were to rend these fantasies, to trample and ridicule them: but they respect them, they are talking about themselves, not the Other.

The first play chosen for our new nationalisation programme at Arena was Machiavelli's *Mandrágora* (The Mandrake), directed by myself. The lyrics of the songs were taken from *The Prince* – the only 'adaptation' we made to the text, which was otherwise respected. With *Mandrágora*, we discovered Metaphor. We abandoned realism in search of reality.

Mandrágora *and metaphor*

Machiavelli was a 'political scientist', in the best sense of the term. As a politician, he theorises Renaissance princely practice, showing that in the society he lives in – just like those we live in – everything is possible, the only question being the means used to obtain one's desires.

In the battle of politics, power is the supreme good: as long as no impertinent scruple detains us, we will get there. In the battle of love, the supreme good is the loved one: if we dare all, without worrying about morals, we will get there too. In *Mandrágora*, Lucrétia is, metaphorically, power.

Metaphor is the concretion of an abstraction, the transposition of words and meanings. When we speak of 'the root of evil' we are not refer-ring to the buried part of a tree: we are thinking of the origins of that which we consider nefarious. The root, in metaphor, is the origin: it has nothing to do with plants or vegetables.

With the 'nationalisation of the Classics', tired of tautological realism, we went in quest of the metaphor. In contraposition to the notion that 'What you are seeing is exactly what you are seeing' we wanted the 'This is that' and 'That is this'-ness of metaphor. We were tired of repeating similar dialogue and similar costumes. We were afraid of repeating similar thoughts. Horror, horror! With *Mandrágora*, the metaphor came to us made flesh in sensual *história*, rather than abstract fable.

If I were to write a fable about Brazil – like the beautiful 'Raft of Medusa', on which the survivors of a shipwreck devour one another – the

Boal, Juca, Flávio Imperio, Guarnieri after winning prizes for
Machiavelli's THE MANDRAKE *in 1963*

Brazilian spectators would easily recognise our concrete reality in the abstract fable. The fable, however, would not exist without reference to us; it is invented with us as its starting point, and to us it returns. Like animal fables: no one believes that animals talk to each other, fables exist only in reference to us, human beings: they symbolise us – they have no life of their own.

When this is the case, a binary relationship exists. The first term of this equation is the fable, which is the metaphor of our reality and which does not consubstantiate with a new autonomous reality, remaining in the world of symbols – the symbol being a substitute for the thing, not the thing itself, as, for instance, the flag is not the fatherland, only its symbol. The second term is the spectator's reality. Only those two terms exist: unreal fable and our real reality.

However, when it comes to a play written long ago and far away, a play in which the author is not inventing pure fantasy but transubstantiating a living society, there will always be a triangular relationship. First, the author's reality – which exists or existed (Renaissance Florence); second, the autonomous organicity of the story (*Mandrágora*, a story of love and cunning); third, the spectator's reality – today, here.

Story and characters, though metaphorical, have a life of their own. Medieval kings and princesses were realities, they existed in a context; within the play, they retain their human dimension, even transformed into metaphor. In contrast to these kings and princesses, realities now turned metaphors, La Fontaine's fox never had a reality outside the fable, it was never more than metaphor; foxes eat chickens, they do not eat grapes, whether unripe or ripe, except in La Fontaine – gastronomical poetic licence.

La Fontaine and Machiavelli spoke of people who existed; they 'metaphorised' their societies, the former by resort to ethereal fantasy, the latter employing corporeal reality. As the Florentine characters have a human tri-dimensionality, we attribute a living existence to them, which we deny to the Frenchman's animals and fruits. Foxes and grapes are allegories: *they are, but they do not exist*. Timotéo, Lucrétia, Ligúrio *are, and they exist*. These allegories, to the same extent as these people, are also symbols. No one falls in love with crickets and ants . . . – which *are*, but do not *exist* – however beautiful their songs may be; for Lucrétia, everything is possible.

The Renaissance comedy is a carnal story: a beautiful and shy woman, a religious extremist, is the object of desire (and later of love) for the young Calímaco, who aims to conquer her, aware of the near-impossibility of winning her – 'near' does not mean 'total'. With wit and art (and lack of scruples), he gets there. Ligúrio is a character who is virtuoso, i.e. possessor of the Machiavellian *virtú*, representative of the world-view which says 'I can because I want to, not because I should!' and 'My power is my desire!' He is not intimidated by, nor shrinks in the face of, modes of behaviour less concerned with the moral. Ligúrio invents a thousand tricks to pervert Friar Timóteo, the confessor, and to outwit Messer Nícia, the husband, and a thousand crafty wiles to conquer the faithful wife and hand her over to his friend, in exchange for friendship and money.

The characters of *Mandrágora* were symbols of a social reality; however, as characters, they existed independently of that which they symbolised. They *were* symbols and *existed* as people. To be and to exist. Foxes *are*, but do not exist as thinking and plotting individuals. Virtuosi *exist* and *are*.

The metaphor operated on two planes: as political story it was about the struggle for power; at plot level, it became the struggle for a woman's love. Parallel planes. Machiavelli spoke of political power using the language of love. But, in his time, his audiences, who lived in the reality of the play, knew what and whom he was talking about, seeing, in the amorous characters of the drama, the characters of the political life of the time: from the symbol, back to the symbolised. There was transit between these levels. In Brazil, audiences knew nothing of Florence: the play told a story of love and adultery – the connection with Florentine politics, or our own, which would give it its metaphorical dimension, was not made, or at least, not consciously.

Enigma: to what did the play owe its immense success, spicy comedy or metaphorical symbology? Drama of love or political intrigue? We had doubts whether the spectator, on hearing talk of a hunger for love, could make the leap to a thirst for power. To our audience, these Friars and *Messers* were foxes and grapes: symbols; Florence was not Brazil. But, for the Florentine spectator, Florence was the Fatherland! They knew what

Machiavelli was talking about. Was our metaphor too remote? — we used to ask ourselves. I wrote essays explaining the allegorical meaning, the political content. The show was seen by many thousands, my essays read by a few hundreds.

Cervantes' *The Siege of Numância* was played in cities under siege — recently in Bosnia during the Serb bombings and, a while back, in Cuba at the start of the unjust and cruel blockade determined by the US in 1960. In this instance, the relationship between metaphor and reality, stage and auditorium, was plain for all to see.

Mandrágora served to show that we could dress up in silk and satin, without needing to cloak our voices in velvet or turn our actors into mere coat hangers. And it served to pay our overdue salaries: in the first fifteen years of my professional life, we could never consider the aesthetic without first laying a protective hand on our wallets.

Judgement in Novo Sol

With Nelson Xavier, I wrote *Julgamento em Novo Sol* (Judgement in Novo Sol) which was presented at a peasants' congress in Belo Horizonte. The play concerned a successful uprising – in Brazil, only in theatre are revolutions successful. . . . Today, however, with the formation of the MST,[55] hope is renascent.

The actor who played the part of the landowner was persecuted by the congress-goers, even though they knew he was an actor — he was a Communist Party militant who could not by any stretch of the imagination have been considered to share his character's reactionary ideas. Even so, they wanted to persecute the *character* that was lurking in the recesses of the *person* of the actor. They thought that if the actor was capable of such a lifelike representation of the cruel Colonel, it stood to reason that he must have something of that character within him. The actor had to leave through the back door disguised in beard and moustache lent by the fellow-actor who played the priest.

In order to qualify for what meagre subsidy there was, the law obliged us to mount a national classic. We chose Martins Penna's *The Novice*, which offered me the pleasure of total irresponsibility of directing a comedy. At no point did I think 'what does this mean?' It meant *subsidy*, of course!

We returned to Rio with *Mandrágora*. We performed the play in the Teatro Santa Rosa, directed by my friends Leo Jusi and Glaúcio Gil. It was the last time I saw Glaúcio alive: he died of a heart attack in front of television cameras, during a programme he was hosting. He died live.

While we were there, *Auto do bloqueio furado* (The tale of the broken blockade), produced by the Popular Centre of Culture, was written the day Kennedy declared the naval boycott against Cuba, rehearsed the following morning and performed on the steps of the Teatro Municipal less than twenty-four hours after the blockade was declared. It was about breaking the blockade, which was not yet even fully in place. (How about that for high-speed dramaturgy?)

What is interrelationship?

In Rio, Milton Gonçalves was replaced by Ari Toledo, hurriedly. The original show had been rehearsed in minute detail. I even blocked the eye-movements of the actor in the role of Friar Timóteo, in the scene in which Ligúrio (Guarnieri) tries to convince him to convince Lucrécia to make love with Calímaco. The friar is almost convinced, he just needs one final push. Ligúrio jangles some coins: the sound of the gold immediately draws the eyes of the holy man, but his face remains unmoving. The audience, two metres away, fell about laughing. With the help of the actor's coin-jangling, even those seated behind him could imagine the expression on the saintly man's face — when working in the round, the director must block the actors' movements for all sides, 360 degrees. The rigour of the watchmaker. The important thing, however, was the strong inter-relationship between the characters. Not a word was addressed to thin air. Every breath found an attentive ear, every movement a receptive eye. Everything was done *à deux*. You could cut the atmosphere between the actors with a knife, such was its density.

The play begins with Calímaco's long monologue in front of Siro, who barely opens his mouth, tossing out the odd 'I remember it well' . . . 'I think so' . . . 'It is true, Sir . . .'. Nothing more. In São Paulo, Paulo José was a huge success doing this near-monologue; it was theatre. In Rio, the monologue became mere information.

Why? Paulo was the same in both cities. Siro was not: great actor that he was, Milton had rehearsed Siro and every 'Of course' he delivered was replete with layers of intention . . . Paulo and Milton interacted: they dialogued in 'under-waves' of unspoken thoughts. Ari, poor thing, hardly had time to learn the monosyllables before he was thrust on stage where he duly repeated his lines on cue. The interrelationship was broken, the theatre came to an end.

I insist: theatre must be *à deux*! Theatre is love, *à deux* is the only way!

Another example: in *Tartuffe*, Guarnieri was the protagonist, Lima was Orgonte. Tartuffe is declaring his love to Orgonte's wife, when in comes her son Damis. Damis threatens to denounce Tartuffe to his father. Enter the father, who hears the denunciation. Livid, he asks if it is true. In the early days the pause lasted several seconds before Tartuffe would reply: 'God is my witness' – having caught sight of a crucifix on the wall.

The pause grew. Guarnieri developed his sub-text and at each performance he thought longer thoughts while he gazed at Orgonte, Damis, the crucifix. . . . It reached a record two minutes with two bursts of applause mid-scene, in the same pause: colleagues would come to see it, marking the time on their watches. It was theatre: interrelationship, interaction!

The King is the Best Justice

The actors interrelated to such an extent on stage that interrelationships off-stage were inevitable . . . Joana Fomm, an actress from Santa Rosa, fell in love with one of our actors and came with us to São Paulo. A time of great passions! Joana, an intelligent and beautiful woman, played the role of the peasant Elvira, in *O melhor juiz, o Rei* (The King is the Best Justice), by Lope de Vega.

We modified the ending of his script, so that we could restore Lope's central idea – we wanted to establish the bridge between the metaphor and our reality. Pelayo dressed up as King and meted out both applications of justice. Paulo, Guarnieri and I translated the script. Flávio designed, rustling up noblemen's robes from carpets and old bridles and cake stands: recycled refuse.

The nobleman Don Tello falls for the peasant Elvira; on the night of her marriage to Sancho, Don Tello, who was Sancho's best man, arranges for

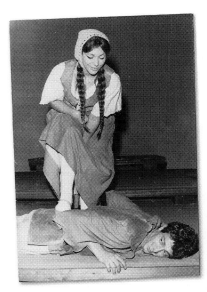

Cecília Boal as the protagonist in Boal's production
of Lope da Vega's
THE KING IS THE BEST JUSTICE,
Buenos Aires, 1966

Boal, Cecília and actors of the IFT theatre,
Buenos Aires, 1966

her to be kidnapped. He wants to exercise his *direito de pernada* ('right to a leg over'). In the Middle Ages, feudal lords had the right to make love to all the brides in their fiefdom, on the first night of their marriage. Tello wanted to exercise his right, because he was in love with her; he had both the traditional and the legal right to do so and, for him, nothing could have been more just.

Sancho and his friend Pelayo, unresigned to this fate, go in search of the King. When they get back with him, Elvira has already been violated. The King magnanimously punishes Tello and regales the bride with presents in compensation for her lost virginity. The King metes out justice. In this way, Lope wanted to venerate the figure of the King who opposes local power: central power against the 'colonels'. Which was a good thing, in Spain, in his time. In Brazil, it could seem like praise of the tyrants, at a time when those plotting the *coup* were already patrolling the corridors of power. In our version, the King was busy with his wars and he needed the support of his faithful ally Don Tello and his hired guns. He did not come: one virginity more or less, what did it matter?

Pelayo dresses up as the King and himself metes out double justice. First, the justice of the nobility – if he is in love, Tello must marry Elvira. At this juncture, when we were in the Northeast, the furious spectators almost brought the show to a premature end. After this came the second justice, the peasants' justice: Tello is condemned to death. Elvira, a widow, her virginity lost and inheritance found, marries her beloved Sancho. Applause. The fact that justice was carried out by a peasant rather than by the King suggested that it was possible for our people to mete out justice. Because of that we were sure that the censor would ban the play – but not a single line was cut. Before it bites, the snake is permissive: censors had suddenly become democratic. . . .

In the Northeast, *O melhor juiz* was played to huge audiences, with people hanging out of trees. And mounted on their infallibly melomanic horses. . . . Sancho's entry on stage (Juca in medieval peasant costume) would provoke laughter and catcalls. Juca, with calm skill, would laugh with them, showing off his costume, and then explain that we were going to present a play about things which happened 'in ancient times', pointing out the similarities of that time with today's situation. The spectators would calm down and Juca would say that he himself was playing the bridegroom, who spoke in verse like the popular singers of the Northeast, for example: 'Noble lands of Galicia / which provide sustenance for our armies / bearing flowers of a hundred thousand colours / birds which sing of lovers / wild ungoverned beasts, etc.' That was it – already he was into the script and the spectators had accepted this kind of show. The audiences automatically decoded the metaphor. In after-show discussions, when any mention was made of the noble Don Tello, the spectators understood this as a reference to a local colonel.

During this time, we were doing an 'educational' theatre and Paulo Freire was spreading his educational method throughout the state of Pernambuco, delivering literacy for all he was worth. The Peasant Leagues were numerous and strong, the Church more and more progressive. President Jango was threatening state ownership of foreign companies, negotiating with rebel soldiers and sailors. Nothing revolutionary, in my view, just democratic. . . . Even so . . .

To tell the truth, I was disoriented. I no longer knew what to do: I compared Lope's play with Santo André factory workers' play — they had written and performed theirs, they had even done a kind of Forum Theatre. They were our much-sought-after 'people' — and they had invaded the stage. In *O melhor juiz* it was only an actor, as middle class as me, in the skin of a fictitious character, who came on stage — the character was supposed to be of the 'people', not us. Pelayo was a pale imitation of the real blood-and-flesh workers of Santo André. Mere fiction!

I felt regret: Pelayo reproduced, in fiction, what Jurandir and his friends had done in reality, so *O melhor juiz* was a regression. We had already taken a step forward: we had given our beloved 'people' the means of theatrical production. We had taught them to do theatre, without putting our words into their mouths, permitting them to express their own thoughts, without our tutelage. With Pelayo, we had taken back the word. Prometheus, regretting having given mankind fire, blew out the flame.

As a child, the young owner of a football, when I lost a game I would take my ball back. We were doing the same thing: abandoning the workers of Santo André, going back to the theatre with its old moral lesson, its famous message. We were saying 'This is the way you should do it!' — to people who had already done better than us! We were artists, we wanted to speak our thoughts. Much later I understood that it is not necessary to make an exclusive choice between doing theatre or teaching. I discovered my double vocation: artist and teacher.

Today, as an artist, I want to write plays, to bear witness — and I do not want anyone to interfere! As a teacher, I want to teach — they bear witness, and I have no desire to interfere.

My father tires of living

During our run of Lope's play, my father died. Ill from the age of 64 on, my father died on the day he completed his seventy-first year. On his coffin, we placed his birthday telegrams: 'Let this happy day be repeated for many years to come. . . .' I saw my father bathed in flowers. I held his icy hands. A memory came to me, of the day his right leg was amputated. My family had spent a sleepless night with him, in the hospital, before the operation.

As I was rested, I kept him company the next night while my family got some sleep.

My father used to say he would rather die than let them amputate his leg. At dawn, he asked if he was still whole: he could still feel the pain in his amputated foot. I answered no, truthfully – he was not. I saw tears in his eyes. He wanted to be sure, wanted to see. I helped him sit up. My father used to say that he never tired of working, but he could tire of living. He had said he would prefer to die – but he preferred to live, even without his right leg.

That night, he remembered episodes of his life, told me things about Portugal. He spoke slowly, slept, woke, started talking again, remembering, like an interrupted dream. He would be talking to me, and then suddenly it was as if his thoughts became submerged in sleep and, when he awoke again, they came back further on, in another story. My father ran through his entire life. He talked of what he had done and of what he thought he should have done. He corrected the sketch of his life.

It reminded me of a character from Chekhov's *Three Sisters* who asks himself: 'And what if our life were merely a draft we could rewrite?' Today, when I am depressed, I think of rewriting mine. In front of this computer, I think of another biography, an invented biography: the life I would like to have lived. But, if it was premeditated, would it be life?

Diabetes is an insidious illness. Years later, the doctors had to amputate his left leg too. Once again I was at his side when he awoke from the anaesthetic, once again I helped him sit up in bed and see what he lacked. Once again I wet my hands in his tears, and mine. When I think the word 'grief', I think of that day.

In his wheelchair, my father used to say that he was tired of living, now that he was unable to work. For him, living was working. As it is for me, today, almost like my father. I love to work, because I love to live.

Looking at the flowers, seeing my father, his eyes closed, I wanted to understand. I always want to understand the meaning of every event. My father, dead: in life we had swapped words and silences, trudging back home from the bakery, or from home to the bakery. Our silences were our most florid language. Our smiles.

There we were again, silent; one of us dead. I wanted to understand. I understood nothing. I wanted to find the meaning: there were no meanings. My father was dead. That was all. That alone. Alone. I was alone.

The Son of the Devil and Ilha Bela[56]

Guarnieri, a city dweller, had written a new play *O filho do cão*[57] (The son of the devil), once again about agrarian reform, the absence of which continues to be one of the main obstacles to life in Brazil; the other is the foreign debt. The external debt of the indebted countries will never be paid, as every politician knows full well. One day it is going to explode – this is the inexorable result of the unscrupulous mathematics of the Market-God! Everyone also knows that the explosion can be postponed with new loans, and new, yet more draconian austerity plans, with cuts in the budget, the closure of schools and hospitals – measures which will simply increase the megaton potency of the explosion to come. The debt is the bond of slavery! In the last century, a master physically owned his slave. In this century, foreign debt was invented. For the masters, this is even better.

At the time of writing, Brazil is paying over one billion five hundred million dollars per month in debt servicing and interest repayments. If we think that every public hospital or state school costs around a million dollars, each month we pay out the equivalent of more than 500 state schools and 1000 public hospitals. Can we live like that? No! Every time the authorities sign the documents transferring these billions into pockets which are already bulging, their gilded pen signs the death warrant for thousands of Brazilians. And the signatories are Brazilians. Inevitable comparison: the people who used to capture Africans fleeing from slavery were black themselves, the infamous *Capitâes do mato*.[58] *Plus ça change. . . .*

I could bear it no longer, I felt lost and needed to rest. I used to listen to the script and feel that I had heard the same lines in other plays. The work that had to be done at the Arena was crude, incessant and assorted: we were doing the administration, the publicity, the programming, the artistic work. And sweeping the stage. And washing the dishes. Sometimes exhaustion overwhelmed us. My colleagues thought I looked lost and pale. I was pale. I was lost. Split between desire and duty, as between two beloved women. This is a metaphor . . . and it is not.

My friends perceived my dichotomy and suggested I rest. I stopped, out of total exhaustion and perplexity. . . . The box-office could not stop: Paulo José took over the direction of *Cão*. I had the right (the need) to take a three-week vacation.

Ilha Bela: no electric light except between 6 and 8 in the evening. After that, candle-light, the moon and the stars.

A light conducive to meditation . . .

The *coup* at the gallop, down the mountain

'There is champagne, I saw it myself' the 'Candidate' said, stretching out in the Professor-in-Chief's armchair.

Three bottles. I counted the guests: fifteen. One bottle between five. The wine was Chilean, French and Spanish. The smell of palm oil promised Bahian delicacies. Multi-culturalism.

'The champagne is for after the General's speech. Whisky or *cachaça* now, to whet everyone's whistle . . .' proposed the Professor.

31 March 1964, waiting for the TV news. The 'Candidate' was the most loquacious of the eclectic bunch present: artists from the theatre, from cinema and music, teachers, journalists (perpetually glued to the phone, speaking in whispers, sharing secrets), a Chilean ophthalmologist, a humanist philosopher, a bespectacled psychologist, and a vet with walking sticks – for which a neurotic horse was to blame. The hosts were the Professor-in-Chief and the Sub-Professor-in-Chief, his wife.

The *coup* was arriving at a gallop from the highlands of Minas Gerais, sending ripples across the plains. Would there be heroic spillage of blood or just threatening telephone calls? Bombs or curses? Bullets or telegrams?

10 p.m. Part of the *mineiro*[59] army that was in revolt was awaiting the end of the negotiations between generals and 'scum-of-the-earth governors' (as Darcy Ribeiro had it) so that they could continue their advance on Rio or return to their barracks. Men and weapons were being counted in the same way as a person might assess his cards in *Truco*,[60] before the deadly bluff.

Brasilia was by then already the capital, and – if they wanted a real *coup* – the army would have to advance on the Planalto,[61] a lengthy journey.

The *coup* would lose its cinematic suspense, which depended on its rapid execution. War tanks used up more fuel than the commanders' Mercedes – the tanks would have to refuel in the Esso or Shell stations, on the roadside. There would be a risk of encountering a stray photographer: a photo of your tanks refuelling in a petrol station is enough to demoralise any army. Especially if the young woman clutching the fuel-hose is wearing a short skirt, a red one, like they do in the USA. . . . It doesn't look virile enough.

The general from Minas Gerais had read in the war manuals that one has to advance, so he advanced on Rio, where the presence of Lacerda's government would make negotiations easier. He could have chosen Espirito Santo – with the symbolism of taking Vitória, its capital – but the invasion of Copacabana and Ipanema,[62] causing stupefaction among the bathing trunks and bikinis, would have a greater impact, even if the tanks ran the risk of becoming stuck in Rio's traffic jams. Having your tanks stuck in traffic, alongside bicycles and soft drink lorries, is enough to demoralise any *coup d'état*.

Troops across the country were up in arms, negotiating. A general in Amazonas wanted to invade neighbouring Acre, but he knew no reason to do so, he just felt like it; another, in Tocantins, was ready to occupy Mato Grosso if necessary – except it wasn't. They desisted because they were convinced that such actions, which would be arduous, would not attract popular support.

The general of the south, General Cruel, who was loyal to the constitutional government, had risen in defence of the legality. Even so, he was negotiating with another general, who was insurgent for the opposite reason, who in turn was negotiating with rebellious or dormant generals right across the country. Generals were negotiating with their peers and with scum-of-the-earth renegade governors. There was no shortage of generals. Or negotiations. Or scum of the earth. Far from it.

We took no pleasure in seeing our general, the faithful Cruel, converse with governors who were conversing with the US ambassador. A bad sign. The people were not negotiating, they were awaiting the outcome. Scum-of-the-earth governors were negotiating with loyal governors, who were not renegades – but who were exchanging ideas with the ones who were. Generals and brigadiers were negotiating with the gringo admiral, who just happened to be in command of a battleship. By an incredible coincidence, this ship, which was anchored five minutes off our coast, had its cannons trained absent-mindedly on our sunny beaches. Full of marines armed to the tonsils, to the oesophagus. By pure coincidence! They were just passing. . . .

The handiest coincidence was that the Admiral had a hot-line to the generals, insurgent or not, and spoke to all of them, in English, a language of which they all had perfect mastery, especially the interpreters.

In the Professor's house, we were waiting for the general of the south to pronounce. Why the delay? We wanted to drink champagne.

Honest Governors carried on negotiating with negotiators who had access to the negotiators who were negotiating with the renegades' negotiators, and so on. Men in uniform continued to negotiate with civilians, civilian nationals with foreigners, and foreigners with renegades, with or without uniforms. And so on. Cruel was the pointer on the scales of power: whichever side his heart swung, whichever side the butt of his gun pointed, that side would win. The Third Army (his army) was Brazil's strongest because it guarded our borders with our arch-enemies at football: Argentina and Uruguay. The nation held its breath as it awaited the end of the negotiations. Like the wronged husband the people would be the last to know, too late.

It's 10.50 on a dark night. 'What time was the General due on?'

'10 . . . now it's 11. I don't like it . . .'

The respondent was the only pessimist in the circle – me. The optimists demonstrated, scientifically, how it was impossible for there to be a *coup* in Brazil. Above all, the Candidate explained, because of an extremely powerful cosmic-religious force, which was called the 'Balance of Power'. With the Balance of Power on our side, no one could hold us back, because it included the entire nuclear arsenal of the Soviet Union, which threatened the world with definitive atomic and hecatombic Armageddon – if the United States should dare to touch one hair on the head of our national sovereignty. Absent-minded cannons were pure coincidence. . . . The Yankee admiral was doubtless taking a little turn on deck, in silk pyjamas, smoking a cigar: nothing could be more peaceful than a cigar and silk pyjamas.

The Chilean ophthalmologist thought that a *coup* in Brazil was feasible because we lacked the ancient democratic tradition of his country: '*En Chile nunca habrá golpes militares! Lo decidimos todo hablando diplomaticamente, como caballeros . . . Golpes en Chile? Jamás!*'[63]

The Candidate thought that once those resistant to the inexorable advance of history — which, he vowed, will never retreat! — once they had done with their ritual baring of teeth, we should be generous with the rebel military. A few days of house arrest to purge their misdemeanour, and they would have paid a reasonable price for giving us such a tremendous shock.

Why a *coup*? Jango was carrying out reforms, but all small stuff . . . promises the wind would blow away. 'The death-rattle of authoritarianism', explained the Candidate.

Candidate for what? Why, for everything! The Candidate was always standing as a candidate. Wherever a vacancy loomed, he was there. A study grant in Turkey or a chair in Botucatu, a position as Legal Adviser to a guarana[64] factory or a free blood test: he was in the queue. He was the Candidate. People like that always end up getting in somewhere. That day, the Candidate was putting himself forward as a candidate for First Universal Explainer: if war was the prolongation of diplomacy, as Clausewitz said, there would be a lot of diplomacy to go before outright war. Those who believed this remained unperturbed. Some of us *were* perturbed.

The humanist philosopher counter-argued: 'We have to accept the universal truth that Man . . .' (People still said 'Man' then. Today it is 'the human being', an advance due to feminism!) '. . . Man is carnivorous, a predatory animal. He crushes and devours. And not only inferior animals: he gobbles up his fellows, he has an appetite. Man is not humanised. The journey for man to become Man is a long one!'

'So?' asked his perplexed auditors.

'In the face of this biological and moral inevitability, men either accept that there is no point in behaving morally, in being nice to our fellow humans. The voice of inhuman nature wins out! — and they dedicate themselves to total butchery, or otherwise they become humanised.'

'Man will never become humanised!' countered a journalist.

'Those who, in spite of everything, become humanised, agree that there is only one indivisible Humanity, and that we have to install socialist regimes throughout the world which will protect the weak and offer equal opportunities to all, to the children of rich and poor alike. Down with Darwin's *The Origin of Species* – impeccable book though it is, it is incumbent on all of us to give the lie to it with our humanitarian actions!'

The philosopher was dialectical, so his reasoning was hedged around with extensive circumlocution:

'We humanists agree with the thesis that the state has a duty to offer education and health to all. These are human rights – we are one humanity, all in the same boat. But . . . those who think otherwise, those who copy Freud in the bad sense – Freud said that Man is a porcupine, he likes to live in packs, but impales and kills when he embraces – those guys put venom on their barbs. Every man for himself and God had better watch out, because not even God is safe from earthly brawls! We are humanist socialists or prehistoric cannibals!'

The intellectual level of the conversation was no more uplifting than recollections of that night. The champagne glasses were still virgins, waiting for the General, but the whisky glasses were already half way through their second coming.

'You should read Marx . . .' announced the Professor, Chief Marxist. Everyone had read Marx, but he alone understood him. 'You cannot compare class struggle with wild boar and crocodile.'

He had a point. Crocodiles and wild boars do not phone each other, and the *coup* was being gestated thanks to the good offices of Alexander Graham Bell. Someone heard people on Radio Tupi tell of eating the wires in anxiety. The nation was just one million dollars short of enabling a decision to be taken which would be serious and committed to True Democracy. No one was saying whose pocket that million would end up in.

The psychologist, with his minuscule eyes and trifocal lenses, like all good psychologists, was schooled in the art of listening in silence, uttering the odd 'mmm . . . mmm . . .' by way of stimulus to the orator. It pained him to say whole words. As the silence became prolonged, he decided to make his small contribution to the party; unwittingly, he provoked a great psycho-ideological crisis:

'Weber is right . . .' he began, instantly capturing everyone's attention. 'Weber said that there is a measurable causal relationship between physical and psychic energies!'

Strange Weberian language. What kind of energy? The psychologist cleared his throat: 'Look: sensation and perception. For someone to feel a new sensation, an increase in intensity of stimulus is required. For each new sensation, a further increase. This increase is fixed in percentage terms. For example, if you have something on your head weighing 200 g you need a variation of 10 g to feel the difference. Well, if the starting weight were 1 kg, you would need a variation of 50 g, indisputably five times ten. Do you not think that Weber is right?'

No one dared disagree with the master. But what on earth did a weight on one's head have to do with tanks from Minas Gerais?

'If the workers are deprived of their basic rights gradually, by less than 10 g each time, they do not feel it, and they accustom themselves to the worst of living conditions; they do not revolt, and the world carries on peacefully. But if this deprivation is of brutal force and comes all in one go, they rebel!'

The sociologists were astonished at this assertion of Weber's and its practical application to the Brazilian situation, which Weber did not even know; shocked at this secret Weber, who now revealed himself as shamelessly siding with the bosses. The humanist, off the leash, dared to contradict:

'Machiavelli said the opposite: the Prince should do all bad things, all in one go, however many grams or kilos or tons are involved, all in one go! If you have to kill fifty, kill two hundred: the subjects are left in the knowledge that anyone who had to die is already buried. Good, according to Machiavelli, should be doled out in small doses, so that the subjects stay hopeful, wanting more.'

The psychologist, with Weberian certainties, counter-attacked, scandalising the majority, sociologists emeritus to a man.

'How do you cook frogs so that their flesh is tasty?' He asked. No one was a cook, nor given to amphibian gastronomy. 'Like this: you put them alive in a clay pan, with a little salt, no pepper, and, so that they do not jump out, you put the pan over a low flame. You raise the temperature slowly; the frogs do not realise the cook's strategy and, by the time they become aware of the heat, their blood has already thickened in their veins, they are unconscious and ready to be served up in a vinaigrette sauce, with garlic, onions, black and sweet pepper . . . they die baked, without protest.'

'Do frogs have blood?' someone asked delicately.

'I don't think so, but for our scientific reasoning, that is irrelevant. . . .'

As no one commented further, the psychologist was able to conclude by saying that that was how it had been in Brazil for years: factory workers had been losing their rights little by little, with inflation eroding their meagre wages. They had already become habituated to this and did not even realise that their suffering was increasing. Which was why a *coup* was improbable: no one would be so bold as to implant dictatorship when bourgeois democracy served the interests of the bosses, anaesthetising the working class.

We could sleep easy: there would not be any *coups*. The frogs were there to prove it!

Unease silenced everyone: the majority disagreed, in lonely embarrassment. *Magister Dixit*! Best to keep quiet until someone broached a new subject. If Weber had uttered this barbarity, maybe he was right. Those present venerated Weber, the celestial one: how could they contradict the Divine Father? Hearing his name, they fell to their knees like Islamic fundamentalists at 4.55 p.m. But . . . on what page of what book had the Master written this savagery about frogs, obliging them, silently, to swallow this distasteful frog-pill? Or was the example of the frogs merely the psychologist's own maladroit contribution? They were treading on eggshells.

The Musician commented: 'Weber, eh? I thought he was only interested in arias, duets, recitatives. . . . And in the dead of night, he's off cooking frogs and sucking their bones. . . .'

'Weber did not like music! For him, psycho-physics was everything!' the psychologist commented, provoking musicological ire and sociological alarm.

The psychologist retorted: 'Weber is one of the composers I most admire. I am sure he never said all that crazy stuff about culinary art of batraquicide. This is slander!'

The drunken musician launched a salvo: 'Debussy even said that Weber was the first composer who was concerned with the relationship which should exist between the soul of nature and the soul of the character, in opera!'

'Which Weber are you talking about?' the psychologist asked.

'Carl Maria Von Weber, the true creator of German Opera! Without Weber *nicht* Wagner!'

'Ahhh, that's not the Weber I am talking about, not at all . . .'

Anxiety increased amongst the sociologists. The Professor and his friends wanted to know which goddamned Weber the psychologist's Weber was. It was Ernst Heinrich Weber, a German anatomist. The psychologist regained the smiling admiration of the company. Laughter. Joy. Whisky!

'Ahh! It is not *our* Weber! I am sure that our Max would never eat frogs, especially if he knew that they had been tortured in that manner!' came the judicious comment of the Professor, more Weberian than ever, ever the Marxist, ever the Chief.

If the leaders of the *coup* take power – I am speaking hypothetically – we have to find a formula to join them. 'If they take power, we were wrong, and they were right. Whoever takes power is right!'

The comments which followed ran the whole gamut, from 'Traitor, masquerading as a nationalist!' to 'Crystal-clear Cartesianism!' A rainbow of opinions.

In decisive moments, the Professor decided on the last word.

'In Brazil, given the complexity of our social fabric – in which the most extreme poverty in the landed estates of the Northeast lives alongside the sophisticated industrial technology of the south – bearing in mind that we live in a democracy . . .' – he looked at his watch: it was midnight and no word from General Cruel – 'a democracy – until midnight, at least, this country was still a democracy – whoever it may be that exercises power in this country, they will have to embrace economic forces, even those of the colonial past. Brazil, without a broad alliance which includes even the most retrograde forces, is not governable. . . . In order for the Left to govern, we have to let the Right govern, too! If we have to join forces with the reactionaries after the elections, why not do so beforehand? In order to carry on being of the Left, we may be obliged to distance ourselves from the Left in order to satisfy some of the reactionaries' desires, because otherwise there will be a *coup* and they will do whatever they want. . . . We have to be realists! To unite the Centre Left with the Far Right might seem like a crazy idea, but it has a *raison d'être* . . . I think Marx, if he were alive. . . .'

'Thankfully Marx died before you came along . . .' someone murmured.

Given that the Professor was a self-proclaimed First Marxist, this statement exploded like a hydrogen bomb. To join or not to join them? Had we of the Left gone too far, beckoning the people with the dream of agrarian reform, Soviets in power, etc., or had we fallen short of what was necessary, not daring to do even what Getúlio Vargas would have done?

I remember hearing a word of good sense – one: 'If they carry out a *coup*, they will not need anyone to join them! If they win without us, why would they make alliances with us afterwards?'

The Professor, never one to lose, took the pulse of the group: 'What do you think?' He always gave the impression of being on the whole world's side, even if that world was exploding all about him. . . . It was important for him to give the impression of power, even in the absence of it . . . but that was a detail. He wanted the pomp!

The conversation fragmented into tangential subjects: being a Statist means finding solutions; if the President thinks that the interest on the debt should be paid, that we should go on being slaves in order to avoid retaliation, what is the use of the President? A good administrator would be sufficient! Enough of intermediaries: Lincoln Gordon[65] for President!

We were waiting for General Cruel in order to be able to celebrate the end of the failed *coup*. If I remember rightly, it was 1 a.m. The newscaster gave notice of an important political pronouncement. A Governor appeared, whose electoral campaign slogan admitted: 'He steals, but he gets things done!' He was portrayed smiling, with his hand on his fat wallet. The General had come on board, and the Governor doled out smiles: lest he lose his thieving habit, he stole our peace, our hope.

The Professor put the champagne away on the shelf. He took a quick decision: 'Best if you all get off now. I will put out the lights so as not to attract attention. Better leave one by one or in pairs. Three could seem like a conspiracy. . . .'

The Candidate, in the forefront of the retreat, said: 'I was sure Max Weber never wrote anything about frogs . . . I only didn't say so in order to avoid embarrassment – don't you agree, Professor?'

'Let's speak on the phone tomorrow . . .' said the Master reassuringly, as he opened the door.

In the dark street, on my way home, for the first time in my life I listened to the silence. And heard it. How full of sounds silence is! It can be heard from kilometres away. The further away, the more frightening. A police siren . . . or was it an ambulance? My shoes on the street . . . a strange noise. I kicked a stone in the road. Would they be arresting people before dawn? It was prohibited by law. . . . What law? Or were they taking wounded mutineers to hospital? Silence.

Alone. No one was passing in the street. Silence. A door closed. I heard a key turning. I heard my breath. I heard the shadow of a woman gliding past a silent window. I heard the soft murmur of my hands skimming the air, cutting the wind. I heard the wind, the breeze. I heard the silence.

After the silence another siren, and then another. . . . Then silence . . . silence . . . silence . . . s . . . s . . . s . . . .

Alone.

war declared, inside and outside of me

Opinion and Zumbi – the musicals

After that solid silence, we were afraid of telephones. Even whispered conversations in the bar across from the Arena – all bugged. We met on the set of *Filho do Cão*.

It was a hellish world. We went through our shelves. Letters from Cuba, diaries, addresses, editions of *Granma*,[1] books by Mao, Chê, Fidel, Marx, Engels, Sartre . . . lovingly annotated, were hidden or thrown in the bin. We had bonfires, an early ideological São João.[2]

The army, parking tanks in the middle of the road; the navy, anchoring ships on the coast; the air force, landing wherever there was a runway – they had abandoned their military duties and converted themselves into a police force. They conducted sweeps, looking for us and for 'the people'. Anyone who had once said anything which might appear similar to left-wing thinking – for example, the affirmation that communists did not eat small children and, if they did, would not necessarily do so in Red Square, in a public celebration! – was imprisoned and taken to specially adapted prison ships, barracks, common jails or neighbourhood police stations. Where there was a door and padlock, prisoners were locked up.

The dictatorship's first measure was a cultural one: the banning of the Centres of Popular Culture throughout the land. As well as the peasant leagues, the trade unions, the student unions, any form of dialogue.

We decided to abandon the Arena for weeks, for months. After wandering from friendly house to house, each night in a different bed – some of us with children – we discovered that the State Police did not know about the deeds of the persecuted in other states, so, if we moved to another state we'd be 'clean'. Thank God computers did not exist then, Bill Gates was still a poor boy sucking lollipops. Whoever moved to another state would have a police record purer than an angel's belly on the day of a debutantes' ball in Heaven.

I spent weeks alone in the mountains, in the house of some friends: books lining the walls! There I read from sunrise to after sunset. Three times a week, I went to the town cinema. A single projector showed one reel at a time: three intervals – popcorn and guaraná. I tried to stop smoking – three packets a day was excessive. I cut down to seven cigarettes . . . and spent every minute thinking of the next puff. (Years later I abandoned the vice, at age 35, after collapsing in the street from the accumulation of nervous nicotine in my lungs.)

For the first time I felt alone, in the world of theatre. I am a man for groups: before travelling to the United States I had friends in the Black Experimental Theatre; in New York, it was the Writers' Group; on my return Gláucio Gil and Leo Jusi; in São Paulo, the Arena. . . . And now, no one. I am a man for groups. One of the most wonderful prizes I have won in my life was in the town of Gävle, in Sweden: it was the *Premio Haddock* – fish which only live in shoals. I have to be in a shoal. In Rio I was a fish out of water, on the hot sand!

The first *coup* was not deadly. They imprisoned, but torture had not yet been instituted as the usual method of interrogation: the armed forces still displayed tenuous vestiges of civilisation. During the democracy, we had our adversaries: now we had enemies. Before, since we accepted the democracy, we were obliged to accept them; now, how could we dialogue with the devil?

I had an idea that I thought ingenious. Before 1964, movie directors had created a style: *cinema-verdade* (truth-cinema); characters were played by the very people who inspired the story. In other words, true documentaries with the appearance of fiction.

If you could have truth-cinema, why not truth-theatre?

The first idea came easily: Kafka's *The Trial* revealed what was happening in Brazil. K. wakes in the morning – as we did on 1 April 1964 – to find his room full of policemen: he is being accused by someone (you do not know who), of something (you do not know what), and will be tried (you do not know when), by a judge (you do not know which), in a court (you do not know where). K. ends up being sentenced to death and is executed.

Nothing seemed more like Brazil in those dark days.

I thought of inviting to make up the actual cast people who, like K., were persecuted without knowing why. There was no shortage of potential cast! Fine actors! In my delirium, I wanted all my friends and all the people I admired, I wanted all the victims of persecution on Earth! (If you are going to dream, why do it in black and white? Gigantic cinemascope, instead. I always wanted to drink the sea – a tempest is just an aperitif!) When I explained the idea, people loved it, as long as . . . the cast was made up of others, not them. No one had the time. Or the skill. Or both. But they thought the idea was great, albeit unaccomplishable.

Tartuffe

The *coup* counted on the support of the extreme Right, organisations with names such as 'Tradition, Family and Property',[3] and 'The League of Catholic Women'.[4] These women organised diabolical 'Marches with God for Liberty', which were menacing ku-klux-klanesque parades with the insolent swagger of the *Galinhas Verdes* of my childhood. Extremely religious people, of the most impeccable upbringing, on discovering the liberty of the streets, they swore at anyone who looked as if they might be 'the people'. Happy as pie, with an escort of mounted police, they vociferated in loud and strident tones: 'Sons of Bitches!' and other delicate utterances p till then they would only have entertained in shameful thought, ...sconced in their bathrooms.

...-heels on the march. Rich women walking excitedly on the prol- ... treets, a thing they would never have done in times of political ... dressed in their Sunday best, reaffirming their condition as 'don't mess with me' Catholics. Behind the bloc of the high-heeled came the bloc of the nannies, governesses, and faithful retainers; behind them, chauffeur-driven cars: each lady brought her vehicle in case of any fainting emergency. Plus just a few armed security guards: the time was not yet ripe for that profession. Today it is so ripe it is positively rotting.

The ladies used the most anti-religious procedure one could imagine: God ceased to be the Supreme Justice and became their ally in the battle against the Left. In truth, these were anti-God marches. In their prayers, they reduced God to their own bigoted level: God as little busybody. If we wanted to continue speaking of our times, investigating the metaphor, the choice of play was clear! Molière's *Tartuffe*.

The seed of the idea of *The Trial* eventually germinated, transformed into *Opinião* (Opinion), a truth-show, in which singers would tell their stories in song.

An *intelecto-popular* restaurant opened, Zi-Cartola, which served up Brazilian food, popular music and assorted non-conformism. Nara Leão presented *shows*[5] in this gastronomico-politico-literary-musical dialogue, with well-known names, such as herself, and the revelations, Zé Keti and João do Vale.[6] The group chose these three artists for the first show. Vianninha and some writers from the CPC started interviewing the singers about their personal lives, to write the script of the show, in Rio, while I rehearsed *Tartuffe* in São Paulo.

Tartuffe was a great success. People who were familiar with the script were shocked by the speech of the Official who comes to imprison *Tartuffe* and delivers a eulogy of the Prince. Molière wrote eulogies of the monarchy so that Louis XIV would authorise the production: the script was critical of the nobility. In the final monologue, the audience was enchanted by the irony of the script centuries after it had been written. People who had never heard of Molière approached us, Guarnieri and I, speaking in secret conspiratorial tones: 'That's a great play you have written! The idea of using a pseudonym to throw the censor off the scent, and that Molière character you invented – it's fantastic, marvellous! Do you know, some people think this Molière really exists? Don't worry, we won't let on to anyone that he is just a pseudonym for you!'

A word is a living being

Vianninha handed me 300 pages of monologues, dialogues and song lyrics. I wanted to tell the truth, but not to take so long over it: our theatre was hot and dusty, in a humid summer. The 300 pages shrank to fifty.

We were creating a new theatre form – I wanted it to be theatre, not just a musical show: the actors had to sing to one another in the same way as they might talk to each other, with passion, rather than singing at the audience or into a microphone, like someone exhibiting themselves, solo. The singers found it difficult to concentrate, looking at each other, eye to eye. For most of them, singing was a solitary act in the middle of a multitude: alone, amidst the crowd. Fine to be looking at footlights – faced with another human being, the singer lost concentration.

The fear of singing face to face was the fear of discovering oneself, of seeing oneself in the other. It is impossible to sing eye to eye without feeling the revelation of the word pronounced; it is impossible to hear only the music, the pure dancing sound, without the live body of the poem. In singing for the microphone the word is sound, rhythm, volume, melody, timbre . . . but the beating heart has less significance. I wanted each singer to see themselves in the others, when they looked at them. I wanted them to mean what they were singing.[7]

To me, *the word is a living being*. In writing this book, I feel a sensual joy, a bodily pleasure as I see the words fleeing from my fingers and reappearing, happy, on the screen of the computer. When they come out of me, out of my head and out of my blood, they first look at me and let themselves gaze, in human dialogue through the screen. Then they beg leave to depart, in search of someone: you, the reader. Words are friends which seek new friends. Words should be caressed, loved. Only thus do they reveal themselves. They are like women: only with love do they reveal themselves. I kiss my words when they depart, as one kisses a child before a journey. They are daughters. Words are sisters: we are born from the same womb, the same blood plays happily in our veins. My words and I

war declared inside and outside of me

want to say the same thoughts, to love the same love. Yet each word has its own irreplaceable individuality. Synonyms are not words which have the same meaning, that is impossible: they just have similar meanings. Even almost identical twins from a single egg, difficult as they may be to tell apart, are not the same person. Each word is unique! Syntax is a form of friendship among words: real friends get something from one another. Every two words together have a third meaning.

My words are loved ones, their pulse beats, they breathe! My words are me, part of me, the best part. If I want to know who I am, I have the best mirror: the words I say, I write. My plays, my books. Are me. Others think differently. Who am I to think that only what I say is right?

Our truth-show was a dialogue: the actor-singers told their lives to one another, sometimes with plain words, most of the time singing songs. João had written a letter to his father when he ran away from home as a boy; he read it to Nara, tears flowing, tears which clothed his words. Nara replied tenderly, looking into his eyes, affectionate: *Carcará*.[8] Capture, kill and eat![9] This was dialogue, theatre, not show-business. . . . (Please under-stand: I have nothing against show-business, I love it, but . . . I do theatre!) I wanted them to use the words of the songs as dialogue, in a dramatic form, not lyrically. This forced me to cut a song in half, to use only some verses. I wanted them to hear not just the music, but the idea in it. *Opinião* was going to be the first show of a new phase. A shout, an explosion. Music alone was not enough.

It was not easy to convince João and Zé to be themselves and characters, not just singers. Nara quickly understood and helped me to convince them. They were excellent singers and bashful actors. It is difficult to play a character, and still more so if it is oneself. They agreed to be one thing or the other, themselves or the characters: both at the same time was complicated.

Each represented themselves *and* their class. Zé came from the hill-side;[10] João from the Northeast;[11] Nara, an intelligent, beautiful lass from Copacabana,[12] represented herself and other young women like her who were more concerned about what was happening in our country than with the body beautiful.

I felt a great affection for all three. Especially for Nara, who helped me so much, as a friend. My personal life was changing in that difficult time. I was separating from my first wife. Nara helped me to see ways forward, she was my counsellor.

Dori Caymmi[13] was the musical director. The band consisted of guitar, drums and flute. Nothing more. The scenery, old timber. Half a dozen lanterns, with cellophane instead of lighting gel. The costumes, our everyday clothes. Three microphones; the sound desk, a warped wooden affair perched on uneven legs, would judder in response to any careless movement, sending out high-pitched blasts of noise. *Opinião* alternated moments of pure beauty with explosive electronic disasters. . . .

It was hard working with 'people/characters'. Imagine a director explaining to an actor his conception of the character, and the actor (the character) replying that it was nothing like that. That was what the rehearsals of *Opinião* were like. I would be speaking to the actor, and it would be the character who replied. Or I would be talking about significance, and it would be the signifier who answered me back.

The rehearsals were difficult also from the human relations perspective. Nara lent us the living room in her parents' house for rehearsals, in Avenida Atlântica, overlooking the sea. The rehearsals were short: João used to tire easily. I said it was the drink, he swore it was not. One day Nara's father realised that his bottles of Scotch – single malt – were going down rapidly. He pointed out subtly that this evacuation had begun after the rehearsals had been transferred to his house. Ashamed, we took the decision never again to touch the bottles, sensuous as they were, tantalisingly within reach of straying hands. João explained, with all seriousness, that he needed to drink because without a little alcohol going down his gullet, his voice would not leave his throat. I proposed that after each rehearsal we go to the bar on the corner to drink *cachaça*.

'It has to be before rehearsal!' João explained. 'Otherwise, my voice won't come! I know my throat better than anyone! It is very temperamental.' He thought a bit, then added: 'The drink after rehearsal idea is possible, but then it wouldn't be the same; that would be the after-work *cachaça*, and I am talking about the before-work *cachaça*. . . . The one helps rehearsals along, the other helps me sleep in peace. . . .'

I argued that, before rehearsal, *cachaça* affected concentration. João promised not to get drunk, he only needed a drop to rehearse properly. I challenged him: 'João: tomorrow I will bring a bottle of good *cachaça* full to the brim! I will give myself as many shots as you do. No more, no less! It is not a competition to see who holds out, but if you fall asleep before me, I will never again allow even a whiff of drink during rehearsal. OK?'

João – who had been drinking since he was a small boy, from early morning onwards – laughed at the challenge and said that I would be fast asleep on the table before he so much as blinked.

I was true to my threat and brought in a very good *cachaça*. João helped himself to a shot, I drank another. The rehearsal went on, him taking one shot, me another; I'd say something, they'd do some singing, whenever one took a shot, the other would too.

I felt groggy, but I held on, I did not want to endure the shame of being humiliatingly routed – until finally João put his head on the table and started to snore. I was astonished: how come I had vanquished such a hardened drinker? Although it was no cause for pride, I did feel proud of myself: what endurance I had shown! I was the champ! Hurray!

Nara threw light on the mystery: on her way to the rehearsal that afternoon, she had found João in the bar, already half-drunk. The shots he'd had at rehearsal had been a gentle finale: he was already half-cut before the 'competition' had begun. . . .

That is what rehearsals were like: tenderness, work, art and . . . childishness.

The opening night arrived. The audience was on our side, which was an essential part of the performance, they shouted out our songs, they sang along to our shouts. *Opinião* was us and our audience! *Opinião* was the first coherent and collective protest theatre against the inhumane dictatorship which assassinated and tortured so many, which so impoverished the people, which so badly destroyed what before we used to call Pátria (Fatherland).

After three decades of alienation, of Pátria only the music remains.

The box-office stops for no one

Nara gave herself to the show. Her beautiful voice had body, the songs demanded body and soul. On stage, the pleasure of singing what the people were shouting in the street. But there was the heat, and the floor was dust. . . . Nara's vocal chords could not stand it: after weeks of splendour, her doctor decreed that she could go on no longer. Nara came up with the solution: in Salvador there was a divine singer, Maria Bethânia. Who? No one knew her. Had anyone seen her? Not one of us had been to Bahia.

Even if it were true, it would be a solution for the long term: with the theatre sold out we could not wait. Bethânia would need a good two weeks' rehearsal. Some disagreed about inviting Bethânia – the show would be disfigured: the text revolved around the different geographical and cultural origins of its participants, and Bethânia, like João, came from the Northeast. Still uncertain, we decided to ring Santo Amaro da Purificação;[14] her family agreed on condition that, being only 17, she be accompanied by one of her older brothers. They came.

That night we sought out Suzana, Vinicius de Moraes' daughter, who was rehearsing with Ziembinski. Protesting that she was an actress who sang (rather than a singer), she agreed to sing with us if Zimba agreed. He agreed to let her go for one week. Suzana would come on board, giving Bethânia time to rehearse. Suzana sang us her life story.

I remember the Thursday when Bethânia (then known as Berré) arrived clinging to her brother's arm. She wanted me to hear her sing: I did not have time. Submerged in rehearsal, I could not listen to her; I was feeling guilty about throwing Suzana into the fire just because the *show must go on* – at least, when it is sold out: when it is not, it stops by itself. . . . The show can stop: the box-office stops for no one.

I apologised to Bethânia, and promised that after the opening night I would listen to as much of her repertoire as she cared to sing me. Only then did I notice her shy, skinny brother, and I asked his name.

'My name is Caetano'.

'Caetano what?'

'Veloso.'[15]

'Ah. . . .'

I went back to rehearsals. Suzana debuted on a Saturday, in the fashion she wanted: as an actress who sang. Such a good actress, playing a great singer. We applauded both. Thankyou, Suzana, and Ziembinski.

After the opening performance, I called Bethânia and Caetano. I sat with my back to the theatre entrance, in the middle of the arena, with the two of them seated in front of me. On hearing the first song I was sure I would invite her to join us. Impressed by her voice, I asked her to carry on singing, and she sang another, and then another. It was no longer a test, but the pure pleasure of a privileged spectator. With Caetano accompanying or alone, she went on singing to my silence, the three of us alone. I wanted more. Sing, Bethânia, sing. Alone? I heard a noise behind me; I looked and saw the stalls were almost full. The spectators, hearing the strange, unusual, beautiful voice from the street or from the bar at the corner, entered in a daze: once again the theatre was full.

That was Berré's true première in Rio de Janeiro: the night of the audition!

Bethânia was an impressive figure: a determined, slim young woman with a solid voice which flew, filling the stage, tumbling down staircases, escaping through the windows, crossing roads, avenues, beaches. Soon, Bethânia's voice would overflow throughout Copacabana, Rio de Janeiro, Brazil, and the world beyond. Her appearance was impressive: I wanted the audience to hear her voice before seeing her. To see her voice before hearing her image.

Bethânia had asked to do *É de Manhã* (It is Morning), by Caetano, as her first song. I asked her to start singing it in the dressing-room. I darkened the Arena so that Bethânia could appear in the dark. First rays of light came gradually, and only when the rooster began to crow, at the end of the song, did the light open up, like the flower of her song, bathing her image in the dawn. It was morning, yes, Bethânia, just as your brother's song said: it was the lovely morning of your beautiful career, which will never turn into night.

The people – found and lost

Unhappy felicity. The Arena, in the Northeast, had found our people; the CPC in Rio had found its people. Though in dialogue with 'the people', we continued to be the owners of the stage, the people remaining in the audience: intransigent. In Santo André, people and characters had come to grips with each other on stage – this happened on one day, a single day: but one swallow does not make a summer – you need more, and eagles and *carcarás*.

Our consolation was that our singers were the incarnation of the people on stage; others disagreed, saying that they were there in their capacity as singers, not as the people. Others redefined the concept of the people to include sectors of the bourgeoisie interested in the national economic emancipation – i.e. the 'good bourgeoisie'. The notion of *the people* was in danger of becoming meaningless. If I, you, he, us, they, if everyone is the people, the people does not exist. The word was at risk of expropriation. The people would lose its identity, its own name: everyone would end up calling themselves José da Silva and Maria Nobody.[16]

The class divide continued – sorry, I mean the divide between stage and audience: one spoke and the other listened. The audience joined in in the choruses but did not interfere in the plot. Now, with the current repression, the people had been expelled from the theatres, from trade unions, associations, parishes – the people was prohibited. Theatre was once again the business of the middle classes and the intellectuals. Each *people* in its own corner, each cow in its own stall. Yielding milk, working.

Opinião provoked the same polemic as our realistic phase: it is not a musical, nor is it theatre – so what is it?

Zumbi, *from Palmares*[17] *to the Third Army*

Zumbi was the crystallisation of the experiments we had been through. We knew we were not going to dialogue with the *people*. We would show our own face. I have never been hungry or felt the cold, I have always lived in relative comfort and I am not ashamed of it.

We were middle class: the set would be a soft red rug, middle class like us (today I detest soft red rugs . . .). And the costumes? Jeans and coloured shirts, each a different hue. The show was as if a group of friends descended on a living room, where some other friends, the audience, were waiting. So that there could not be the faintest shadow of the remotest and most far-flung doubt, the cast sang in unison:

'The Arena tells a story / for you to hear with pleasure: / if you like it, give us a big hand / and if you don't, you can please yourself!'[18]

It had to be clear: the teller of the story was the whole group of us, the Arena!

I created the *Sistema Coringa*[19] (Joker System): no character would be the private property of any one actor. All had the right to play any character, men in women's roles and vice versa. Actors were detached from characters, which passed from one actor to another. *Verfremdungseffekt* taken to its ultimate consequences.

So that a character would not be associated with any particular actor, it was never played by the same actor in successive scenes, and everyone had to maintain the same social mask of behaviour for each character. Each character had its own way of being, a preferential image, which would be recognised by whoever was interpreting the role at the time.

In *Opinião*, singers were confounded with characters, each being both former and latter; in *Zumbi*, the actors retreated from the characters and revealed them, at a distance: it is he, not I.

Opinião was a truth-show. We could not go on doing truth-shows, inviting three *coup* generals, three well-heeled senhoras, three unemployed factory workers, three malnourished peasants farmers, three out-of-work university lecturers, three whatevers, to give testimonies: they would not come. The characters we wanted to present had to be separated from the actors. That was the point of this collective interpretation, the taking of turns.

Collective interpretation allowed the separation of the essential from the circumstantial. In our realistic phase, much of the actor's work consisted of developing singularities of the character which did not have an impact on his social meaning. Here, this meaning was shown as social mask, social behaviour. The singularities belonged to the actor; the essential to the character.

The show was interrupted by the Joker, master of ceremonies, explainer, director of the scene, stage-manager, like the Kabuki's *kurogo*[20] – he could play any character, when necessary. He explained hidden meanings. The Joker – always the same actor – represented us, Arena. This was the beginning of the dialogue with the audience, which I would later develop fully with the Theatre of the Oppressed. The presence of the Joker allowed us to embrace aesthetic chaos: all theatre styles and genres would be allowed within the same show. This variety, given that we did not have stage sets and few costumes, was limited to the actors' performances.

The Joker, that multifarious function, was born with *Zumbi*. We began rehearsing the first act of the play while the script was still being written;

I was blocking the first act when the dialogue of the second was still half complete. In *Zumbi*, once again, we used metaphor. We used the Black Republic formed by slaves who freed themselves. Palmares occupied an area larger than the Iberian Peninsula, for almost a century in the northeast of the country till its destruction by a joint Portuguese–Dutch force when its commercial power threatened white hegemony. Palmares resisted down to the last man. We wanted to resist!

The script used newspapers. A speech by the illiterate commander Don Ayres, Palmares' destroyer, was copied verbatim from the dictator Castelo Branco when he addressed the Third Army: our army would become a gigantic police force, the true enemy (us!) being within rather than beyond our borders. A monstrous idea! *Zumbi* was a joy for us, even financially. For years when a show was not attracting houses we would return to *Zumbi*: as if by magic, the theatre would be full to overflowing.

A strange thing: the Arena had a sort of air exhaust system through an open pipe. We never understood why when the cast launched into *Upa Neguinho*[21] – this one number and no other – a gang of large rats would thrust their snouts into view at the entrance of the pipe, and listen to the music in respectful silence. Animals like music: Saint Francis of Assisi sang so tunefully, the whole bestiary would come to listen. But rats? Strange. On the last strum of the guitar, the rats would turn their backs on us and would not be back till the following day, for the next *Upa Neguinho*. . . . Who knows what strange winds blow in the soul of a rat?

Bahia, in time of war

Bethânia wanted to help her Bahian friends and launch them in the south, where they were unknown. Apart from Caetano, she introduced me to Gal Costa, Gilberto Gil, Tomzé and Piti. We did our new show, *Tempo de Guerra* (Time of War), with all of them, at *Oficina*. After this, we decided to do another musical telling the stories of Northeasterners coming south in search of work, in flight from famine.

The songs of *Arena Canta Bahia* (Arena Sings Bahia) were chosen for their words, to tell the migrants' story. It was not a selection of the most beautiful Bahian music: I wanted to show drought-stricken families chasing mirages of hope. People afraid to dream in colour, dreaming in black and white. Dreaming of dew drops, not daring to dream of oceans.

Plínio Marcos and the one-armed censor

The rehearsals bolstered my belief that the word is a living being. We were rehearsing on the stage: musically it was perfect. The singers sang the music, but nothing was coming from within them, apart from their voices. I asked them to rehearse the whole act again, but . . . without the music: just the text, trying to feel it, to understand it. The atmosphere changed and the singers' attention focused not on musicality, but on the content of what they were singing. It spoke of people like themselves. 'I came from Bahia . . . but one day I am going back there. . . .' Gil could not contain himself, and cried.

It was beautiful to see a singer crying because no one can say 'one day I am going back there' without thinking of the 'there', of their reasons for leaving, the people they left behind. Why leave, go back to whom?

Gil cried; the cast was damp-eyed: the show had a heart. Theatre has to be in flesh and blood. Otherwise, it is *entertainment*.[22]

Maria Bethania, Gal Costa, Gilberto Gil, Caetano Veloso, Piti, Tomze and the musicians
of ARENA CANTA BAHIA *directed by Boal, Sao Paulo, 1965*

Our political intent was evident; before the première, the censor cut whatever could be deemed critical. We reconstructed the score five times, masters in the art of metaphor, and he ended up accepting the last version.

Success! And perdition – in that the audiences understood meanings which had escaped the censor, and he came back with further cuts. Caetano's memory for songs was prodigious, he had masses to choose from; we took those that, even if they were not ideal, fitted with our metaphors. The duel with the censor had its creative side.

Until one day we found ourselves at risk of running out of repertoire to replace what had been cut. I tried to convince the censor: he resisted energetically – subversion, never again! Down with socialism, communism, anarchism, Thomas More's Utopia, Campanela's City of the Sun, Plato's Republic, down with everything!

São Paulo newspapers used to put blank spaces in place of the censored articles, and soon they were forbidden to publish blank spaces. Another paper printed cookery recipes in the censored spaces and, on not so rare occasions, the reader would find himself reading that 'The military junta met secretly and decided that . . . aubergines should be left to soak in hot water before going in the oven, at which point the parmesan cheese can be sprinkled on the top'.

The censors prohibited culinary art. The newspaper went on to verses from Camões'[23] *Lusíadas*: 'Having met with the President, the economic team decided that . . . with arms dispensed and lords apportioned, barons who from Lusitanian beaches of the Occident, by waters formerly uncharted, have passed even beyond Taprobana. . . .'[24]

I decided to take a leaf out of the censor's book and gave him an ultimatum: either he allow the songs or I would make ridiculous substitutions which he would not be able to prohibit. Such as? *Happy Birthday to You* and *God Save the Queen*![25]

The censor reassured me: I could go, mind at ease: I was off the hook. I went to the School of Dramatic Art.

My friends phoned me: the censor, lying to me, had called the police and the singers were going to jail straight after the show: they could not be arrested while they were working. They took the opportunity to sing songs that had been banned – since they were going to be arrested anyway, why economise on transgression?

By the time I got back, everything was already sorted out, the actors freed. But not before various comical episodes. Plinio Marcos, the author of *Navalha na Carne* (Razor in the Flesh), was the administrator of our company. A bluff fellow, he spoke his mind in language close to that of his lumpen characters – in each phrase there were two or three swear-words which made no concessions to the censor's mother's past life. The latter, a one-handed man – he only had his right arm, which he used to grab Plínio by the shirt, with his only hand – threatened: 'If you don't stop cursing my mother, I'm going to punch you on the nose!'

'I doubt that!'

'Why?'

'If you want to punch me, you are going to have to let go of me and if you let go of me, I'll run off. . . .'

In the interval, the cast informed the audience that they were going to be arrested as soon as the event was over; as an act of solidarity, the spectators went and bought sandwiches which they left on the stage, like bouquets of flowers on opening night. . . . 'You wouldn't happen to have a little cognac to go with this?' asked a female voice, and then bottles of *cachaça* appeared at the footlights.

In the following days, the same routine: cuts. Within a month the show came off for lack of public support. Today, each one of those singers can fill three Maracanãs[26] on their own.

Heroism and *Inconfidência* [27]

Zumbi was, for us, a revolution. We needed to understand it before moving on. A well-known critic wrote that our play was not a play, our show was not theatre, and our actors were dancers. *Zumbi* was not a revue: it had no chorus singers, no multicoloured waterfalls; it was not a Broadway musical: it had neither romantic couple nor grandiose settings; it could not be an opera without arias and duets, and lyrical voices with a five-octave span; it couldn't be circus as there were no clowns. It was not anything. It was just *sound and fury*.[28] To copy Shakespeare, he only had to add . . . *signifying nothing*. But *Zumbi* signified something, though he did not know what.

Colleagues said similar things, praising our acrobatics, our choreography, though it was not a ballet; our voices, though we were no Ellis Regina.[29] So what was it then? (Each time I have invented a new style I have been told: 'What you have done is great, but it is not theatre!' I have a strong desire to say: 'I am theatre! Theatre is what I do!' – a repressed desire!)

These opinions sometimes mean the absence of subsidy. In France, we went to the Ministry of Culture to ask for money and were given the highest praise – our work was extraordinary, innovatory, divine, marvellous! For all matters to do with money, we should refer ourselves to the Ministry of Education, our theatre was so magnificently pedagogic. In the Ministry of Education, praise abounded, cries of enthusiasm, hip-hip hurrah! Money? We should go to the Ministry of Health: our work was therapeutic, there was nothing better than Theatre of the Oppressed to cure neuroses, psychoses and Down's Syndrome. . . . We went to Health, they suggested Foreign Affairs: our method was used in all the ex-French colonial countries in Africa. If we staged *Hamlet*, we would surely have been sent to the Ministry of Metaphysics, because that business about being or not being, frankly . . . it's not theatre. . . . Entreaties from beyond the grave, etc. . . . Religion, occultism, spiritualism – not Art with a capital A.

The Government Inspector

We found a new metaphor: *The Government Inspector* by Gogol. We did not need to modify the script, it was already crystal clear. Gogol's Governor was our Governor. During our 'Nationalisation of the Classics' period, the metaphor worked in a different way, sometimes soaring high above – as in *Mandrágora*, where the relationship between love and power was vaguely discernible – and at other times stuck on to the skin of contempory characters.

Our Governor admitted to being a thief, but with mitigating circumstances: he was the dynamic builder of São Paulo. *He steals but he gets things done* – a slogan he invented (which to this day other Brazilian politicians use unashamedly!). The plotters of *coups* are voracious; and our Governor was the greediest. He was one of the first to be swallowed up by the *coup* he had helped give birth to. *The Government Inspector*, a skin-tight metaphor, was always sold out. In the midst of his mandate, the Governor was caught with his hand in the till and suffered impeachment. From that day on our houses at the theatre were less than half sold . . . ironically, the play had opened on the anniversary of the liberation of the slaves, which occurred in 1888.

Liberation? It had simply become more economical for the masters to employ free workers – to whom they paid nothing except their meagre wage – than to keep slaves in their houses and plantations. In the latter the masters were obliged to offer food and shelter. With 'free' workers, the masters were freed from the onerous bondage of slave-owning. Slaves were put out on to the streets with no compensation for their time spent in captivity, with no guarantee of food or housing. To this very day, they live in our *favelas*!

During *The Inspector*, I was invited to direct in Buenos Aires, at the Jewish Theatre. I chose *The Best Justice*: it was fun to translate the lines we had created, into Lope's style in the rest of the play. I learned nothing new, and taught little; the important thing for me was that I came back from Buenos Aires with Cecília Thumim, as my wife, and Fabián Silbert, my son.

I remember the exact moment I felt I was a father. Fabián was a year and a half old when we met. He got into the habit of bringing me the newspaper in bed in the morning. He used to imitate the newspaper seller beneath the window: '*Diariôôôô* . . .'.[30] Reading that *Diario* in the morning, I felt I could be a father. I became one. From that moment on, I have been a father. Thanks to Fabián Silbert's *Diáriooooo*. I became more of a father when Fabián learned to say the magic word: Daddy. To hear that word said by a child, eye to eye – that is powerful. It moves you, it makes you responsible. I was adopted by him. I set out alone . . . and returned to Brazil as a family. My own father appeared in dreams to tell me about paternal responsibilities. It was not just me I had to look after. Life was hard, theatre increasingly marginalised, and we needed security! I tried to organise my new life.

Jokers and heroes

With *Tiradentes*, the Joker System acquired definition. We were happy with the separation between characters and actors. In Brecht's distancing effect, the character was incarnated in a single actor: Helene Weigel was the only Mother Courage. In *Zumbi*, each character floated from actor to actor. At the strum of a guitar, actors and characters swapped partners.

But we regretted the loss of empathy and its tremendous power to convince. We wanted to get it back. We decided that the protagonist of *Tiradentes* would always be the same actor. The rest took turns.

Reason and emotion, we wanted it all, in the greatest intensity, high voltage. The Joker provided *Explanations*, so that there could be no doubt about the social and political situation of that time and of our time. We also introduced *Interviews* — the Joker interviewed characters, when necessary, mixing levels of consciousness and time. The Joker, as a citizen of the here and now, knew about our time and, when in the past, had a consciousness of the future: the characters, far away in time, knew only what they could know there and then.

The *Interviews* replaced the monologues. If we had done *Hamlet*, the Joker would have questioned the Prince about the relative advantages of Being or Not Being, and the reasons for his choice. We also introduced the final *Exhortation* in order to stimulate the spectators to resist the fascism that was taking hold. During or in *Tiradentes* — the music entered our lives once and for all. Our actors sang well, even if Carlos Castilho, our musical director, used to say maliciously: 'A singer, the musician *accompanies*; an actor, he *chases*. . . .' In recitals, the singer can follow the orchestra. In the heat of the drama, it is the orchestra which must be sensitive to the actor's emotion: it chases the actor, yes Castilho, and so it should. The actor's emotion is the true conductor of the orchestra!

This already happened at the outset of opera as a theatrical and musical genre. In 1600, with Peri and Rinuccini's *Eurydice*, and even before with the Camerata Fiorentina (1585) when the father of Galileo, Vicenzo Galilei, proposed the individualisation of the song (monody versus polyphony) and the predominance of the meaning of the word over the music: music should serve in exaltation of the poetry. Let us stop here: I do not want to promote discord between poetry and music — I want to marry them![31]

Two kinds of polemic were at play, the first being about the role of the intellectual in times of turbulence or peace. The scenes of the intellectual rebels were inspired by the night of 31 March 1964, in the Professor's house. That useless night had stayed with us as a symbol: intellectuals gave themselves the right to suggest ways forward . . . and fold their arms.

As if being intellectual meant the acquired right to do nothing more than think.

We were cruel dramatists, merciless critics. We invited the participants of that night to readings of *Tiradentes*. Some recognised themselves and were not bothered by it. Others did not take themselves to be present in the script. We were conflicted: we accused intellectuals of engaging in cosy revolutionary chit-chat, but we were doing nothing more than that. We were intellectuals. Just like those we criticised: we wrote, but . . . no one took up arms. Some of us started thinking about effective action: cursing insane dictatorships was not enough! Some wanted to do what they judged was their duty.

The second polemic came from Anatol Roselfeld's article questioning the use of empathy. I responded, and we continued responding to each other, stimulating each other. What a joy to disagree, without deprecating the other's opinion, without considering oneself the sole owner of truth. I respect all intelligent opinions, even if I disagree. What displeases me is the papal infallibility of some critics. When their word is condemnatory, it destroys the show. In Brazil, the majority write like a judge doling out a sentence, without the artist having the sacred right to a defence. I love polemics, but not criticism. It would be wonderful if, in the same space as the journalist, the artist could give his or her opinion. Not retaliation: dialogue.

When in 1960 I was invited to be a theatre critic, I initiated a column full of debates, of which I was the moderator. I used to put in my penny-worth. It was great: everyone could write in, readers included.

In *Tiradentes*, the critics condemned the cult of the hero. Brecht said 'Happy the people who do not need heroes'. I might add: Brazil is not happy, dear Bertoldo, we do need heroes! May they proliferate, prolifically!

For me, myth is not mystification *per se*. Myth is the simplification of the historical individual, retaining the fundamental traits of his character, his essence, so to speak, which becomes magnified. However, it becomes mystification if non-essential circumstances are magnified and what is important is thrown into the waste bin of history. The picturesque remains, the principle is lost.

Take Christ. If one were to show only his suffering on the cross, his stoicism – if his power to mobilise the people was kept from view, this would be *mystifying the myth*. Take Chê – only showing his corpse, eyes half-closed, surrounded by his assassins, this is *mystification*: the man defeated. Showing Chê as the hero who overcame Batista will then be *myth* without *mystification*. In neither case is it necessary to tell the hero's entire life story, to speak of paternal carpentry in Jesus' case, or family medicine in Chê's – however, it is crucial to choose what you wish to show – in that choice will be *myth* or . . . *mystification*.

While we are on the subject of Chê, as we are; and Jesus, as we have mentioned him; and of revolution, since that is what we are dealing with . . . let's proceed.

Armed groups

In 1966 armed groups began to be formed. Sincere religious people began to subscribe to the idea of armed struggle: it was an immediate way of serving Christ, as Father Batalha preached from the pulpit and practised what he preached. The Communist Party lost important members who did not believe in the thesis of two bourgeoisies, one national, one foreign. Marighela and Toledo, my friends, founded the ALN;[32] Amazonas and Arruda founded the PC do B (Communist Party of Brazil)[33] . . . Many more left in disgust. . . . Students and factory workers lost everything except hope. Banished from their habitual terrains, they had to meet somewhere. Somewhere clandestine. Seen from this angle, responsibility for the armed struggle lies with the dictatorship itself, which left no other door open. You would be involved in a furtive conversation and before you knew it you had slipped into the armed struggle. A meeting, a secret, and soon the person already felt committed: which is why I say you did not join the guerrilla movement; you slipped into it.

Armed conflict was the natural extension of political encounters: you had already become a militant before you noticed how it had happened. There was no ceremony, as there is today when you join a political party, with toasts and speeches, and little prawn pastries. It was enough to do someone a favour or to do an errand for a combatant – carrying a confidential and dangerous letter, offering your home as a hiding place one night – and that was it, you were already part of the resistance. Step by step, your commitment deepened.

Many carried out guerrilla actions without calculating the danger. When the repression came, then they realised: they were playing with their lives.[34] Being a guerrilla meant risking your life. Some fled or died; others had second thoughts – too late.

Chê proclaimed: *to be in solidarity means to run the same risks*! Some people knew that the risk was death. Create one, two, three, a thousand Vietnams – beseeched Chê. That was the revolutionary desire: to confront all imperialist violence throughout the world, simultaneously! The CIA was afraid that one solitary Vietnam, however limited – Brazil, for example – would already be the thousand Vietnams dreamed of by Chê.

Of course, there were some honest patriots who preferred not to enter the armed struggle because they were aware of their own limits or because they did not believe in it. They lived in accordance with their beliefs – their right. Those who had subverted democracy – who used to call us 'subversives' when they themselves had overthrown the legitimate government! – knew that the military did not have the support of the people, so they became more and more violent.

On our side, there were too many parties and dissident groups, dissidents of dissident groups, and dissidents of the dissident dissidents, factions and micro-factions, micro-factions of the factionalised dissidents. Forgive me, my *companheiros*, but it was difficult to know who was in which organisation, who was allied to whom, which organisation was more Marxist, more Maoist, more Trotskyite, which the most Guevaraist. And which was the most *Brasilianist*.

The literary guerrilla: Regis Debray,[35] though not to blame, was at the root of grave errors. His book about the theory of 'foci', based on his Bolivian dialogues with Chê, did immense damage to the armed struggle in Brazil. It was taken literally. The Battle of Santa Clara (in which Chê cut the territory of Cuba into two), for some Brazilian combatants, could be reproduced here: all we had to do was create many small foci, and then . . . in our dreams . . . it would be easy. Awake, we were able to perceive that Cuba was a long sausage and Brazil was rounded; Cuba was very small, we were gigantic. It was comfortable to dream . . . why open one's eyes?

I remember when an important guerrilla leader, seeking to convince me of the correctness of his strategies, laid out a colourful map of Brazil on the table, all mountains and rivers, and indicated the inexorable progress of our popular victories: focus by focus, all that we needed to do was cross the São Francisco river[36] and all the revolutionary forces would reunite in a glorious Army of National Liberation, marching on Peking, I mean, Brasilia. I asked him a straight question: weren't there alligators and crocodiles in that river? Would it be so easy to cross? On maps there are no such things as malaria and typhoid, mosquites and yellow fever: just swathes of blue and yellow and green. On maps, wars are beautiful.

No dictatorship can tolerate popular structures, however precarious. The first decree of dictatorship is always the Curfew: deserted streets. As a warming towards popular resistance started to become evident, the cold dictatorship prepared its greater *coup*, the second one.

The Circle *and the* Moschetta

Thirty years have gone by and I still do not understand how it happened. *The Caucasian Chalk Circle* is a beautiful play, our actors were good, it was a fine show. . . . What happened? I do not know. We opened off-Arena. The next day, Guarnieri and I sat on the stairs, thinking: 'We cannot do this to ourselves or to Brecht. . . .'

This has only happened to me once in my life: pulling a show after the first night. It happens in cooking: you follow a recipe faithfully, the cake turns out shamefully bad, inedible. It happens in theatre, too.

I have a hypothesis: excess of respect was to blame. I did not want to do anything at which the author's ghost – as it roamed about the Arena, in the dead of night, sending out good vibes – could turn up its nose in disgust. Betray Brecht, never! I showed such a canine fidelity to the script that, even with the right recipe, the show came out burnt to a cinder.

How I envied the European theatres, funded by the state, which could allow themselves the luxury of failure: we could not. When failures happened – which was inevitable – *Zumbi* was revived at high speed.

In a hurry, we rehearsed Ângelo Beolco's *La Moschetta*. It went fine, the sort of *going fine* that moves no one. Everyone praised it with that murderous phrase: 'Well, do you know, I liked it. . . . Yes . . . I did . . . you know, I liked it.'

We needed a parallel company for experiments, one not dependent on the ticket office. In 1967, we founded the young *Núcleo Dois* (Nucleus No.

Two), with the acting students of Cecília and Heleny Guariba. Cecília opened her first show as director with *A Granada* (The Grenade), by the Argentinean Rodolfo Wash, who was later assassinated by the Buenos Aires dictatorship. There were many armed groups. And many possible paths. Which way should we go?

The atmosphere was ripe for *A Feira* (The Fair).

Censorship: bad to worse

Ever since childhood, I have hated censorship. Penha, where I was born and bred, was as conservative as Trás-Os-Montes.

In 1922, during the 1st Feminist Congress of Brazil (in which the inventor of Samba, Chiquinha Gonzaga, was a participant), for the first time in Rio, a young woman wore a hooped crinoline skirt, which was all the rage in Paris; she was nearly lynched. Even though the hooped skirt covers up more body than a normal skirt. In that same year, a Week of Modern Art took place in São Paulo, the PCB[37] was founded, the Soviet Union was created . . . but a woman could not wear a hooped skirt. Ten years later, women won the vote – until then, they had been under the tutelage of father, husband or brother.

A strange conservatism: topless sunbathing on the beach shocks people to this day, and is tacitly forbidden. Women in Ipanema[38] – I can see them out of my window right now – wear '*fio-dental*' (dental floss) bikinis, which live up to their name and reveal the whole bottom in all its glory. The lower hind parts can be shown in their entirety; the upper parts are sacred.

When I returned from New York in 1955, I brought some jeans with me. When, at the urinal, my colleagues discovered that my trousers had a zip rather than the traditional buttons, they ridiculed me: 'That's what poofs wear. . . .' Even though I am not gay, I went on sporting my zip trousers, but I avoided public urinals.

As a child, everyone took the mickey out of everyone. I used to go to the beach before sunrise: I did not go brown. My friends called me whitey and vim and the like. No one noticed that, though they were white, my legs were muscular from playing football. Even today they are not ugly.

I was 9 years old when my brother discovered a note I had written to a friend and which I had not had the courage to give her: 'Alice, how old are you? If you are 7, I will marry you!' – an audacious and precocious marriage proposal. I think it deserved to be met with encouragement: instead I was mocked all week, until a fresh mockery consigned it to oblivion.

I invented a *Book of Inventions*. I used to invent everything, even war tanks which ran on gunpowder – like cannon and cannon-ball at the same time: they would leap over the enemy and beat a retreat, only to leap forward again, like a deadly grasshopper. This invention was accompanied by drawings to explain how to construct this destructive and indestructible war machine. I invented rational urban development of a great capital city of a country of the future. If I had done it, Brasilia would have been more convivial . . .

I used to hide the *Book of Inventions* under the mattress, for fear of someone discovering it. The maid would come to clean my room and laugh her head off.

A teacher decided to take his pupils to collect plants to study. Tired and parched, the boys sat down in a bar. No one had any money. I had a little. In a spirit of brotherhood, I asked the waiter for 'One lemonade and nine glasses . . .' – we were nine boys. I overdid it. But it was no reason to be subjected to such mockery as followed: the whole school ended up hearing about my ridiculous philanthropy.

Pretend it doesn't hurt!

Christening my new bicycle, I decided to test what it was capable of, going up and down hills, until I fell off in the middle of the road. I heard the screeching of a truck's brakes and a woman shouting 'Hey, kid, you have just been born again. . . .'

Shaken I escaped with my life, and a bleeding knee. The next day I went limping to school, thinking about the risible comparisons which people would make with motor-racing champions. I took a decision: 'Augusto, you are going to pretend it doesn't hurt!' I went into school treading firmly, making out it did not hurt. Inside, I was giving vent to groans of bear-like proportions, savage cries of pain.

During my life, a thousand times I have said to myself: 'Augusto, pretend it does not hurt.' Reading mendacious reports from unscrupulous political journalists, hearing rejections of funding applications, under interrogation in court or in the torture chamber: 'Augusto, pretend it does not hurt.' It continued to hurt, but my pride anaesthetised the pain. . . .

Five shits and one fucking hell

Even as a child I detested censorship, so imagine the adult me, obliged to discuss with a censor, the owner of the last word, the cuts he was going to impose. When the censor was '*good*', he might even let himself be convinced. If he was '*bad*', the following day he would send the script back to us, scrawled all over with authoritarian comments: the light cannot be so bright; the scenery must be repainted to hide the pornographic figure. . . . The dialogue you liked cut completely. (When a censor allowed a full-frontal nude to appear for the first time in Brazil in *Hair*, he decreed that the stage had to be left in such a shadowy half-light that one could barely see the actors' genitals: the actors might as well have been wearing tailcoats for all one could see. Well-informed spectators said to their friends: 'You can't see, but those young men and girls are starkers . . . I read it in the paper.')

There are no good or bad censors: only awful, terrible and the worst censors. The function of a censor is immoral, no matter who undertakes it. The function of an executioner is immoral, irrespective of the personality of the one who does the killing.

In the general rehearsal of *Chapetuba FC*, along came a 'good' censor. 'Good' though he was, he felt that the playwright had exaggerated by including five *shits* in the script and, horrors, a sonorous and explosive *fucking hell*![39]

Vianninha, aged 22, was making his debut as a playwright. Nervous, smoking like a chimney, he offered to advocate our cause. He sat before the 'good' censor and launched into vehement discourse, gesticulating wildly. He spoke of what he knew about the history of theatre, Aristophanes and licentious language, the Roman Fescennine poetry,[40] he talked about anonymous and shameless medieval farces which cast aspersions on the doctrine of the Immaculate Conception. He left the censor open-mouthed with his disconcerting erudition. Making the most of a pause, and the fact that he was open-mouthed anyway, the censor spoke: 'This is true, but it is also true that *shit* five times in a two-hour show is too much *shit*! If you were a little more restrained. . . .'

Vianninha showed his willingness to collaborate:

'Let's analyse all these *shits*. The first one doesn't count, because here we are talking about a football player who accidentally kicks a door and is not going to say "Praised be the Lord . . .". He exclaims *shit* and is fully justified in doing so on account of the pain to his foot. This is an introspective *shit*, do you understand? As for the second *shit*, you don't have to worry because the actor has a serious diction problem, he is in treatment with an esteemed speech therapist, and we ourselves were thinking of replacing him because no one can understand what he is saying, and you only understood his *shit* because you read the script, but no spectator is going to hear that *shit*, I guarantee you, that *shit* is invisible, inaudible, odourless. . . . You can leave it where it is, it is inoffensive *shit*. . . .'

'That's what I said: a bit more restraint. If you leave in just those two *shits* and wash all the rest out of your mouth, you can open, no problem. I liked the play!'

Happy with the progress he had made, Vianninha thought a little. He continued: 'Those are the two incontestable *shits*. Now, the third is one of the most important *shits* in the history of universal theatre, because over in Europe they are free to say as many *shits* as they like, without having to answer to anyone. And in the United States there is *shit* all over the place! *Shit*, and *fuck* are common as muck. *Son of a bitch* is our daily bread! And we who want to do art, pure art, you understand, aesthetics, yeah?, we can't say *shit*, let alone *fuck*!'

'I have already let two *shits* go as proof of my good will . . .'

'But the third *shit* comes at a psychological moment of the greatest relevance. . . . It is when the centre-forward fails to score from inside the area! It's obvious he can't shout out "Help me, Our Lady of the Immaculate Conception!" – it would be heresy. *Shit* is more hygienic. More Catholic! Look: missing what should be a guaranteed goal, at the end of the second half! Of course he has to come in to the changing rooms shouting "*Shit!*" It would be highly improbable for him to say anything else.'

'You have smooth-talked your way to a 3–2 lead, but the last two *shits* I cannot let you get away with. . . . It would be an indication of moral weakness on my part,' the censor lamented, trying to close the subject and fearing the worst.

Vianninha was valiant to the point of recklessness, and would not give in. 'The fourth *shit*, well, let's look at it . . .' and he went on with his arguments. To tell the truth I cannot remember the reasons he lined up, only that he trotted out more stories about Molière and Beaumarchais, *Fanny Hill* and *'Tis Pity She's a Whore* – texts he had never read. He invented writers who had never written, invented a story in which a supposed Pope Leo XXXVII had personally intervened to let pass a text by the Count of Cagliostro (who?) written in partnership with Casanova, and he said so many things, referring to so many precise dates with absolute conviction, so many historical facts that had never happened, so much Mad Black Man's Samba,[41] with such passion, that the pale censor agreed to allow the fourth *shit* and, and in a rare accession of a stunning and acute generosity and altruism, offered the fifth *shit* gratis, with the argument that if the innocent ears of the spectators had already been assaulted by four justifiable *shits*, one *shit* more or less would make no difference.

'Now don't come to me with any more stories! It will be years before *fucking hell* gets to be pronounced on a Brazilian stage. Our people is not ready for the *fucking hells*! . . . Europe is another story, different geography, civilisation . . .' the censor warned him, intimidated.

He did not know Vianninha, who gazed blankly at the wall, with the *tristesse* of an eighteenth-century romantic poet, the kind that dies of TB, the kind they don't make any more. He agreed that the Brazilian people was not prepared to hear such an impropriety on stage. But . . . was the art market ready to understand Van Gogh in his time? Van Gogh died without having experienced the joy of selling a single painting – or perhaps just one, and they suspect it was to his brother, Theo, who arranged for it to be bought. Were the eighteenth and nineteenth centuries ready for Shakespeare, who had had so much success in his own century? No: the critics judged him to be a bloodthirsty butcher. Was science ready to hear Galileo proclaim that the Earth revolved around the Sun? . . . *eppur, si muove!* And was the whole world ready to understand Darwin and accept that we, even the most elegant and refined of us, are descendants of grotesque monkeys? No! So how come we, the descendants of monkeys, almost as much monkey as they are, how come we can't hear a pure and simple *fucking hell*! delivered with Stanislavskian emotion memory? A monkey can, we can't.

The people was not ready and a young man starting out was going to be forced to give up his play because he would never give up his truth. And his profound truth, at that crucial moment in his life, was that *fucking hell*, which he would stand by even in the knowledge that his play would be banned! No to castration: he would never be a eunuch, a tenorino, a castrato! Like Darwin, Galileo, Van Gogh and other illustrious foreigners – he only spared Jesus Christ, Buddha and Mohammed – he would suffer on account of a people who was not yet ready, an ignorant rabble. He would have to wait for generations to come. A monkey can, we can't. . . .

Overcome with emotion in the face of the inflexible censor, Vianninha terminated his peroration with an outrageous proposal: 'How about this: I'll return the five *shits* you so generously made me a present of, and you let the *fucking hell* have its freedom! Is that a deal?'

Vianninha almost wept. As for the censor, I am sure I saw tears in his red eyes as he threw the script in the air, rose in fury and left the theatre shouting: 'I am jacking in this profession. I want to do honest work, to censor only what needs to be censored, to defend morality, but also I do not want to destroy anyone's career. Do what you like. Say as many *shits* and *fucking hells* as you like. . . . But you take responsibility. Because I'm not. . . . Never again! *Fucking hell*!'

We were happy with our five *shits* and the first *fucking hell* ever to be uttered on a Brazilian stage . . . Vianninha the Great!

Things weren't always like that. The censor could administer ruthless cuts, without discussion. In *Black-Tie*, Lélia Abramo was playing the part of a factory worker's wife. When she discovered that her husband was in the custody of the political police, her character would shout: 'He is in the DOPS?[42] They are going to beat my husband to death!'

The censor cut that. Lélia had no doubts: on the opening performance she cried out: 'In the DOPS? Oh Mary Mother of God!', burying her head in her hands. The impact was much more theatrical.

Negotiation was one of the inevitable chapters of the staging process.

Routine. But theatre shows were not alone in being subject to censorship: visual art exhibitions, readings, ballet, musicals, television programmes. Anything which had an audience. The larger the audience, the greater the rigour.

A friend of mine was directing a TV programme called *Collage*: images and music juxtaposed. He used to mix the roar of an African lion with the waves of the sea on Hawaii, rain falling on the roof of a hut with the whining of a disconsolate hound. The censor was always discovering hidden subversive messages, even in neutral scenarios. My friend was getting ready to go on holiday and keen to get away. He called his assistants together and asked them to imagine the most inoffensive script – nothing that could be accused of being subversive or political. But the censors saw subversion even in a white cloud in the blue sky, because it subtly showed controversy: why was it not blue like the rest of the sky? Subversion!

An assistant, looking at a pot-plant, noticed a worm extending itself languidly: 'A worm stretching is visual. It is aesthetic. Let's film the worm.' Director and assistants observed the worm's movements. 'Yes . . . there is something sensual about it . . . mysterious . . . blind as a bat! Worse, it does not have a bat's radar. Worms don't even know which end their head is.'

'It asks us questions about the essence of humanity. . . .'

'Essence of humanity, my foot! I want to make this programme right now and get to the beach. Take the worm to the studio.'

Unfortunately the worm was frozen in shock. Then, sensing the attention it was attracting, the worm began to wiggle and gyrate. Cameras running. They finished and went to watch the rushes. The first minute, fantastic! Congratulations! The second minute, tedious: always the same choreography – the blind worm did not have a clue how to occupy the space harmoniously, it stayed in a heap in one corner of the glass case, like a timid ballerina. The third minute, unbearable: wearisome repetition, *ipsis movimentus*, the same gyrations. Discouraged, someone had a cruel idea. 'If it is monotonous, the fault is not the worm's. . . .

'When it starts repeating itself, we stimulate it, as if it were a human actress. All actors need to be stimulated.'

'Oh boy! Tell me, how do you stimulate an actress who, apart from being a worm, which is already a disadvantage, has the aggravating feature of also being blind?' 'Let's record it again. When it gets boring, we get a dropper full of sulphuric acid, and let out one drop . . . and then another, and another . . .'

No one had the courage to take the cruel decision. Not out of affection for the worm: out of fear of the Society for the Protection of Animals.

'The Society only protects fat animals. Cockroaches, fleas, worms, grasshoppers, crickets, ants, even rats, are all exempt from protection. You can maltreat them at will, stab their eyes, pull their legs off. It is neither a sin nor a crime. Small creatures do not have neurons, they are insensitive!'

They went back to the studio and the machine of television cranked itself up again: lights, cameras, microphones and . . . action!

The first minute, well rehearsed, came off better than first time round and then, as predicted, the interest waned.

The first drop of acid. Panic: the worm gave a jump, and further drops were needed to make it wriggle and to keep it within the rectangle of glass. The emotion redoubled with its ornamental leaps. Fatally wounded, the worm lost elasticity in inverse proportion to the drops of sulphuric acid that fell on its back. Happily, by then the second minute had come to an end.

They carried on dripping acid. Though peaceful, the third minute was horrifying: the svelte body of the worm dissolved in the liquid, slowly, until it disappeared. It was mysterious: having dissolved the animal, the acid seemed to have acquired a kind of life of its own and throbbed, pulsated, breathed. It was beautiful! Could that worm have had some rudimentary kind of soul?

In funereal silence they examined the glass case. If it was possible to ignore the matter of the Society for the Protection of Animals, no one could fail to accept that – from the strictly aesthetic perspective (I repeat, in the absence of ethical or biological consideration) the video could be considered a minuscule work of art.

But they needed sound: collage is about sticking one thing to another, the image to the music. 'What music?' the assistant asked. 'Take the first record you come to on the shelf. When it comes to combining with a worm, no one kind of music is more appropriate than another. There is no such thing as worms' music!'

Without looking – that was part of the collage aesthetic – the assistant took the first record that touched his hand: Wagner's *Ride of the Walkyries*! It was mixed and dispatched to the censor. The Director went to load his suitcases with swimming costumes, flip-flops and straw hats.

As he was about to get into his car to set off for the beach, the telephone rang. The Director answered it, in his shorts: the censor found his *ophidian*[43] programme overly politicised in its obvious subversive message. (That's always the way with holidays: last minute problems, every time.) He had to negotiate.

The censor began by praising the sophistication of the subversive messages. Brazilian artists were masters in the art of allegory, ellipsis and metaphor. And he, the censor, was a specialist in their detection.

'Where did you see subversion in my programme?'

'In the worm: as a symbol. A worm lives below ground. An allegory, by which you mean that the Brazilian people, poor, sad worms, live in hiding, humiliated. That was the second symbol I detected.'

'What was the third?'

'The sulphuric acid. For you subversives, acid signifies the military government which for you is the torturer of the population.'

The Director, without the will to respond, nevertheless asked 'And Wagner. . . . Did he by some chance symbolise something?'

'Of course: that is where I began, that was the first symbol. The music of Wagner gave me the key to interpret the rest.'

'What does Wagner symbolise?'

'Hitler had a great affection for Wagner. For you, Wagner means Nazism, because you think that we, the military, are Nazis! But we are not, we are simply selective democrats!' exploded the censor, forgetting that he had no military rank and was just another common-or-garden civilian.

Censorship tightened the siege on those who feared to speak of reality, of the unjust distribution of income (by which measure today, Brazil ranks even lower than Botswana). It reached a grotesque sublimity with *Antigone* in Porto Alegre: the censor called the director of the play to his office, said he liked the script and would do everything he could to allow it to go on, with some minor surgery: Creon comes out of his confrontation with Antigone tainted, and the public would see in that strong criticism of the Brazilian situation.

'Come back with the playwright and we'll find an amicable solution: the play deserves it . . .' he proposed, conciliatory.

After his initial shock, the director said it would give him the greatest pleasure to come back with the playwright . . . were it not for the minor inconvenience that Mr Sophocles was long dead.

'What a shame! I didn't know,' the censor replied, moved. 'All the more reason to let it go on: in rightful homage. You bring me the person who gets the royalties in Mr Sophocles' name, and we'll talk!'

It was hard to explain that, over the course of twenty-five centuries, as might be expected, track of his direct successors had been lost. The play ended up being allowed to go on when the censor convinced himself that Sophocles was not making any oblique reference to our beloved Fatherland!

Uncultured censors abounded. Ladies recruited from the reactionary Tradition, Family and Ownership organisation, or simple career police-men. When the imprisonments began after 1968, police used to raid people's houses and confiscate suspect books as proof of subversion. One would expect works of Marx and others to be confiscated. But they also confiscated Stendhal's *Le Rouge et le Noir* (The Scarlet and the Black), because the police thought that it had to do with the colours of communism and anarchism; the art book *The History of Cubism*, with its clear insinuation of support for the Cuban revolution; an engineering book entitled *Resistance of Materials*, an obvious study of the explosive power of Molotov cocktails. . . .

The climax of the struggle for freedom of expression came in 1968 — the year of the students! It was the last year of relative brightness, before the darkness which took hold of Brazil, as a result of *Ato No 5* (the 5th Act), which officially instituted fascism in the country, bringing with it laws such as the famous *Lei Secreta* (Secret Law). In official accusations, they published only the number and not the content of the laws which had supposedly been infringed by the accused, which enabled the dictatorship to accuse and condemn whoever they wished, alleging infraction of a law, to which not even the lawyers had access. Condemned without knowing why: Franz Kafka's *Joseph K*.

Then came the *Lei da Delação* (Law of Denunciation): university lecturers who did not denounce their 'subversive' students would incur the same punishment as them. Then came the compulsory retirements, the annulments of civil rights, kidnappings, tortures and assassinations. We did not know what to do. Everyone had their own opinion. Which was right? For this reason, our thoughts turned to holding a *Feira*, which would be a fair of opinions.

The theatre's guerrilla war

Stage sets versus guns!

At this ideological and aesthetic crossroads there were choices to be made; lacking a compass, we spun round and round in search of true North.

Before looking forward, we looked back: at Arena we had delivered a repertoire which bore our own face and our own voice; after the realist mirror, we saw ourselves in the metaphor of the Classics; in Santo André, the spectators wrote plays and, to crown that liberation, invaded the stage, actors and characters mixing together. Along came the *coup*; we drew back; singers sang about their lives, each one representing many; *Zumbi* enabled us to make a synthesis, singing our history.

We could not show certainties. Which should we choose from among so many possible paths? All of them! Why not do a mural show, a *Feira paulista de opinião* (São Paulo's Fair of Opinions)? Playwrights, composers, visual artists. . . . We should answer the question: What do you think of the art of the Left? We asked ourselves why we existed. Did gentle artists such as ourselves serve any purpose in those tough times of war? We questioned our art, our function in society, our identity, our lives.

In stable countries, artists know where they stand – serene and unperturbed. They know what they want and what is expected of them. In a Brazil cast adrift, everything was and is possible: we asked where we were, who we were, where we wanted to go.

What do you think? The reply had to be a work of art. Lauro César Muniz wrote the story of a fisherman imprisoned for being literate: as the only one on his beach who knew how to read, he was considered a subversive. Jorge Andrade wrote about sickness and lack of medicines; Guarnieri, about the means of communication and their destructive power; Plínio Marcos, about colonels dressed as gorillas, censoring his play, defecating and wiping themselves with the censored pages; Bráulio Pedroso, a parable about the rotten part of the bourgeoisie; and it fell to me, the director, to close the event with a collage of texts about Guevara: by Cortazar and Neruda. Each composer had his song: Edu, Sergio Ricardo, Caetano, Gil.

Visual artists scattered beautiful works of art, from the streets to the dressing-rooms. One made a sculpture called *O milagre brasileiro* (The Brazilian Miracle), patterned on the dictatorship's propaganda: the spectator entered a green and yellow[44] tunnel and sat in a wheelchair which slid around, in the dark, until he or she reached the end of the tunnel, where the wheels triggered a switch which illuminated a tasteless image of the Virgin Mary. The spectator stood up and walked away: that was the miracle at the end of the tunnel!

Jô Soares[45] painted a picture inspired by a celebrated advertisement for cough mixture, in which a crazed man cried out: 'Let me loose! Let me shout!' Another artist dreamt up something involving bits of coloured wood which could show the Brazilian flag transforming itself into that of the United States; another, a collection of rubber-stamps which allowed spectators to make their own works of art from elementary designs; another, a two-metre banana. . . .

If we were painters of still life, *nature morte*, we would be blameless; theatre is *nature vivant*, life; when it is shown, it has meaning, direction, destiny — we were responsible for what we were saying.[46] This was our certitude: uncertainty. How to utter it? A mural show, contradictory thought, diverse options. A kaleidoscope.[47]

The script went to the censor eighty pages long. It came back with sixty-five pages cut and 'AUTHORISED' stamped on the remaining fifteen. Authorised, with sixty-five pages banned. A macabre sense of humour. The show bore everyone's signatures: censoring it would mean censoring all the artists of Brazil.

When a playwright had had a play banned, someone would always say: 'So-and-so went over the top . . . we are living in exceptional times.' Everyone was against censorship, but when each case was taken in isolation, there was always someone who thought that we were the ones who had gone too far. Now it was all of us.

If anything was 'over the top' it was our very existence, as creators: how can an artist work under a dictatorship if the artist is the body who, when free, creates the new, and the dictatorship is the body which, by shutting people up, preserves the old? Art and dictatorship are incompatible. The two words loathe each other!

On the day of the banned opening, up rose the most wonderful movement of artistic solidarity there has ever been in Brazil. The artists decreed a general strike in the city's theatres and came to join us. Never before had there been such a concentration of artists per square centimetre: no one was missing. Even the most timid turned up.

Up on stage, Cacilda Becker,[48] with the artistic community behind her, assumed responsibility for the 'civil disobedience' we were proclaiming, in the name of the dignity of Brazilian artists. The Feira was presented without permission, disrespecting censorship, which would not be recognised by any artist from that day forward. The theatre class abolished censorship! A thunderous ovation: the victory of art against mediocrity! A victory for freedom of expression. Democracy!

We arrived at the theatre early the next day, the police arrived earlier still – the theatre was surrounded. We made a pact not to give way – civil disobedience! It was our duty to disobey: we were obeying our desire!

We whispered to the spectators that the show would take place at another theatre where Fernanda Montenegro[49] was on. With her support, we marched into her show, revealed what was happening and, as proof of our disobedience, sang songs which had been prohibited. The public, happy at our courage, offered us friendly applause.

Day three: all the theatres of São Paulo were surrounded by soldiers and

Boal at Chapagua, New York, 1970

marines. Accompanied by those spectators who had vehicles, we went on to a theatre in Santo André: there we presented the complete script! Newspapers published our courage on their front pages: The Theatre's Guerrilla War! On the legal front, we entered a plea of habeas corpus.

On the fourth day, the theatres of Santo André were surrounded. At our theatre, an hour before curtain up, our lawyer turned up, euphorically shouting that that play had been provisionally authorised by the Judge! Victory.

Months later this judge was imprisoned: he was part of a guerrilla organisation . . . and no one knew.

From that day on, we did the complete script and added whatever we felt like – censorship having been routed and humiliated. This was when the physical aggression began, kidnappings and raids.

The **Feira** *of all violence*

The dictatorship dressed its savagery in the livery of legality. It called its sordid *coup* a 'Revolution'. We, the legalists, were called subversives. They justified censorship by calling it law. It had to be obeyed, just or iniquitous. With the habeas corpus they were beaten on their home ground: a judge authorised the show, we could say whatever came into our heads. Freedom!

Legally, there was nothing more that could be done: clandestine actions began. Chico Buarque's *Roda Viva* (Live Wheel) was in a theatre on the second floor of the same building where we were. One night, alarmed by shouting and commotion, we went up the spiral staircase and were able to give fight and capture one of the aggressors: paramilitaries had burst in and destroyed the scenery, beating up the company. The police arrived. Naïve as we were, we handed over the prisoner to the police, who later gave him back his freedom.

They threw sulphur gas bombs into our theatre, provoking a stampede: the door was narrow, people were hurt. Students came to do security guard duty. Every day, fifty students or more searched the spectators on their way in. They offered security . . . in exchange for seeing the show for free. Whole faculties came.

At the Arena, they kidnapped Norma Bengell as soon as she came off stage. A few days later she was set free in Rio de Janeiro – she had been kidnapped by the army. From that day on, Norma only went out into the street to travel from the hotel to the theatre, accompanied by two elite bodyguards: Maurício Segall and myself. Hands in the pockets of our jackets, finger on the trigger. A minor detail: none of us was qualified to shoot. It would have been a disaster if we had been pounced upon: our own feet were at considerable risk.

Following the *Roda Viva* incident, the cast of the *Feira* began to do an additional warm-up routine: physical and vocal exercises, then down to the basement for target practice. Since we were armed, better learn how to use our weapons.

On stage, actors worked with their finger on the trigger – really! One day, a rifle appeared in the theatre, from who knows where. The person who had the best aim inherited the rifle. It was not paranoia, I swear! It was tragic: in the *Commedia dell'arte*, actors used masks to hide from the police – we used revolvers! In what other country, in what other epoch, would such a thing have happened?

At the end of a show, actors prepare themselves for the applause. We prepared ourselves nervously for invasion: there were two students on either side of the stage, watching the audience, one arm inside the curtain, with us lined up behind, revolvers and rifle pointing at the auditorium. The students had orders to make a signal with their arm if armed spectators were to advance on the stage. That would be the moment to raise the curtain, take aim . . . and may God's will be done. Thank God, he did *not* will.

Madness! How could we play characters with so much danger and fear around us? When the *Feira* went to Rio, people in the audience, alarmed by an object rolling about on the floor, shouted out, causing the show to stop and the lights to be switched on. We went to look: a grenade had been thrown at the stage. Fortunately, being *Made in Brazil*,[50] it did not explode . . . but imagine if it had been of Czechoslovak construction?

The grenade was photographed and the picture shown in the newspapers, revealing the side exposing its number and origin: the National Navy. 'Like a white swan, on a full moon night. . . .'[51]

★ ★ ★

Guerrilla warfare

General strike in France: *Imagination en pouvoir* (Imagination in power), *Sous les pavés, la plage* (Under the paving stones, the beach), *Interdire est interdit* (Banning is banned)! Edson Luis, a student, was killed in the university restaurant in Rio, in a protest for better food, in March of that year, well before *les événements* of May in France and Mexico.

Our confusion revealed itself in the disparate variety of plays and shows we did: *O Comportamento Sexual do Homem e da Mulher, Segundo Ari Toledo* (The Sexual Behaviour of Men and Women, According to Ari Toledo), *A Praça é do Povo* (The Square Belongs to the People), with Sérgio Ricardo, *MacBird* (in which Barbara Garson parodied Lyndon Johnson and the Vietnam War). The *Feira* in Rio.

This confusion was not confined to us: José Celso invited Julian Beck and Judith Malina's Living Theatre to do a joint experiment – the whole company came over, and, for a year, they discussed how to do a piece of work together, and concluded that the only piece of work they could do together was to discuss, together, why it was impossible to make a piece together. They came, together, to the conclusion that it was best not to do anything . . .together. The Living Theatre left its mark.

Hegel, my uncle

The intense preoccupation with ethics in our aesthetics was making us suffer. We were seeking beauty; yes, Hegel, my uncle, we wanted beauty, just as much as you, believe me. But we could not keep quiet in the face of the dictatorship's crimes: apart from inventing kidnappings (today carried out by drug-dealers in need of money fast – the invention belongs to the military, the first kidnappers, who taught these delinquents the know-how), the dictatorship also put an end to workers' rights, and increased the foreign and national debts, slavishly applying the recipes of speculatory capital. It surrendered itself subserviently – as the elected government still does today – to the IMF.

What was to be done? In the theatre, it was difficult to respond. Outside the theatre, guerrilla warfare beckoned. Guerrillas began to think, to dream, that all the people needed was a 'focus' for them to start organising themselves into larger foci and, moving from focus to focus, guerrilla action would turn into national war. If the first Independence Day had been whispered modestly on the banks of the Ipiranga stream, this would be proclaimed in the colossal *pororoca*[52] of the waters of the Amazon fighting the Atlantic.

Dreaming, they were killed

It was in this way, dreaming, that many leaders were killed. The desire for freedom was so great, so sincerely felt, that they were blind to the hazards of the rapids, the inclemency of nature, the firepower of the uniformed enemy.

They were tortured, assassinated in cold blood. Killed in combat — according to the armed forces: 1968 was the beginning. Worse was yet to come.

Navigating the world

In France, students believed they would carry out the French Revolution 200 years later — a General Strike would do the trick. In Mexico, students believed that they would overturn a half-century of dominance by the PRI, the oxymoronic Institutional-Revolutionary Party! We believed that the theatre class would proclaim a new independence or death: only the white horse, sword and brook were missing.[53]

Cacilda Becker — wonderful actress! Impossible to forget her fragile form, her tremulous voice, her clear words: civil disobedience. Every night the class would gather again in euphoric assembly. Antônio Pedro and I took turns in the chair. We represented Arena and *Roda Viva* targeted by the repression.

I have never seen anything like it: the class talked deep into the night on theatrical subjects: how could we avoid being raided or kidnapped? How could we protect ourselves from tear-gas bombs, what kind of bicarbonate should we use on our handkerchiefs? What should we do with spies infiltrating our martial midsts? How could we avoid attacks by enemy cavalry – would it be ethical (to the horses) to scatter marbles to trip them over, with the resultant risk of their being sacrificed?

Some said no: animals do not have ideology, they do what they are told, they are innocent. Others argued for the marbles: horses do have ideology, sure they do. Just look how horses, in an ethically flawed allegiance, take the side of the bullfighter against the bull. Animals ought to ally themselves with others animals, not with humans. Police dogs bite anyone not wearing a uniform! They even respect the uniforms of mosquito-killers and cinema doormen: confronted with anyone in civvies, they dig their teeth in deep. A pitbull terrier is still worse, more reactionary. Our final verdict was that, from the political perspective, being an animal is not an extenuating circumstance. Marbles to the ground and barbed wire in their veins!

This reasoning fired an anti-ecological fury: 'The use of barbed wire and marbles in the street to make horses pay for their crimes is a matter of civic duty, a demonstration of patriotism! The mounted animal assists the animal who mounts it to beat us up: let it get its just punishment!'

Apart from these bellicose subjects, the meetings questioned what was the right repertoire for such an uncertain situation. What plays should be done in the period between *coups*, when the next *coup* was imminent?

Brazilians like to celebrate a goal before taking the penalty. We were already celebrating our new independence: censorship abolished, all we needed was agrarian reform and a moratorium on the foreign debt. Cacilda wanted it, and that would be enough for it to come to be! Easy. We just had to take the penalty. This guerrilla warfare, the need to defend ourselves, was isolating us from the worker and peasant people we had been seeking. We were penned in our corral, we and our audience, fellow members of the middle class.

Actors from the interior, who had never heard of Molière, began to appear at the theatres, in the universities, in cinema queues, at bar tables. They liked listening and asking questions; not about Sophocles, but about friendships. Some of us were suspicious: could these people be actors who had never heard of Shakespeare?

At the end of one of these permanent assemblies, Ítala Nandi and I were the last to leave the theatre, wrapped up in talking politics. We got into a taxi and saw that a car was following us. We asked the taxi driver to go round the block and come back to the same place – if they were still behind us, it would be clear that they were following us. They were. We asked the driver to take us to the *Gigeto*. Artists came to the door of the restaurant, and the grey car disappeared; happy days: they were still afraid of us. Later, they lost their fear, and ours grew.

The well-heeled ladies were becoming alarmed. One of them, a very rich woman, inadvertently found herself in the audience of *Roda Viva*. She had been told that the protagonist was the Virgin Mary, and she was fanatically in love with the Virgin. Except that no one had told the lady that the virgin in question was a circus virgin! Since, apart from being well-heeled, she was both Catholic and a state Deputy, she generated an archdiocesan scandal. Politicians were alarmed by her quivering alarm. Journalists were alarmed by the alarm of the alarmed politicians, and one TV station, in the very apotheosis of alarm, organised a discussion of politicians and artists. Its objective: to crush the artists in the full view of public opinion!

We chose our debaters: the impetuous Plínio Marcos as striker, spearheading the attack; the mature and responsible Fernando Torres in defence, dominating the area; and me, acting as link man, able to shift between defence and attack. A balanced team. My memory of the opposition is limited to Dona Conceição, the well-heeled lady. There were two others, but they made no impact – she was enough.

We scored some goals which were gifts. A marvellous example of this was when Fernando was talking about the wonderful scatology of Caesarian Rome, of the profane farces of the Middle Ages which called into question the divine virginity, etc., when the mortified Conceição shouted with great ferocity: 'You see, you see? And what did all that lead to? What? What did it all that pornography lead to?'

'The Renaissance, dear lady, the Renaissance . . .' Fernando Torres replied, smooth as only he knew how, kindly. Dona Conceição took off, levitating from her chair, shouting apoplectically and banging her fist on the table. No one could say anything – she did not let us. Our glasses of mineral water trembled, plastic bottles tumbled over! One of us would put up a hand to speak, and be on the receiving end of scattershot sprays of hideous shouting and blasts of spit. I took advantage of the open microphone, and began to broadcast on Dona Conceição's behaviour. The TV director, Luiz Galón, excellent artist that he was, started to play around with images of her from all angles, in co-ordination with my broadcast. At home, the viewers only heard my voice – not hers – commenting on her aggressive and bad-humoured antics: the flying spit, the clenched fist, the overturned glass of water. The effect was a work of art. In footballing parlance, we took them to the cleaners.

Newspapers told of our knockout victory in that memorable debate; in the headlines, they said we confused liberty with libertinism. . . . The press coverage had repercussions in our assemblies. One writer, who had never won a prize, proposed that we return awards we had won from a newspaper. These were prestigious awards, the *Saci*.[54] Returning them would be a slap in the face for the newspaper, but would also cause a certain sense of loss for those to whom they had been awarded. I myself did not want to return mine – they were mine, after all! The majority, not being award-winners, chanted rabidly for the beautiful statuettes to be thrown to the ground in the hall of the newspaper. A slap in the face and a kick in the balls.

Antônio Pedro and I came out against returning them. Whether or not to return them should be the personal decision of each person so honoured. The assembly had no right to propose that some artists should rid themselves of their awards, as a means of redress for everyone else. What's more, we were already at war with the censors and the reactionary politicians. Why open up a new front against one of the most influential newspapers in the country?

Pedro called another assembly meeting for the following day with the massed presence of all award-winners. The following day, the crowd would have been a tight fit in the Maracanã. By 4.30 a.m., no one had left. I was hoarse, voiceless. With Pedro in the chair, the voting took place: those in favour of throwing them away won. The next day, the newspaper building was overrun with police. We arrived, each award-winner with his or her trophies, I with my two, ever-so-pretty little statuettes. They would not let us in. The majority decided that we should chuck our statuettes into the newspaper's gardens.

Ironically, the newspaper proprietor thought that it was I who had instigated this act of return: he ordered that my name never again be published in full in his newspaper, only ever in the abbreviated form *aboal*. It's water under the bridge now, but at the time, that *aboal* hurt. The prohibition lasted for decades: I survived. Today, my name appears in full.[55]

Travel is inevitable!

The noose tightened. I was invited to visit Cuba, which had long been a dream of mine. Departure date was 14 December 1968. On the evening of the 13th, Costa e Silva, taking his turn as our tormentor, promulgated *Ato Institucional No 5* (Institutional Act No.5) – the suspension of all civil liberties. Fascists showed their faces. Fascism: power in the hands of a bunch of scoundrels, the power of the *fascio*. It happened in Brazil too.

Who was Costa e Silva? Popular anecdote claimed that he was such a donkey that he had to wear sunglasses to stop him eating his green uniform – irresistible temptation. Travelling by aeroplane one time, he heard the air hostess explain that they were flying at 10,000 metres. He revealed his surprise: 'I knew that Brazil was large, but I did not imagine it was so high. . . .' Under this man's reign, the systematic use of torture began.

I travelled to Havana the night after the proclamation of the Fifth Act. Once again I heard the silence, amidst the din of the airport. Tumultuous silence – it surrounded me, amidst the shouts. I asked myself: 'Does anyone suspect me? Is "destination Cuba" written all over my face?' I thought it was. Within this noisy confusion, the shoving and pushing, I did not want to hear the voice of prison. Like Joseph K. Were the military eavesdropping on my thoughts? I was sure that my loathing of despotism shouted itself from the rooftops, even when my mouth was shut.

I got on a plane for Paris, to whom I was introduced on 15 December 1968, a cold, dark morning. Love at first sight, reciprocated. I spent days drinking *Bourgogne rouge* to ward off the cold, eating long Gruyère sandwiches, meeting exiled friends, savouring the joys of pluralism: kiosks offered newspapers all the way from Right to Left. I bought *Classe Ouvrière* and went to visit Émile Copfermann, a theatre critic, one of the directors of *Éditions Maspero*, my first French editor. I spoke to Émile, who became a brother of mine, about my admiration for the freedom of expression in France: books by all kinds, revolutionary music, *gallo negro*, *gallo rojo*,[56] street-corner conversations – everything was permitted. Émile tactfully advised me not to display my newspaper – this total freedom was more apparent than actual.

I got on a plane for Rome, and telephoned the Cuban Consulate on my arrival. They just told me where to meet, such and such road, such and such a corner, at midday. Not a minute earlier, not two minutes later – Swiss time. I was to arrive on the stroke of 12 noon and to make as if I was going to cross the street, without actually crossing; someone would ask me the time. My reply was to be 'My name is Juan'.

Midday: the hand of a passerby tapped me on the shoulder – '*Per favore*. . . .' Of course my name was Juan: it was midday. We went to a bar, I handed him a *cruzeiro* note, small change. My new friend checked the number on the note against the one he carried in his pocket – it matched – and gave me a plane ticket to Prague. At the airport in Prague, I changed my name, identity, address, passport, everything: a real New Man. At the Hotel Intercontinental, I was not to talk to anyone. No danger: they were Czechs. Snow was falling – I had not seen snow since I had left the USA, fourteen years earlier.

I jumped on a tram and went to the end of the line, to get to know the city. The cold was biting and I wanted to go back to the hotel on the same tram. The driver came along and insisted that I get off the tram. I used gestures to explain that I was unaccustomed to the cold, being a *carioca*. He indicated, by gesticulation, that I had to dismount the tram and get back on it a hundred metres further along. With gestures so crystal clear as to leave no room for doubt, I explained that to do so would be proof of the most ridiculous bureaucracy: why get off, freezing, and then back on again to sit in the same seat, when I was already sitting there? He explained that one does not argue with orders.

I walked a hundred metres, the tram advanced the same distance, I took the same seat again, the driver smiled, his authority satisfied. My first contact with East European bureaucracy was not amusing.

To recover from my sign language argument, I went into a bar. Everyone was drinking beer – I asked for one too. The waiter said no. I showed him my money. He showed me the door. To this day, I have never understood why everyone else could drink beer and not me. One day I shall return there, even if it is only to kill the thirst which sticks in my throat! I don't want to see cathedrals, or bridges: I want my beer! I swear I still have to have a Czech beer in Prague! On a hot summer's day.

From Prague to plague: a snoring aeroplane-ette belonging to *Cubana de Aviación*, an anaemic wounded hangover from the Soviet Revolution, featuring the following itinerary: Prague – Shannon in Ireland; Shannon – Halifax in Canada; Halifax–Havana. More than thirty hours with stops to fill the tank and Band-aid over any cracks. I am not exaggerating: I swear I saw Band-aid on the outside of the plane! Blockade: heroism! Band-aid holding the plane together!

It was fantastic seeing Fidel speak in Revolution Square, for seven hours, no break, explaining the economy to the people. How beautiful and simple some things are! Fidel explaining and us understanding.

Of course the world economy is complex. Even so, we are capable of understanding it: the question is knowing how to explain it. Astronomy is among the most complex of sciences but certain facts are easily under-standable: I know that the sun will rise in the morning and set at the end of the day – never the other way around. With the help of two green lemons and one yellow orange, astronomy is comprehensible.

Fidel explained things using simple words, and when things became more difficult he would explain the words, which made it simple. Any word, when understood, is simple. Even my old friend 'flabbergasted'. Simplicity itself! *Verfremdungseffekt*, easy as pie – you just have to look at the clown Piolim's face.

In Fidel's voice and gesture, I saw his love for words: Fidel loves his interlocutors, the Cuban people. The word was the love which united the two. His speech was an act of love. Which was reciprocated.

Sojourn in New York

After a month of Cuba, theatres, walks and talks, I returned home. Few people knew what I had gone abroad to do – only those who needed to. And a few others who shouldn't have. . . .

By a happy coincidence, Richard Schechner, a Professor at New York University and the Director of Performance Group and Editor of *The Drama Review*, came to Brazil with Joanne Pottlitzer, of Theatre of Latin America. Schechner was thinking of dedicating an issue of his magazine to

In Sao Paulo in July 1968, the entire artistic community went on strike, declaring a state of civil disobedience and refusal to accept censorship any longer. The show, A FEIRA PAULISTA DE OPINIAO *(São Paulo's Fair of Opinion), was directed by Boal and included short pieces of his own, songs by Gilberto Gil and Caetano Veloso, and contributions from hundreds of visual artists.*

Latin American theatre. We became fraternal friends. Joanne invited *Zumbi* to New York. In August 1969, Arena boarded a plane: colourful shirts, guitar, drums and flute. Saint Clement's Church. The one-week run turned into a month, the church hyper-overcrowded. The *New York Times* published an eulogistic review in the early hours following the opening: you hardly had time to put the phone down before it would ring again, bouncing happily in its cradle. Dining in Joe Allen's, Pedro, Lima and myself, we would economise on food and order chilli con carne, at 99 cents. Our daily allowance was US$11. And to drink? Well . . . Chateauneuf du Pape – and there went our US$11 down the hatch.

A Mexican impresario, Manolo, read the rave reviews and invited us on a Mexican tour. He invited us without seeing the show. . . .

We returned to Brazil: the noose was tightening. International solidarity could be useful. Dictators are ashamed of what they do: if they are denounced, their acts of evil diminish. May they always be denounced!

The unforgettable señor *Quezada*

The trip to Mexico was a disaster, the next trip to the United States a tragedy! From the artistic point of view, they were both great successes.

ZUMBI
New York (Times Square), 1969

The disaster: Manolo, a commercial impresario, wanted shows to suit the *señoritas* who came to matinées. In ecstasies after having read our reviews, but not having seen the show, he had no idea what he was booking: *Zumbi*, and another play of mine, *Bolivar*, music by Theo de Barros.

Zumbi opened at the *Palácio de las Artes*, all 1500 seats full, a sea of *decolletage* and tails and girls with pink ribbons in their fair hair. Our Mexican audience was entirely lacking in Aztec, Mayan, Oaxacan or Chichimecan faces – the look was pure Belgian! Our show was unfit for such finesse. . . . Apart from the virulence of the script, it showed scenes of dubious morality: Lima, the destructive Captain Don Ayres, made orgasmic gestures, his hand stroking his sex, rhythmically. A show for fair-haired girls with ribbons in their hair it was not. The *New York Times* had liked it; the girls' parents not one bit!

Couples stomped out, vocalising their indignation; girls were dragged out by furious parents, glancing back in curiosity. The Papal Nuncio, the carrier of three heart bypasses, almost had the definitive collapse. Military men vociferated. Elderly ladies stumbled on the red carpet, and Mr Manolo went white with shock and fainted.

Manolo decided to withdraw the advertisements he had arranged to be published. The show went on, clandestinely. Mexico City is 2 km above sea-level: the actors would tire easily; as artistic director, my sole task was to wait in the wings with an oxygen pump pointing at the stage: when the actors came off, they came straight to me, pump at the ready, and I would hold the nozzle over their noses. After a deep breath, back they would go to the rarified air of the stage. But it was a national tour – and Manolo honoured his contract. He appointed the unforgettable *señor* Quezada as our companion.

In Puebla, San Luis de Potosi and Guadalajara we performed to audiences of twenty-odd – not even the employees of the theatres were warned of our arrival. As for posters, we drew our own and stuck them on the front of the theatres. We went into the streets to announce our arrival. The theatres were desolate. When, by chance, we were performing in student towns, such as Guanajuato, we were packed out. Sometimes, *señor* Quezada asked politely: '*Por favor, hoy hay muchas niñas en el publico. Modere sus pelotitas. . . .*'[57]

SÃO PAULO'S FAIR OF OPINION

In Plínio Marcos's play, a colonel clad in a gorilla costume censors one of the writer's own plays whilst defecating and using the censored pages to wipe his bottom.

Lima took the note, and that day, the orgasms were less rhythmical and more silent. One day, Quezada asked us to go easy on the *pelotas* when a long-standing lady friend of *señor* Manolo was coming; he himself was still consigned to bed after his fainting fit. Same again another time, because the Bishop was coming. On other occasions, the *pelotas* had free rein. Before each show, Lima would ask: '*Señor Quezada, hoy será con pelotas o sin pelotas?*'[58] Quezada would advise us, according to the audience. On the last performance in the last town, Quezada said: '*Hoy es la última función: hágalo con todas las pelotas que quiera.*'[59]

During this trip, there was love and romance. In Morélia we met a dark-skinned gypsy bullfighter, distinguished by one impressive detail: his right foot had been cleft in two by a valiant animal. Even when intact of foot, *toreros* exert a certain attraction on women – I do not know why, but it is so. Imagine this gypsy *torero* with lacerated foot and crutches: irresistible. Isabel Ribeiro fell in love. When we got to Lima, Peru, the end of our journey, Isabel asked me if she could change her Lima–Rio ticket for one back to Mexico. Isabel married the cleft-footed Mexican bullfighter. We lost an excellent actress, the Mexican theatre gained one.

Loves, and hates. At four o'clock every morning, in our hotel, with its beautiful verandas of flowers giving onto the *corralón*,[60] in the selfsame Spanish colonial town of Morélia, we were woken by a mad guest who blasted out the *Reveille* on his bugle. Out on the veranda in our pyjamas, we would protest against this military musician, who hid before we got there. Most furious of us all was Renato Consorte, a marvellous actor, who would rage against the *Reveille*, complaining to the manager. We all loathed the bugler, and Renato loathed him most. Till one day we decided to wake before four, hoping to surprise the implacable bugler. At four on the dot he appeared. Can you imagine who he was? Dead right – Renato Consorte!

This was Renato's way. We forgave his jokes. Even Zé Bicão and Hélio Ary forgave him, I am sure. One dawn, they leapt out of bed, awoken by the infernal din of an orchestra of *mariachis*, with wide brimmed hats, singing *La Cucaracha* and other Mexican gems. They forgave Renato, but not the music!

Renato later had a tragic accident: he was in an aeroplane crash and was one of the two survivors. He spent six months in hospital with burns of all degrees, one leg and both arms in traction. Then he graduated to a wheelchair. At night, the doctors were in the habit of going up the hill next to the hospital in order to drink *cachaça* in the bar at the top. Renato, feeling better, asked if he could join them. After the understandable hesitation, the doctors set off up the hill, pushing Renato in his wheelchair. In the bar, the physicians drank more than was advisable. On the way back, the doctor pushing the wheelchair gesticulated with even greater vehemence, and the wheelchair careered down the steep slope at high speed. Renato crashed into a wall. Another six months in hospital, re-mending the freshly broken bones. . . .

The postmen's strike

We opened the show in Berkeley, California and went on, applause, and happiness.

The US postal service – whose motto proudly announces that not even earthquakes, floods, snow or storms can interrupt its work – had its first and, to this day, only general strike. Lacking any direct mail services, universities cancelled our shows. We passed the time playing football in the snow – with bottles of brandy to fight the cold. We ate our fill thinking that the food was included in our contract. It was not: we spent the season's profits. Luckily, Joseph Papp[61] offered us a small space in the Public Theatre in New York, almost for free. That was what saved us. Solidarity!

But on return to Brazil, I felt anguish. I did not want to live abroad, and it was impossible to live in Brazil. We could not speak about what we really wanted and, under dictatorship, who could think about metaphysics? There is a time for metaphysics. Some threw themselves into the armed struggle and disappeared. We tried to resist. It is difficult to confront tanks with stage sets, guns with music. We lost.

Nucleus Number Two

Cecília Thumim and Heleny Guariba organised an Acting Course in 1970. In December, some of their pupils decided to carry on. An old idea I had developed with Vianninha came into my head: from the newspapers every morning select topical material which could be theatricalised, rehearse it in the afternoon and, each night, perform a different show.

We opened our new experiment in September, in a minuscule theatre with a capacity of seventy, which we christened *Areninha*! Sábato Magaldi wrote that our show was an exercise in freedom – in the middle of dictatorship, imprisonment, torture and death.

Teatro Jornal: primeira edição (Newspaper Theatre: First Edition) taught organised groups, of parishioners or students or slum-dwellers, how to do theatre for themselves, using the twelve techniques we had developed. We wanted to offer our audiences not the finished product but the means of production. In Santo André, the seeds of TO were sown; here the embryo took form. We would not give up making theatre. We offered the population our know-how. If we did not know what to say, we did know how to teach people to say what they wanted. Liberty had been lost, but not dreams. We had lost plays, theatre, grants, costumes, everything. Except our dreams.

There was no difference between us and our audiences, now that we had no vestige of our artists' trappings; we were citizens, mere human beings. We – us and them – could do theatre. Because we were theatre. We offered our knowledge, we sought theirs. An exchange.

We started forming Newspaper Theatre groups, more than thirty of them. We performed anywhere, away from the police: behind the church, in the anatomy room of the Faculty of Medicine – the unbearable smell of formaldehyde kept the military away – in the houses of factory workers, priests, teachers. . . . We would write our shows and, two hours later, they were ready for the audience. Instantaneous Theatre, lightning-quick. Then we helped them to do their own show.

Our dream was to propagate the techniques so that everyone could use theatre, the richest of languages.

Arturo Ui *and escalopes* alla milanese

Working with *Núcleo Dois* (Nucleus Number Two), forming groups all over, we still had to carry on with our professional company. To speak of our times. What better than Brecht's *The Resistible Rise of Arturo Ui*: it showed that the rising tide of fascism oppressing us was resistible. The Dictator on shift at the time was called Garrastazu, known as the Dictator of Death: it was our duty to fight him.

ARTURO UI

By Brecht adapted by Guarnieri. The last play directed by Boal at The Arena
in São Paulo before his exile, 1971

Guarnieri played Adolf-Arturo. Weinstock made the set out of iron: boots struck the ground hard, the sinister sound of fascism. The siege tightened, both on-stage and off!

The Argentinean Association of Actors had a festival in Buenos Aires. We took *Zumbi* – instead of one performance, we stayed there for a month and a half. We also took the Newspaper Theatre, which helped in the formation of local groups. Meanwhile, back home, another invitation: the Festival at Nancy. Our internationalisation was beginning. Anguish. The siege was closing, pincer-like. Danger.

I was working. Cecília rang me: escalopes *alla milanese* awaited me. I walked along the wet pavements. It was dark and raining – three armed men got out of a VW Beetle. I recognised two of them: 'actors from the interior' who had never heard of Euripides. Twisting my arm behind me, they asked if it was going to be necessary to handcuff me or if I would come quietly.

I had no choice: I was kidnapped.

I was imprisoned.

Imprisonment and jail: the freedom of Prometheus

Imprisonment

Windows had bars. Tables, machine-guns. Men, weapons. Faces, frowns. Words, hate. I answered different questions with the same words: No! It was not me, I did not see, I have never known anything about anything, no!

They were going to free me: I pre-smelled escalopes *alla milanese*. The unshaven sub-chieflet phoned the stoned super-chief: he was happy, and ordered them to house me for the night. I wanted to make a phone call. No! After all, it is only for one night . . . the brutalised reasoning of brutish boors.

The jailer came along, singing old love-songs. In the corridor, doors barred the way to shared cells, suffering faces.[62] At the far end, another door led to a short corridor linking four cells for solitary prisoners. Maximum security. I was not dangerous; the cell was: thick bars, invented for fearless warriors. I was locked up under maximum security. When I say *doors*, I mean iron, heavy, creaking! When I say *cells*, I mean people piled on top of each other, sad people. When I say *sad*, I mean extreme sadness, feeling like death.

The cell that housed me was on the corner: through the little windows – mine and the corridor's – I could see the long path: I imagined the short one, to the right. The cell was two quick steps long, less than two timid steps wide. Basin and latrine, rats in the drain. Unlike this narrowness was the silence – ample, immense, infinite. For the third time in my life, I heard silence, bellowing: in there you yelled without sound, a silent movie. I wanted actual sound, real noise, and the silent din I listened to without hearing shocked me: I threw my shoe on the floor, and heard it. I threw my shoe at the ceiling, kicked the camp-bed, in my silenced rage. Through the thick walls I imagined tortured groans. Tortured for real, they did groan: but far away, I did not hear them. I listened to my imagination imagining cries – cries which existed, on the third floor. Cries made and cries yet to be made. There would be more. And they would be mine too.

The number eight, flat on the page, is symbol of the infinite. I walked around making a figure of eight on the floor of the cell, jostling the walls, brushing up against the latrine, traversing a thousand infinite eights so that my walk would be infinite.

In a cramped cell one has the sense of walking through deserts, tracing a figure of eight. I was going forward and coming back to the same place. Was that not what I had done all my life? Run fast, swiftly, without leaving the spot; fly without taking off? Hear noises, while deaf? Move my immobile body, bellow mute speech? What had my life been? *Lavrador do mar* (Farmer of the Sea), like Simon Bolívar?[63] I farmed words. I farmed desires, hopes. I farmed waves, I farmed the sea. Farmer of the air! I had done so much – but I had nothing: a man alone, empty-handed. A body surrounded by concrete on all sides . . . except inside.

I closed my eyes and the faces of Cecília and Fabián exploded into memory, my wife and son. I opened my eyes wide: I did not want to see them in the narrow cell, see them imprisoned, even imagine them so – I opened my eyes so they went away! Where would they be? I did not want to see them prisoners, even in my encaged memory. I closed my eyes, back they came, Fabián and Cecília. Coming to with a start, I lifted my eyelids with my fingers: I spied dirty walls, and son and wife disappeared. If I blinked, they came back: I wanted to see them flying, distant, far from bars and walls, beyond limit. In safety.

Suddenly, a song: '*É doce morrer no mar*' (Tis sweet to die at sea) – Caymmi. In another cell, a *mineiro*[64] song. In another, a *gaúcho*[65] tune. Before they slept, the prisoners proffered songs to one another. The jailer asked if I wanted to sing. I could not.

Tired, I did not sleep; the burning bulb – it never went out! – dazed the darkness, without illuminating my fear. I thought of my son: he used to like hearing me telling stories of the magic guitar and the Emperor of the Birds. That night, Fabián went to sleep without birds . . .

Not only is the prisoner imprisoned . . . family and friends are imprisoned, though free, their memories, their smiles, locked in the cell. A single prisoner is a heaving crowd.

Unrestricted solitude, immured

A hypnogogic state: neither sleep nor waking. In the dark haze of that region, I remembered my childhood at the gate, alone, watching the world go by. That loneliness recurred. In childhood, possible paths to tread lay before me, spaces opened up. Now, walls encased me, locked doors. I have always liked to have keys in my pocket: they had been confiscated.

The neurotic always plays the same role, like actors lacking in imagination, repeating themselves, in every part the monotonous same. In my hypnogogic reverie I swore that I would never be the neurotic who acts out the same torment, the same loneliness: I do not want to be alone! Is it possible to keep that promise? Not to be alone, so unaccompanied? I looked at my body and asked in which part of me the loneliness lay, dissolved. Not in my hands, my face. Not in my gaze, so full of people. Hidden in the liver, the kidneys, the spleen? Oh, loneliness: if it could only be extracted, like an inflamed appendix, pulled out like my long hair! Oh if only. . . .

If by the love and grace of some stray god it were possible for the divine hand to tear the loneliness out of my body . . . what a void it would leave! Perhaps I would be too alone, without my faithful companion, solitary loneliness.

Night frightened me and I feared the dawn

In the morning, morning voices. Next to me, a friendly woman's voice, a prisoner's. I was fearful of recognising it. The friendly voice, which had heard me without seeing me, in the cell next door, asked: 'Augusto?' I said: 'Heleny?'

It was she. For months she had been in the military prison; she had been recalled to the political prison for questioning with recent prisoners.

Heleny gave me advice. Firstly: never confess, anything. Not even the slightest confession of a petty inconsequential detail. She called to mind Nelson Rodrigues: even if the husband surprises his wife naked in bed, her lover by her side, naked, even *in flagrante*, she should deny it, always: it was a misunderstanding. Even naked: a misunderstanding. Same with the police: always deny it. With this advantage: the husband is cast into disquiet even at the sight of his wife's nudity; the torturer has seen nothing, he knows nothing: he merely suspects. If he interrogates, it is because another tortured person, not able to hold out, has denounced you. History was full of false denunciations . . . and new, true, torments.

Deny it; say no: lying is a civic duty!

The second piece of advice was Brechtian: Heleny said that the tortured used to exaggerate the effects of torture in order to save themselves from greater ills. Stanislavskians, they simulated to perfection and magnified the small pains they felt. It reminded me of Pessoa:[66]

> *O poeta é um fingidor, / finge tão completamente,*
> *que chega a fingir que é dor, / a dor que deveras sente.*

> (The poet is a make-believer, he makes believe so completely,
> that he even makes believe that the pain he truly feels is pain.)

She told me not to be anxious on seeing Albertina, my first wife, a prisoner, learning to walk again. Easy now: she was exaggerating the pain, it was not as great as all that. The tortured were Stanislavskians; I, however, must be Brechtian: rational distancing, *Verfremdungseffekt*[67] aplenty, not believing in what I saw.

That helped me to cope with the sight of Albertina, learning to walk again. I took it as staged melodrama: the actress was 'overacting' and yet sincere. I learned later that this was not the case: Heleny wanted to spare me the pain of seeing the truth in that place. Today I suffer that fragile image.

Morning. Weak coffee, *teaffee*. The bread was yesterday's, paupers' bread. At midday: spaghetti, strands all stuck together, like bunches of hair, impenetrable braids. I could not eat. I waited all afternoon, night fell. Supper, the remains of lunch. I slept a fitful sleep, waking at every puff of wind: it rained, the wind whistled at the window, higher than I could jump, my desire leaping still further beyond.

The big Chief sent for me. I feel sick when I write his name[68] – assassin, violator, drug-addict and -trafficker, he was in command of the struggle against guerrillas. Inventor of the *Esquadrão da Morte* (Death Squad), corrupt 'elite' gunmen, specialists in killing handcuffed prisoners in the back. The *Esquadrão* had begun its activities by assassinating common prisoners. As they proved efficient, the Dictatorship decided to use them against the guerrillas. When ambushing their unarmed victim, they were invincible. They never involved themselves in fights between equals.

I was taken to an office with barred windows, where there were three other inspectors. To get there, I passed through aseptic-looking bureaucracies: typists typed, office boys served coffee, staff discussed football. They were taken aback at the sight of me in handcuffs.

The Chief was on the telephone: me being a well-known artist, he was proud of my capture – it fed his vainglory. Without looking at me, he examined his 'information'. Adjectives: subversive, rebellious, author of anti-government texts, published abroad. Not one incriminating fact.

He asked if anyone could recall a more significant accusation. No one did. Why had they arrested me? I could smell the escalopes. The bearded man, cleaning his gun, remembered. Under torture, a prisoner had spoken of me. I trembled.

I sat down, waiting for the book to arrive – computers did not exist in those days. The Chief read, tossed his pen down on the table, simulated a frown: 'Don't waste my time!' João, a *companheiro*, had denounced me as bearer of a Cuban letter describing armaments. José, on the *pau-de-arara*[69] had confirmed the allegation: 'There's no small talk with me: when in doubt, beat up the accused!'

I am proud to say I followed Heleny's advice down to the last word, come hell or high water, to the letter: I did not confess. Anything. Ever! Not even strung up on the *pau-de-arara*; not even to the military, in the sham of a tribunal at which I was tried. I harbour no bitterness towards those who did confess: I know the pain – it is hard to resist. Nor do I judge myself a hero because I managed always to deny: I do not know how close to death I would have come and still resisted. I just know that I did resist. And I am proud of that . . . without pride! I do not know if you understand me . . . I understand myself, at least on this occasion.

That day, realising it was useless to persist, the Chief sent me back to my cubicle. Two days passed before I went back upstairs. As I waited, I noticed that one of the policemen was wearing my green sweater – in spite of its being summer, it was cold. On the table I saw my two – legally owned! – revolvers, and my trousers, shirts, books, photos, newspapers, documents, letters. I saw my industrial chemistry ring, a present from my father and mother, proud of their *Doutor* son. That was the last time I saw my ring.

They had raided my house. With anguish, I thought of my family. For sure they had escaped, since they were not here. Relief. A common practice was the group torture of relatives: husband and wife, parents and children.

João and José arrived, downcast. It is strange: thirty years have passed and I remember, like it was this morning, their sad faces and crumpled shirts – there were no irons in the cells.

Once again I followed Heleny's advice: I explained that the confession of the two was to be expected. I justified the false declaration they had given with statements which, without incriminating me, did not accuse them. I tried to cobble together plausible explanations. The big Chief did not believe me. Two more days, two more nights.

The torture room

Three mastodons came along. Handcuffed, I ascended the stairs, familiar with the route. On the third floor there were two corridors – I headed for the usual one. They asked me if, this time, I was prepared to confess. I answered that I did not know anything. A gorilla ordered me to change paths. He opened the door: four orangutans were waiting. Last chance: will you confess? 'No!'

They terrified me by describing various tortures. Tupac-Amaro, the Peruvian indigenous hero, was tied to four horses by the Spaniards; a stampede set the horses to flight in four directions: he was torn to death. In Brazil, it was jeeps instead of horses. The *Cadeira do Dragão* (Dragon's Chair) made of aluminium: the naked prisoner was bound – fire was applied. Scorching heat, the prisoner could lift himself up, encasing his head in an electrified helmet . . . or suffer the fire to the buttocks. The *Psicodélica* (Psychedelic) was done in a room little larger than a lift, with mirrored walls: loudspeakers blasted out rhythms at the highest volumes, lights flashed on and off. After minutes, the body spasmed, out of control. For the rest of his life, the victim was deaf and half-blind.

There was more: drownings in buckets of water, nails torn out, eyes pierced. . . .

Torture is a hateful process. Like love-making, it is done naked. The *pau-de-arara*, straightforward and popular (in both senses of the word), is used even today for common prisoners throughout Brazil: anyone who says otherwise knows they are lying! Electric cables are attached to fingers and ankles; the electricity runs through the body assisted by the salt-water in which the prisoner is bathed at the beginning of the session: later on, salty sweat takes over the job. The electric current varies in accordance with the rheostat and the anger or haste of the operators. The body is hung by the knees on an iron pole running under handcuffed hands which in turn are crossed under the knees, taking the weight of the tortured person who is effectively tied in a knot. In the beginning the pain is bearable. Then it is not. The fingers become violet balls of blood not circulating. Cries resound in the solid silence, death-wishes.

The stabbing pain was too much. To buy time, I asked them what they were accusing me of. They did not know: the teams which did the torturing were not those which did the arresting – each to his own deathly speciality; the bearded man alone belonging to both. He looked at the list of serious accusations. The first said that I had defamed Brazil while abroad. I asked how. Reading on, he said that I had defamed the Fatherland by stating that there was torture in Brazil. (Impossible not to laugh, even hanging there. . . .)

The rheostat increased the charge. My weak smile dried up. I argued that if I was denouncing torture, I was telling the truth: I was living proof, hanging there. The chimpanzee agreed. Tempering the violence, he explained: as I was a famous artist, they were torturing me, yes, but . . . 'with all respect'. What would torture *without respect* be like? He replied: the electric cables could have been placed in the anus or the penis, or on a tooth, in an exposed cavity. Cigarettes could be put out on living flesh, instead of in the ashtray.

Sweat ran into my eyes, clouding my vision. I could hardly see the Cro-Magnons conversing with the Neanderthals, while the impatient Homo Habilis carried out orders. The whole tribe of prehistoric humanity was waiting for confessions to justify their day's work. After centuries hanging there, I was let down, my knees out of joint, my breathing explosive. 'More to come tomorrow. Here everyone confesses: sooner or . . . too late, in a shallow grave.'

The body and the soul remember. The images do not fade! The voices keep shouting: they never shut up.

My brother

Albertino and I did not agree about politics. No matter: he was my brother. My family had been searching for me for seven days and seven nights. In hospitals, police stations, the morgue, the asylum, no trace of me. But he was an army officer, in the reserves. He was entitled to carry a gun. Out of intuition he wanted to visit the DOPS.[70] My name did not appear on the list. They had given me a false name – I was there incognito. In cell F-1 was the dangerous miscreant Francisco de Souza – me.

One investigator, fresh from martyring someone, asked: 'What shall we do with the body?' My brother thought I was dead. A bag of nerves, he whipped out his revolver, swearing he would shoot someone if he could not see me, dead or alive! In the face of this unexpected explosion – and out of surprise at the unaccustomed threat – they decided to show me to him. I was with my brother for three minutes, in the midst of the gorillas. Cecília and Fabián were safe, he told me. My kidnapping had turned into imprisonment. Before I confessed what I did, the death squad confessed what they had done: I had not been imprisoned, but kidnapped.

Thanks to my brother, it got into the newspapers: my thanks, belatedly.

International solidarity

The news spread far and wide. In Brazil, there was little anyone could do, apart from look for a lawyer. Garrastazu *das mortes* (of the deaths)[71] had ordered even the Diocese of São Paulo radio station to be closed[72] for defending political prisoners. To whom should you complain, when the government was the outlaw?

In the United States, Arthur Miller drafted a letter which was published in the *New York Times*, demanding my freedom. Hundreds of illustrious names signed it: Richard Schechner, Michael Miller, and teachers at New York and other universities; Joanne Pottlitzer and members of the Theatre of Latin America; Robert Anderson, and reams of famous people in solidarity. In England and France, Émile Copfermann, Bernard Dort, Peter Brook, Jean Louis Barrault, Sartre and Simone, John Arden, Arianne Mnouchkine, Antoine Vitez, Gabriel Garran, Simone Signoret and Yves Montand, hundreds wrote to the Embassies. Jack Lang, President of the Nancy Festival, asked participants to protest. Telegrams poured in even from Japan, which impressed the military: Japan is exactly the other side of the Earth and they knew that the Earth was still round – fascists do not like that, they prefer to think of it as square! If artists were concerned about me even in Japan . . . I must be extremely important!

The scale of solidarity impressed the dictators. A prisoner could be incarcerated for two years, without accusation; and three or four without trial. My case was heard after only a month. They wanted to transform me into a dangerous guerrilla, to attribute to me actions I would never dream of undertaking. During the interrogation I was so sure I would be freed that I did not pay attention to what the scribe was writing. Craftily, he asked if I admitted having delivered the Cuban letter to our leader: I replied that I did not. He wrote that I admitted I had not delivered the letter to the leader: I therefore admitted to having brought the letter . . . I signed it, without reading it. I was happy, I became sad.

The judge concluded: my crime was proven. I should be heard in a tribunal. Two months went by in the *Tiradentes* military prison. I learned: when you talk to judges, scribes or journalists, you must say, clearly, what you want to see published or written in the statements. When you say too much, the person who is writing it down can use genuine words to compose false texts. I paid for it.

Jail

I went in to the collective cell and was greeted by fifteen *companheiros*. One prisoner told me: 'The Arena bed is empty; Isaías has been transferred. You inherit a bed, a cup, and flip-flops. . . . He took the toothbrush. Selfish man.' Since 1969, that cell had always housed a member of Arena: a captive bed.

The Left united in jail: members of parties of the Left, dissident tendencies, dissident dissidents from fragmented dissident tendencies. Why did they have to wait for prison before they were united? Political cells were organised. In the morning, from seven o'clock on, you could talk out loud. From nine to one, in whispers: time to meditate. After lunch, lessons. Each taught what he or she knew: guitar, French (I learned the rudiments!), the history of the parties (pupils disagreed with the masters . . .), theatre (with me as teacher!), philosophy, and cooking (I learned how to make *feijoada!*[73]). People knew *capoeira*,[74] but we didn't have enough space . . . martial arts: memories.

Frei Betto, a long-standing prisoner, had the privilege of visiting cells. Being friends, we used to converse. It was he who taught me the right way to read the Bible; as well as being a religious book, the Bible is history.

We had to work: in a replay of Atlantic City, I had a dazzling career: I started out sweeping the floors, graduated to pot-washer and ended up cook, once a week. I like an eclectic kitchen; in France, *feijoada* with *champignons*, *vatapá*[75] with truffles – delicacies I know how to make. And can teach.

Visiting day: my mother came from Rio every week, bringing a nephew or niece: Ângela, Sílvio, Sônia, Luiz and Luciana got a taste for aeroplanes. I took advantage of the visits to send out drawings done to remember episodes to write about, when free. My mother used to tell them that the drawings were for my son. I wrote a novel, *Milagre No Brasil* (Miracle in Brazil), and *Torquemada*, a play.[76]

At visiting time we used to see imprisoned *companheiras*. I urged Heleny that when she was freed – an imminent possibility – she should travel to

Buenos Aires, where we had friends. She spoke of her duty, to return to the struggle. She was assassinated days after her release. The dictatorship did not arrest a second time, it killed.

A *camburão*[77] fetched us for the hearing: a windowless vehicle. On the sidewalk, from the car to the tribunal, lines of young soldiers with machine-guns were awaiting us, as if we were Guevaras. For the judges, João and José gave a different version of events – they were not afraid of torture. The accused would often say different things in court to what they had said when in the secret prison. Before the final sentencing, the judge granted me the right to travel and join the cast. In Nancy, this would give the impression of magnanimity: the dictatorship needed to show a less sordid face.

I signed a document promising to return after the Festival and to be present at the tribunal at the time of sentence. The official who made me sign the promise advised me: 'We do not arrest the same element twice: we kill them! Never return. But sign on this line – promising to return.'[78]

That was the only piece of advice from the dictatorship I followed closely: I returned only in December 1979, a few months after the Amnesty.

Written and spoken memory

The word is a living being. It lives within me, between people, it floats. I cannot give someone my word: I can give myself. I am my word. The spoken word – to which we bid farewell – that word dissolves in the person who hears it and consumes it: it is pronounced without return. A gift. A part of me that takes its leave. What comes back – the response – is another word, not the same one. The written word is different: nurtured by its writer just for himself, to him it returns. Naked and pure, as it left him. The reader is a contingency.

The word is richer when written than pronounced, it has more personality. Contemplating what is written, the writer discovers related words. Some are friends, others hate each other. Either they exchange pleasantries, or they are blind to each other. *Love* and *hate* love each other; *intelligence* and *dictatorship* hate each other. The imagination drawn, the painted face of thought, the body of emotion – the word is these! A living being, it breathes – it trembles in my hands, in lovers' discourse. It is mine!

Words have feelings: I want them to love me. I need to care for them so that they do not mix with bad company, with words that do not deserve them.

The word pronounced is never the one heard; the word I wrote, that is the same one, it carries my memories, not other people's, and comes back to me without interferences. When I read what I wrote, I am speaking to myself. Or misunderstanding myself, another form of understanding.

About torture and prison, I have spoken to friends, journalists, strangers, my analyst. To denounce is imperative. To understand is urgent and necessary!

All crimes must be revealed – not to reveal them is a crime.

This is the fourth time – or the sixth! – that I return to this subject which I portray in words. I need to understand what happened. For this, it is necessary to see that reality drawn in the profile of the written word; to see it arise transubstantiated on the computer screen: magic. A ritual in search of lost purity: he who writes purifies himself, liberates himself, bathes naked, seeing himself. Before putting my clothes back on, to meet the world, I want to meet myself. I want to know my hand's reach, the remoteness of my foot. I want to know: I write. This book is my purification.

On the couch, I remembered: but that is not enough! The silence of the analyst is the word which returns, transformed. I have to write my word – to see the word of my choice, to touch it with my fingers. I have *saudades* for *nankeen*[79] ink.

I want to daub myself with blue words.

Infinity, within walls!

As a child, I lived in a large house: in the garden, friends of mine discovered a rat's nest. A rat-icide expedition was organised: the rat family was stoned to death. Pitiless slaughter. I did not throw a single stone, but I felt guilty for not having prevented the rodent hecatomb.

Today we know that music stimulates human or animal activities: children who listen to Mozart become more intelligent than those subjected to Heavy Metal; cows listening to Bach produce more milk – not better quality, with more vitamins and mineral salts: just a greater quantity – that itself is progress.

The influence of music on lactation and physical labour is so well attested that multinationals use a varied repertoire to stimulate their workers according to the product they are making. Tractors and trucks demand Wagner and Verdi; delicate textiles require Monteverdi and Italian madrigals; sensitive computers, Chopin and Debussy. Bossa Nova is good for going to the beach, preferably Ipanema. . . .

I saw a snout peeping out of the drain in the cell. Days later, the small head of a mouse. Confidence grew; one fine summer's afternoon, the whole, minuscule body appeared. Encouraged by my tender gaze, the little animal ventured out. Every day he came to see me, before dusk. A short visit, not face to face: face to snout. A deep gaze, the mysteries of nature.

This was the only mouse with whom I have had any kind of affectionate relationship. He knew I liked him; I felt he liked me. I never sought to frighten him: in his restless eyes, I tried to disentangle the mystery of life. Though I had not gone mad – I swear – I conversed with the creature. I had the courage to tell him what I would never say to my equal. That mouse guards my unconfessable secrets! When I was transferred to a larger prison, I was sad, not having time to say goodbye to the creature who had been my only friend in four weeks of solitary confinement. My secret confidante. Why not?! And you? Have you never spoken to an animal?

I drew a self-portrait on crumpled paper and threw it into the drain, in the hope that the mouse would see it and, who knows – no one knows the deepest mysteries of the rodent psyche – perhaps he would understand my gesture of affection, perhaps a furtive tear would fall from his eyes. I do not know if mice cry: I was not imprisoned long enough to ascertain this. I only know that, when they are not afraid, they are affectionate. After the cell, rats and mice went out of my life once and for all. Nevertheless, I remember those creatures, who made me feel both guilt and affection. Especially that little prisoner. It was in prison, faced with that animal, that I discovered myself as Augusto. I swear!

I discovered, with alarm, that I was not my master. I could not programme myself. The *tomorrow* was the same as the *today*, no different to the *yesterday*. Nothing changed, unless someone – not I – decided to the contrary. All the power lay with the jailer! My body was imprisoned: I, however, comprise more than the moment! My feet tethered, my imagination wandered. Of the *me* past, of that I was master. Of the *me* of the distant future, I was also master. In the cell I found Proust looking for his *temps perdu*. I had lost mine. Within the walls, I recovered my liberty. A certain liberty. In prison, I found freedom. A certain way of being free.

In the quotidian grind of life repeated, I did not see myself – I was in a hurry, coming and going. In the cell, I watched and saw myself – it was obligatory. Out there, there were schedules, duties – those rituals did not allow me time to reflect, to say good morning to the mirror, to talk to myself. Where there was space, I did not have time. Now I had time – and space was lacking. There, in the diffuse disintegration of time – *now* without *before* or *after*: only the eternal instant – and the small space, I thought about myself, I heard the sound of the silence, for the fourth time in my life!

In the cell, the words I caressed had no other recipient – their right address was me and back they came. The jailers called me delinquent – for them, I was an impurity that would have to be removed from social inter-course in order for the world to purify itself of my existence. I was judged according to their ideology. The worth of an act does not depend on the act itself, but on the circumstances in which it is carried out. I always craved legality, which was subverted by those who judged me.

Prison suspended me in time and confined me in space, but there were no walls within me: I am infinite. They can raise mountains around me and press them to my chest, handcuff my feet and bind my hands with wire: my thought is free, like Prometheus[80] bound. He gave fire to mankind, democratising access to the flame. The Gods, however, were not ready for democracy. They feared that, feeling the caress of the fire, men would also want the water that quenched thirst and the fruit that kills hunger: they feared that men would also want the Earth, the Sky and the Sea. The Gods wanted Prometheus to recognise his crime. The theft itself could be forgiven, there was fire enough for everyone, more than enough: but not liberty! His crime was the example he gave.

Prometheus was free to say no to the greatest God, and said so: to Zeus he repeated that mankind deserved fire. In his heart he had desire and courage. In hearts less Titanic than Prometheus', less deified, like mine – besides our few virtues, we have illusions. In the cell, I was able to rethink these. My body was imprisoned, my imagination free. Winged, I passed through walls. Boxed in, I thought about alternatives. What paths could I have followed and did not? What life had I wasted?

Metaphorically, the Theatre of the Oppressed was born in prison. I like to say: in this kind of theatre, the citizen – in the present – studies the past and invents the future. The stage, the arena, like the cell or the prison yard, can be a place of study; and the theatre can be a fit instrument, a proper language for that discourse, that quest for oneself.

Prison should be a time for reflection, space and learning. In hospital, the body cannot just cure itself of its own accord – it is assisted. In hospital, the doctor; in prison, the educator. We political prisoners were our own educators: we came out better, more determined to reject the dictatorship. The cell should not turn into life in suspension – that would be a crime! The bear hibernates; when it awakens in spring, it is the same bear that went to sleep in Autumn. When the prisoner is freed he or she should be different. But how can one be different if one has merely been hibernating?

While a *political* prisoner I thought about the *common* prisoners, in their *common* cells. Proportional death sentence: part of their lives is killed in there, the part equivalent to the duration of their sentence. Young men are assassinated between 18 and 30 years of age, between 20 and 35! If, beyond those walls, social structures exist – the kind of structures which we know to be generative of delinquents! – inside the walls, a form of social organisation must be invented. In our cell, in the ironically named *Tiradentes* jail, we were political and we educated ourselves; in the common cells, the people were chained up. The people I was seeking, piled on top of each other in there. Even in prison, the class divide existed. There were even divisions between political prisoners: in front of my cell there was the *Cela dos Lordes* (the Lords' Cell) – for guerrillas from rich families, whose meals were brought to them from their homes. Common prisoners are delinquent. In prison, their return to society is prepared. They must adapt themselves to a society, to which they were clearly not adapted before! Theatre can accomplish the task of teaching people to learn through action. And what allows the passive spectator to transform him or herself into an active Protagonist is the Theatre of the Oppressed.

In the magic alchemy of art and social life, theatre and prison – both limited in space and time – can become synonyms of freedom. And the word freedom, which is so beautiful, is less beautiful only than the act of being free.

Danger and dictatorship in Buenos Aires

No one could travel without permission from the police, who would check criminal records, tax returns, physiognomy, fingerprints. . . . It would be impossible to leave on the first plane. In São Paulo, I went to the flat where I had lived for seven years to say my goodbyes. I filled two suitcases with intimate things. *Saudades*. I noted the destruction of furniture, the disappearance of objects, photos, money, documents – I was enraged!

I travelled first to New York, then to Europe. Thank-yous galore. I met my actors. Our farewell full of hopeful 'see you soon's.

Buenos Aires, without a salary. Luckily my in-laws were moving and left us a furnished flat, on a mortgage. I had inherited four rooms in Penha from my father – they brought in US$300 a month in rent. The mortgage cost US$90: on US$210, we could live well. Ahh, the old days . . . who would not have *saudades*?

In 1966 I had gone to Buenos Aires for five weeks, and stayed for five months. This time, I imagined five months, and stayed five years. An odd sensation: Buenos Aires did not need me! If I had not existed, I would not have been missed. In my country I made a difference, however minimal. In Buenos Aires, no difference.[81] I felt invisible. I looked for myself in the deserted mirror: all my selves had departed – even me! Difficult to shave when your face escapes from the mirror.

Oppressed in New York

While I was still in prison, Schechner invited me to direct at New York University. I asked if the offer was real, or just a cordial stratagem. It was real. Off we went and for three months we lived near NYU, and then on Second Avenue.

I went to thank Arthur Miller, and through him the signatories of the letter that had demanded my freedom. The *New York Times* documented the encounter, and the Brazilian Embassy spied the article. I met Dore Ashton, an art critic and campaigner for human rights. The Embassy stayed on the lookout! At NYU, *Torquemada* – spies in the audience; at Saint Clement's, the *Feira Latino-Americana* (Latin-American Fair), with diplomats lurking; spies all around me.

I wrote a novel, *Milagre no Brasil* (Miracle in Brazil) – the miracle of the survival of the people, in spite of the government. The students could not imagine the anguish of a prisoner in a cell. The University agreed to let them spend twenty-four hours on the set: the actors and I, eating, sweeping, playing the guitar. Talking to each other in character the whole day long – marvellous.

Feira bewildered its audiences. Simultaneous scenes, songs, poems. Spectators chose their own paths through it: the show would go back to the beginning, over and over.

In the show, after an hour and a half, TV screens on stage showed the interrogation of a 'kidnapped' spectator. Our questions were based on a report by the North American Senate on criminal relationships between Latin American dictators and the CIA. We altered nothing: our conclusions were those of the US Senators. After each frightful affirmation, we would ask: 'Did you know?' the invariable reply being: 'I did not even suspect!' Last question: 'Did you know that in Nuremberg the reply the tribunal heard most from the accused was: "I did not know"?'

TORQUEMADA
Written by Boal in prison in 1971,
directed by him with students of New York
University a month later

Workshop in Germany, 1977

performed.

Wonderful to see sculptures by our artists: tortured South Americans beside the sacred images of Jesus at Calvary, Peter on the Inverted Cross, Sebastian and his wounds. Julian Beck wept. He and his company had been imprisoned in Brazil — they knew what we were talking about.

★   ★   ★

Solidarity

What astonishes and enchants me, in times of crisis, is solidarity. Paco Urondo, journalist, playwright and poet, made me an offer: 'You are a writer and have lost your typewriter: a painter without arms. I'll give you mine. I can use the newspaper's.' I accepted the newspaper's typewriter, my heart beating samba. Paco was assassinated by the gorillas – I will never forget.

Tigre Cedrón, brother of the tango singer Tata, was making a film and had money in the bank. I was looking for producers for *O Grande Acordo Internacional do Tio Patinhas* (The Great International Agreement Of Uncle Scrooge Macduck) which parodied Lanusse. Tigre suggested he produce my play: 'If you get the money back, pay me; if not, I'll film a few scenes less . . . my film is very long. . . .' The play ran for six months. Tigre committed a strange suicide in exile in Paris – I cannot forget.

Baden Powell's guitar

A play made me reflect on the moral duty[82] of the director. What ethical duties take precedence over aesthetic choices? If I were a director in Bangladesh, I would not do what I did. Do I make shows for myself or do I think about the audience? What is the use of art? Does art have a use?

There was a celebrated debate in Brazil in the 1970s centred around a popular Brazilian guitar player and composer (named after the founder of the Boy Scouts). Was Baden's guitar right-wing or left-wing? Is there ideology in art? Some said that there was no ideology in *do-re-mi*, or Van Gogh's sunflowers or Rembrandt's *chiaroscuros*. Others said: for whom are the notes played? Whose ears will hear them? To whom are the paintings addressed? Whose eyes will kiss them?

Rhythms, melodies and voices have no ideology – any more than yellow, blue and green.[83] Words, on the other hand, are logos, concepts. When they join together in a phrase, it carries meaning, intention. It contains an opinion on the society in which it lives. Poem, story, novel and play are all representations of the real, created from a point of view not situated in the Cosmos, where we are not, but well and truly earthbound: in which trench do we fight, and for what? Or do we naïvely think that humanity lives in peace? Does peace exist, has it ever existed?

Seven children murdered while sleeping in front of the closed doors of the Candelária Church, in 1993, reveal a country at war. Eritrea is here, Sierra Leone is here, Haiti has always been with us: even when people 'merely' die from hunger, a silent death, without bursts of gunfire – death whispered is not peace!

Peace is an incessant, dynamic search. Reality is war, divided humanity! Peace is a dream. We want that dream, we want peace! Let us be dreamers . . . with our feet on the ground. Peace, yes; passivity, never!

Sounds, in themselves, have no conceptual content[84] – offered to a someone, at a particular time and place, concepts can arise from them: from their relationship with the *other*. If Baden's guitar had been offered to the generals – thank God it never was! – it would be as fascist as the military. Offered to the people, it would be of the people.

Guitars do have ideology: it depends who they are playing for.

I was in transit. What plays should I choose and for whom? I was seeking my people: not any people. What could I say to the Argentineans, not being one? With what right, by dint of what duty? Should I do a play for its amusement value? Should I do *Torquemada*, because it was true?

In Buenos Aires, I continued to speak to Brazilians.

The birth of invisible theatre

In Argentina all theatre directors were also teachers. I too earned my daily bread this way. With my students, I prepared scenes for the street based on a law that allowed any hungry person to go into a restaurant, however luxurious, and eat and drink whatever they liked, dessert and wine excepted; on showing their identity card, they could then leave without paying. A beautiful law, a humanitarian law! We wanted to let people know about this law – it is so rare to be in favour of a law, we wanted to prove that we were not against all laws.

Brazilian friends warned me. Already in the pipeline at this stage was Operation Condor, by which Nazis in Argentina, Chile, Uruguay and

Brazil, in obedience to the CIA, offered mutual assistance in the form of actions, information and assassinations. If arrested, I would be sent back to Brazil. I should not even entertain the idea of watching the première of this piece. I remembered the policeman who said goodbye to me: 'We do not arrest the same element twice. . . .' I decided to stay home.

An actor had the idea of playing the scene as 'invisible theatre', inside a restaurant: this would remove the need for a stage set – it was there already – and for publicity – at midday, the house was full. No one would know of the clandestine première, the police would not turn up, and it would not be known who was an actor and who wasn't. Spectators would see the show, without seeing it *as* a show.

Consternation: the reason we do theatre is to be seen, isn't it? The actor explained: I would be there, eating my lunch in peace. Meanwhile, the actors would sit at some distance from one another, in order to involve the maximum number of customers, and, at an opportune moment, the piece would be played as if it were a spontaneous act.

Our actor versions of *waiter* and *manager* would inevitably be replaced by the real waiter and manager working there. It happened: they said, almost word for word, what we had scripted. They even threatened to call the police: which also figured in our script.

From my table on the other side of the room, I was able to observe this extraordinary thing: the interpenetration of fiction and reality. The superimposition of two levels of the real: the reality of the quotidian and the reality of the rehearsed fiction.

Reality took on the characteristics of fiction, fiction appeared like reality. The professionals, having rehearsed; the spontaneous 'performers', improvising – all playing truth. Arguing passionately: if there is food, why are people dying of hunger? The country is rich: why are the people poor? The debate was more intense than it would have been in the street. A lawyer, one of the company, explained the humanitarian law.

Our objective was not to get a free steak: one of us paid the bill and it all ended peacefully.

Fiction does not exist: everything, if it exists, is real – all fiction is true. The only fiction that exists is the word 'fiction': it designates something that does not exist. But the word fiction, itself, exists as signifier and signification: it signifies our desire to tell the truth, lying!

We began to develop this second form of the Theatre of the Oppressed, the first having been the Newspaper Theatre. The third and fourth forms, Image and Forum, developed in Peru in 1973, a decisive year in my life.

Artist in transit, divided

I did not integrate myself into this alien culture – apart from its wine. I had friends, family, I spoke the language. What was lacking? I felt myself dissolving. Quicksands did not swallow me up; but they made walking more difficult. My desire to return home grew – back to my mug of coffee, my language. When I looked up at the sky, I did not find my stars. The stars there were, were not mine. That was not my moon. That river was not my sea. I was in transit. I took my shoes off on a strange floor, every night.

I directed *Torquemada*. I could not believe what I had been through. I needed to see it happen outside me, on stage, so I could see myself, separate myself from me. Me and the word, me and the actor. Only in this way would I understand myself.

A mirror was not enough, memory was not enough: I needed to see myself in someone who would steal my name, the Augusto Boal I thought I was, the Augusto Boal I carried stuck to my face, my hands, my chest. I no longer knew who I was nor who I had been. I wanted to hear words I pronounced under torture. The cultivated voice, producing hoarse cries. To see myself from a distance. To direct myself directing actors.

I took pleasure – was it morbid or healthy? – in directing the actor who played me. Hamlet directing the actor playing the assassinated father, as *Gonzaga*: how could he speak to the character without seeing his father? How could I speak to me without seeing me? I wanted the actor to suffer what I had suffered, and I was jealous of the pain, which was mine alone. I wanted to invent suffering for the actor, similar to mine, but far away from the real thing. I learned that to make theatre is to dominate pain! The cruellest pains become beautiful! I wanted to re-create myself. To be reborn. I did not want to admit that the tortured person was me, that that scene had happened to me.

When I was living in Portugal (1976–1978), where once again I felt too alone, I wrote a play in which I saw myself from afar: *Murro em Ponta de Faca* (Blows at Knifepoint). Distant, in the mist – the wind and the cold of the journey without end. A circular play, in which I am no one: I am all of them, I am the one who commits suicide and also those who survive.

I wrote *Murro* in Lisbon at a time when exiles were committing suicide. A tribe of solitary people, so together, in the same boat: so alone. Exile is half-death, just as prison is half-life! The appearance of liberty masks ties of love broken by distance, moral parameters destroyed by the fight for survival, projects for the future contorted by time. Corroding within. Termites! The body an empty form.

In Buenos Aires people talked about assassinations, spectacular escapes, shootings in the street. In Portugal the talk was of surrender, suicide, no way out. Conversations had a whiff of formaldehyde. I remembered the theatre we used to do in anatomy rooms: violet corpses, crushed flowers!

Without apprehending the horror of what they were saying, candidates for nothingness talked about the multiple forms of the pursuit of death, from eating your own tongue (there were people who tried it!) to a philosophy student who dreamed of ending like Epicurus, the philosopher who died sweetly in a bath of tepid water, talking to his friends, taking tea (or *cachaça*?). To die in sweetness: pleasure . . . non-orgasmic! Conversations about death assailed one, tore one apart, pale shadows of death. Courage wilted,[85] arms fell to the sides, fists unclenched.

Some killed themselves because of the after-effects of their experiences, from thinking about the past – events recurred, fresh horrors to horrify them, nails dug into the memory clawing out chunks of the future, daggers in the chest of the imagination. Others drowned themselves in confusion, eyes to the wall – the future – surrounded by the present, seeing nothing ahead of them.

Solitary suicides: disintegrated families, functions reversed, who is who? Exile disintegrates – takes away from each person their primary role, negates the individual, their function, their intimate *I am*. No one is: the father, the mother, the son, the friend – no one is what they have been, nor what they will be. You float. Over the structures of family, of friendship, of ideological identity, of difference – is superimposed a *tabula rasa* equality, freed of all nuance – *exiles*. Prisoners in freedom: that was what exile was. Dead Man Walking.[86]

An easy death: in the pharmacy, one bottle would do the trick. A rope, a tree. One act of carelessness: the train! Jumping out of a very high window – one second! *Murro* tells of death, the vicious circle. It tells how Death passed so close by me that I felt its cold sweat brush my skin.

I held warm hands in mine. The following day, they were cold. When would mine turn cold? The dead gave a lead! Incentives: why live? It is all over, isn't it over? Well then, better once and for all! The same argument used by those (OK) false *guerrilheiros* who denounced others to get things back to normal more quickly.

I thought of death. I visited suicide locations. I remembered dead loved ones. Expected deaths and premature deaths. Painful deaths and accidental deaths. Natural causes and bullet causes. The Mexican skull, beside that vertiginousness, is a caress.

I sought out friends, I wanted to hold tight to the duty that I knew to be mine. Trips for work distanced me from those I most loved and cast me even further adrift from myself. I clung on to those who also wanted to hold on. There were not many of them.

That was in Portugal in 1977, but I am still in Argentina in 1975, where the emptiness began.

Perón on stage: he should not have been

My third play was done while the Peronists were in power – proof of my insane derangement! *Revolução Na América Do Sul* (Revolution in South America) provoked indignation; the characters were corrupt politicians, all of them! Peronists and communists alike hated the play. It came off as surreptitiously as it had gone on. No one noticed . . . less risk.

The return of Perón, after his fat Spanish exile, was a hecatomb. In the weeks preceding his return, the tragedy was already foretold, Peronists were threatening Peronists; death, with no quarter given.

Followers of the *caudillo* were supposed to show their loyalty by going to the airport to welcome him, and they felt a justified panic; they wanted to fall ill– God bless sickness! They telephoned each other anxiously: 'Thank God I am throwing up, I think it is typhoid, may the Lord will it! What about you, are you bedridden?' 'Not yet . . . but I am hopeful, what with the weather changing, who knows, it's turning cold. . . . A good dose of pneumonia before Sunday would be my salvation.' I heard conversations like this – *peronistas* glorifying hepatitis.

Before the aeroplane had landed, 400 lay dead in the be-flowered parks of the airport. Peronists killing Peronists. The police, superfluous, were passive: their dirty work was being done. I had made mistakes in Brazil, I did not want to make them in other countries. I participated in demonstrations only when they were just against the Brazilian dictatorship: the furrow I had to plough! In Buenos Aires I grasped the meaning of the word roots . . . when I lost mine.

In Chile, I met Geraldo Vandré.[87] We thought about doing an *Opinião*, in Luna Park, the stadium in the centre of Buenos Aires, with four composers: him, from Brazil; Victor Jara,[88] from Chile; Cedrón, from Argentina; Daniel Viglietti, from Uruguay. A surefire hit, if it got to be staged; financial means to mount the show, nil! With Cedrón and his quartet, I did an italo-*portuñol*[89] show – I have always liked mixtures! – *Soy Loco Por Ti América* (I Am Mad About You, America), in a prestigious venue, despite its name: *La Cebolla*.[90] With Brazilian exiles, I did *Caldo de Cana* (Sugar Cane Juice).[91] Nothing could have been more appropriate: we were the mangled leftovers. . . .

Journey to Peru

There was no space for me, being neither Peronist nor communist. As an ex-political prisoner, the TV people gave me no work, nor did I ever get a call from the impresarios of the Buenos Aires boulevard. The directors of the state theatres, balancing on their own tightrope, were even less forthcoming. A political prisoner? You had done something. . . . It was a stigma.

I continued travelling, like the proverbial errant Dutchman on his wandering boat, with no port to shelter him. I lectured in US universities. I worked in Mexico, Colombia, Venezuela and Peru. I have never written so many letters. The man at the post office used to help me lick and stick stamps. Once, I wanted to send a book to a foreign editor, but the cost under galloping inflation meant that I had to put more stamps on the envelope than would fit on its surface. My postman friend did not hesitate: he tore the book in two, placed each half in a different envelope and covered both of them with stamps.

My family followed me around, when they could. If Fabián's schooling or Cecília's work got in the way, I would go alone. Exile divides, it does not add – it separates, distances. It cuts short dialogue. It isolates. The family suffers. An exile is many people dispersed: too many! The punishment you suffer exceeds the sentence.

In Peru I carried out the experiment which I recount in *O Teatro do Oprimido* (*The Theatre of the Oppressed*).[92] That is where Forum Theatre was born and where I systematised Image Theatre. The Theatre of the Oppressed became a book. I was directing a theatre workshop as part of a literacy programme. Forum was born when I could not understand what a spectator was saying to me when she wanted us to improvise her ideas, and I invited her to come up on stage – fantastic transgression – and show, herself, what she had in mind. I invited her to *enact* her thoughts, instead of just *speaking* them. She entered the scene, taking on the role of the character, dividing herself: she and the character.

I grasped that it was not just that woman whom I couldn't understand: I couldn't understand anyone, ever. The word pronounced is never the word heard. When she came into the scene, I could *see* what she was thinking. 'Doing is the best way of saying!' said José Marti, Cuban poet and hero of the war against Spain. Invading our space, she concretised her truth. Long gone was the time when we used to teach, know-alls that we were. When she broke the rules of the game I felt relief: I was not obliged always to know the right way. I did not have to feel guilty about it!

Workshop at Chacacayo, Peru, where the Theatre of the Oppressed was first systematised in 1973

Cecília, Fabian, Augusto and Julián, Buenos Aires, 1975

I experienced the pleasure of asking. Before, I thought that the Artist was master of the truth. I discovered that I was merely an artist, that's all! What a relief to discover that I was…merely myself! My theatre would be, from then on, the theatre of questions. Socrates, *Maiêutic*.[93] The people who would have to give the answers would be the *spect-actors*! Forum taught me the art of asking the right questions.

Images

Image theatre was born because my Peruvian students spoke forty-seven mother tongues. Spanish was a stepmother to them, as it was to me. To understand them, I asked them to make an image. One image of the real and one of their desire. Another image of how you can move from the real to the ideal. I asked them to do it . . . and, as they made images, the techniques were born, from the simplest, the image of word, to the complex introspective techniques.

In Peru, I wrote *Técnicas Latino-Americanas De Teatro Popular* (Latin American Techniques of Popular Theatre) and *Categorias Do Teatro Popular* (Categories of Popular Theatre). Theatre of the Oppressed did not yet have that name. Why the title? Booksellers argued that no one would buy a book called *Poéticas Políticas* (Political Poetics). Poetry or politics? I changed it to *Poética do Oprimido* (Poetics of the Oppressed), in homage to Paulo

Freire.[94] Another rejection: which shelf should it go on? Poetry? Anyone flicking through it would realise their mistake. Theatre? No one would open it, they would think it was poetry. When I pronounced *Teatro do Oprimido* for the first time, it sounded strange. Still today, for some, it sounds like *Deprimido* (Depressed), although it is about uprising, about what you consider worth struggling for, about being happy. Imagine if I had called it *Theatre of Happiness*, *Theatre of Revolution*, *Theatre of the Invented Future*! — pretentious. It stayed as it is, and now I like it: *Theatre of the Oppressed*!

In September 1973, Allende was shot dead, *La Moneda*[95] burned down, and Chilean democracy buried. What was to happen in Argentina over years happened in Chile in a few days. Thousands were imprisoned in the national stadium, hundreds were killed. Neruda died of sadness.

Passport and terror

There was a recrudescence of terror after Perón's death. All forms of torment were then practised. The Prata River swallowed up living men tied to rocks, dropped from military aeroplanes. To this day, *Las Madres de la Plaza de Mayo* (The Mothers of the Plaza de Mayo), *Las Locas* (The Madwomen), continue with their blessed madness, parading every Thursday at noon, with white handkerchiefs covering their heads, and photos of their sons at their breasts. Without memory, it is impossible to be.

I wanted to leave, the destination did not matter. Not being able to work is terrifying. To have every day free — is tragic! I shall never retire, ever. If one day I die — and I hope not to! — I want to be like Molière, and die on the stage! But I will be nice to the audience and wait till the end of the show.

Cecília was writing a children's programme for TV; Fabián was studying — his departure from the school in São Paulo had been traumatic, it would be good to prepare the next exile gently. Carlos Porto, a respected Portuguese critic, invited me to work in Lisbon, following the *Revolution of Carnations*.[96] The Portuguese government promised me a contract. My passport had expired. I went to the Brazilian Consulate in Buenos Aires. The Consul said that the authorisation had not arrived. Have patience. But in a low voice, he told the truth — the passport would not be granted.

Money was scarce, inflation doubling at every turn. In the morning, I wanted to buy a suitcase (with the idea of departing) and I noted the price. I went to buy it in the afternoon: it was more expensive. I returned the following morning, with the right money for the previous afternoon's price; it was already not enough. I gave up.

I competed for a bursary from the Guggenheim Foundation in the USA. Dore Ashton explained to the rest of the judging panel who I was. I was selected. This allowed me to write.

I wrote nine books in three years, while waiting for my passport, including *Crônicas De Nuestra América* (Chronicles of Our America) and *A Deliciosa e Sangrenta Aventura Latina de Jane Spitfire, Espiã e Mulher Sensual* (The Delicious and Bloody Latin Adventure of Jane Spitfire, Spy and Sensual Woman), a fiction. In the first I recounted actual facts, transformed into chronicles; in the second I used a James Bond style, with sex, mystery and blood, to tell the story of the *coup* in gestation.

In *Tio Patinhas* I told of the Fifth Act, before it had been decreed. In *Jane Spitfire*, I told, premonitorily, of the Argentinian *coup*.

As well as producing nine books, we had a child, Cecília and I – Julián Boal, writer.

Idibal Piveta

The repression increased, and became explicit. Two Uruguayan ex-Senators were gunned down in the entrance hall of a central hotel in Buenos Aires: cleaners mopped up the blood, and life went on, in silence.

As well as killing, the military wanted to frighten people: they were in love with terror. They drove around the streets in unlicensed blue cars, machine-guns in view; they would change to a lower gear and trail a pedestrian – by way of provocation. If he felt guilty, he would run: then the soldiers, airmen, sailors, would run after the victim to investigate – which meant torture. In the street, I used to sense blue cars gliding about. If you want a mild word to describe the sensation, I will give you one: terrifying! Death stalked the streets in blue cars which mounted pavements and crashed red lights. When the doorbell rang, I used to tremble until I saw a friendly face.

When Julián was born we moved to a larger flat: with the money from plays and books abroad, the bursary, and with Cecília's savings – her children's programme was a big hit – we bought an old flat. There we received exiled Brazilians, on Saturday nights, to remind ourselves of *feijoadas* and charred meats which the poet Gullar could do to perfection, or fish from Amazonia, the speciality of Thiago de Mello – another poet.

Our main subject was the terror. One Brazilian pianist on tour went downstairs to buy cigarettes at the corner by the hotel and did not come back. Deaths happened, with or without explanation. Going downstairs with Fabián as a little boy, on our way to the cinema, a man passed us, running; two others came after him, shooting: we threw ourselves to the ground. Episodes like this were not uncommon.

Idibal Piveta, a dear friend, pupil, brother, telephoned me saying that he would take the matter to court and oblige the Minister of Foreign Affairs to give me a passport. It was risky, but there was a chance. I agreed. For months I got letters from Idibal relating the legal proceedings. Argentinean newspapers published the news in a distorted way, as if I were the one being proceeded against, and not the Ministry. They increased the risk.

But at last my passport was granted. *Viva* Idibal Piveta! After he got mine, Idibal managed to do the same for more than three Brazilians stuck in Argentina in exile, by jurisprudential means.

The Consul explained that he was only obeying orders when he refused to grant passports. I had already heard that argument from a torturer: it was his duty.

I booked a seat on the first plane and went to Lisbon. Little did I know. . . .

I do not want to close my eyes. I want to live, I don't want to die. The past is not extinguished, if forgotten: it hides, like ulcers. That is why I write, that is why I speak – I want to wrench it out of me! To bring it to the light of day.

The military dictatorships went away: economic dictatorships took their place.[97] The tenebrous Latin American night, tired of darkness, turned to dawn. But before daybreak, there come the shadows of a new night.

Globalisation has already been invented, to create unemployment, and destroy the minimal rudiments of social security – always the first victims of economic repression! Globalisation imposes the will of the market: mediocrity! Witches and demons tend their cauldrons. Day has not yet broken . . . and already it is night! Theatre is light, it is the dawn. In times like ours, we need to reaffirm our identity: we must not let ourselves be globalised, robotised. Let us be who we are. I know that my nose is large, my ears are different sizes: but I know that that person is me! I will not surrender!

Theatre is desire, bodily struggle, personal defence. Theatre, if it tells the truth, proffers a quest for oneself, oneself in others and others in oneself. It proffers the humanisation of humankind. This cannot be done without struggle.

Today, theatre is a martial art!

exile, banishment, palm trees, birdsong

Exile and Theatre of the Oppressed

Looking at my life up to now, I can see: there has been coherence! I sought a Brazilian style in the laboratories and playwriting seminars I led: I wanted us to speak in our own voice, with our own face. I did not like theatre that was imported, gift-wrapped for us – I believed in *pátria* (fatherland). In the Classics I found metaphor. Not in order to vulgarise universal culture, but as an attempt to find, in distant works, our face of today. In the musicals, I sought relations between a supposed heroic past and the pusillanimous present. My theatre has always been moral!

I dreamed of the spectator-protagonist. In the Newspaper Theatre we abstained from giving the public the finished product and offered instead the means of production – everyone needed to discover the theatre they carried within. In Peru, I saw vibrant life invading the immobilised stage.

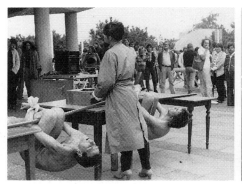

Demonstration against the methods of torture used by the Brazilian dictatorship in front of an art exhibition, Berlin, 1980

Boal giving a theatrical demonstration at Ariane Mnouchkine's Théâtre du Soleil at the Cartoucherie de Vincennes, 1980

It was the transgression any form of liberation requires. With Forum, the Theatre of the Oppressed (TO) acquired structure.

The TO allowed me to return to writing about myself, as witness. I used to say that everyone can do theatre. As I am part of that 'everyone' I can also do theatre, not only teach it. I wrote *Murro*, and a novel, *Suicida com medo da morte* (Suicide with fear of death). In Europe, *The Rainbow of Desire* — the police patrolled the streets and hid in our heads.[1]

When later I returned to Brazil, I saw it was necessary to articulate *O Teatro Legislativo* (The Legislative Theatre). I wanted to see our desire transformed into law.

The TO did political events, it was politics; it withdrew into the intimacy of internalised oppressions, it was psychotherapy; in schools, it was pedagogy; in the cities, it legislated. The TO superimposed itself onto other social activities, invaded other fields and allowed itself to be invaded. Where was the theatre?

It was in the exercise of liberty. This is the major coherence informing my work: I have exercised and defended the freedom we must have to be ourselves, and to allow others to be themselves. All my life I have been in search of peace — never passivity!

★　　★　　★

*'On a toujours cents ans!' A play about the trade
unions' centennial in Paris, 1982*

Teaching at the Bubble Theatre, London, 1992

Casa Portuguesa, com certeza[2]

In the year 1976, I left Argentina, and with a good part of the Arsenal[3] in my suitcase, I went to Portugal full of hope. I was not aware that the Portuguese revolution was called the revolution of carnations. Carnations are flowers; flowers wither. When we arrived, the revolutionary carnations were dessicated, their perfumes sad.

Faded, they exhaled memories. Having invited me, the government delayed signing the employment contract. They had promised me I would train local actors. Céu Guerra and Helder Costa, directors of one of the best Portuguese groups, *A Barraca* (The Hut), proposed I became its artistic director. The Gulbenkian Foundation agreed to pay my salary and we started rehearsing *Tiradentes*: on Portuguese colonialism. In Brazil, actors imitated Lisbonites; in Lisbon, it was the other way around.

The government signed the promised contract, under pressure from the theatre people, but reduced it to six months. By the end of two months, artists were up in arms against measures taken by the Ministry of Culture. I had no hesitation in standing alongside the artists in public demonstrations. The Ministry rescinded my contract. I lost a third of my salary, the rent.

On a panel in Seoul, Korea, 1995

Boal and Paulo Freire.
Doctors Honoris Causa, Nebraska University, 1997

I rehearsed *Zé do Telhado* (Zé of the rooftop), by Helder, music by Zeca Afonso, and *A Feira Portuguesa de Opinião* (The Portuguese Fair of Opinion) by dozens of artists, in the Museum of Modern Art. I gave classes at the National Conservatory. Another government department, the Ministry of Education, invited teachers, including Carlos Porto and myself, to draw up a plan for the reformulation of the Conservatory. In six months we arrived at what seemed to us to be the perfect programme. The Minister received us with great ceremony and fine biscuits. He listened to our plans enthusiastically, he almost decorated us with heavy patriotic medals. At the door, bidding us farewell, he remembered an important detail: in the morning, he had signed a decree relieving us of our duties. We were out on the street, all of us. If we wanted to come back, we would have to submit ourselves to an examination by a panel made up of the most reactionary teachers in the country. I lost the second third of my salary.

The carnations met the tragic destiny of all flowers: the dustbin.

In the two years I spent in Portugal, I did nothing new in relation to the Theatre of the Oppressed. Only one Forum show, in Porto, in the street where a secret service torturer had been captured and, after popular discussion, set free; at liberty, he killed a revolutionary the next day. A group mounted a staging of the capture and the Forum took place, in the same street as the actual event. The fact of its being done years later, in the place where it happened, intensified the debate; a diachrony which, rather than having the effect of melancholy, elevated the event. The past revisited. Reflection.

I visited Justes, land of my forefathers. I met Aunt Barbara, a hunched 90-year-old, clad in heavy mourning. She served me wine, bread and ham. The journey was worth it: I visited the window from which my mother watched my father. Blessed window! I walked in the street in which they had held hands for the first time. I imagined the smile, the goose-bumps.

Lisbon, for two years, was a long wait. Lunching at my house in the company of Paulo Freire, his first wife Elsa, some of his assistants and Darcy Ribeiro, my mother (recently arrived from Brazil), said she brought a letter from Chico Buarque. I had written to Chico two or three times, and received no reply. I asked to read it, and she gave me a cassette: *Meu caro amigo* (My dear friend), in his voice and Francis Hime on the piano. We listened in silence to the recollections they sent us.

Collective catharsis. Chico sang: do not come back, it is not time yet. I

At the Royal Shakespeare Company, 1998

will not tell you the tremendous emotion, for all of us, to hear his sung advice. You will have to guess the importance, for the exiled and the banished, of the solidarity of those who stayed in the country. A letter from a friend, even scrawled in pencil, was consolation and stimulus. Those who have never been exiled have no idea how much good it did us when people wrote, even telling of the everyday and the banal: it was enough. In pencil. . . . Imagine a sung letter. . . .

I never threw a letter away. If new ones did not arrive, I used to reread the ones I had.

I love actors!

In Portugal, I penned sorrows. To mitigate my Lusitanian limbo, I worked in other countries creating Theatre of the Oppressed groups. Jack Lang invited me to work in Nancy. It was curious: my pupils, coming from a variety of professions, all fell in love with the idea that 'we are theatre, even if we do not do theatre'. My two assistants – a couple of Venezuelan students – abominated everything that was not Beckett, Artaud, Ionesco. Though I also liked them, I wanted to invent another theatre, urgently. My assistants only understood theatre that had been awarded the academic seal of approval. Anything outside this sacramental status seemed like amateurism. This made me furious. It was to them – against them – that I dedicated the sentence that caused me some problems: *Everyone can do theatre: even actors!*

It was an insolent sentence, written in relative anger, and yet a sincere sentence. Sadly, it has been misinterpreted by some who read contempt into it, when it has the opposite meaning: I am a director who loves his actors. For me, the actor is the centre of the theatrical universe. The sentence was designed to make clear that all of us have the vocation for theatre. In real life we use the languages of theatre – body, space, voice, ideas, passions! Like Monsieur Jourdain[4] who spoke in prose without realising it: we speak theatre! Theatre is the human language *par excellence*. I wrote that in *Jogos para atores e não atores (Games for Actors and Non-Actors)*. Even the title seemed a spiteful provocation to some people, suggesting that games could be used by anyone, that specialisation was unnecessary. Actors complained.

I tried to mend the damage by amending the sentence and wrote: *Everyone can do theatre: even good actors!* God help us. The purport of my words was honest, clear and simple. Bad actors always play but one character — themselves. They are excluded from true theatre by their incapacity for the adventure of creation, for that is the actor's art. Even marvellous 'entertainers', if they are always the same as themselves, are not actors in the technical sense of the word.

Of all professions, the actor's is the most beautiful: while each is who he or she is — though schizophrenics may divide themselves into two or more obsessive characters, they are always the same ones! — the actor can be Einstein, Chaplin or Gandhi today and, tomorrow, a refuse-collector, a grave-digger, an illiterate pariah. What I wanted to say — and said! — is that the human being is capable of diving into the depths of self and emerging with undreamed-of characters, hidden potentialities submerged in the recesses of the person.[5] Being an actor means immersing oneself in this plunge into self, awakening the characters bubbling away in the pressure cooker[6] of our unconscious. It is wonderful to be an actor. We are all capable of it — except those who, in their profession as actor, enact only their own character.

Loreta and Carlos Valadares, exiled in Sweden, convinced Inger Ziefeld, Claes Von Rettig and Maragareta Sodeberg to invite me, though they did not know me, to lecture at the Institute of Dramatic Art in Stockholm and to direct workshops at the Skeppsholm Festivals. Henry Thorau convinced German directors about the importance of the work; Anne Martinoff took me to trade unions of Belgium, and from friend to friend, town to town with her. I went through Sweden, Norway, Denmark, Italy, and ended up in Bollene, the South of France, in a workshop for teachers of the Freinet Movement,[7] showing pedagogical techniques from the TO. I directed a workshop for professional actors in Paris, at the Aquarium of the Cartoucherie at Vincennes.

Invitations which would have a decisive effect on my life arrived: from Émile Copfermann to publish *Théâtre de l'Opprimé* with Editions Maspero; from Bernard Dort, to occupy a chair at the Sorbonne-Nouvelle in Paris for a year. In September 1978 we went to live in Paris. From Portugal, I took *saudades* of everything that did not happen.

Paris

The Sorbonne was important. The material for my Chair was me myself: I lectured on the Theatre of the Oppressed. The comfortable salary allowed me to live well and work abroad.

Copfermann suggested I create a centre. If I alone was responsible for communicating the TO to the outside world, it would spread slowly. I agreed. He and his wife, Jacqueline, put together a group of twenty teachers, actors, psychologists and social workers. For months, I taught games and techniques from the Arsenal. In January 1979, 300 people signed up, way beyond all expectation. We did four workshops of forty trainees each, and formed four teams of five aspiring Jokers – each team led one workshop through the week. On Saturdays and Sundays, the groups met for a marathon of Forum Theatre.

The following month we repeated the process, with another 140 apprentices, and in March we founded the *Centre d'Étude et Diffusion des Techniques Actives d'Expression* (CÉDITADE), an unnecessarily complicated name – those French. . . .

We took the decision that I would work abroad, leaving the ground clear in France for the members of CÉDITADE. An error: I should have stayed centred, I should have forgone the vocation of flying Dutchman; I should have created a school in Paris, permanently established. That is what I think now.

In France in 1981, a fleeting visitation of hope: the socialists won. We were sure we would be helped in our work, it being pedagogical, therapeutic, social and artistic: France esteemed the arts, sciences and humanities. The socialist government promised fair treatment for groups such as ours. We were all the happier when I was awarded an honorific title: *Officier des Arts des Lettres*! Émile explained: 'Bad sign: when you get given honorific recognition, it means the money is going to be sparse.'

He was right. We never got enough from the Ministry of Culture to pay the rent for the spaces we were using. The grant structure is so stratified that cultural groups end up getting just enough for them to go on always doing the same thing. Budgets hardly change, cultural projects likewise, with the exception of the pharaonic monuments: *Opera de la Bastille*, *Grande Louvre*, *Très Grande Bibliothèque*, *l'Énorme something-or-other*. . . . Pretty and large.

In France, apart from its cultural importance, art has enormous economic potential; tourists are attracted by the traditional museums, operas, concerts, ballets and theatres. They expect to see *Mona Lisa* and *Venus de Milo*, Rameau and Lully,[8] *Gisèle* and *The Nutcracker* – they do not want surprises. Masses of tourists, apart from consuming culture, eat in restaurants, sleep in hotels and take taxis to make purchases in *Galéries Lafayette* . . . they spend.

The budget for culture, in France, is about 1 per cent of government spending – an enormous sum. The Paris Opera alone manages a larger sum than the entire budget of Burkina-Faso, an African country with nine million inhabitants. Culture in France is big business. In Brazil, subsidy aplenty is poured into Carnival. The reason is the same: tourism. Here, the 'classic culture' does not attract Japanese or Germans. Charter flights do not arrive jam-packed for the Imperial Museum. They come for the samba, they come to go down the *avenida* with Bahian beauties spinning around them! It's another kind of culture.

Somewhere in the middle are the popular art groups doing work which is necessary and useful, but not spectacular: and not for the shop window. In the 1960s there were State Commissions of theatre, cinema, circus, opera, visual arts, made up of artists, journalists and people put forward by the government. Subsidies were awarded publicly – projects were discussed and scrutinised. Today it is private economic power that guides the decision-making process. Artists have become dependent on their patrons and sponsors – these people hold the power. Culture has again become privatised, as in the times of kings and feudal lords: companies can spend up to 3 or 5 per cent of what they should pay in tax on the arts. It stands to reason that the owner of a supermarket is not going to feel the slightest temptation to finance a play about starving people, nor is a clothes company likely to produce a show played in rags. Each firm will look for artists with whom it would like to see its products associated; they want to sell soap associated with the body of Such and Such an actress so that, whoever desires that body will wash themselves with their soap. Artists run the risk of identifying themselves with the products: their masters' voices instead of being masters of their own voices.

In a meeting with the Minister of Culture (1997), I heard a well-known supermarket owner expressing his gratitude: 'Now we can choose our artists.' How awful! This is the privatisation of culture: the same sensibility that chooses the groceries, decides the art. I have nothing against any particular *taste*; I love *feijoada*, but there are different tastes: *Bacalhau a Brás*[9] and modern dance have nothing in common, like a cigarette and a naked woman!

Barracks in the head

In Europe, I started hearing about species of oppression not discussed in Latin America: loneliness, isolation, emptiness, lack of communication – very different from strikes, shortage of water, hunger and violence, but . . . many people were committing suicide because they could not cope with these things. There were more suicides in Scandinavia, where matters of basic subsistence were resolved, than in the southern hemisphere, where dictatorships murdered people, but where fewer people pointed weapons at their own heads. I felt obliged to invent new techniques that could help the victims of these forms of psychological torture to theatricalise their oppressions, in order to understand them and fight them.

In Paris in 1982, with the help of Cecília, now a psychoanalyst,[10] I began an *atelier*, *Le flic dans la tête* (The cop in the head): if the police were not right there in front of the victim, where were they? In Latin America, oppression was the police. And in Europe? The new oppressed carried their own police in their heads. They needed to be dislodged.

The introspective techniques I describe in *The Rainbow of Desire*[11] take an individual account as their starting point and seek to pluralise[12] – we want to discover the police and their headquarters or barracks. If this thing is in one person's head, it could be in others': where had it come from? Which crack had it crept in through? How could it be expelled? How could its path of entry be closed off? The *atelier* lasted for two years.

★   ★   ★

Saudades

The story of my return to Brazil, in 1986, can be found in its entirety in *Legislative Theatre*. In short, I joined the Workers' Party, was elected City Councillor, in four years we formed nineteen groups doing theatre as politics, as opposed to the old political theatre, we presented thirty-six bills, and promulgated thirteen laws.

Thirteen times, in Rio de Janeiro, the desire of the population became law. Perhaps that has been the Theatre of the Oppressed's main conquest: transforming desire into law.

Law is always someone's Desire.[13]

When will it be ours? What is the object of our desire?

Who are we?

the impossible return and the strangeness of the familiar

I RETURNED TO THE HILL
Contrary to all expectation, I saw no dogs. . . .

Whenever I arrived in a new country, new language, metabolism, everything new, I used to think: one day, I will go back to my mug of coffee, mine, all mine.

After the amnesty, in 1979, in transit – alone, with my family in Paris or with my French company – I used to visit Rio, and found it strange; I had no time to look at what I saw. Everything was different: voices, timbres, thoughts.

In 1986 I returned there to live, and realised the impossibility. No one returns from exile, ever.

My country was no more, neither were the people the same people, nor I, Augusto. Even the sea was not the sea. Buildings casting the beach into shade, making night before the sun set. Memories of light, now dark sand. A sarcophagus of a cathedral, the ugliest in the world! Even in this we are at the top of the league: the ugliest cathedral league!

Mesbla's[1] clock

I thought: Mesbla's clock. Salvation! The clock would be just the same. As a young man, I used to pass it on my way to chemistry. An image burnt into my memory. Unless they had stolen or destroyed it – or, who knows? – perhaps the military had imprisoned it in a deep dungeon because its hands refused to go backwards! Reactionaries hate clocks: they always go forwards! Into the arms of the clock I could return, coming home. It guarded my secrets.

Armed with fear, I went to see it, eyes glued to my feet tracing curves on the patterns of the pavement. I covered the ground with the emotion I used to have when confronted with a woman I loved. I raised my eyes, in slow motion. My heart jumped: the clock, suspicious, looked at me coldly – Sisyphus without a stone. The clock eyed me uneasily like a factory worker when someone sees him working. I smiled familiarly back, recognising the friendly hands of the clock – how many times they had quickened my step! The clock, insensitive, did not remember me. Shock: was that my Mesbla clock, my very own? I stared at it: passers-by examined me, concerned about my mental health: 'Are you ill or are you always like that?' ventured one doubtfully.

I replied that that was how I was, God did what he could, he must have just had an off-day with me. 'Listen: is that the original Mesbla clock? Has nothing changed about it?' It was the measurer of my anxiety, of plodding love, of hasty hate. Has it really been there all these years, and not taken sides, and just stayed on the wall? It is the clock of my flight, of my first *'I love you, me too!'* A few people gathered round, curiosity aroused. I explained: the clock, an old friend, was looking at me with strange hours and minutes, unwarranted aggressive sideways glances.

With sadness, I saw precious buildings from my childhood. *Candelaria* (the city centre church) barred its heavy doors like someone closing weary eyes from a heavy weary sleep. *Maracana* (the Stadium), its stray cats abandoned to neo-liberal survival. *Pão de Açucar* (Sugarloaf Mountain) invisible behind dozens of tourist brochure loaves: tropical tours, bananas, pineapples, brown-skinned thighs. I could not see Christ on the *Corcovado*:[2] he was covered by advertising hoardings screaming imperatives such as: 'Brazil, Love it or leave it!' You couldn't see him; they had draped gigantic orders on his wide shoulders: 'Drink Diet Coke', 'Eat Fast Food', 'Die of Cancer and Cholesterol!' 'Drop Dead! Now!' I looked for Rio in Rio and could not find it: I was in Rio. The only place where Rio de Janeiro no longer existed.

Carmen Miranda

On return from the USA, Carmen Miranda sang '*Voltei pro morro*' (I returned to the hill); she came to find her dog, her slippers – so said the song. What dog, Carmen, what slippers? How can you return to a place you have never been to? That which exists is not that which existed! Carmen's hill was virtual reality. She saw Rio, a hill, a dog. Pure imagination. A clock: on to it, I projected chemical hopes, childhood crushes. Amazing that the clock could mark the time without knowing if it was very early or too late, if the wait would be long or soon over. It delivered hopes and fears . . . without having them.

Carmen, we will never return, you and I, the both of us, never again will we re-encounter dogs straying *sans* lead, *sans* us, the legitimate owners of lost illusions and abandoned dogs: our most intimate hills never existed, nor our beloved, much sought-after dogs. We invented dog and slipper with our desires. You went back to Hollywood unaware that Rio never even saw you: what you were seeking exists only within you. My Rio, within me.[3]

I am convinced: we can only return to places where we have never been – only paradoxes are true. There, where we have never been, in that country, city, corner, there we can nurse our imaginary images. How many times, on arriving in a place in which we have never before set foot, do we say: 'I remember . . . I have been here before . . .'?

I am convinced: we only remember what has not happened.

★　　★　　★

MURRO EN PONTA DE FACA
A play Boal wrote during and about his exile, performed in São Paulo, 1978

I tried

My first show, after exile, was *O Corsário do Rei* (The King's Corsair). A simple play, set in a bar where tables would be boats; table-cloths, sails; drunks, pirates. Simple like *Zumbi*, poor like Arena.

Our courageous producers spared no effort – more's the pity! A circus dwarf became a giant; a ragged corsair became an invincible Armada; Brancaleone, the Seventh Army. The cast swelled like elephantiasis: thirty-seven actors, fifteen marvellous master-musicians conducted from the pit, dozens of strapping stage-hands in the understage manipulating warships, cannons dispatching balls of fire, blue smoke. Beautiful.

But not the play. If it had been Christ's Last Supper, this millionaire's production would have had 120 apostles in place of the synthetic dozen; there would have been waiters carrying pigs, poultry, fish and olives to satiate the hunger of convivial multitudes; there would have been evangel-ical women greedily filling up on bread and wine and – oh yes – there would have been dozens of Judases! A single solitary Judas would be incapable of such treachery – a faithful portrait of Brazil!

A small play is supposed to *be* small! My return, however, had to be grandiose. When I went back after the Amnesty, in 1979, the customs inspector was taken aback, wanting to know 'Who on earth are you, that you get so many famous people turning out at the airport for you?' The

At the end of a workshop, shortly after Boal's first return to Brazil, December 1979

crowd included Chico Buarque, Paulo José, Dina Sfat, Rui Guerra, Beth Mendes, Fernando Peixoto, Tessy Calado, Ian Michalski, as well as my family and other friends who were at the door of the aeroplane awaiting my embrace.

I wanted to explain that I was just me, leave it at that. But no one can be only who they are, they have to be others. For me, my friends were my friends. They came to greet me: so the customs man wanted to know what kind of celebrity I was – I *had* to be one. And my return on the stage was doomed to be the return of a *Celebrity*! The play, which was a little fishing smack, the merest raft, became *Titanic*. It had to sink, even without icebergs! And many icebergs were launched at that show.

Seduced by the ease of it – and by the moral imperative in trade union terms: the employment of the maximum possible number of actors was a matter of urgency, these were times of crisis! – I felt like Ingrid Bergmann in Hollywood. 'If I asked for a pink elephant, alive and jumping through hoops, the next day they would give me dozens of coloured elephants to choose from,' she said.

The elephant I was given was white.

When I look back, I remember a beautiful show, beautiful music and words, beautiful sets and performances, pure beauty. The only thing it lacked was blood coursing through its veins and a beating heart. Criticism rained down, which was normal enough. Not so normal was that they said that, after so much time in exile, I was not in tune with *carioca* reality – a reality which at the time encompassed French boulevard plays presented alongside alcoholic North American comedies written by authors who had never been in tune with anything at all and did not even know if Brazil was in Buenos Aires or vice versa. I was a foreigner in my own home. No: simply, I was me! I have no reason to be the same! The same as who? Is anyone the same? We are not even the same as ourselves.

Fernanda

In 1985, I directed Fernanda Montenegro in *Fedra* (Phédre). It was the first time that this author had been produced professionally in Rio. In the light of the success, Carlos Kroeber joked: 'The *carioca* adores Racine!'

For a year and a half we toured around Brazil. I have never seen anyone so fond of rehearsing as Fernanda. If, at midnight, exhausted after a rehearsal, I suggested running the whole play, her voice would ring out, the first to speak: '*Vamos!*'

Peter Brook and his daughter Irina participate in a game led by Boal in Rio de Janeiro, 1980

MURRO EN PONTA DE FACA
At the Schauspielhaus, *Graz, Austria, 1980*

Fernanda has enormous talent, that much is obvious; but as important as her immense talent is her immense desire to work. For a director, it is wonderful: an artist creating, wanting more! Fernanda is one of those actresses who make us understand theatre, or, if you will pardon the platitude, make us love it! It is lovely to see Fernanda onstage: we discover what a marvel the human being is. Hope is reborn: perhaps the human being is viable.

Our show was as savage as if the play had been written by a distant great grandfather from the time of Greek tragedy, ten centuries before Christ, thirty before ours, and not by the rigorous alexandrine Racine, attender at the Court of Louis the Sun King. This roughness was possible because the script, translated in blank verse, went with the trunk of a tree simulating a wild beast – the single scenic element, apart from the floor of cowhide, ringed by a border of bamboo poles.

I would say to the actors: 'Outside here, we spend our whole life doing theatre, all the time; once you cross the bamboo line, on stage, you cannot do theatre: here it is life!' I said what I think: that on stage, one lives. Society grumbles: 'No, it is not so, no, you can't, don't do it, you don't want it, don't say it!'

Theatre, by contrast, is the art which says Yes!

PHAEDRA

By Racine, directed by Boal with Fernanda Montenegro, 1980

New endeavours

I did *La Malasangre* by Griselda Gamboro which I also directed in Nuremberg. There it was a geometric show, straight lines, Germanic; in Rio a variable random geometry! Both here and there, the play dealt with dictatorial mechanisms as seen from the dining-room.

Actors needed to earn their livings in TV and cinema – theatre pays little. We would often be waiting to rehearse and have to give up because a recording was delayed, or because people had a shoot far away.

I spent eleven years without directing straight plays, apart from the short pieces I did for my Centre of the Theatre of the Oppressed (CTO).

The legislative experience

I am not going to tell this story here: it is all in my book, *Legislative Theatre*. Suffice it to say that, on my return from Paris, I wanted to found the Factory of Popular Theatre. I organised a programme in the state schools. Cecilia and Rosa Luíza Marques, director of the *Teatreros Ambulantes de Puerto Rico*,[4] helped me direct thirty-five cultural animators.

The Governor elected in Darcy's place did not want to know about the project. We almost 'suicided' the CTO. We sought out the PT[5] and offered to help in the 1992 elections – it would be the final act of the CTO. They agreed, on condition that I put myself forward as a candidate. Sure that I would not win, I accepted.

I won. For the next four years, I lived exiled from professional theatre and knew the bloody arena of the Chamber of Deputies; I learned what I already knew – that that is the place where you go to fight on behalf of personal or corporate appetites, not on the people's behalf. There you even find bankers of *Bicho*[6] and members of death squads, and drug barons. In the midst of which there are good people, as anywhere, even saints. As anywhere.

In four years we created dozens of groups – landless peasant farmers, homeless children, hopeless elders, black students, *favela*-dwellers, unionised factory workers, battered women – and we did TO with them. Their ideas were taken to the Municipal Chamber, where my lawyers

Boal receives the title of Benemeritus Citizen of Rio de Janeiro at the local Legislative Chamber of Deputies, 1991

(working for my mandate and for the Commission of Human Rights, of which I was President!) 'metabolised' suggestions, transforming them into bills of law: more than thirty of them!

Thirteen of these bills were promulgated to become municipal law.

Legislative Theatre[7] was the conclusion of the search, born out of perplexity. In Forum Theatre we wanted the population to express its desire. That was not enough. So . . . we wanted them to transform that desire into law. Thirteen times, this was possible.

I did analogous experiments in Munich (*Rathaus*), The City Council, Paris (with an anti-racist group, MRAP), London and Bradford (in England).

In London we did a Solemn Symbolic Session. Organised by Michael Morris,[8] it was a condensed session of *Legislative Theatre*. Three subject groups – directed by Adrian Jackson (Transport), Paul Heritage (Homelessness) and Ali Campbell (Education) – presented short pieces in the Debating Chamber of the Greater London Council, which was closed down during Margaret Thatcher's reign. I presided over the session, seated in the imposing Chairman's Chair, so heavy as to be immovable, surrounded by well-known public figures and writers – Lisa Jardine, Tariq Ali and Paul Hallam – and a lawyer (Mark Stephens). Julián Boal and a young woman linked the table to the public, who were installed in the erstwhile seats of the legislators. At my side, Orlando Seale, an actor from the Royal

Boal at his office at the Chamber, Rio de Janeiro, 1995

Shakespeare Company, and Tim Wheeler, director of Mind the Gap, an arts and disability organisation, dressed as my guardian angel.[9] A band improvised the music.

The Solemn Session consisted, first, of the invocation of divine protection (I sought protection, as you can imagine, from the two excellent friendly gods, Apollo and Dionysus); this was followed by the presentation of each of the three scenes, with spectators intervening in search of legal solutions. At the end of each forum, spectators drafted the laws in their own manner, writers gave them a literary form, lawyers added the legal trappings; at the end of the evening I put these to the vote.

It was theatre, fiction. Even so, it showed possible paths: by means of theatre, law can be made. Theatre as politics, not just political theatre.

Other experiments started happening around the world. In Bradford, a Solemn Session in the Chamber of the local council, promoted by Tim Wheeler, concentrated on a single play, performed by people with Downs Syndrome, in the presence of the Mayor of Bradford and elected legislators, in April 1999. In Rio, the Congress of Theatre and Development, in June, organised by Paul Heritage, did their session on local issues. In October, in Cardinal König House, Vienna, at a TO Festival organised by Lisa Kolb and Theatergruppe Wiegl, the first Solemn Session took place in the presence of a Minister of State (the Science Minister) and four state deputies — all of whom participated in the final panel discussion.

These Solemn Sessions serve only — and this is already a lot — to show

*Santo André just before the school
of samba in the participatory budget,
1998.*

what is possible. Someone makes the law: why not us? Solemn Sessions are symbolic . . . but without symbols, what would civilisation be?

The TO, without abandoning where it has been, seeks new paths: Forum Theatre has already been done on Canadian television, via satellite (Headlines Theatre, David Diamond); in English and Brazilian prisons (TIPP Centre, Paul Heritage); in hostels, schools, and on the streets with homeless people in London (Cardboard Citizens, Adrian Jackson). Other people have tried similar experiments throughout the world. For example, the fusion of TO and popular traditional dances done by Jana Sanskriti (Sanjoy Ganguly) in Calcutta, India.

Executive theatre

Since 1997, in Santo André, popular assemblies, which decide on the city's budget, have invariably begun with the presentation of Forum plays mounted by groups organised by the CTO, and relating to that budget. An experiment which promises to blossom. Today, the municipal government of Santo André already has its Theatre of the Oppressed Group, entirely institutionalised – effectively, we are talking about executive theatre. In Rio, the CTO collaborates with the Forum of Municipal Budget (a non-governmental organisation) and is already taking its first and middle steps. In Porto Alegre . . . Minas Gerais . . . Bahia . . .

O TRABALHADOR
(The Worker), 1995, at Favela Julio Otoni

Crossroads

When I started out in the theatre I was speaking about myself, my neighbourhood. I knew the truth: I doled out advice. But I discovered that you could not liberate anyone by occupying their space, taking their decisions. I systematised TO in such a way that the oppressed might make their own theatre – not I talking *on behalf* of the oppressed nor I talking *about* them. Paternalism is on its way out. However, we artists are necessary. Without paternalism but, in some way, as parents. Our relationship with the oppressed artist is not paternalistic, but continues to be paternal.

Julián Boal, in his book *The Images of a Popular Theatre*, recognises the importance of the Theatre of the Oppressed; still, he asks: what form will the relationship between the artist-intellectual and the people-artist take now? How will it be possible to develop that relationship democratically, when one knows that a method, any method, is elaborated according to a living and earthbound ideology, and not in the ideologically aseptic purity of a laboratory? How will it be possible to offer that method to the oppressed without it arriving already impregnated with the ideology which inspired it?

I agree with Julián, but I would add: TO is not evangelising like the old political theatre, it brings no pat answers: it poses questions. Like Socrates, who did not put ideas into his interlocutors' heads but rather made them give birth to the ideas they already had. That is what the philosopher said.

Julián contests this: by the very act of choosing the questions, Socrates restricted the field of possible answers. He may not have put ideas into anyone's head but he stimulated the emergence of ideas which responded to his own questions. There was inducement, though not coercion. Nevertheless, in the case of TO – I believe – the structuring of that method is already the result of an ideological dialogue. I did not invent the Theatre of the Oppressed by myself, in my house, nor did I receive it as tablets of stone from God: it was in the interaction with popular audiences that the TO was born, little by little. It did not come out of me ready and finished: it created itself by a process of exchange.

The method was structured through decades of work just as, in a two-hour Forum Theatre session, the Joker structures the interventions of the 'spect-actors' without manipulating them. Of course, between the actors and the audience, there is the Joker and his/her ideology, but the live audience is there to counterpoint and disagree![10] TO was structured on the basis of the interventions of live popular audiences. The desires of those organised populations are integrated in the very structure of that method. The desires belong to the people, I gave them structure. My work was, in part, interpretive and systematising – not catechising, although it may be true that the relationship between artist and popular audience is delicate.

But of course I exist – that much is evident![11]

The first law arising from the Legislative Theatre (and originated by the blind people's group) to be promulgated in the Legislative Chamber: small, raised concrete platforms built under phone kiosks to alert the blind to the impending obstacle

This is what currently exercises my mind. As a child, I once used a stone to break open eggs which were trembling with their near-hatching chicks, to help them be born without effort: I killed them. I learned the lesson: I no longer kill chicks. But . . . how can I help them be born, to grow up, without breaking the eggs? I do not know. I do know that as artists, we should be like the magician who performs his magic tricks and teaches others how to do them. I like magic tricks: I do them; I am a teacher and like to teach them.

I want to write plays, to stage them, to speak of what I know, feel and dream. The Theatre of the Oppressed, which aims to liberate the artist in each one of us, liberated me to be able to feel what I feel, without remorse; to speak of myself, without vanity (if possible); to give my testimony truthfully.

Today, in a new century, I like to do different things, not out of infantile rebellion, but because I like to do things my way – I am different, just as, in fact, everyone is! I began the year by mounting, with Cecília, a musical show with tangos and boleros with people who had never done theatre before: psychoanalysts, diplomats, teachers. . . .

I directed by first *Sambópera*, in which the *Carmen*, without ceasing to be Bizet, acquired Brazilian rhythms: *samba*, *baião*, *maracatu*. . . .

We performed two pieces of aesthetic surgery. On the music: while staying faithful to the original melodies (the DNA of music) and harmonies – though with different sonorities for the same notes, since the instruments we used, alongside the piano and guitar, are Brazilian: *cuica*, *agogo*, rain stick . . . – we translated the original rhythms into our own cultural rhythms, those we carry impregnated in body and memory. In the staging we tried to be more theatre than opera, dramatic and not lyrical: action is driven by the conflicts and confrontations between characters and not by the lyrical and slow exposition of arias and duets.[12]

I am preparing other *Samboperas*: Verdi's *Traviata*, in which I intend to stage the characters' desires, their sub-texts, while the script remains the same – in the last act, while the priest, the father, Alfredo and the maid sing eulogies to Violeta's health, they place the sick woman in her coffin and toss flowers on to her body; Mozart and, one distant day, Wagner and his Valkyries in Bossa Nova. . . . Or the first opera ever written, *Eurydice* by Jacobo Peri and Octavio Rinuccini, premièred at the wedding of

Henry IV of France with Maria of the Medicis, daughter of the Count of Tuscany, in 1600 – four centuries ago now . . . like *Hamlet* which was premièred a year later. The first part of *Quixote* was published around then.[13]

Life, up to now

Thank goodness I was born! Otherwise, who would see the world as only I do? Who would tell the story that only I can tell? Who would be as unhappy as I am at my unhappiness, or as happy at my happiness? Who would be able to say: 'Augusto, thank goodness we were born.' Only me!

In writing this book, I relived the life I have lived. I tried to make a clean copy of it, a final draft, but that is impossible – I can rewrite encyclopedias, but not my life. I read biographies of others: if they could, they would do it all again, the same way. For myself, if I was to start again, I would never do anything the same way: I know now what I did not know then. My life has been a draft, unfinished sentences, unexpected syntaxes. But I neither can, nor want to make a clean copy: I did what I could. If I could have done more, I would have.

I do not regret even the mistakes. Each deed done was what it was possible to do. Today, it would be a different deed, not the same: time has passed. But, at that time, the time had not yet passed. May those whom I offended forgive me.

I crossed continents, oceans, alleys and footpaths – I stumbled on rocks, so many were there on the way! I can say to myself, in the solitude of the written word: 'Thank goodness you were born, Augusto. You made a difference.'

Epidaurus: the feast of the word

I went into the great theatre of Epidaurus, and remembered the first time I had been there, twenty years earlier. In the stalls, I thought of *Ephigenia in Aulis*, which I had staged in Paris, the wind brushing her virginal neck, before the deep cut of the blade. Why such bedazzlement? I felt it, not just in thought, but in my body – the force of the sea on the rocks – I felt

Theatrical demonstration against the rise in university fees: nuns at Ipanema beach prepare for a class on philosophy and theology

Greek tragedy as if it were the feast of the word. The Greeks achieved extraordinary feats in war and in peace, extending frontiers, inventing democracy; in architecture, Acropolises and Parthenons were built, statuary was humanised; everything was grandiose, in deed and stone. Still greater were the conquests of their thought: words and numbers. With Pythagoras, they discovered the fundamental secret, kept under 7000 locks by jealous Gods: the idea of numbers does not depend on the thing numbered. Fantastic! You, who read my words, may think that was a small achievement: but it was monumental!

Today it is easy to imagine that two and two is four, without enquiring as to the identity of these two twos: it is enough for us to know that two, whatever they may be, plus any other two, add up to four, no matter what they are. Before Pythagoras it was necessary to see the thing before counting it, like children who learn on abacuses, with balls sliding along rods: children learn to add and subtract by sliding stones. *Calculo* = a stone: in order to calculate, stones were necessary.

Before Pythagoras, adding sacks of rice and beans was easy: sacks stayed still, not exhibiting a will of their own. But how can you add up fifteen cows and seven bulls, all ravenous? Animals, not having the patience for algebra or other philosophies, wanted to graze: which is what they were born for. Pre-Pythagorean arithmetic suffered from such bovine hunger: calculations came out wrong, on account of an impatient cow or wandering bull.

The Mandate's Band: spreading butter on the bread, an allusion to their way of playing drums . . . they have improved a lot since

Pythagoras separated the number from the thing numbered, and human thought took a giant leap forward: the quadripedal abacus was rendered unnecessary. So vertiginous was this progress that the philosopher created a religion in which the number was raised to the status of omnipresent God. Pythagoras went mad – naturally: even I would go mad if I discovered the number!

The IMF does craftily what Pythagoras did innocently: it separates profits and rates of tax (abstractions) from poverty and hunger (which are concrete!): the human being does not count – what counts is the Market-God-Number-Rate of Tax-Interest-Profit. When the directors of the IMF, the real governors of Brazil and of a good part of the world, come to our country, they never go up the hill to see the tragedy they cause with their gilded pens: they do abstract sums – for them, only the market exists.

Philosophers wanted to explain the world and numbers were not enough, they were merely quantities; the Greeks wanted to know about qualities. They thought about human relations, they wanted to understand the individual, separating occasional behaviour from its perennial significance, which could be applied to all situations of the same genus. They created morals. From the phenomenon – the isolated fact – one arrived at the law that governed it: *ascesis*.

Greek tragedy never showed acts of violence on stage – deaths, killings, suicides, eyes gouged out, thuggish brutalities: they showed the reasons for

*Chapéu Mangueira: one of the nineteen permanent groups of the mandate, 1993 to 1996.
The costumes were made of newspaper and beer can tabs*

them *in words*. The tragedies happened through the medium of the word.
The opposite of the Rambos and James Bonds – in Greek tragedy, cold
daggers never penetrated warm flesh in front of the audience: words, yes,
words pierced hearts. Words were entities, living beings, they felt envy,
fought duels, made peace, made love and killed. Everything happened by
and through words. Action was the word. Saying was doing.

The opposite of those North American films which never show reasons
and exceed all limits in scenes of violence, where cars tumble from iron
bridges, flying off and sinking in torrential rivers; buildings explode tearing
bodies apart, the eyes popping out. Hollywoodesque cinema seeks to
shock, to obfuscate, to paralyse – a million miles from bringing understanding. Greek tragedy wanted to comprehend: words! This kind of
cinema, to confuse.

In Epidaurus, seated in stalls which could take 20,000 citizens at a
squash, I heard voices 2500 years old. Even if the Theatre of Epidaurus
was built only in the third century BC, after the death of the most famous
tragedians, I swear that sitting there in the stone stalls, by the alchemical
miracle of memory and imagination, I heard their grave voices amplified
by the masks, saw their words which danced on the orchestra (stage). I
heard Iphigenia accepting iniquitous (heroic?) death in order to save her
father; Oedipus, swearing he would find Laius' murderer, knowing, unconsciously, that he was the murderer whom he was seeking. I saw Antigone

challenging the tyrant, disavowing the state and proclaiming the family, blood! I imagined silent multitudes hearing words, in the burning sun, seeing the ballet of concepts, the acrobatics of *logos*, the dance of words in the cold mouths of the tragic masks. I saw the feast of the words.

How beautiful that Greek discovery was; with the Greeks, the human being became human: dialogue was born.

Word of honour!

On that same journey, I went up to the Athenian Acropolis – *acro* = the highest place; *polis* = city. In it, I saw the Parthenon dedicated to the Virgin Goddess Athena. Below, the vast Agora, where traders traded, citizens argued, philosophers taught: social life existed – democracy. I saw the Theatre of Dionysus – where Aeschylus, Sophocles and Euripides did actually stage their plays. First made of wood, which time devoured; then reconstructed in stone, which we see in ruins. Facing the stage where the chorus danced and protagonists evolved, I saw a marble seat, a single solitary seat, flanked by other smaller seats – the powerful sat in the latter; in the former, the High Priest of Dionysus. Tragedies were performed before him: before the greatest religious authority, flanked by the powerful heads of the city.

I could not sit in the High Priest's seat for two reasons: one of which was a moral consideration – I didn't think it would be good to wear down the marble, to profane history; the other, a practical consideration: when I tried to sit there, even though I knew I shouldn't, the guard blew his whistle.

I could lean up against it, place my body so that my head was level with where the sacerdotal skull would have been. I could see, my eyes in place of his, the duel between Creon and Oedipus, Oedipus banishing the blind Tiresias, Antigone disobeying Creon, Agamemnon killing his daughter and being killed by his wife, Clytemnestra, murdered by her son Orestes, assisted by his sister Electra, both pardoned by Athena, there, in the virginal Parthenon (or was it down below in the Areopagus?[14]) In the Acropolis: the highest place!

The Dionysian High Priest watched and approved: the long saga of crimes was a chain of obediences. Not to commit certain crimes would be a crime – disobedience to filial duty. The Greeks wanted to understand the nature of that abstract thing – *Duty* – beyond *Power*. Duties which

today are considered monstrous: filicides — could anything be more tragic?
— parricides, and matricides — could anything be more repugnant?
Nevertheless, they were duties inserted into a civilising code. Crimes
necessary for the construction of a moral order. Crimes and punishments
— further crimes! — which engendered criminal punishments.

The emancipatory pardon announced the dawn of civilisation. The
discovery of pardon — the overthrow of the *Moira*,[15] of fatalism! — was the
beginning of civilisation. Religion — represented by the priest seated in a
comfortable marble seat — was, initially, a way of knowing. Human beings
sought knowledge. Where there was an unanswerable question, they placed
a symbol, a God, deity, titan, supernatural force. So that these symbols
could be understood, and loved or hated, religion gave them human
features: Gods had faces, frowns.

Mortals and immortals, men and Gods were taken to the theatres
to confront each other. If the people wanted to celebrate in the fields,
aristocrats wanted to immobilise themselves in the stalls to hear stories of
Gods and men, with catastrophe by way of warning: they should not run
the risk of disobeying the laws. The powerful flanked the priest, the great
solitary one who represented Dionysus — a God who, however, loved good
companions, Bacchants who loved him and danced with him! There, the
priest sat alone. Surveyor. Censor. Guard. It was in that aristocratic theatre
of stone that the popular theatre of the wind was incarcerated.

In the ruins, I recoiled within on seeing the prison of the theatre of
stone! I felt the hot wind on my body, wind which carried to oblivion the
spontaneous poems of the people inebriated with the good wine of
Dionysus; wind which dissolved the verses of poetry flowing freely from
the drunken lips of the labourers.

It was windy — the wind which took spontaneous creation with it.
Today, I read poets who used to write for the theatre of stone, but I imagine
drunken poems, poems that dissolved in the wind. I imagine desires. I do
not disdain any theatre, either of wind, or of stone: each has its time and
place. I dream of the two in dialogue: Dionysus and Apollo.

I have lived my life intensely; in this book, I write about it and describe
it. I began recounting details, minutiae about myself and my family: I end
speaking of abstractions, generalities: always using words, word, words —

as Hamlet would say. Words: for me, writing is a feast – living has not always been so. Words which, I hope, have life.

Of all the inevitabilities, death

In the great theatre of world politics, the great lie is proclaimed by the great fat ravenous one: inevitable globalisation. Those who govern say: It is already inevitable, best adapt ourselves to it. International finance carries out an inhuman Pythagorean operation. Pythagoras allowed us to think without the burden of objects. He created an abstraction: the number. The global economists are carrying out a Pythagorean revolution the other way around: they reify the number which thus becomes autonomous. For them, the number exists, the human being not necessarily.

It is our duty to shout in the ears of our governors that all economic decisions are, first and foremost, ethical decisions! For an understanding of ethical behaviour, numbers are not enough – words are necessary too: humanism, justice, democracy – there are words!

When unemployment rises from 10 per cent to 15 per cent, for global economists, the difference is 5 per cent – not much. For them, in that number five, tears, anxieties, fears, hunger are non-existent. Just the number five exists – a new divinity!

Global economists divide humanity into three groups. The first controls the market – a God adored above all things and beings! The second is humanity inserted into the deified market, producing or consuming. The third, discardable humanity. This last exists not only in Bangladesh, Rwanda, Eritrea and Ethiopia – where tractors shovel corpses into common graves – it even exists within rich countries. In the United States – and these are their own economic data, not mine – 20 per cent of the population lives below the poverty line: the wretched. Of course, most of the wretched are Latino or black.

Profit is the post-Berlin God. On the fall of the Wall, nicknamed the Wall of Shame, other walls were erected, with no shame. Around the rich mansions: out with the poor and starving, out, out! – and at the frontiers of rich countries: out with the foreigners, out, out! Profit, not human beings, is what determines the relationships between countries, encumbered with walls of shame. Profit, not love, determines human relations.

They say it is inevitable. A lie! There are people who do not feel repugnance for human solidarity, in contrast to the great fat famished one. Even the Bible recommends a periodic pardoning of debts, the great Jubilee! Let's be biblical: let us not pay anything! Jubilee 2000!

The great fat famished one proclaims the inevitability of globalisation, a euphemism invented to hide what has already been called interdependence, Imperialism, Colonialism, Hitler's Thousand Year Empire, *Pax Romana* . . . names which hide the true nature of the universal phagocytation which is underway.

Inevitable? Not true! Even if it were, nothing would justify us giving in to it. Of all the inevitabilities, the most inevitable is death, but that is no reason to shoot ourselves in the head. Down with suicide! Down with inevitabilities: they are all avoidable. Even death is postponable. Some governors of subjugated countries, *Capitães do Mato*,[16] preach national suicide in the same way as they would advise slaves to remain in captivity: liberty brings dangerous responsibilities – it brings choice! We must fight against this surrender to fatalism, which spreads as if there were no other option. Writing this book – words! – I play my minuscule part, I take a step. It is not a timid one, though it is short. If you have longer legs, take a longer step.

The man who did not learn to die

In the interior of São Paulo I met an aged backwoodsman, of an age impossible to ascertain without documents, an old man of olden times, age itself. He said he did not know his age, but he was certain of one thing: he was immortal: 'I never learnt how to die . . . death has no relations, I have never met anyone who knows how to die properly, no one has ever taught me.'

That is not the case with me – they have already taught me how to die, they even wanted to help me go more quickly. Autobiography is not life: it is an account. I suppose I know what it is like to die, but I have not learned how to end this book. Just as the old man had not learned how to die, no one has taught me how to stop writing.

This book does not end here, although it lays bare a good part of what I have lived. Perhaps a second volume, when I give up trying to go on or already lack the strength . . . when I can no longer work, I promise to work, to work intensely on a real book of memories. Yes, that book already even has a title: *Closing Statements*! That is for later, for when it is getting late.

It is still too early. . . .

From birth, I was a solitary child, sitting on the bridge at the gate of my house, watching the world go by. I feel these confessions going by, fleeing from my hands. The words escape from my fingers and reappear on the screen, taking the best part of me. Where to?

Words escape carrying thoughts. They are going to find you, who I do not even know.

My words flee from me. Like this book, which I now bring to a close.

It is no longer mine. . . .

PS: Whoever read the footnote in the previous chapter must have asked themselves why I was so detailed in relating future projects. In this book I wanted to show my life, just up to now. From here on and right up to the end will be told in *Closing Statements* which I shall begin to write a minute after I write the final word of this one: *End*.

I do not believe in that word: nothing ends, you can be sure. Believe me. Nothing ends. . . .

Ever!

END

Closing statements

My name is Augusto Boal. . . . I was born on 16 March, very early in the morning, on a summer's day, in my parents' bed. . . .

My star sign is Pisces, in Hot Sands. . . . A very strong Sign!

A long time ago . . . In 1931 . . . in the Penha-Circular . . . in Rio de Janeiro . . . Brazil . . . Brasil . . . brésil. . . .

. . . One day, I saw myself in the mirror and realised that

I was alive . . . How strange . . . From that day on, I have never been able to stop living . . . never . . . ever . . . never. . . .

notes

Introduction

1 Sweets – biscuits and cakes. The first two translate as 'holy marys' and 'monks' bellies'; *Iáiá* is Yoruba for elderly black woman, and *quindins* are moist cakes with coconut, traditional in some African countries.

2 Something between 'companions' and 'comrades', with a connotation of 'fellow fighters'.

The landscape, the family

1 A white tulip-like flower particularly used to honour the dead, literally 'glasses of milk'.

2 A quintessentially Brazilian–Portugese feeling which combines longing, missing, and fond memories, but more positive than sulking from the lack.

3 A diminutive of *Joaquin*, the diminutive usually being demonstrative of affection, condescension or familiarity.

4 'Big little *Joaquin*'.

5 The *zao* added to his name, again for familiarity.

A long time ago, I was a boy

1 In Portuguese the two spellings sound the same.

2 A kind of small crab found in marshland and sand, as opposed to in the sea or on rocks

3 Jellyfish in Portuguese are *aguas vivas*, which means 'living waters'.

4 *Trocaria de mal* in Portuguese: each child wraps their little finger around the other's, saying they have broken friendship and will never speak again.

5 When it happened, once in a while, that I agreed with myself, solely out of love of argument, I would even argue with God. But I did not like it much: when He lost He was furious, and would frown. . . . Dangerous discord, to defy the powerful. [Author's note.]

6 Apart from having broken his collarbone, my brother often came home with a football injury, exacerbating my envy. Sometimes his injury would become infected and produce an ulcer. When the chemists made up the medicines they would follow the recipe exactly, but only for the top half of the pot of cream they gave you. When we used that part of the pot, my brother's wound would almost heal; but when we innocently used the bottom half of the pot, into which Penha's chemists put all sorts of strange substances, the wound reopened. It was already in those times dangerous to use medicines with the designation *Made in Brazil*. . . . [Author's note.]

7 Literally 'dirty blocks'; a carnival 'block' is a tightly packed troupe of people.

8 High-alcohol sugar cane rum, very popular and much drunk during Carnival.

9 *Cuíca* and *pandeiro* are traditional Carnival musical instruments, both with a tight drum-like skin on top, though the *cuíca* is not percussive.

10 In Brazil, people go to registry offices to formalise statements, register signatures as well as births, marriages and deaths.

11 *Salve Rainha*, nothing to do with the British national anthem.

12 Two of the most popular Brazilian football teams.

13 Famous Fluminense players of the time.

14 Peripatetic barrel-organists keep a parakeet on top of their instruments, which uses its beak to pick out a piece of paper inscribed with a prediction relevant to the paying customer's future.

15 Both French words approximate to 'whatsit' or 'thingummybob'.

16 See Genesis 31.

17 Louis de Camões, 1524?–1580, Portugal's national poet – *como Jacó servindo Labão, pai de Raquel, serrana bela, que não servia ao pai, servia a ela.*

18 Television entertainment programmes used to go out live, so the studio audience was paid to laugh at appropriate moments.

19 There is a Portuguese saying to the effect that whoever is lucky in gambling is unlucky in love, and vice versa.

20 Cantareira is a neighbourhood of Rio served by boats which could dock on either side.

21 The show I did immediately after the *coup* in 1964, with Nara Leão, and later Maria Bethânia, Zé Keti and João do Valle.

22 *Arena conta Tiradentes* (The Arena Tells of *Tiradentes*) (tooth-puller) – nickname of the Brazilian patriot, José Joaquim da Silva Xavier (1748–1792). Leader of the *Inconfidencia Mineira*, a revolutionary movement against Portuguese rule, executed in Rio de Janeiro in 1791.

23 *Arena conta Zumbi* (The Arena Tells of *Zumbi*), probably the company's best-known production. Zumbi (1655–1695) was leader of Palmares in the northwest, one of a number of independent areas or *quilombos* established by runaway slaves together with indigenous peoples; martyred in 1695, he is a major focus of black consciousness movements in Brazil.

24 Great singer/*sambista carioca*, b.1921.

25 Integralism was the Brazilian nationalist movement of the 1940s which supported Nazism.

26 *Galinhas Verdes* means 'Green Chickens' and was the popular term of disrespect used for this paramilitary group.

27 The distancing technique invented by the German theatre-maker Bertolt Brecht, usually translated as 'alienation effect', more properly 'estrangement effect'.

28 Santa Catarina is a state in the south of Brazil.

29 Essentially the system described here, where various different actors can play the same part at different times. See *The Theatre of the Oppressed* and *Games for Actors and Non-Actors* for further explanation.

30 As in Boal's famous *Arena conta Zumbi* (cf. note 23 above).

31 A berry from a tree in the Amazon, used in health drinks and the like.

32 (Edward Henry) Gordon Craig (1872–1966), British theatre theorist, director and designer, famous for his anti-naturalism and apparent desire to replace the human actor with 'uber-marionettes'.

33 *Cachaça* is raw sugar cane rum, the most commonly drunk spirit in Brazil. *Parati* is also a variety of rum.

34 Sebastião Bernardes de Souza Prata, actor of mineiro origin, b.1915, given the nickname 'The Great Othello' by Orson Welles, which he Brazilianised to Grande Otelo.

35 Distinguished black academic and civil rights activist of humble origins, b.1914, founder of the Black Experimental Theatre in Rio (1944), the Black Arts Museum (1968) and Federal Congressman (1982–). 'When he was a child his dream was to arrive at the age of 18; now he is more than 80, was a senator of the republic and is secretary for human rights of Rio' (AB).

36 A small state in the Northeast of Brazil, one of the poorest and considered 'backward'.

37 *Busca-pés* – fireworks which run along the ground, literally 'feet-seekers'.

38 There is a vast stock of Brazilian jokes which poke fun at the Portuguese, based on characterising them as stupid and/or pedantic.

39 Synonymous with 'Portuguese', Lusitania being another name for Portugal.

40 *Vossas Senhorias*: formal archaic Portuguese style.

41 *Macumba* and *Candomblé* are Afro-Brazilian religions.

42 People with the power to conduct Afro-Brazilian ceremonies.

43 *Galo Preto* literally means Black Cockerel. It is the animal which esteems Exu, one of the Afro-Brazilian evil spirits.

44 The most northerly of states in the Northeast, bordering on Amazonia.

45 Traditionally, large landowners in the Northeast of Brazil have been called 'Colonels'. This signifies their power and their sympathy with the military in government, rather than their own military standing.

46 The name given to the sites where *Candomblé* rituals are observed.

47 Allan Kardec (1804–1869), a world leader of a Christian tendency of Spiritism.

48 'Light' (*sic*) is the name of the principal electricity company in the state of Rio.

49 Carmen Miranda (1909–1945), a Brazilian singer-actress famous for her elaborate fruit-basket head-dress, who performed in the USA during the war period, becoming a Hollywood icon and symbol of Latin American spirit.

50 The National Siderurgical (Iron and Steel) Company.

51 *Vale do Rio Doce* was, and still is, the main company exploiting minerals in Amazonia.

52 The National Motor Factory.

53 President of Brazil 1930–1945 and 1951–1954. Following failure in the 1930 presidential election he overthrew the republic and in 1937 set up a totalitarian, pro-fascist state, known as the Estado Novo; ousted by a military *coup* in 1945, returned as President 1951, committed suicide 1954.

54 *Padim* is the word in the text, indicating a northeastern pronunciation of *Padrinho* – Godfather. Father Cicero was a populist Catholic Priest, and his proximity to the poor rural population led him to be referred to as Godfather. In Ceará State, neighbouring Piauí, there are still huge annual processions to pay tribute to him.

55 *Ôh gente* literally means 'Oh people', and is a typically northeastern exclamation.

56 Nobody, myself included, can remember the second part. . . . [Author's note.]

57 *Uái* is an expression used to mean 'Don't you think so?' in the state of Minas Gerais.

58 A state in the west of central Brazil.

59 The national anthem begins with the words *Ouviram do Ipiranga às margens plácidas/De um povo heroico o brado retumbante* ('The peaceful banks of the Ipiranga heard/the resounding cry of an heroic people . . .') In popular delivery, the first few words tend to merge into one.

60 In all the countries of my exile, the first thing I constructed was the library. A properly prized library must have paintings on the walls. As a family in exile, we always carried with us two 'naive' paintings, bought in Argentina. The painter of these, Ana Sokol, a Romanian, who used to make her living as a barber before becoming known as an artist, when we complained about the high price of her paintings, pounded on the wood – she painted on wood, not canvas – and exclaimed: 'It is expensive, but the wood is good! It won't get termites!' [Author's note.]

61 Noel Rosa (1910–1937).

62 José Barbosa da Silva (1888–1930), 'King of Samba'.

63 The famous Sugar Loaf mountain which overlooks Rio.

64 Couple-dancing typical of Rio de Janeiro.

65 'Louder, louder! Rascals!' (in Italian)

66 André Antoine (1858–1943), French director renowned for his interest in scenic realism.

67 Fluminense's strip – red, white and green.

68 The Moscow Arts Theatre.

69 People dwelling in or originating from Rio de Janeiro.

70 Fish and shellfish marinaded in lemon juice.

71 'Of course, Sir'.

72 Simon Bolivar (1783–1830) led the movement for independence from Spain of five South American countries: Bolivia (named after him), Peru, Ecuador, Colombia and Venezuela.

73 Underlined passages English in original.

74 The *São Paulo Courier*.

75 The Amazonian tidal bore – when its waters explode against the water of the ocean, the noise is heard several dozen kilometres away.

76 Spanish for 'That is what I am like'.

In the arena of Arena

1 A tabloid newspaper critical of the military system.

2 In 1998 my son Julián, having heard so much about it, finally went to visit the place. 'Dad, is this the Arena? You did all that stuff here?' I have never seen such amazement. Which was quite justified! [Author's note.]

3 Pertaining to (intellectual) midwifery, i.e. to the Socratic process of assisting a person to bring out into clear consciousness conceptions previously latent in his mind (*OED*).

4 In dialogue with other actors, Helene Weigel herself, Brecht's wife and one of the foremost actresses of the Berliner Ensemble, asked: 'How could I "show" at a distance (*Verfremdungseffekt*)

Mother Courage's pain if I had not felt it before, myself?' Stanislavski and Brecht are not incompatible: in the creation of the character by the latter, the former precedes him!

5   Black bean stew with meat (particularly pork) offcuts, originally made by and for slaves.

6   A cocktail of *cachaça* and lime.

7   Since then I have thought of writing an essay on 'Alcohol and its curious effects on ideology'. I start writing, drink a glass of Burgundy and I forget.

8   School of Dramatic Art.

9   We have a popular saying, 'An old parrot does not learn new words'.

10 French in the original. *The Incredible and Sad Story of Erendira and Her Diabolical Grandmother*.

11 Brecht wrote about the clown Karl Valentim, who much influenced him. My Valentim was Piolim!

12 Dercy was the first person I heard say: 'I like life a lot because I like myself a lot'!

13 Reference to *Mrs Warren's Profession* by George Bernard Shaw.

14 There were excesses. The actors would occasionally do 'laboratory' even when they were alone. . . . One day I arrived early at the theatre, to find the arena illuminated: one of my best actors was there on his own, playing his part opposite 'invisible characters' (which was one of our rehearsal techniques). Usually, in a scene of three or four actors, we used to exclude one of them: there he was, having excluded all the rest . . . and he managed to 'see' the entire cast, although they were absent. Excessive, yes, but when you are young, who doesn't go for excess?

15 An Italian director who worked with TBC.

16 *Dirty Hands*, Jean-Paul Sartre's 1948 play about political expediency.

17 In Portuguese a yellow smile is a false one.

18 Spanish equivalent of Portuguese 'então', meaning 'well then'.

19 Expression typical of the Chaco region (covering a small part of South Brazil, plus Uruguay, Paraguay and Argentina). Adopted by Ernesto 'Chê' Guevara, born in N. Argentina.

20 Gaúchos, people from Rio Grande do Sul, customarily share an infusion of *mate* tea (*chimarrão*) from a gourd (*cuia*).

21 From the state of Minas Gerais.

22 Northeasterners are referred to as *cabeça chata* (flat-headed).

23 Rio was at that time the capital city.

24 Jam with high gelatine content, eaten on its own or with cheese.

25 Later the writer of hit soaps on Globo TV, such as *Pantanal*, *Rei do gado* (King of the cattle).

26 The Cog-Wheel.

27 *Centros Populares de Cultura*, a nationwide movement of local cultural centres.

28 National Student Union.

29 One of our actor-playwrights.

30 Not adequately translatable: the manner, the way of being, the knack, the 'something of' a characteristic.

31 The Landless Workers movement, a powerful current popular movement which combines the squatting of unproductive land with an agrarian reform agenda.

32 Part of the Secretariat of Culture of the state of Pernambuco in the Northeast.

33 Percussion instrument used to provide the music to *capoeira* – the martial art brought to Brazil by slaves from Africa. A long curved wooden bow with one string and a gourd in the centre.

34 Other percussion instruments approximating to shaker, tambourine and keg.

35 *Images of a Popular Theatre*, Julián Boal, Hucitec Editions, 2000, a close reading of which I highly recommend. [Author's note.]

36 The life of the *people* was getting better and they wanted it to get better still. When their living conditions are reasonable, the *people* becomes more conscious; when living in abject poverty, hunger and fear prevent them from expressing themselves. This, i.e. abject poverty, is what is still happening today. [Author's note.]

37 A kind of rural trade union.

38 The word used is *latifundiarios*, the owners of 'latifundia', extremely large landed estates.

39 Companions in struggle – the Latin American equivalent of 'comrades'.

40 Large landowners of the Northeast are often referred to as 'Colonels', alluding to their connections with the military and their style of business.

41 In Roman and Civil law the acquisition of ownership by long use or enjoyment (*OED*).

42 Men apportioned land by the Portuguese Court were called Captains. Ownership of their estates was hereditary and not to be sold.

43 Captains of the forest, literally; pursuers and catchers of runaway slaves.

44 Sweet cassava or manioc.

45 A word of advice to my friends: when in the house of a priest, consume a lot of soup! [Author's note.]

46 Metaxis – Gk, signifying for Boal 'the state of belonging completely and simultaneously to two different, autonomous worlds' (Augusto Boal, *The Rainbow of Desire*, Routledge, 1995).

47 Santo André, São Bernardo and São Caetano, three neighbouring municipalities in São Paulo, noted for their trade union organisation.

48 *Partido dos Trabalhadores* (Workers' Party).

49 Pertaining to fat.

50 Augusto Boal, *The Theatre of the Oppressed* (Pluto Press, 1979).

51 Augusto Boal, *The Rainbow of Desire* (Routledge 1995).

52 The Anthropophagic Theatre.

53 English in the original.

54 *Favelas* are slums, shanty towns on the periphery of cities. In Rio, they are on hillsides overlooking the beaches.

55 *Movimento Sem Terra* (Movement of Landless Peasants) is a non-party organisation formed in the 1980s which campaigns for agrarian reform. It is perhaps the most important social movement that Brazil has known this century.

56 'Beautiful Island', off the state of São Paulo coast.

57 Literally, The Son of the Dog, here meaning also the Devil.

58 See earlier footnote 43.

59 From Minas Gerais.

60 Also *Truque*, a Brazilian card game involving the collection of tricks.

61 Highland region in which Brasilia is located. Also the name of the Presidential Palace.

62 Rio de Janeiro's most renowned popular beaches.

63 'In Chile there will never be military *coups*! We decide everything through diplomatic talks, like gentlemen . . . *Coups* in Chile? Never!'

64 Carbonated drink made from an Amazonian berry, renowned for its health and vitality-giving properties.

65 US Ambassador to Brazil at the time.

War declared, inside and outside of me

1 A Cuban newspaper, named in homage to the boat in which Fidel and his *companheiros* arrived in Cuba.

2 Saint John is commemorated on 24 June with bonfires, in celebration of the maize harvest.

3 *Tradição, Família e Propriedade*.

4 *Liga das Senhoras Católicas*.

5 English in the original.

6 Popular black singers.

7 The eyes are the most vulnerable part of the body – that is why, unless they are doing it as an act of will, people do not look each other in the eye for long. They know that the eyes reveal even unconscious thoughts, that flow of thought which never reaches the point of verbalisation by the thinker. Eyes emit messages, the nature of which we do not know. We do not want to offer our eyes to others, our gaze, because we do not want our interlocutor to read in our eyes that which we ourselves cannot read; we do not want to reveal secrets we keep hidden even from ourselves, and which our eyes, traitors, shamelessly divulge. [Author's note.]

8 A bird of prey like a small eagle.

9 Words from a song by João do Vale.

10 The hills of Rio are where the bulk of the *favelas* (shanty towns) are located.

11 Along with Amazonia, the Northeast is the poorest region of Brazil, from which many migrate south in search of a better life.

12 Copacabana is one of the beaches in Rio, frequented by many parading their beautiful bodies.

13 The Caymmi is a family of highly esteemed Brazilian singers and musicians.

14 Maria Bethânia's birthplace.

15 Caetano Veloso would later emerge as a songwriter, singer and poet of great importance.

16 José and Maria are the most common Brazilian forenames; da Silva is the equivalent of Smith. And José da Silva was the name of Boal's protagonist in *Revolution in South America*.

17 Zumbi was a leader of a seventeenth-century rebellion, by a colony of escaped slaves, forming the *quilombo* (Republic) of Palmares.

18 A loose translation of: *O Arena conta a história / pra você ouvir gostoso / quem gostar nos dê a mão / e quem não tenha outro gozo!*

19 The first incarnation of the '*coringa*', the Joker (as in a pack of cards); later to appear in a somewhat different guise as the facilitator / difficultator / referee / MC / go-between in Forum Theatre.

20 An actor from the Japanese Kabuki theatre and similar to forms from other countries, who is dressed in black and supposedly invisible, and carries out tasks such as removing corpses or props from the scene, so that the action can continue without obstruction. [Author's note.]

21 'Stand up, young black child'.

22 English in the original.

23 Fifteenth-century Portuguese writer, the *Lusíadas* being his magnum opus.

24 For the Camões scholars: *As armas e os barões assinalados, que da ocidental praia lusitana, por mares nunca dantes navegados, passaram ainda além da Taprobana . . .* (For geographers, Taprobana is a cape in Africa).

25 English in original.

26 In its time, the world's largest football stadium, built for the 1950 World Cup in Rio de Janeiro.

27 Disloyalty – the name given to the uprising in Minas Gerais was the *Inconfidência Mineira*.

28 English in the original.

29 A much-loved singer of Brazilian popular music, who died in 1982.

30 Daily.

31 I return to this subject at the end of the book.

32 *Ação Libertadora Nacional* (National Liberation Action): one of the clandestine groups active during the period of military dictatorship 1964 to 1986.

33 An outgrowth from the PCB, the *Partido Communista Brasileiro* (Brazilian Communist Party).

34 It is true that there was an excess of irresponsibility. I remember a young man known as Barão – no one was sure of his real name, just that he was rich – he called himself a recruiter of guerrillas. He offered meetings to explain guerrilla strategy, in his comfortable house, where he would serve up beer, wine and cheeses. Without further formality, Barão would declare that those present were part of the patriotic fight to overthrow the dictatorship. No one ever really knew who this madman was; they drank their fill, ate his exotic cheeses, and no one took the nobleman seriously. Not even him: the only person who did was his mother, who used to serve the wine. [Author's note.]

35 The Belgian activist who spent time with Chê Guevara in Bolivia, and wrote about his guerrilla warfare.

36 A large river which traverses the otherwise drought-ridden interior of the Northeast, which was the centre of Peasant League activity in the 1950s and 1960s.

37 *Partido Communista Brasileiro* (Brazilian Communist Party).

38 A district of Rio de Janeiro, with a well-known beach by the same name.

39 In the original, *Puta que pariu!*: literally, 'whore who has given birth' – used as an exclamation of frustration and disagreement, rather than derogation, i.e. not 'son of a bitch'.

40 Pertaining to *Fescennia* in Etruria, famous for a sort of jeering dialogue in verse. (*OED*)

41 *Samba do crioulo doido*: refers to a famous song about the eponymous mad black man who wrote a samba in which personalities and historical facts are confused.

42 Political prison where I myself was held.

43 Belonging to the order *Ophidia*; pertaining or relating to, or resembling that of, a snake or serpent (*OED*).

44 The colours of the Brazilian flag.

45 Well-known comedian, now host of a popular TV chat show, and a novelist.

46 Theatre is not the reproduction of reality, it is its representation and, as such, is made from a particular point of view – this point being situated in society, and not in the cosmos. [Author's note.]

47 In exile, I did other *Feiras*, using the same mural idea, the same bewilderment: Latino-Americana, in Saint Clement's Church in New York, near Times Square (which was when I first heard about the existence of the Obie Awards: we won one, during the 1971–1972 season), and the Portuguese *Feira*, with the *A Barraca* group, in the Lisbon *Museu de Arte*. '*Feiras*' are important. It is good to know what others think! [Author's note.]

48 Prominent Brazilian actress, one of the first to move from theatre to TV soaps. Died at the end of 1960s.

49 Theatre, film and TV actress. Won the Best Actress Award at the Berlin Film Festival in 1998 for her part in *Central Station*.

50 English in the original.

51 *Qual cisne branco, em noite de lua*: opening words of the Brazilian Navy's Anthem.

52 The tidal bore at the mouth of the Amazon.

53 On the banks of Ipiranga brook, Don Pedro the First was riding a white horse when he cried 'independence or death!' and raised his sword. So they say – I do not believe them, though. [Author's note.]

54 Named after Saci Pererê, a figure of Brazilian myth – a one-legged, pipe-smoking black boy, who lives in the forest and punishes people for injustices.

55 I later learned that most of the award-winners were able to reclaim their trophies once it had all died down; if anyone knows the whereabouts of mine, please contact me. [Author's note.]

56 Spanish revolutionary anthem. [Author's note.]

57 'Please, there are a lot of young girls in the audience today. Moderate your ball games. . . . '

58 'Señor Quezada, will it be with or without balls today?'

59 'Tonight is the last show; do it with all the balls you want.'

60 Patio.

61 American director and producer, founder of the New York Shakespeare Festival.

62 We carry museums in our memories: wax museums, history museums, and also museums of horror. All the scenes and images I describe here are archived in my memory, and easily consulted: it is enough to remember a name, colour, sentence or word, for them to come flooding back, as vivid as when they happened.

 Twenty-eight years later, in November 1999, I went to see a play Lembrar é Resistir (To Remember is to Resist), performed in the very cells I describe here, in the DOPS of São Paulo. I heard a song we used to sing when one of us was taken up to be tortured: 'My boat is setting out to sea. . . . ' I could hardly concentrate on what the actors were saying: my eyes were staring at those painted walls in pain and revolt. I hit the wall, as I had done twenty-eight years earlier. [Author's note.]

63 Nineteenth-century 'Liberator' of Spanish American countries – which are still enslaved by another means.

64 From Minas Gerais.

65 From Rio Grande do Sul.

66 Fernando Pessoa (1888–1935), most celebrated Portuguese modernist poet and essayist, who wrote under seventy-two 'heteronyms', literary alter egos supporting and criticising each other's work.

67 See note 27 on p 357.

68 'Fluery'.

69 Literally, the macaw's rod: the victims is hung upside down from a metal pole behind their knees, with arms tied or handcuffed around their calves.

70 Departamento de Ordem Política e Social (Department of Political and Social Order), lair of official bandits, paid for by the taxpayer.

71 Garrastazu Medici, the Dictator of the time, during whose rule there was the highest number of recorded deaths.

72 This radio station was only officially reopened on 18 March 1999. [Author's note.]

73 Brazilian national dish. Beans stewed with pork and sausage – originally food made by and for slaves with the parts of the pig discarded by their owners.

74 Martial arts practised with distinctive musicwhich has evolved from a type of combat introduced by slaves from Africa.

75 Crushed brazil nuts and peanuts cooked up with manioc flour and palm oil to form a paste, some-times with added prawns. Typical of Bahia state.

76 Tomás de Torquemada (1420–1498), First Grand Inquisitor of Spain, notorious for his cruelty.

77 Slang for police van, equivalent of 'Black Maria'.

78 In 1998, obliged by federal law, the Military Office of the Presidency of the Republic handed over to me an account of all the information the secret service of the Dictatorship had collected about me: there you can read that the Dictatorship considered me officially banished – not

merely exiled: banished. Prohibited from returning home. *Banished*: deracinated, extirpated! [Author's note.]

79 Indian ink.

80 In Greek mythology, Prometheus was a Titan who stole fire from heaven for the human race. In revenge, Zeus had him chained to a rock where an eagle came each day to eat his liver, which grew back each night, until he was rescued by the hero Heracles.

81 The personality of the exile is in danger of disintegration – I need to be missed to know who I am: I am the lack I make by my absence. If I make no lack, I cease to be! The worst thing that can happen to someone is to become anonymous to themselves. [Author's note.]

82 The science of duty; that branch of knowledge which deals with moral obligations (*OED*).

83 Or they have been transformed into symbols, whose meanings we can ascribe to them! Black is mourning? In Asia, it's white. A rose in the forest is not a rose unless it finds eyes to see it and a nose to smell it. Or is it a rose, on its own? Is a rose a rose for itself, or for me? [Author's note.]

84 They can carry symbolic concepts which necessitate prior agreement: by such agreements, a sound may come to signify the anthem of a country, a nuptial celebration, a funeral. [Author's note.]

85 Among macabre stories of suicides which left the most lasting impression on me was one concerning a lake on the outskirts of Bangkok, Thailand: there they say that when a young woman is impregnated by a man who does not take responsibility for the child, and she is abandoned by her family, the solution is to throw herself into the crocodile-infested lake. The animals do not eat the drowned body straight away: fresh meat is tough and unflavoursome – using their snouts, they push the corpse under the stones and wait a few days before feast-time. [Author's note.]

86 On Death Row in the united States, when the prisoner sets off on his walk to the electric chair or lethal injection, the representative of Justice must call out 'Dead Man Walking!' so that the executioner won't feel that he has killed a living man.

87 Brazilian singer and composer who wrote the anthem of resistance to the Brazilian dictatorship.

88 It is said that the Chilean dictatorship killed Victor Jara by cutting off his hands, the only way of separating him from his guitar, his life! Others say that he died from thirty-five bullets in his chest.

89 Portuñol: synthesis of Portuguese (*português*) and Spanish (*español*).

90 The Onion.

91 Made by squeezing sugar cane through a mangle – leaving the cane useless. Poor people's fare in the countryside of the Northeast.

92 Pluto Press, 1979.

93 See note 3 on p 356

94 Brazilian educator, pioneer of a revolutionary and influential educational method, whose *obra prima* was 'Pedagogy of the Oppressed'. Died 1998.

95 Chilean Presidential Palace.

96 *Revolução dos Cravos*, the popular name for the Portuguese revolution, so-called because soldiers put carnations in their rifles. (They did not shoot anyway. . . .)

97 A country with a minimum salary of US$100 a month cannot call itself a democracy. The minimum salary, as a politician from Bahia remarked, is worth less than an Italian silk tie – the comparison is magnificent in its monstrosity.

Exile, banishment, palm trees, birdsong

1 A reference to *The cop in the head*, one of the first techniques of *The Rainbow of Desire*.

2 Literally, *Portuguese House, of course* – a popular saying taken from the words of a fairy-tale used in a song *Casa Portuguesa*, sung by Amalia Rodrigues.

3 The name given to the full repertoire of games and exercises of the Theatre of the Oppressed.

4 From Molière's *Le Bourgeois Gentilhomme* (1670).

5 In *The Rainbow of Desire*, I articulate a triad of person (the whole), personality (the socially acceptable persona revealed to the world), and *personnage* (other possible characters one could choose). [Author's note.]

6 In the systematisation described in the preceding note, the regulator of these roles is analogised as the nozzle of a pressure cooker, loosened or tightened according to circumstances.

7 Followers of method of Celéstin Freinet (1896–1966), influential educationalist.

8 Jean Philippe Rameau (1683–1764) and Jean-Baptiste Lully (1632–1687), Baroque composers.

9 Cod cooked in the Portuguese style.

10 At home, Cecília and I used to talk about psychoanalysis, Stanislavsky and related subjects. Julián, a boy at the time, when asked about his dreams of the previous night, after in an onset of anxiety he had fallen out of bed, not unreasonably answered that the reason for it was in the hidden part of his head. What was that hidden part? '*Le désir!* (Desire!)' he said, aged 9. Cecília, trying to calm him down, explained that she herself went to her analyst precisely to discover that hidden part. Julián responded, in a discouragement of analysis: '*Tu perds ton temps, maman: ce qui est caché, doit rester caché* (You are wasting your time, Mum: what is hidden should stay hidden)'. [Author's note.]

11 *The Rainbow of Desire* is the name of a particular technique and the generic title of the chapter of TO which relates to introspective techniques, like the Screen Image, the Projected Image, the Image of the Antagonist, etc.

12 Our process is therapeutic without being therapy. There is the function of the joker, who organises the session, but does not interpret it: we use the multiple mirror of the gaze of others – no one has more interpretive authority than anyone else, each person merely reflects the image they see with their own eyes, by their sensitivity, in the light of their story. Our point of departure was an individual account – one particular story. However, from that point on we sought not to singularise the story in the person of the protagonist, but to pluralise it in the participants of the group. [Author's note.]

13 Hammurabi, who promulgated the first existing Penal Code in the world, in the eighteenth-century BC, used to say that the laws therein came to him directly from God – whose desire was law.

The impossible return and the strangeness of the familiar

1 Large Brazilian chain of department stores.

2 The famous figure of Christ on the hill overlooking Rio.

3 Carmen swore she had not returned Americanised; I swear I returned North and Latino-Americanised, Portuguesed, Frenchified, Germanised, Scandanavianated, dark-skinned, slant-eyed. I did not conduct my travels clad in a diving suit: I went around with my skin exposed to the sun, in the flesh. [Author's note.]

4 Literally, the Travelling Theatre-Makers of Puerto Rico.

5 *Partido Trabalhadores* (The Workers' Party).

6 *Jogo do Bicho* (Game of the Animal) is an unregulated gambling game popular throughout Brazil

and run by a mafia. Each animal represents a number, on which people bet in accordance with superstition, often including the animals which appear in their dreams.

7 *Legislative Theatre* (Routledge, 1999). *Teatro Legislativa*, Civilização Brasileira.

8 Co-director of London-based arts organisation Artangel.

9 I said that in Rio, when I presided over a Solemn Session in the Chamber, there was always some good soul who was expert in the ceremonial aspects of the house, a true guardian angel, who would show me what to do at every step. Tim had an angel costume and agreed to do the celestial honours. [Author's note.]

10 Julián thinks that, in the vertical relationship between the aesthetic vanguard (artist) and the popular audience, TO eliminates the first term of that equation, without resolving it. From that point of view, he is right, though we should consider that the artist remains an integral part of the process, in the formation of those popular nuclei, which are co-opted by their ideological similarities to us – we do not agree to work with any group. Our jokers initiate the process from which we should progressively distance ourselves. [Author's note.]

11 That is why TO can only be practised by audiences desirous of change in their world. I sometimes say that only Jesus resuscitated Lazarus. We only help those who are already combatants – we give rocks to David! [Author's note.]

12 The person who started this idea of valuing the word against the music, which would become a mere accompaniment; who said that only in that way could you validate human sentiment, when expressed by a single human being in recitative, solo and aria, was Vicenzo Galileo – father of the Galileo who, faced with the threat of the Inquisitorial bonfire said: '*Eppur, se muove . . .*' (Nevertheless, it moves . . .) Galileo Senior defended his musical ideas in *Dialogo della musica antica et della moderna*, written in 1581, shortly before Shakespeare began writing his tragedies in which abstract medieval devils became concrete people: Iago, Richard III, Lady Macbeth . . . characters became multi-dimensional (Hamlet, Othello, Lear . . .). The heavy Roman style had already given way to the lighter Gothic. The creators of opera wanted to restore the classical Greek tradition – from the time Greek commerce was developing, its bourgeoisie was gathering strength. Look at the parallel: Thespis proposed the protagonist against the choir; the inventors of opera, the aria against the polyphonic choir. In both cases, the victory of the individual! [Author's note.]

13 Henry IV, for political motives, annuls his marriage to the famous Queen Margot, Marguerite de Valois and marries by proxy Maria de Medici, daughter of the Duke of Florence, a prosperous city. To ensure that the nuptials would mark both a clear break with Protestantism and his recent re-conversion to Catholicism – 'Paris is well worth the Mass' – he commissioned an original programme of music, which resulted in that first opera. In the plot of this, Orpheus goes to find Eurydice in hell – she had died after being bitten by a serpent.

Orpheus, marvellous poet and singer, enchanted human beings and animals, plants and stones with his song – he enchanted the infernal potencies who agreed to return Eurydice to him on condition that he did not look at her until they returned to human conviviality. Orpheus looked at her, and Eurydice died a second and last time.

Henry married from a distance, without seeing his wife! When he heard of this plot, the king thwacked Peri and Renuccini and said: 'Not that, never! You do not know to whom you are speaking! I want Orpheus to grab Eurydice, by the hair if necessary, and look back as many times as he likes, and she will come to live with me in Paris! All mythological dispositions to the contrary are revoked!'

The singular desire of a single king is always more powerful than the vast Greek mythology! [Author's note.]

14 Hill of Ares, NW of Acropolis; the ancient Council associated with the Acropolis.

15 The Greek concept of destiny.
16 Literally, 'captains of the jungle', who were pursuers of runaway slaves.

illustrations